CANADIAN SOCIETY
IN THE TWENTY-FIRST CENTURY

CANADIAN SOCIETY IN THE TWENTY-FIRST CENTURY

AN HISTORICAL SOCIOLOGICAL APPROACH

THIRD EDITION

TREVOR W. HARRISON

JOHN W. FRIESEN

Canadian Scholars' Press
Toronto

Canadian Society in the Twenty-First Century: An Historical Sociological Approach, Third Edition
by Trevor W. Harrison and John W. Friesen

First published in 2015 by
Canadian Scholars' Press Inc.
425 Adelaide Street West, Suite 200
Toronto, Ontario
M5V 3C1

www.cspi.org

Library and Archives Canada Cataloguing in Publication

Harrison, Trevor, 1952-, author
      Canadian society in the twenty-first century : an historical and sociological approach / Trevor W. Harrison, John W. Friesen. — Third edition.

Previously published by Women's Press, 2010.
Includes bibliographical references and index.
Issued in print and electronic formats.
ISBN 978-1-55130-735-0 (pbk.).—ISBN 978-1-55130-736-7 (pdf).—ISBN 978-1-55130-737-4 (epub)

      1. Canada—Civilization—Textbooks. 2. Canada—Civilization—21st century—Forecasting—Textbooks. 3. Canada—English-French relations—Textbooks. 4. Native peoples—Canada—Textbooks. 5. Native peoples—Canada—Government relations—Textbooks. I. Friesen, John W., author II. Title.

FC95.5.H37 2015   971   C2015-901655-X   C2015-901656-8

Text design by Brad Horning
Cover design by Gord Robertson

Printed and bound in Canada by Webcom

Canada

Dedicated to our wives:

Terri Mae Saunders and Virginia Lyons Friesen

CONTENTS

ACKNOWLEDGEMENTS

As with the first two editions, I want to thank the many students whom I have instructed in courses on Canadian society, first at the University of Alberta and, since 2002, at the University of Lethbridge. Their keen interest and probing questions have led me to think hard about the nature of societies and Canadian society in particular.

Thanks go to Canadian Scholars' Press Inc., in particular Daniella Balabuk, Natalie Garriga, Andrea Gill, and James MacNevin, with whom John and I worked closely in putting together this edition. I would also like to thank Martha Hunter and Emma Johnson, with whom we worked in the final stages of the text's preparation.

Thanks go also to a host of friends and colleagues for their many contributions to my thinking over many years about Canadian society, and to my departmental colleagues for their general support.

I would also like to acknowledge Dr. P. B. Waite for the use of his words quoted in Chapter 5 and John Robert Colombo for the use of various quotations from *Colombo & Company*.

Finally, I must also acknowledge the support of my wife, Terri, and my children, Jayna and Keenan. They are a constant source of inspiration and the cause of my dedication to a better Canada.

I apologize to any whose contributions I have unintentionally overlooked. I take sole responsibility for any errors or omissions contained in the text.

T. W. H.

To begin, I want to acknowledge the consistent support of my wife, Dr. Virginia Lyons Friesen, who shares my research interests and with whom I have co-authored more than a dozen books. Virginia shines in the areas of computer technology, Internet research, editing, and putting up with my whims. I owe her a debt that cannot be repaid in this life.

Second, I want to say thanks to the Aboriginal peoples who have graciously hosted us while we were conducting research through the years on reservations (reserves) from Alberta and Saskatchewan to Texas and Mexico. Locally, our gratitude must be extended to the Four Band Plains Cree, Siksika, Stoney (Nakoda Sioux), and Tsuu T'ina First

Nations from whom we have learned a great deal. My own formal attachment to the Stoney First Nation as minister of the Morley United Church from 1986 to 2008 gave me the opportunity to be mentored by some of the most accepting individuals I have ever met. This includes a lengthy list, some of whom have since passed away. They are: Chief John and Alva Snow, Lazarus and Lily Wesley, Frank and Glenda Crawler, Ivan and Trudy Wesley, Rod and Reatha Mark, Lucy Daniels, Clara Rollinmud, Fred and Beatrice Powder, and Reba Powderface. There are many more people to list, but space will not allow, and I apologize for that. Still, I want to express my thanks for their influence on my life.

I also want to thank the students at the University of Calgary and Old Sun College at Siksika who have enrolled in Canadian Studies classes conducted by my wife, Virginia, and myself. The courses include CNST 311 (Plains Indigenous History), CNST 313 (Native Art in Canada), and CNST 315 (Native Education in Canada). Our students deserve thanks because often we learn as much from them as they do from us. True learning is always a sharing process.

Finally, I want to thank my colleague, Trevor W. Harrison, for the hard work he put into this project. He never seemed to weary of deadlines, but worked prodigiously and perseveringly to bring this production to its birth as a book. I only hope that our readers will appreciate the effort involved in producing this work.

J. W. F.

INTRODUCTION

WHAT IS SOCIETY?

Ours is not the only nation which has out-travelled its own soul and now is forced to search frantically for a new identity. No wonder, for so many, the past Canadian experience has become not so much a forgotten thing as an unknown thing.

—novelist Hugh MacLennan, 1974

How could we have believed that there is such a thing as time, the self, or the nation?

—author John Gray, 1994

Any place is only a landscape until it is animated by the stories that provide its identity.

—novelist Noah Richler, 2006

Introduction

Since its founding in 1867, Canada's imminent demise has been regularly predicted or encouraged. Throughout much of the 19th and early 20th centuries, two threats were particularly prominent: the internecine battles between Canada's French and English communities, and the equally looming presence of the United States. The English-born journalist Goldwin Smith (1891/1971) enunciated the first of these threats in 1891 with the publication of *Canada and the Canadian Question*, a text that somewhat too gleefully pronounced the conflict between English Canada and French Canada as intractable. The second threat, that of American absorption, found its voice in a duet sung across the borders, from the Canadian side by Sarah Jane Duncan (1904/1971) in *The Imperialist* (1904) and from the American side by Samuel Moffett (1908/1972) in *The Americanization of Canada* (1908). Later, as the western provinces were opened up for agricultural development, a third peril reared its head—that of western alienation.

In one form or another, these same threats found an echo in later years. Quebec's escalating demands for recognition, if not outright sovereignty, after the 1960s resulted in a plethora of books predicting as before an end to Canada's national experiment. One of them, Peter Brimelow's (1986) *The Patriot Game*, faithfully replicated Goldwin Smith's arguments of nearly a century previous. Similarly, changes in Canada's political economy after the Second World War led George Grant (2005 [1965]), in *Lament for a Nation*, to decry the loss of British influence as a buffer against the American embrace. The adoption of free trade after 1988 heightened these warnings: Witness, for example, Lawrence Martin's *Pledge of Allegiance: The Americanization of Canada during the Mulroney Years* (1993). As before, these twin pillars of discontent were joined in the late 1980s by rising western discontent, then in the guise of the Reform Party (Harrison, 1995). These more traditional fears were joined in some quarters by warnings centred on Aboriginal demands for the redress of historic wrongs (Smith, 1995). And though a new confidence—even cockiness—has in recent years emerged, there are voices still heralding Canada's demise, to whit columnist Diane Francis's (2013) recent tome on the benefits of a merger with the United States.

Canada faces challenges and always will. As with individuals, the scars that define nations are always ripe to be opened again. To the historic and more recent internal challenges and threats must also be added the growing and interrelated challenges of globalization, terrorism, resource scarcity, and climate change (especially global warming). These issues—some old, some new—and the processes by which Canadians have attempted to resolve them frame this text. In particular, this text deals with the thorny problem of Canadian society.

Given Canada's geographical vastness, its historical and cultural diversity, and its political and social complexity, one might ask how it is possible to grasp Canadian society. What sense does it make to even speak of "Canadian society" at a time when—we continue to be told—cultural, economic, and political borders are breaking down (Ohmae, 1990)? The vastness of the problem led one sociologist some years ago to comment that "the task of 'constituting society,' of creating knowledge about, and articulating a wholist account of, the total society, is no longer central to current concerns of sociologists in Canada" (Whyte, 1992:313). To paraphrase Frisby and Sayer (1986:121), Canadian society would seem "too grand an abstraction by far for modern sociological tastes."

The reader is thus forewarned: In opening this text, you begin the daunting task of journeying into a territory that many scholars avoid, where existing maps may be unclear, where the terrain is constantly shifting, where fact and myth coexist, and where abstractions run wild. To assist in this journey through Canadian society, this introductory chapter provides a set of rudimentary tools: terms, concepts, theories, and an explanation of historical sociology as a method of study. Learn to use these tools well. The chapter begins with an attempt at defining the object of study.

The "Problem" of Society

What is society? At first, the question may seem strange. After all, we use the term *society* frequently. But try to touch it or point a finger to it. It cannot be done, of course, because—unlike a rock, for example—society is not a concrete thing; it is an abstract concept.

This comparison touches on the first problem with the concept of society. Abstract concepts are very powerful and necessary tools for assisting us to think about complex social phenomena. Abstract concepts become problematic, however, when we engage in **reification**, the process of believing that our mental constructs actually exist materially. Many of the terms we will deal with in this chapter, such as *state* and *nation*, share with *society* the frequent problem of being reified.

A second problem with the term *society* is its diverse meanings. Take, for example, the following definition of the term appearing in *Merriam-Webster's Collegiate Dictionary* (2003:1115):

> **1** : companionship or association with one's fellows : friendly or intimate intercourse : COMPANY **2** : a voluntary association of individuals for common ends; *esp* : an organized group working together or periodically meeting because of common interests,

beliefs, or profession **3 a** : an enduring and cooperating social group whose members have developed organized patterns of relationships through interaction with one another **b** : a community, nation, or broad grouping of people having common traditions, institutions, and collective activities and interests **4 a** : a part of a community that is a unit distinguishable by particular aims or standards of living or conduct : a social circle or a group of social circles having a clearly marked identity <literary society> **b** : a part of the community that sets itself apart as a leisure class and that regards itself as the arbiter of fashion and manners **5 a** : a natural group of plants usu. of a single species or habit within an association **b** : the progeny of a pair of insects when constituting a social unit (as a hive of bees); *broadly* : an interdependent system of organisms or biological units.

Such a definition is very broad. Clearly, Canada is not a society like that of a group of plants or the progeny of insects, or even that of individuals who believe in a flat earth. Moreover, the problem of definition is only partially remedied by adding a descriptive modifier, such as *Canadian*.

When sociologists refer to society, they often mean something more narrowly defined, yet conceptually larger. A popular introductory text in sociology (Brym, 2014:49), for example, states, "A society involves people interacting socially and sharing culture, usually in a defined geographical area." Another introductory text (Kendall, Murray, and Linden, 2007:4) defines society as follows: "A society is a large social grouping that shares the same geographical territory and is subject to the same political authority and dominant cultural expectations." This definition suggests that a society's social boundaries are coexistent with its political boundaries. But which political boundaries are to be used: federal, provincial, or municipal?

This question points to a third problem with the concept of society: Where does one society end and another begin? Denis (1993) notes, for example, that while Canadian society courses are common throughout Anglo-Canadian universities, Quebec's francophone universities focus on Quebec society courses, while a popular anglophone text (Fournier, Rosenberg, and White, 1997) also deals with Quebec society. Add to this the fact that the University of Calgary has for some years offered an Alberta society course, and we may acquire some understanding of the frustration voiced by Denis (1993:255):

> Where does it stop? If "English Canada" and Quebec can both be distinct societies within Canada, which is itself a distinct society relative to (or within?) the U.S., does this also mean that American society is within . . . etc.? In this socio-geographic chain, shouldn't a number of statements be mutually exclusive?

A fourth problem with the concept of society is its conflation with several other concepts, notably those of country, state, and nation (see Denis, 1993). Note above, for example, the inclusion in *Merriam-Webster's* of *nation* in its definition of society, and Kendall and colleagues' (2007) equation of the concepts of country and society. How can we distinguish among concepts such as country, state, and nation? And how are they related to the concept of Canadian society?

Country, State, Nation

Turning once again to our *Merriam-Webster's* dictionary, one of its definitions of *country* is as follows: "a political state or nation or its territory" (Merriam-Webster, 2003:266). In other words, country *equals* nation *equals* state. There are problems with this formulation, as we will see. For now, however, we will define a **country** as a territorial area, politically recognized as a country both by people within the territory and by governments outside it, on the basis of historical, material, and geographical factors (see Lane and Ersson, 1994; Deutsch, 1980).

In these terms, Canada is a country consisting of 10 provinces and 3 territories, spanning a total land area of 9,984,670 square kilometres (*Time*, 2013:232). This makes Canada the second-largest country in the world, next to Russia, which spans 17,098,200 square kilometres, and just ahead of the People's Republic of China (9,572,900 square kilometres). Compared with Russia and China, however, Canada is quite sparsely populated, with roughly 35 million people (see Table 0.1).[1] By comparison, Russia's population is 143 million, while China's population is 1.3 billion (*Time*, 2013:403, 240).

Defining Canada, Russia, or China as countries is unproblematic because each has diplomatic recognition of its sovereignty from the rest of the world. Contrast this reality with that of the Kurdish people—whose would-be homeland is divided among the countries of Iran, Turkey, Syria, and Iraq—or, for that matter, the small but militant Aryan Nations movement in the northwest United States. While the former has established a quasi-state within northern Iraq, there is no likelihood of the latter gaining a similar homeland in the foreseeable future.

A term frequently employed offhandedly as synonymous with *country* is that of *state*. However, *state* is also often used when referring to issues of governance and the use of political power. In the former sense, an individual might argue that Canada *is* a state. In the latter sense, however, the same individual might ask what kind of state Canada *has* and what its characteristics are.

The latter meaning of *state* is rendered even more diverse in scholarly accounts. For example, pluralist theorists tend to ignore the state altogether, choosing instead to narrowly analyze the formal institutions of government (such as parties, legislatures, bureaucracies), which they view as open to the influence of competing political interests (see Orum and Dale, 2009:169–170). By contrast, neo-Marxist scholars, such as Miliband (1969) and Poulantzas (1973), have tended to view the state more broadly, the former seeing the state as an instrument of capital accumulation, the latter as a relatively autonomous ensemble of social and political institutions. For others, like Skocpol (1979), the state is a wholly autonomous actor with its own powers, goals, and interests.

In each of these interpretations, the state is described more or less as a thing. Recent definitions of the state, however, have taken a more radical turn. Beginning with Abrams (1988), the state has increasingly been described as an abstract concept, the reification of which is a weapon for enacting, legitimating, and ultimately condoning "violence" (Sayer, 1987; Denis, 1989).

Table 0.1: Canadian Population, by Province and Region, 1851–2013 (in Thousands)

Year	Canada	NL[1]	PE	NS	NB	QC	ON	MB[2]	SK	AB[3]	BC	YT	NT	NU[4]
1851	2,437	n/a	63	277	194	890	952	n/a	n/a	n/a	55	n/a	6	n/a
1861	3,231	n/a	81	331	252	1,112	1,396	n/a	n/a	n/a	52	n/a	7	n/a
1871	3,690	n/a	94	388	286	1,192	1,621	25	n/a	n/a	36	n/a	48	n/a
1881	4,325	n/a	109	441	321	1,360	1,927	62	n/a	n/a	49	n/a	56	n/a
1891	4,833	n/a	109	450	321	1,489	2,114	153	n/a	n/a	98	n/a	99	n/a
1901	5,371	n/a	103	460	331	1,649	2,183	255	91	73	179	27	20	n/a
1911	7,207	n/a	94	492	352	2,006	2,527	461	492	374	393	9	7	n/a
1921	8,789	n/a	89	524	388	2,361	2,934	610	758	588	525	4	8	n/a
1931	10,377	n/a	88	513	408	2,875	3,432	700	922	732	694	4	9	n/a
1941	11,507	n/a	95	578	457	3,332	3,788	730	896	796	818	5	12	n/a
1951	14,011	361	98	643	516	4,056	4,598	777	832	940	1,165	9	16	n/a
1961	18,239	458	105	737	598	5,259	6,236	922	925	1,332	1,629	15	23	n/a
1971	21,963	531	113	797	643	6,137	7,849	999	932	1,666	2,241	19	36	n/a
1981	24,821	575	124	855	706	6,548	8,811	1,036	976	2,294	2,824	24	48	n/a
1991	28,033	580	130	915	746	7,065	10,428	1,110	1,003	2,593	3,373	29	61	n/a
1996	29,698	561	136	931	753	7,274	11,101	1,134	1,020	2,781	3,882	32	68	25
2001	31,021	522	137	932	750	7,397	11,898	1,151	1,000	3,057	4,078	30	41	28
2004	31,996	517	138	938	752	7,549	12,420	1,171	995	3,208	4,204	31	43	30
2005	32,311	514	138	936	751	7,598	12,565	1,174	990	3,281	4,260	31	43	30
2006	32,872	511	138	938	746	7,632	12,662	1,484	992	3,421	4,242	32	43	31
2011	34,343	525	144	944	756	8,008	13,264	1,234	1,066	3,790	4,499	35	44	34

2012	34,755	527	145	945	757	8,084	13,412	1,250	1,088	3,889	4,543	36	44	35
2013	35,159	527	145	941	756	8,155	13,538	1,265	1,108	4,025	4,582	37	44	36
% (2013)	100	1.5	0.41	2.7	2.2	23.2	38.51	3.6	3.2	11.45	13	0.1	0.13	0.1

Notes: 1. Newfoundland figures before Confederation in 1949 are not included. 2. Population figures for Manitoba before 1871 are included in figures for the Northwest Territories. 3. Population figures for Saskatchewan and Alberta before 1901 are included in figures for the Northwest Territories. 4. Population figures for Nunavut before 1996 are included in figures for the Northwest Territories.

Sources: Adapted from Statistics Canada. 1983. *Historical Statistics of Canada.* Cat. no. 11-516, Series A2-14. Ottawa: Statistics Canada; Statistics Canada. 2001. *Canada Year Book.* Cat. no. 11-402, Table 3.2. Ottawa: Statistics Canada; Statistics Canada. 2011a. *Focus on Geography Series, 2011 Census* (www12.statcan.gc.ca/census-recensement/2011/as-sa/fogs-spg/Facts-pr-eng.cfm?Lang=Eng&GK=PR&GC=10).; and Statistics Canada. 2013a. Annual Population Estimates, Table 1.1-1 (www.statcan.gc.ca/pub/91-215-x/2013002/t002-eng.pdf). Totals rounded up by authors.

Despite important differences, the definitions reviewed here agree that the concept of state has something to do with the exercise of political power. In this text, therefore, a **state** is defined as a set of institutions successfully claiming a monopoly over political rule-making and the legitimate use of violence and coercion within a given territory, that is, a country (see Weber, 1958:78; Lane and Ersson, 1994:30). The important question of globalization's impact upon states is taken up below.

The third term requiring definition is *nation*. Note, at the onset, how the terms *nation* and *state* are often linked together, that is, as *nation-state*. (Note also how the *Merriam-Webster's* definition above equates the concepts of country and nation.) We have looked at the meanings of *country* and *state*. What exactly is a nation?

A **nation** is defined as a mass of individuals who define themselves collectively as a people. But on what bases might individuals define themselves as a nation?

Scholars differentiate between two types of nations: civic nations and ethnic nations (Webber, 1994). Civic nationalism is determined by citizenship. Membership in the civic nation, at least in theory, is open to anyone. By contrast, ethnic—sometimes also termed *tribal*—nations are based on supposedly fixed biological (e.g., racial) and cultural (e.g., linguistic or religious) markers. Note, however, how malleable even these markers are. Biological descriptors are particularly uncertain measures of difference, and people can readily acquire a new language, convert to a different religion, or adopt new cultural practices.

Both civic and ethnic nations are tied to a specific territorial homeland. In the case of civic nations, however, the territorial referent is quite concrete: no territory, no citizenship. By contrast, ethnic nations may continue to exist, even thrive, after the territorial homeland has disappeared from political maps. Both civic and ethnic nations, however, constitute what Anderson (1983) terms "imagined communities." A person can never know all the other members of his or her nation. Rather, the other members are idealized figments, our relationship with them the product of collective stories that we tell each other.

As stated above, the term *nation* is often conflated with *state* to produce *nation-state*. This conjoining of these terms is both unfortunate and imprecise. The term *nation-state* suggests that every nation must be a state, and that every state must consist of only one nation. The actions of the Nazi regime in Germany (1933–1945) and the Balkan and African wars of the 1990s suggest the dangerous consequences that may result from such a belief. Beyond these extremes, however, the term *nation-state* is simply misleading in describing reality. As Hobsbawm (1992:186) notes, no more than a dozen of today's 180-plus nation-states house only a single ethnic or linguistic group. Indeed, van den Berghe (1992) argues that only Japan, Swaziland, and Somalia are genuine nation-states—and even these are, today, finding their "purity" challenged.

As Laxer (2000:56) points out, most countries are heterogeneous and "cannot, even mythically, pretend all citizens are kith and kin." A lot of countries, in fact, are "state-nations," that is, nations organized—indeed, "created"—under the guidance of the state, while other nations are "stateless." In short, the assumption that country *equals* state *equals* nation is historically, politically, and socially constructed. Determining the exact fit between these terms in any particular case is a matter of empirical reflection. This point brings us to Canada.

A central thesis of this text is that, while Canada is indisputably a country, it is one founded on not one but three historic nations—English, French, and Aboriginal—and consequently requires a complex federal state structure. Efforts to make Canada conform to the European model—for example, repeated attempts by the English majority to coerce and otherwise assimilate either the French or Aboriginal peoples—have usually foundered, threatening Canada's continuance. The text's second thesis, however, is that these internal differences over nation and state, combined with external threats of absorption by the United States, have rendered Canada unique among 21st-century countries. The result, in turn, is a country in which civil and state relations are also unique; in short, something that we may consider a society.

Back to Society

The concept of society emerged in the 19th century. **Sociology**, meaning the study of society, arose at the same time. For early sociologists, the concept of society was meant to locate the site of the many changes wrought, both directly and indirectly, by the Industrial Revolution and the rise of capitalism. For Karl Marx (1818–1883), feudal relationships, based on tradition and fealty, were being replaced by capitalist relationships, based on private property and the cash nexus (Marx, 1977a). For Ferdinand Tönnies (1855–1936), rural and small-town life was being replaced by urban life, and kinship and tradition were being replaced by anonymity and self-interest (Tönnies, 1887/1957). For Émile Durkheim (1858–1917), the changes were marked by a transformation in the basis of social solidarity from similarity-in-kind ("mechanical solidarity") to differentiation and, hence, greater interdependence ("organic solidarity") (Durkheim, 1893/1964). For Max Weber (1864–1920), traditional authority was giving way to legal-rational forms of authority, reaching its apex in bureaucratic institutions (Weber, 1958).

Early on, however, the concept of society also came to define "one half of an antithetic tandem in which the other is the state" (Wallerstein, 1997:315). Wallerstein adds,

> In this formulation, the state could be observed and analysed directly. It operated through formal institutions by way of known (constitutional) rules. The "society" was taken to mean that tissue of manners and customs that held a group of people together without, despite or against formal rules. In some sense, "society" represented something more enduring and "deeper" than the state, less manipulable and certainly more elusive.

This perspective is very much alive today. Consider, for example, how often you have heard someone—perhaps on a radio talk show—denounce the state or the government for doing something at variance with the interests of society. For many people, including some academics, society is an abstract concept defined by its opposition to another abstract concept, the state.

It was not always the case, however, that society and state were viewed as separate (and perhaps opposed). Knuttila and Kubik (2000) suggest, for example, that both

Auguste Comte (1798–1857), who first coined the term *sociology*, and Durkheim, who held the first chair in sociology, viewed the state as an integral part—*but only a part*—of a functional modern society. From this perspective, society and state are not merely "coterminous" (Giddens, 1984); they are indivisible.

Denis (1989) has argued forcefully for a restoration of the links between the two concepts. For him, "'states' are a historically specific type of society, whose institutions take the legal-constitutional discursive form which has enabled capitalism to rise—*a state is not in (or above) society, a state is a society*" (Denis, 1989:347–348, italics added). Similarly, Teeple (2000:15) argues that the form of state that has emerged since the Second World War in most Western countries, the welfare state, "can also be seen as a capitalist *society* . . . " (italics in original).

This formulation may seem at first extreme, positing that the capitalist state is everything, and everything is the capitalist state. Yet it is hard to think of any activity today that is not codified, regulated, and occasionally prohibited in some way by the state, often for the purposes of enabling markets and ensuring profits. This is true whether speaking of a state-capitalist country such as the "communist" People's Republic of China, the social democratic country of Sweden, or the laissez-faire capitalist country of the United States.

It is also true of Canada. The creation of Canada—of Canadian *society*—cannot be understood separately from the role of the state. A prime example of this is the National Policy of 1878 (see Chapter 6), which dramatically altered Canadian economic development and immigration policy. The real challenge in conceptualizing state and society as one thing involves determining which social actors have gained either influence or outright control of the state's machinery at given times and what this has meant, in turn, for defining and shaping socio-cultural, economic, and political relations within Canada.

What, then, is society? A **society** is defined as the product of relatively continuous and enduring interactions, within a political territory, between people more or less identifying themselves as members of the society, these interactions being maintained by an ensemble of political, economic, cultural, and other institutions, the sum of such interactions being in excess of interactions occurring with similarly defined societies external to the given territory.

This definition raises several points requiring elaboration. First, note that societies, like states and nations, are processes, not things. Whether any of these labels has substantive meaning for a group of people is dependent upon the maintenance of "relatively continuous and enduring interactions." We may presume further that, on balance, positive interactions are more fruitful than negative interactions. Second, note also that individuals may have either greater or lesser attachment to a society, just as they may have greater or lesser attachment to other social groups (such as the family) or may have different reasons for feeling they are part of a group. Third, note the important role of various institutions in acting as intermediaries between individuals, small groups, and society as a whole. Fourth, note that no society today is hermetically sealed off from external influences. This last point is brought home by globalization.

Globalization, the State, and Society

The term *globalization* became popular in the late part of the 20th century as a short-hand means of describing global integration. But what does globalization actually mean? In brief, **globalization** is defined as a series of interrelated economic, political, and cultural changes, sometimes contradictory and even opposed, occurring throughout the world (see Harrison, 1999). Economically, globalization—often prefaced with the word "neo-liberal" (see Chapter 8)—involves a complex series of worldwide exchanges in labour, trade, technology, and capital (Stubbs and Underhill, 1994; Laxer, 1995) and the reorganization over space of production itself (Mittelman, 1996; Lairson and Skidmore, 1997). Politically, globalization similarly manifests itself in increased interconnectedness and interdependence among countries, though not necessarily unification (Boyer and Drache, 1996). Culturally, globalization involves the spread of primarily Western liberal practices and notions of individualism and civil and political rights, as well as consumerism (Mittelman, 1996; Boyer and Drache, 1996; Sklair, 2002; Robbins, 2014).

A central debate surrounding globalization has been its impact upon the state. One school of thought holds that globalization has severely curtailed the power and capacity of states, if not actually signalled their outright demise. Economic historian Eric Heilbroner, for example, states,

> The global market system stretches beyond the political authority of any single government. Faced with a network of connections that escape their powers of surveillance and regulation, national governments become increasingly unable to cope with the problems that arise from the intrusion of the global economy into their territories. (1992:60)

Or, in Daniel Bell's words, "the national state has become too small for the big problems of life, and too big for the small problems" (1993:362). In partial consequence, the state is being "decomposed" by globalization from above (by transnationals, the World Bank, the International Monetary Fund, and so on) and the re-emergence of smaller communities from below (McDonald, 1994:241). In effect, nation and state are viewed as decoupling (Paquet, 1997:36), perhaps devolving into smaller, regional states (Ohmae, 1995). While hardly a case of peaceful devolution, the breakup of the former Yugoslavia in the 1990s provides an example.

Note that not everyone views the state's supposed decline equally. In the early days of globalization, some applauded the decomposition of the state as allowing for greater economic efficiency and consumer choice (Ohmae, 1995) and the end of state-orchestrated violence (Rummel, 1994; van den Berghe, 1992). Others, however, fear that the state's eclipse will result in the sweeping away of 200 years of hard-won civil, political, and social rights (Teeple, 2000). Likewise, some believe that the fragmentation of states signals the decline of civic nationalism and its replacement by renewed forms of tribalism (Barber, 1996), perhaps even anarchism and terrorism as witnessed in the attacks on New York and Washington in September 2001 and since (see Chapter 8).

If traditional states are in decline, does this mean their powers of regulation and coercion have been dispersed? A second school of thought disputes this, arguing instead that the powers previously held by territorial states remains concentrated but has been transferred to undemocratic quasi-states—transnational corporations—and other unaccountable international organizations (see Robbins, 2014; Strange, 1996; Korten, 2001). From this perspective, the state itself is being globalized (Albrow, 1997:172). In the words of David Korten (2001:54), "Corporations have emerged as the dominant governance institutions on the planet."

Clearly, either the outright demise of the state or its resurrection at the global level would have important implications for societies such as Canada's. What might be the fate of Canadian society in such a world? Malcolm Waters (1994:233) provides a succinct answer: "If the nation-state is dissolving, or at least attenuating, then so too must national societies." One logical extension of this dissolution is that national societies will be replaced by a global society, also known as "the global village." Is such a thing possible, or is this merely utopian theorizing?

A third school of thought argues that the death of the state has been greatly exaggerated (Laxer, 1995). From this perspective, the world economy has not been globalized but rather "internationalized," with states themselves the architects reorganizing capitalist production. While many of the world's wealthiest economies are not countries but corporations (Robbins, 2014), the latter are not stateless, let alone "virtual." Most multinationals retain headquarters in the economically dominant states, especially the United States. Put another way, states peripheral to the world capitalist economy were weak before globalization and remain so now, while states that were central to that economy remain powerful actors, not merely despite, but as a *consequence of*, globalization (Burbach, Nunez, and Kagarlitsky, 1997:19).

Finally, from an historical perspective, it should be noted that globalization is not a new phenomenon (Laxer, 1995). Of an earlier episode of capitalist globalization in the mid-19th century, Marx (1977a:224) wrote, "The need of a constantly expanding market for its products chases the bourgeoisie over the whole surface of the globe. It must nestle everywhere, settle everywhere, establish connections everywhere." At the same time, however, capitalist expansion has not always proceeded in a straightforward manner; there have been periods of contraction, such as during the Depression of the 1930s. Faced with increasing challenges brought about by war, resource scarcity, and climate change, some argue the world may experience de-globalization and a return to localism (Bello, 2002). The credit crisis that spread like a virus through the world economy in the fall of 2008, leading to the widespread nationalization of banks and the overnight depreciation of stock values, bears witness to the negative side of global interrelatedness and dependency.

Whatever its final disposition, the recent period of globalization has not left states unscathed. Technological and organizational changes and the freer flow of capital associated with the growth of multinationals have had an impact on state roles, functions, and policies (see Jessop, 1993; Teeple, 2000). At the same time, states remain central actors, organizing economic life, providing political legitimacy, employing means of coercion, and generally exercising control over their populations (Boyer and Drache, 1996).

This fact remains true for Canada. Globalization has not left Canada and Canadian society untouched. As a wealthy but semi-peripheral country, Canada faces the additional challenge of residing next to the United States, the chief engine of recent globalization. Yet Canada also remains a sovereign country, its cultural symbols and political state intact. And within these geographic and political boundaries, Canadian society also continues to exist as an object worthy of study. Sociology is particularly suited for the task of carrying out this examination.

Theorizing Social Relationships

Students approaching sociology for the first time are frequently confounded by an array of theories. This reaction is both unfortunate and unnecessary. Theories are like tools. A wrench is a poor instrument for hammering nails. Likewise, a hammer is useless for sawing wood. But, used properly, a wrench or a hammer can be very helpful.

The same goes for theories. Theories are neither good nor bad. They are either useful or not in assisting us to sort out and understand particular phenomena.

The sociological "tool box" contains several theories for understanding how individuals and groups (large and small) interact. For students at a beginning level of instruction, four theories, with their own perspectives on human behaviour, are particularly useful: structural functional, conflict, symbolic interaction, and post-structural theories. **Structural functional theory** has roots in the work of early anthropologists, including Herbert Spencer (1820–1895), an English sociologist who adopted evolutionary theory for the study of human societies (the idea of Social Darwinism, or the "survival of the fittest"). It was the American sociologist Talcott Parsons (1902–1979) who primarily codified the theory's tenets, however. Drawing upon earlier work by Weber and Durkheim (among others) and emerging ideas of systems theory and cybernetics, Parsons arrived at a grand theory of social action that emphasized the relationships among various institutions—the Church, family, schools, the state—each of which, he argued, fulfill specific functions necessary for the continuation and survival of a given society (Parsons, 1951). An institution's function may be *manifest* or *latent* (Merton, 1968). For example, schools are manifestly intended to educate students, but they also control young people and socialize them for later participation in the labour market.

Structural functionalism draws our attention to how various social elements are interconnected. A change in one part of society—for instance, a downturn in the economy—may thus have unforeseen consequences for other parts (Merton, 1968), such as family structure. Where change in one sphere occurs, and other spheres are not able to adapt, or do so slowly, disequilibrium or *dysfunctions* may occur. In general, however, the theory suggests that the interconnectedness of functions slows the rate of social change.

The second perspective, **conflict theory**, has its roots in the work of Karl Marx and Max Weber. Marx, whose writings champion social revolution, argued that world history was the result of class struggle and, more widely, of structural contradictions. Weber's contribution to conflict theory was to suggest that conflict is not necessarily based on class alone, but also upon differences in status and power. Conflict theorists today recognize the many non-class bases of inequality and conflict, such as ethnicity, language, region, age, and gender, and that conflict frequently cuts across several lines (Curtis, Grabb, and Guppy, 1999). For example, labour conflict at a bank may involve workers and owners/shareholders (class conflict). At the same time, it is likely that the majority of low-level employees are female while upper-level managers are male (gender conflict).

Within the Marxist stream of conflict theory, particular emphasis is given to the notion of **praxis**, defined as purposeful action in contrast to abstract theorizing. As Marx (1977b:158) himself said, "The philosophers have only interpreted the world, in various ways; the point is to change it." This tradition of activism continues today in feminist and anti-oppressive approaches to research (see Box 0.1).

Box 0.1: Feminism and Anti-Oppressive Research

There are several types of feminism: liberal, socialist, radical, cultural, and post-modern feminism. Despite some differences, however, each of these types of feminism encourages activist research, especially meant to oppose **patriarchy** (the system of male domination in society) and **sexism** (the belief that one sex is inherently superior to another).

The tenets of anti-oppressive research, as described by Potts and Brown (2012:103–105), similarly invokes the notion of praxis:

1. Anti-oppressive research is social justice and resistance in process and outcome.
2. Anti-oppressive research recognizes that all knowledge is socially constructed and political.
3. The anti-oppressive research process is all about power and relationships.

Source: Potts, Karen, and Leslie Brown. 2012. "Becoming an Anti-Oppressive Researcher." Pp. 103–116 in *Rethinking Sociology in the 21st Century*, edited by M. Webber and K. Bezanson. 3rd ed. Toronto: Canadian Scholars' Press.

Structural functionalism and conflict theory are generally viewed as the yin and yang of sociological perspectives. Nonetheless, the theories also share similarities. Both are macro theories, examining society as a whole using broad social categories, such as class, occupation, or gender. Both emphasize the interrelatedness of society's parts. Both also emphasize the social reality of the objects of study (e.g., class, family). By contrast, the other two theories examined here—symbolic interaction theory and post-structuralism—argue that social reality is largely constructed.

Symbolic interaction theory generally deals with interactions within small groups or organizations. Symbolic interaction is a sociological offshoot of social psychology. While social psychological concepts are embedded in the work of Marx, Weber, and Durkheim, symbolic interaction theory is chiefly a product of American pragmatism, particularly the work of George Herbert Mead (1863–1931) (see Morrow, 1994:13; also Collins, 1982). Whereas both conflict and structural functional theories emphasize the structures within which action occurs or is constrained, symbolic interaction theory emphasizes that all human behaviour is meaningful, but that these meanings are collectively constructed and defined in the course of interaction. To give an example drawn from Durkheim (1912/1978:228), the flag for which a soldier dies represents symbolically more than a piece of cloth. In this sense, the methodological approach of Weber (1958), known as *verstehen*—that is, an understanding of the meaning that others attach to events, symbols, and experiences—is entirely congruent with this theory.

Like symbolic interaction theory, **post-structural theory** deals with the social construction of meanings. Unlike the former, however, its origins lie in the structural linguistics of Ferdinand de Saussure (1857–1913), hence the theory's primacy of language as the medium by which reality is understood. Specifically, post-structural theorists argue that language operates through a system of signs that point not to a definite referent but gain their meaning through difference from other signs. In turn, any text (written or spoken) involves a combination, or string, of signs, each pointing to another sign, such that any "meaning" is both arbitrary and unstable. Put another way, there is an endless slippage between the words we use and the meanings (we think) we are conveying and the meanings that others derive. From a post-structural perspective, humans may engage in meaningful behaviour, but such meanings are not precisely decipherable.

At the extreme, post-structuralism would suggest "the impossibility of sociology" (Scott and Marshall, 2005:512; see also Giddens, 1987). Especially as practised by theorists such as Jacques Derrida (1930–2004), post-structuralism questions the possibility of establishing taken-for-granted meanings (as suggested by symbolic interaction theory) or apprehending objective reality (as sought by structural functionalists and conflict theorists).

The work of theorists such as Michel Foucault (1926–1984) restores post-structuralism's radical potential, however. In a series of books, Foucault (1973, 1977, 1980) examined the discursive practices that define and categorize individual behaviour. Take criminal behaviour, for example. Rather than existing per se, Foucault argues it is a category produced by a social discourse produced within a set of social institutions (prisons, the criminal justice system) using a set of historical statements (theories, statistics, etc.). More important, however, post-structural theorists such as Foucault connect language with a rethinking of ideology and power (Fairclough, 1989:15). Post-structuralism thus provides a link to structural functionalism and conflict theory and to the work of theorists such as Antonio Gramsci and Noam Chomsky. To give an example, a post-structural analysis might question the role of data gathered by Statistics Canada (a source we will use throughout this text) in formulating our notion of Canadian society—a question made particularly salient by the Conservative government's order in 2011 that Statistics Canada not conduct its Mandatory Long-Form Census (see Box 0.2).

Box 0.2: Statistics Wars: The Mandatory Long-Form Census

The first census on Canada's present territory dates to New France in 1666; the first census after Confederation was conducted in 1871, and has been done regularly since that time (Statistics Canada, 2013b) Over the years, the census has grown in importance and scope to not only enumerate Canadians but to provide a statistical profile of Canadian life.

Key to this larger profile was the Mandatory Long-Form Census (MLFC), introduced in 1971 to complement the Mandatory Short-Form Census (MSFC). The latter was thereafter given to 80 percent of all Canadians while the former was given to the remaining 20 percent of Canadians. This more extensive information was used in a wide variety of ways, including social planning, marketing, school construction, and social transfers—not to mention genealogical research.

In June 2010, however, the federal Conservative government ordered Statistics Canada to drop use of the MLFC. The decision was made without consultation with any experts or affected community leaders, and was quickly denounced by virtually every segment of Canadian society, including several of the provinces, union and business leaders, nursing and religious organizations, non-profit groups, and university administrators and academics. The head of Statistics Canada resigned his position on a matter of principle.

In defending its decision, the government cited privacy concerns and complaints it had received about the MLFC being coercive—a state intrusion into personal liberty. Critics noted, however, that the confidentiality of census data is protected by the Statistics Act and that there had only been two complaints about the census in recent memory. Many critics argued the decision appeared to be based on the government's desire to control the information available to Canadians, particularly disadvantaged groups who might use it to promote their claims for greater social justice (McDaniel and MacDonald, 2012).

The MLFC was replaced in 2011 with the (voluntary) National Household Survey (NHS). The difference between a census and a survey is important to note: A census is a record of an entire population, while a survey is only a sample, which may or may not accurately reflect the population. This means that data collected in 2006 or before is not methodologically comparable with that collected in 2011—an important point as many of the updated tables in this text take information from the NHS.

The MSFC was completed as required by 98.1 percent of Canadians while the voluntary NHS was completed by only 69.3 percent (compared with the 93.5 percent of Canadians who completed the MLFC in 2006). Fewer respondents also completed all of the questions on the NHS than on the earlier MLFC (Statistics Canada, 2012). In consequence, the statistical reliability of 2011 data, especially at the local level, has been questioned.

In the bigger picture, as McDaniel and MacDonald (2012) argue, the loss of the MLFC data deprives Canadians of the ability to know something about themselves and about each other. The decision also betrays an anti-intellectualism (Ramp and Harrison, 2012) that, in a manner turning Foucault's dictum (i.e., knowledge is power) on its head, suggests that power may also flow from a lack of knowledge—or, more accurately, a lack of evidence—by which the state or other powerful interests may make assertions and policies without any basis in empirical reality.

Sources: Statistics Canada. 2012. "Final Report on 2016 Census Options: Proposed Content Determination Framework and Methodological Options" (www12.statcan.gc.ca/census-recensement/fc-rf/reports-rapports/ r2_index-eng.cfm); Statistics Canada. 2013b. "History of the Census of Canada" (www12.statcan.gc.ca/census-recensement/2011/ref/about-apropos/history-histoire-eng.cfm#a1); McDaniel, Susan, and Heidi MacDonald. 2012. "To Know Ourselves—Not." *Canadian Journal of Sociology* 37(3):253–272; Ramp, William, and Trevor W. Harrison. 2012. "Libertarian Populism, Neoliberal Rationality, and the Mandatory Long-Form Census: Implications for Sociology." *Canadian Journal of Sociology* 37(3):273–294.

How might a sociologist use structural functional, conflict, symbolic interaction, and post-structural theories? A typically Canadian example makes the case.

Thinking Theoretically: Canada's Game

The theory you choose as your lens for examining a topic will provide you with particular questions and insights. Let's take hockey as an example. From a structural functional point of view, a sociologist might examine the functions that hockey plays in our society. She or he might emphasize that hockey provides a source of national pride and cohesion, such as occurred in 1972 when Paul Henderson scored the goal that clinched Canada's defeat of the Soviet Union. Our sociologist might also remark on the role of hockey (and sports in general) in providing a safe outlet for male aggression, both at the interpersonal level and as a substitute for war between countries. (The 1972 series was widely viewed in the context of the Cold War as pitting the respective communist and capitalist systems against one another.) She or he might finally note that hockey has traditionally provided a means of social mobility for working-class youth.

A conflict perspective forces us to examine professional hockey quite differently. The 2012–2013 dispute that saw half the National Hockey League (NHL) season wiped out highlighted a conflict between capitalist owners and workers (albeit very well-paid ones). Analyzing the events that led the Winnipeg Jets to move to Arizona in 1996 (see Silver, 1996)—then return in 2011–2012, the result of the relocation of a team from Atlanta— provides a similarly provocative view of corporate capitalism in an age of globalization. Alternatively, a conflict theorist might note that professional hockey seems stratified along ethnic lines. For example, most players in the NHL are white, whether Canadian, American, or European. The first Black player in the National Hockey League was Willie O'Ree, with Boston in 1958. Since then, other Black players (such as Evander Kane and P. K. Subban), as well as some Aboriginal players (such as T. J. Oshie), have entered the league, but ethnic minorities remain few and, as in other arenas beyond sports, have often faced racist taunts from other players and fans.

Likewise, a conflict theorist employing a feminist critique might note how women's hockey remains marginalized (despite the Canadian women's team's four consecutive Winter Olympic Gold-winning performances, beginning in 2002). The feminist approach might also draw our attention to how women in hockey, and sports in general, receive publicity only when they are sexually attractive and that mainstream sports appear often to enforce and reward a kind of male machismo whose aggressiveness is sometimes carried into the personal lives of players, with dire consequences for girlfriends, spouses, and children.

A symbolic interaction theorist might concentrate on the meanings that fans bring to hockey. What, for example, is the process by which an individual becomes a fan? How is it that people come to see their own success as reflected in a team? How do people at a hockey game learn to act like fans (and not like uninformed wannabes)? From the players' point of view, what is the process by which one becomes accepted as a team member? What is team bonding, and how is it achieved?

Finally, a post-structural theorist might begin by examining a set of binary elements surrounding hockey's place in fans' psyche (the individual versus the team; play for fun versus play for money; gentlemanly play—for which the NHL awards the Lady Byng Trophy—versus often violent aggression) and how these are connected to other shifting signs. A post-structural theorist might also note the role played by sportswriters, cultural institutions (e.g., the Hockey Hall of Fame), and record keepers in lodging hockey within a series of classical tropes dealing with athletics, sport, and society. Finally, post-structural theorists, as well as those versed in feminist approaches (see Allain, 2012), employing discourse analysis, would undoubtedly note the remark of Mike Modano, a former NHL player who, leading up to the women's 2014 gold-medal-deciding game between Canada and the United States, said that there was "nothing like a good cat fight."

Note that none of these theories is exclusive. For example, a sociologist might argue that fan disenchantment during the 2004 NHL lockout resulted from a specific set of cultural meanings (a symbolic interaction perspective) manufactured through a set of discursive statements within the institution of professional sports (a post-structural argument) that were upset by the increased corporatization of professional hockey (a conflict argument) and the subsequent breaking of the irrational—but very real—emotional bonds of solidarity (a structural functionalist's concern) that male fans in particular (again, a feminist insight) have traditionally felt for their teams.

Methodology: Sociology and Why History Matters

The methodological approach used in this text is termed **historical sociology**. Historical sociology combines historical detail with sociological generalization. Harrison (1995:261) notes the following specific characteristics of the method:

- deliberate use of time as a variable;
- the explicit use of narrative structure;

- the tendency to deal simultaneously with events and processes at different levels; and
- the use of comparisons of distinct cases or between elements of a single case.

Many students are familiar with sociology as the study of society, but often this understanding is focused on society as it exists *at the moment*. This focus is comparable to that of a digital camera taking a single shot. By contrast, the focus of historical sociology is comparable to that of a video camera. An underlying assumption of historical sociology is that *our material institutions, actions, and beliefs are shaped, though not determined, by past events and our understanding (or misunderstanding) of those events*. Some of the sources of historical material a researcher might examine include official government and organizational records, including statistics; newspapers and magazines; public speeches and sermons; private letters and diaries; photographs, drawings, and audio recordings; cemetery tombstones; and interviews with participants.

For a time, the study of history fell out of fashion. At the end of the Cold War, the title of a bestselling book proclaimed "the end of history" (Fukuyama, 1992), meaning that the victory of capitalism over communism had resolved the major questions of how to organize society. About the same time, a line from a popular song by the British band Jesus Jones spoke of "watching the world wake up from history." Some people appeared to view history as a kind of personal affront to their claims of individualism and self-achievement. Many agreed with Henry Ford Sr. that "History is more or less bunk." Others, reflecting the legitimate concerns of post-structural theorists, questioned the "taken-for-granted" categories—men/women, black/white—that historians have traditionally employed in constructing their accounts (Mills, 2005).

History has made a recent comeback, however. The eminent historian Margaret Mac-Millan (2008:3) notes that history is "widely popular these days, even in North America where we have tended to look toward the future rather than the past."

To understand the value of historical sociology as a methodological approach, think for a moment about the role of history—and memory—in your own life. Consider your own personal relations with others. Do you begin each meeting with your friends anew? Of course not. Your friendship is based on experiences, ideas, and feelings you have shared. In short, you have a history together. If you were to suddenly lose that history—if you contracted total amnesia, for example, like the protagonist in the film *Memento*—the friendship would also be lost.

Looking around us, we can see where history continues to play a role in shaping current events: long-simmering disputes in Ireland, the Middle East, and Kashmir provide ample evidence. Likewise, the echoes of history can be heard in the breakup of Yugoslavia in the 1990s. Not even the United States—surely the world's most proudly modern country—can escape history, as witness the plethora of Hollywood movies that continue efforts at coming to terms with *the* meaning of the Vietnam War, while several more recent movies about the Afghanistan and Iraq Wars, such as *The Hurt Locker*, similarly appear designed to provide meaning, as history unfolds, to a catastrophe that most Americans and others find incomprehensible.

What of Canada? In an oft-quoted remark, Prime Minister William Lyon Mackenzie King (1874–1950) once stated, regarding Canada, "If some countries have too much history, we have too much geography." As John Gray (1994:124) notes, such arguments really mean that Canada "lacks *European* history," conveniently ignoring 50,000 years of Aboriginal existence in North America. But even by Eurocentric standards, the argument is false, as one glance at Quebec's licence plates will attest: *Je me souviens* (I remember). Remember what? History—though which particular historical events and how they are remembered often differs between groups of people.

We need not refer, however, merely to centuries-old history. Ask Aboriginal Canadians about the continuing impact of residential schools, some of which remained open until the 1990s. Or ask Albertans about the National Energy Program of 1980–1986 and how it still colours a widespread understanding of political relations between that province and Ottawa (or at least the federal Liberal Party).

Note, however, that the facts of history often vary with people's understanding, valuation, and interpretation of history. People may agree on the former, but not on the latter. Alternatively, they may disagree about *both* the facts *and* the meaning of events.

The late Palestinian scholar Edward Said (1993:xiii) remarked that "nations are narrations." But the history that makes up our narratives is often contested terrain (Francis, 1997:12). History, in this sense, is not "dead" but, rather, a source of constant rediscovery, recreation, reinterpretation, and *power*. As George Orwell (2008:37) wrote in his novel *1984*, "Who controls the past controls the future: who controls the present controls the past."

Every society possesses a dominant narrative. Always, however, there are also counter-narratives seeking expression. Among the questions a historical sociologist asks are the following: Who determines the "official" historical narrative? How does this narrative square with the facts? Are unofficial, alternative, and even multiple histories heard and respected within the society? What are the lessons—myths, really—that a people construct around their collective histories? In what forms (institutions, laws) is history enunciated in the present?

Of course, our historical narratives can sometimes trap us. It *is* possible for some countries to have "too much history," to be (as it were) stuck in the past; but not remembering—living in a state of amnesia—is also a trap.

History *determines* nothing (Carr, 1990). But our understanding—our *imagination*—of it locates us, both individually and collectively, in time in the same way that geography locates us in space. Put another way, our understanding of history organizes material in a manner that helps us interpret current events. Meaning and meaningful action are impossible without a temporal context (see Rickman, 1961; Dilthey, 1961).

Moreover, the consequences of historical events (as set down in institutions, treaties, laws, etc.), as well as our understanding and interpretation of these events, often set off chains of meaning and action long after the specific events themselves have ceased. Thus, in Canada, two lines can be drawn—one leading directly, the other indirectly—from the Royal Proclamation of 1763. The first of these lines leads to the Oka crisis of 1990 and the passing of the Nisga'a treaty in British Columbia (Chapter 12). The second of these lines leads to the Meech Lake Accord and the Quebec referendum of 1995 (chapters 3 and 4).

One way to comprehend the role of history in shaping Canadian society is to employ a methodological technique termed **counterfactual history**, defined as a simulation based on calculations about the relative probability of plausible outcomes (Ferguson, 2003:85; see also Showalter and Deutsch, 2010).

What is counterfactual history? While often condemned as a parlour game, counterfactual history properly employed is not just history "made up." Rather, it is based on factual information and interpretive and extrapolative logic, held together by an historical sociologist's imagination.

The use of counterfactual history is not new (Honan, 1998). Recalling, for example, the events that led to the dissolution of the Austro-Hungarian Empire in 1918, Oscar Jaszi (1961:380) wrote,

> Opposed to the materialistic point of view, I accept the . . . reversibility of the historical process, and regard the chief utility of all historical and sociological investigations to be to admonish us of the alternative possibilities of history.

Counterfactual history provides a means of separating what is important in history from that which is merely incidental. It alerts us to the importance of history by asking the question What if people involved in an event had made different decisions, or events had otherwise transpired in different ways? The reader is invited throughout this text to ask similar questions about Canada. What if New France had not been surrendered to the British in 1763 (Chapter 1)? What if the Meech Lake Accord had been passed in 1990 (Chapter 3)? What if the Liberals had won the 1988 election and not signed the Free Trade Agreement (Chapter 7)? What if Canada had entered the Iraq War in 2003?

Finally, counterfactual history also alerts us to the fact that individuals and the decisions they make matter, again, that history does not determine the present. For Canadians, repeatedly advised that globalization is inevitable and that the invisible hand of the marketplace cannot be resisted, reminders of personal efficacy are to be valued.

Outline of the Text

The book is divided into three sections. These sections deal with what Canadian philosopher John Ralston Saul (1997:81) argues are Canada's "three deeply rooted pillars, three experiences—the aboriginal, francophone, and anglophone." Each of these pillars is a kind of "master narrative" that is used to structure the overall text while, at the same time, dealing with other important relationships, based (for example) on differences of gender, ethnicity, race, and class.

Part 1 (chapters 1–4) examines francophone Quebec's relationship with the rest of Canada, while Part 2 (chapters 5–8) examines English Canada's relationship with the United States. In a manner calculated to disrupt the usual historicized narrative of Europeans' arrival and Aboriginal peoples' gradual disappearance from the scene, the Aboriginal/non-Aboriginal relationship is dealt with in Part 3 (chapters 9–12).

At another level, each of these sections deals with larger issues impacting all societies in the early 21st century: nationalism, neo-liberalism, and cultural values of social solidarity that persist, despite modernity, because—some would argue—they define what it means to be human. These larger themes are returned to in a final chapter that again examines the complex relationship between the state, globalization, and society, and compares Canada with other world countries on issues of inequality, social development, and democracy.

Conclusion

Sociology is the study of society. But what is society? This chapter has established a framework and a set of theoretical and methodological tools for answering this question. The remainder of this text applies these tools to the study of a specific phenomenon—Canadian society.

In keeping with the narrative structure employed by historical sociologists, the story of Canadian society that follows enlists all the usual literary devices: myths (the Conquest); metaphors (are Quebec and Canada "two solitudes," in the phrase made famous by the novelist Hugh MacLennan [1998], or "Siamese twins," as described by Saul [1997]); symbols (Canadian hockey, the maple leaf, the fleur-de-lis); heroes, villains, and tragic figures (Louis Riel is all three, depending upon whom you ask); and recurrent subtexts (regional alienation, Americanization, ethnic divisions).

For hundreds of years—longer in the case of Aboriginal peoples—people in this part of North America have been creating, together and alone, a story as broad as the prairie landscape, as deep as the Hudson Bay basin, and as rich as ore from the Canadian Shield. It is a story worthy of many books. This is one of them.

Notes

1. Statistics Canada (2010a) has devised three projections of Canada's population by 2060–2061. The low-end projection is that Canada's population at that time will be 43 million; the high-end projection is 63.8 million.

Key Terms

conflict theory
counterfactual history
country
globalization
historical sociology
nation

patriarchy
post-structural theory
praxis
reification
sexism
society
sociology
state
structural functional theory
symbolic interaction theory
verstehen

Critical Thinking Questions

1.   Is higher-level thinking possible without employing abstractions?
2.   In what concrete ways is the world both globalizing and becoming more localized?
3.   Should sociologists strive to change the world?
4.   How might you apply the four main theoretical perspectives discussed in this chapter to current issues in your community?
5.   How does a historical-sociological methodology help in studying a society such as Canada's?

Recommended Readings

Anderson, Benedict. 1983. *Imagined Communities*. London: Verso.
Imagined Communities remains a central book in nation studies, its title capturing a central idea of nationhood as a social-psychological construct.

Ferguson, Niall. 2003. *Virtual History: Alternatives and Counterfactuals*. London: Pan Books.
This book provides a fun and interesting introduction to the idea of counterfactual history.

Knuttila, Murray, and Wendee Kubik. 2000. *State Theories: Classical, Global, and Feminist Perspectives*. Halifax: Fernwood.
This book is an excellent review of theoretical perspectives on the state.

MacMillan, Margaret. 2008. *The Uses and Abuses of History*. Toronto: Viking.
MacMillan's short and very readable book is an excellent introduction to the importance of the historical perspective in social research and a warning regarding the improper uses of history.

Robbins, Richard H. 2014. *Global Problems and the Culture of Capitalism.* 6th ed. Toronto: Pearson.
Robbins's text provides a comprehensive sociological examination of globalization, including numerous case studies.

Related Websites

Canadian Historical Association
www.cha-shc.ca
Founded in 1922, this is Canada's leading bilingual organization for the scholarly study of history.

Canadian Sociological Association
www.csa-scs.ca
Founded in 1965 as the Canadian Sociology and Anthropology Association (CSAA), but renamed the Canadian Sociological Association in 2007, the CSA is Canada's pre-eminent organization for sociologists. It holds professional meetings every year in a Canadian city and works closely with other international organizations in the field.

Statistics Canada
www.statcan.gc.ca
The Dominion Bureau of Statistics was created in 1918. In 1971, it was renamed Statistics Canada. Despite the problems discussed in this chapter, it remains the primary source of statistical information for the Canadian public about their country.

Canadian Society on Video

Postcards from Canada. 2001. National Film Board of Canada, 41 minutes, 20 seconds. A breathtaking photographic sweep of Canada, narrated by the late Peter Gzowski, from the frozen vistas of the Arctic to the frenzy of rush-hour traffic, from deep within the Canadian Shield to the orbiting Radarsat satellite.

PART ONE

CANADA AND QUEBEC

To many today, the threat of Quebec separating from Canada seems remote. This was not the case only a few years ago, however. For a brief moment, on the evening of October 30, 1995, it seemed the endless debates between English- and French-speaking Canada had reached a climax. Like deer caught in winter headlights, stunned Canadians watched the results of Quebec's referendum on sovereignty unfolding on their television screens.

In the end, the *No* side narrowly defeated the *Yes* side by just over a percentage point (50.6 percent to 49.4 percent), a mere few thousand votes. For supporters of sovereignty, the sadness of defeat was lessened by the true believers' faith that next time their side would win. For federalists, nervous relief dampened the ecstasy one would expect of victory. By the skin of its teeth, Canada had narrowly escaped a venture into unknown, uncertain, and, some argued, dangerous territory.

The time since the 1995 referendum has seen a different Quebec and a different Canada emerge. Much of what French-speaking Quebecers had demanded for decades has come to pass, including the Canadian House of Commons' recognition of the province in the fall of 2006 as a "nation." It would seem the issues that have historically aroused the separatist spirits have been rendered dormant. Nonetheless, many Canadians inside and outside Quebec believe separatism will re-emerge one day as an issue.

Part 1 examines the history of English-French relations in Canada, how those relations have structured both Quebec and Canadian society as a whole, and why a country reputed by many outsiders to be "the best in the world" has so often teetered perilously close to dissolving over the years.

CHAPTER 1

LIVING WITH THE CONSEQUENCES OF 1760

Valour gave them a common death / history a common fame / posterity a common monument.

> —words engraved on the Wolfe and Montcalm Monument, Quebec City

I expected to find a contest between a government and a people: I found two nations warring in the bosom of a single state.

> —Lord Durham's *Report*, 1839

[T]he human tragedy, or the human irony, consists in the necessity of living with the consequences of actions performed under the pressure of compulsions so obscure we do not and cannot understand them.

> —Hugh MacLennan, 1959;
> words later recorded by The Tragically Hip in their 1992 song "Courage"

Introduction

The 1980 and 1995 Quebec referendums on sovereignty and the threat of others in the future bring into sharp relief two very different views of Canada. Is Canada a partnership of two founding peoples, the French and English, or even a third, the First Nations peoples, as discussed in Part 3 of this text? Or is Canada a federation of 10 equal provinces: Quebec, and what has been termed "the rest of Canada" or ROC? Most francophone Quebecers believe the former, sometimes referred to as the "two nations theory." They further believe that as a minority nation within Canada, they have an historically distinctive patrimony that must be protected; that they constitute a "distinct society" within Canada.

Thanks to decades of political wrangling, many people in English-speaking Canada know something of the history of Quebec-Canada and French-English relations. But this knowledge is often partial or inexact. In any case, facts do not automatically produce meaning; even less do they constitute truths.

This chapter goes beyond the historic facts to explore the emotional and symbolic meaning of English and French relationships in Canada, and the early evolution of this unique relationship. Embedded in the discussion are important sociological questions regarding dominant-subordinate relationships and the responsibilities and consequences imposed by history upon conquerors and conquered alike.

The Age of Mercantilism

Between 1689 and 1763, the French and the English fought a series of wars. The last of these wars (1756–1763) was known in Europe as the Seven Years War, but in British North America as the French and Indian War (Hofstadter, Miller, and Aaron, 1957:64). North America was merely one outpost, albeit an important one, in these wars. To understand these wars, it is necessary to reflect briefly on the political economy of European expansion beginning in the 15th century.

Before that time, the basic structures of European society had remained fundamentally unchanged since (roughly) the collapse of the Roman Empire (see Manchester, 1992). In Thomas Hobbes's (1651/2014) memorable phrase, life was "poor, nasty, brutish, and short." People lived predictable lives in small rural communities. Families were large, class structures and age and gender roles were fixed, trade was local, and barter was the chief means of exchange.

Slowly, however, European feudal society began to change. Central to the changes were the growth of states in which power was centralized and monarchs became all-powerful, a corresponding decline in the temporal power of churches (though religion itself remained important), and the emergence of a new merchant class. In earlier times, churches had frowned upon trade, especially such practices as the granting of monopolies, usury, and profiteering (Hofstadter et al., 1957:4). Between the 16th and 18th centuries, however, there arose a new economic arrangement. Now the new merchant class and the state encouraged commercial trade. Merchants paid the state levies and taxes, and even lent money at favourable rates to support the state's armies. In return, merchants induced states to enact policies, including war, designed to protect their business interests (La Haye, 1993:534).

The new economic arrangement was called **mercantilism** (Hofstadter et al., 1957; La Haye, 1993; Norrie and Owram, 1996:17–18). The chief aim of mercantilist policies was to preserve the mother country's supply of precious metals and to make it less vulnerable during times of war. Colonies were fundamental to mercantilist policy. In practice, because mercantilism and colonialism also meant the enrichment of one state and its merchant allies at the expense of other states and their business friends, conflict was a frequent result. In North America, the conflict primarily involved the English on the eastern seaboard and around Hudson Bay and the French in Nova Scotia and along the St. Lawrence, the colony of New France. The Aboriginal peoples of the region soon found themselves caught up in the conflict.

The Rise and Fall of New France

The history of New France begins in 1534. That year, the French explorer Jacques Cartier (1491–1557) first made landfall on the shores of the Gaspé Peninsula (see Miller, 2000). Like the Spanish far to the south, Cartier came in search of gold. He was discredited, however, when the "gold" he brought back from his third voyage in 1541–1542 turned out to be iron pyrite. Diverted by a series of European conflicts, France temporarily forgot about North America (Morton, 1997:24).

Early in the next century, however, France returned in the person of Samuel de Champlain (1570–1635). A "navigator, soldier, visionary," "a Protestant turned Catholic by conviction," and "a man of Renaissance curiosity and eternal fortitude" (Morton, 1997:25), Champlain in 1608 founded a trading post at what is now Quebec City. Thus New France began.

From the beginning, the post's survival was perilous. Life was harsh. Champlain's efforts to forge alliances with the Huron Confederacy brought the colonists into conflict with the Huron's chief enemies, the tribes of the Iroquois Confederacy. Despite Champlain's efforts to build a colony, Quebec City in 1627 still had fewer than 100 people. In that year, France's chief minister, Cardinal Richelieu, formed a private company made up of 100 merchants and aristocrats. The *Compagnie des Cent-Associés* was given a monopoly over the fur trade in exchange for promises to colonize the territory (Moore, 2012).

Still the settlement did not thrive. Military threats continued. In 1629, an English trading company seized Quebec City; the city was returned to France in 1632 only after diplomatic negotiations (Moore, 2012). The fact is, Quebec City and the surrounding area were far less politically and economically valuable to France than its posts in Cape Breton, Nova Scotia, and Newfoundland, which protected the valuable cod fishery. Dickinson and Young (2008:16) note that, until 1760, "France imported far more cod than fur and the fishery employed many more seamen and ships than all other French colonial trade combined" (see also Eccles, 1993a:163). By contrast, New France's fur trade economy was unstable. European demand fluctuated according to fashion. Supply was equally unpredictable. Weather conditions, the needs and good fortune of Aboriginal suppliers, the actions of middlemen (Norrie and Owram, 1996:43), and conflict between Aboriginal tribes, exacerbated by competition between the French and Dutch trading companies in Port Albany, all affected supply. In the 1630s, disease ravaged the Huron population, delivering a severe blow to the trade (Dickinson and Young, 2008:20; Innis, 1962; Morton, 1997).

In 1650, about 1,200 French European colonists lived in New France (Dickinson and Young, 2008:65). In theory, the Huron Confederacy's destruction opened up new opportunities to attract French immigrants into the fur trade and agriculture. However, war and the *Cent-Associés's* near bankruptcy prevented the colony from taking advantage of the changed circumstances (Moore, 2012:110–111). In 1663, the colony's population was still only around 3,000 people. That year, Louis XIV dissolved the company and made New France a royal colony. An active immigration policy was pursued. Encouragement and financial inducements were given to disbanded military officers and their men, civilian workers, and—in an effort to redress a long-standing gender imbalance in the colonies—women. By 1681, the population of New France was 10,000. Most of Canada's francophone population today traces its roots to these original 10,000 inhabitants (Moore, 2012:119; also, Dickinson and Young, 2008). New France's population thereafter increased primarily from births rather than immigration.

Growth and development create their own problems and natural contradictions. After 1663, the internal contradictions and conflicts facing New France mounted: the Catholic Church versus the state; rural versus urban; fur trading versus agriculture and industry. In the words of historian Desmond Morton (1997:27), "Were the people of New France to be habitants, cultivating their small colony in the valley of the St. Lawrence, or were they to be voyageurs, carrying the fur trade, Catholicism, and French influence throughout the continent?" Yet the colony also began to develop. Visitors to

New France in the mid-18th century regularly commented on its growing prosperity and cultural sophistication (Eccles, 1993b).

In 1756, however, New France faced a growing threat from England and its southern colonies. The 13 British colonies that eventually became the United States had a more developed and diverse economy than New France. Agriculture and commerce were thriving. The English colonists—roughly 1.5 million compared with New France's 75,000 (Eccles, 1993a:171)—were eager to expand into the Ohio Valley. There however, they faced a belt of French forts constructed along the Ohio and Mississippi rivers, established both to support the fur trade and to hem off British expansion (Innis, 1962:88–89; Morton, 1997:30; Eccles, 1993a:163). In 1754, a series of armed clashes occurred between British and French forces. These events partially set off the Seven Years War in Europe, which began two years later (Dickinson and Young, 2008:46; Eccles, 1993a:163).

As the war began, the English in North America possessed several advantages over the French. Besides a larger population in the colonies, the English also had a larger and more powerful navy, with which they could blockade the French colonies, and a larger standing army. In 1756, there were roughly 22,000 English regulars and militia in the colonies, to which were later added another 20,000 regular troops. By contrast, New France had no more than 7,000 regular troops, along with several thousand militiamen and Aboriginal allies (Dickinson and Young, 2008:47; Moore, 2012:177; but see also Eccles, 1993a:171).

Despite these overwhelming odds, the French in the early stages successfully defended their colony, in part because the British had difficulty in marshalling their superior resources. Gradually, however, the British gained the upper hand. In 1758, the British seized the fort of Louisbourg in Nova Scotia. The following summer, a British fleet sailed up the St. Lawrence, while troops on the ground scorched the countryside (see Box 1.1).

Box 1.1: State Terrorism, 1759

Terrorism is the deliberate use of acts of violence or the threat of violence by individuals, groups, or the state for the purpose of furthering political ends. We tend to think of terrorism as a recent phenomenon. In fact, terrorism—especially state terrorism—is quite old, as shown in the following excerpt from the written account of the sergeant major of the 40th Regiment's Grenadiers (part of the Louisbourg Grenadiers). The passage deals with Wolfe's campaign against New France in the summer of 1759, leading up to the Battle of the Plains of Abraham in September of that year.

The 15th of Aug. Captain Gorham returned from an Incursion, in which Service were employ'd, under his Command, 150 Rangers, a Detachment from the different Regiments, Highlanders, Marines, &c. amounting in the whole to about 300, an arm'd Vessel, three Transports, with a Lieutenant and Seamen of the Navy to attend him, of which Expedition they gave the following Account:

"That on the 4th of August they proceeded down to St. Paul's Bay, (which is opposite to the North Side of this Island) where was a Parish containing about 200 men, who had been very active in distressing our Boats and Shipping—At 3 o 'Clock in the Morning Capt. Gorham landed and forced two of their Guards; of 20 Men each, who fired smartly for Some Time; but that in two Hours they drove them all from their Covering in the Wood, and clear'd the Village which they burnt, consisting of about 50 fine Houses and Barns; destroy'd most of their Cattle, &c. That in this one Man was kill'd and 6 wounded; but that the Enemy had two kill'd, and several wounded, who were carried off.—That from thence they proceeded to Mal Bay, 10 Leagues to the Eastward on the same Side, where they destroyed a very pretty Parish, drove off the Inhabitants and Stock without any Loss; after which, they made a Descent on the South Shore, opposite the Island of Coudre, destroyed Part of the Parish of St. Ann's and St. Roan, where were very handsome Houses with Farms, and loaded the Vessels with Cattle; after which they returned from their Expedition."

The same Day 1 of our Schooners went from the Fleet below the Fall, and the French fir'd 8 or 9 Shot at her; but miss'd her. This Day a Party of young Highlanders came to the Island of Orleans from Gen. Monckton's Encampment; on Purpose to destroy all the Canada-Side.—The same Day our People set one of the Enemy's Floating-Batteries on Fire;—and in the Night General Monckton set the Town on Fire, (being the 4th Time) and the Flames raged so violently, that 'twas imagin'd the whole City would have been reduc'd to Ashes.

August 18th a Sloop and Schooner went below the Falls; the French hove Shot and Shells at them, but did 'em no Damage. The same Day the Enemy hove a Bomb from the Town, which kill'd one Man and wounded 6 more,—one Man had his Arm cut off by a Piece of the same Shell.

On the 20th the Louisbourg Grenadiers began their March down the main Land of Quebeck, in order to burn and destroy all the Houses on that Side.—On the 24th they were attack'd by a Party of French, who had a Priest for their Commander; but our Party kill'd and scalp'd 31 of them, and likewise the Priest, their Commander; They did our People no Damage. The three Companies of Louisbourg Grenadiers halted about 4 Miles down the River, at a Church called the Guardian-Angel, where we were order'd to fortify ourselves till further Orders; we had several small Parties in Houses, and the Remainder continued in the Church.—The 25th, began to destroy the Country, burning Houses, cutting down Corn, and the like: At Night the Indians fired several scattering Shot at the Houses, which kill'd one of the Highlanders and wounded another; but they were soon repulsed by the Heat of our Firing.—It was said that the Number of the Enemy consisted of 800 Canadians and Indians. Sept 1st we set Fire to our Houses and Fortifications, and marched to join the Grand Army at Montmorancy; the 3 Companies of Grenadiers ordered to hold themselves in Readiness to march at a Minute's Warning.

Source: Henderson, Robert (ed.). n.d. *A Soldier's Account of the Campaign on Quebec, 1759*, taken from *A Journal of the Expedition up the River St. Lawrence*. Originally published in 1759. Manotick, ON: The Discriminating General (services@militaryheritage.com). Reproduced with the permission of The Discriminating General, www.militaryheritage.com.

Gradually, Quebec City was isolated from the surrounding territory, and the siege began. Throughout the following months, the British, led by General James Wolfe (1727–1759), conducted a constant bombardment of the city in hopes of forcing the French under the Marquis Louis-Joseph de Montcalm (1712–1759) out of their defensive position. Much of lower Quebec City was laid to rubble. The British also torched the surrounding countryside (Dickinson and Young, 2008; Dufour, 1990; Moore, 2012), yet the French did not surrender.

Frustrated, Wolfe tried a final tactic. On the night of September 12, the British forces seized a path up the cliffs to west Quebec City, setting the stage for the historic battle of the next day, as related by Moore (2012:178):

> On the Plains of Abraham, Wolfe's red-coated army formed one line, facing east towards the city. After some fierce skirmishing, Montcalm's troops in their white coats moved west towards them, drums beating, regimental banners flying. The two armies were roughly equal in numbers. These were precisely the conditions Wolfe had sought all summer, and in a battle that lasted barely fifteen minutes, the close-range volleys of his skilled regulars tore the French army apart.

Wolfe died that day in battle, Montcalm succumbed the next day to his wounds, and part of a national mythology was born (see Francis, 1997:55–56). In effect, the war was over, although fighting continued for another year. In August 1760, Montreal capitulated, the French humiliation completed by a public surrender of arms (Dufour, 1990). The Treaty of Paris in 1763 formally ended the war. France ceded its former colony along the St. Lawrence to Britain.

The Royal Proclamation and Quebec Act

In 1760 New France, now known as Quebec, was in a state of ruin. Roughly a tenth of the colony's population had been killed (Moore, 2012:180). Quebec City and the area around it were in ruins, the colony's economic infrastructure destroyed. Famine and disease were rampant. All in all, the war and its immediate aftermath were terrifying for the residents of the colony.

Adding to their abject circumstances was the French's fear of their conquerors. The French had good reason to fear the British. The torching of homes and villages along the St. Lawrence gave ample proof of the enemy's barbarity. The forced expulsion of roughly 7,000 Acadian people in 1754 from what is now Nova Scotia, without compensation for their land, was also fresh on French minds (Dickinson and Young, 2008:47; Conway, 2004:22). (Many of the Acadians resettled in Louisiana; hence, that region's "Cajun" culture.)

The French were surprised, therefore, by the generally courteous and respectful behaviour of the British. In the years between 1760 and 1764, Quebec was under martial law. Yet the British did little to interfere with French traditions, and indeed they helped in the province's reconstruction. In the words of Dufour (1990:27), the conqueror's behaviour was "correct. Even exemplary."

The Royal Proclamation of 1763, however, gave the French a taste of the iron fist. Designed to assimilate the French, the Proclamation declared that British institutions would henceforth govern Quebec, with an elected assembly and British laws. British immigration would be encouraged. Finally, in an effort to head off further wars with Aboriginal peoples, the interior hinterland of the Ohio Valley was made a vast Native reserve (Innis, 1962; Dickinson and Young, 2008).

In an act of surprising civility, however, the British governor, James Murray (1721–1794), refused to enact many of the Proclamation's provisions. In part, Murray's actions were based on his recognition that the provisions were not enforceable. Eighty-five percent of the colony's inhabitants lived in rural areas beyond administrative control (Dickinson and Young, 2008). There was little likelihood soon of a wave of English immigration that might change the colony's predominantly French and Catholic character. Under existing British law, no Catholic could hold office, making impossible the notion of a representative legislative assembly. Montreal fur traders were already demanding that the Ohio Valley be reopened for business. Moreover, given growing unrest in England's southern colonies on the continent, the last thing the British needed was agitation in the north. But it is also true that Murray himself *actually liked and admired the French* and, setting a tradition followed for a time by his successors, acted, albeit paternalistically, as a protector of French interests (see Conway, 2004). Conqueror and conquered were mutually seduced (Dufour, 1990).

Thus, in 1774, the British passed the Quebec Act, which reversed much of the Royal Proclamation. The law was changed to allow Catholics to hold elected office. Seigneurial land tenure was confirmed. The colony's territorial boundaries were increased to include some of the First Nations territories. Catholics were given the right to practise their religion. The Catholic Church was once more allowed to collect tithes. And while English criminal law was retained, French law was allowed in civil cases (Dickinson and Young, 2008:55).

In a curious sense, the Conquest seemed to have changed little. Nonetheless, its effects were real. In the most profound sense, the Conquest forged a people, a sociological—but not a political—nation.

Being *Canadien*

A people somewhat distinct from the European French were arising in the colony even before the Conquest. In contrast to the town-dwelling French administrators, the peasant farmers—*habitants*, as they described themselves—were mostly rural. In their everyday lives, they experienced greater independence and social equality, including gender equality, than people living in France (Rioux, 1978:17–18). This basic equality, combined with isolation, the harshness of their existence, and the constant fear of attack by Aboriginals, developed a strong sense of solidarity among the *habitants* over time (Dickinson and Young, 2008; Rioux, 1978). By the 1750s, visitors to New France "claimed that a new kind of French people was emerging along the banks of the St. Lawrence" (Morton, 1997:28), a people distinguished by different beliefs, customs, behaviours, and even dialect (Rioux, 1978:24–25; see also Eccles, 1993b; Thompson, 1995). They called themselves *Canadiens*, and their country Canada. There was no need to copyright the *Canadien* identity. By definition, *Canadiens* were French-speaking Catholics settled permanently along the St. Lawrence. Moreover, in their own minds at least, the territorial boundaries of their nation extended well beyond their colony's borders into areas traversed and imagined by French voyageurs and missionaries.

But distinctiveness, though necessary, is not a sufficient basis of nationalism. The Conquest transformed—though not all at once—New France's distinctiveness into nationalism (Cook, 1995:86).

Try to put yourself for the moment in the shoes of a *habitant* after 1763. You have been conquered, not merely defeated, by the English (Dufour, 1990:31). Equally, you have not been merely orphaned by the mother country, but, as the Treaty of Paris cruelly attests, abandoned. The past cannot be reversed. Finally, to add to your confusion, your enemy is actually magnanimous in victory. As a conquered subject, you welcome the difference; the fact that you are not tortured, raped, and killed is clearly important. Still, as Dufour (1990:31) remarks, the conqueror's magnanimity changes nothing; indeed, it actually makes your subordinate status more humiliating because now you must also be grateful.

New France in 1760, like the British colonies to the south, was growing apart from France and no doubt one day would have sought independence, but the Conquest truncated this normal development. Quebec's sense of self-identity was not positive in the sense of one chosen by the people; rather, it was an identity thrust upon them, forged in war, trauma, and the torturous severing of the colony's umbilical cord from France. Time and circumstances conspired to make Quebec's French population a distinct people—*les Canadiens*—before their time. By contrast, the few hundred British who occupied Quebec after 1763 remained, even to themselves, "the British."

The political circumstances were unstable, however. As the British feared, the American colonists in 1775 revolted. In consequence, 40,000 United Empire Loyalists fled to the northern British colonies, about 10,000 of them settling in Quebec (Dickinson and Young, 2008). The contest for political, territorial, and economic power and national identity began again.

The Loyalists and the Constitution Act of 1791

Imagine now that you are a United Empire Loyalist recently arrived in Canada. The American revolutionaries have stolen your property and distributed it among themselves, their friends, and small farmers in order to garner political support for the new republic (Zinn, 1995:83). Your financial circumstances and physical health, and that of your family, are poor. By contrast with the 30,000 Loyalists who arrived in Nova Scotia by ship, you came to Canada by horse cart overland and on foot, bearing little. You are bitter and angry; an historian will later remark that "quarrelsomeness" marked your character and that of your compatriots (Brown, 1993:246). You were loyal to Britain (you say to yourself and anyone who will listen) and now have lost everything (Morton, 1997:65; but see also Francis, 1997:56). The free land, clothing, and farming utensils supplied by the British administration (Dickinson and Young, 2008) do not assuage your bitterness.

Such, in part, was the view of the Loyalists as they arrived in the northern British colonies. Like the French, the Loyalists were a conquered people. In Canada, however, the roughly 10,000 who arrived found their humiliation increased by the fact that they were a minority surrounded by more than 70,000 French Catholics. For their part, the French were no more thrilled with their new neighbours, viewing them as an advance guard of future anglophone settlement. In an age when ethnic and religious bigotry were rife, the arrival of the Loyalists was like gasoline thrown on a fire.

Elsewhere, the arrival of Loyalists created similar tensions. In Nova Scotia, the arriving Loyalists quickly swamped the existing population of 4,000 New Englanders and Acadians. The 1,000 Loyalists who arrived on the Island of St. John (renamed Prince Edward Island in 1799) equalled those already living there, while the 400 Loyalists who arrived on Cape Breton doubled that island's existing population (Brown, 1993:241–242).

Anxious to prevent conflict, the British thus segregated the respective populations. Nova Scotia was divided and a new province, New Brunswick, created, while Cape Breton (temporarily) became a separate colony. The colony of Quebec, formally New France, likewise was divided.

The instrument of this latter division was the Constitution Act of 1791. The Constitution Act amended the Quebec Act, but left intact many of the latter's provisions protecting the French language, the Catholic Church, French civil law, and the seigneurial system. The Constitution Act, however, divided the colony into Upper Canada (where many of the Loyalists had settled) and Lower Canada (French Canada), the term *Canada* having historically been a loose synonym for New France. The act further maintained strong executive power in the office of the governor, an executive council (made up of the governor's advisers), and a non-elected legislative council (a colonial House of Lords). But it also allowed, for the first time, popularly elected assemblies in both Canadas and extended the franchise. Finally, the act envisaged the creation of a colonial aristocracy, a state church, and public education. The first idea was soon abandoned, but substantial land holdings were set aside for the Anglican Church and education (Careless, 1970:119–121; Dickinson and Young, 2008:59).

Even at the time, the Constitution Act pleased few people. The merchants of Montreal had not wanted Canada divided. The English in Lower Canada did not like being separated from the English in Upper Canada. The agrarians and rising bourgeoisie in both provinces did not like the act's openly mercantilist bent. Democrats, believing that the elected assemblies did not go far enough, railed against oligarchic rule. But perhaps the major flaw in the Constitution Act was that it institutionalized ethnic conflict (Cook, 1995:87). Thereafter, as Quebec premier Pierre-Joseph-Olivier Chauveau would later remark, the English and French met each other only "on the landing of politics," frequently in conflict.

The Conquest's Impacts

Social stratification is the system by which a society ranks categories of people (e.g., by occupation, race, ethnicity, or gender) in a hierarchy involving inequalities of various sorts. At the top of New France's stratification system before the Conquest were royal officials: the governor, the *intendant* (the business manager), and the senior military officers. The clergy were somewhat parallel to the royal officials, but after 1663 clearly subordinate in the final instance to the state. The *seigneurs*, some of whom came from the French nobility, came next in the social order, followed by a sizable middle class (composed of merchants and small vendors), the urban working class, then the *habitants* (Eccles, 1993a:42). (Note that this stratification system does not include women or Aboriginal peoples.) The Conquest changed Canada's economic and political order. The degree and type of changes, however, are somewhat disputed.

One dispute involves the actual number of people who left New France. The articles of capitulation in 1760 gave inhabitants the right to return to France. Perhaps only a few hundred took advantage of the opportunity (Dickinson and Young, 2008:49), perhaps 4,000 (Eccles, 1993a:173). Most of those who left were French bureaucrats and soldiers (though some decommissioned soldiers remained), quickly replaced by British bureaucrats and soldiers.

A second, more important dispute arose during the 1950s and 1960s over the Conquest's impacts upon New France's economic classes and the colony's future. Early on, scholars of "the Montreal School" (Saul, 1997:19)—Maurice Seguin, Guy Fregault, and Michel Brunet—developed the **decapitation thesis** (Cook, 1995:92; Dickinson and Young, 2008). This thesis holds that the Conquest had destroyed New France's "embryonic bourgeoisie" (Brunet, 1993; also Rioux, 1978:39; Conway, 2004:24–25). The English and Scotch merchants subsequently stepped into the void left by the French bourgeoisie, while the French who remained retreated to a rural existence. There, dominated by the Catholic Church, they espoused conservative values inimical to capitalist development (Norrie and Owram, 1996:61; Dickinson and Young, 2008). Thus Lower Canada's economic development was truncated.

In direct refutation of the decapitation thesis, a second argument holds that New France in 1763 had no "viable business community" (Dickinson and Young, 2008:51), no middle class (Hamelin, 1993) to be destroyed. More recently, a synthesis of both arguments has emerged. This third argument suggests that the Conquest resulted in the departure of agents and merchants directly connected to France's trading companies, but that local merchants, storekeepers, and traders stayed. That is, the transatlantic French bourgeoisie was eliminated, but the local French bourgeoisie, albeit small, remained (Norrie and Owram, 1996:63; also Dickinson and Young, 2008).

More broadly, these debates point to how historical interpretations can have current sociological and political significance. For example, while the decapitation thesis lends itself to support for the Quiet Revolution (Chapter 2) and sovereignty (Cook, 1995; Saul, 1997), the second and third arguments provide much less support for the belief that the conquest held back Quebec's early development.

There is no dispute, however, that Canada's economy immediately after 1760 was in crisis. The war's devastation, the permanent disruption of its mercantile (metropolitan-hinterland) arrangements with France, and the outbreak of wars with Aboriginal tribes on the frontier were all contributing factors. Within a short time, however, Lower Canada's economy began to rebound. The colony was rebuilt; the Aboriginal wars ended in 1763 (see Chapter 9), restoring the Ohio Valley fur trade; and trade links were re-established, this time with Britain. Capital also began to enter Lower Canada from Britain and merchants in England's southern colonies.

The direct economic impacts of the Conquest should not be minimized. In the long term, however, the Conquest's social and political consequences were more important. After 1763 the English held the balance of **power**, defined as someone's ability to impose his or her will upon others even against their resistance (see Box 1.2). The imposition of English will was a fact of life in Lower Canada, despite the newcomers' frequent conciliations and sensitivity to the French majority. With the arrival of the Loyalists after 1775 (see Chapter 5), ethnicity came to play an even greater role in Canada's social structure. The effects of ethnicity, however, were mitigated somewhat by the granting of elected assemblies under the Constitution Act of 1791, which opened up opportunities for a nascent *Canadien* political class.

Box 1.2: Means of Exercising Power

Power can be exercised by three means. Each means may be effective depending on a particular situation, but each also has limits and none is effective in all situations. Often one means of power is used in combination with another. The three means of power are as follows:

Force or the threat of force: The English expulsion of the Acadians in 1754, the Canadian government's use of the RCMP against protesters at Regina in 1935 (Chapter 6), the use of the Canadian military to deal with the FLQ Crisis in 1970 (Chapter 2), and the use of military troops to deal with the Oka Crisis in 1990 (Chapter 11) provide examples of the use of force.

Reward: Whereas force involves use of the stick, reward involves the use of the carrot. Rewards may be material (e.g., money), but not always; status, for example, is also a form of reward. Because systems of social stratification differentially reward individuals and groups on the basis of class, race, ethnicity, gender, and so on, such systems are themselves means of power. (Note that withholding instrumental rewards results in economic coercion—the use once more of force.)

Authority: Authority gains its power by being recognized as legitimate. Authority frequently coincides with the means of force and reward, but often includes elements of tradition, law, status, or prestige. The **dominant ideology** (see chapters 2 and 7) of any period tends to legitimize current power relations.

By the early 19th century, ethnicity had become a defining feature of Lower Canada's system of social stratification. The English controlled the executive and judicial branches in the political realm, but the French dominated the legislative branch. The English controlled the upper reaches of the economy: international trade, banking, and finance. The French business class was restricted to local trade. At the lower levels, British labourers, contractors, and producers—often favoured by British administrators—competed with their French counterparts (Dickinson and Young, 2008:114; Innis, 1962; Norrie and Owram, 1996). Finally, the *habitant* majority occupied the bottom level of Lower Canada's social structure (Rioux, 1978:35).

The ethnic division of Lower Canada was not merely social, but also demographic. Gradually, the English "captured" the urban portion of the colony, while the French retreated to the colony's villages and rural farms (Rioux, 1978). Early in the 19th century, 40 percent of Quebec City and 33 percent of Montreal were anglophone (Norrie and Owram, 1996:98). In this context the Catholic Church, especially its parish priests, grew in importance.

By the 1830s, these social, political, and economic divisions, built on a foundation of Conquest, had nurtured among Lower Canada's French population a growing sense of grievance and a rising spirit of nationalism. Finally, the grievances boiled over.

The Rebellions of 1837–1838

In 1837, after years of political discord, and in the midst of a prolonged recession, rebellions broke out in both Upper and Lower Canada. The causes of the rebellions in the two Canadas were similar. Popular anger focused on the corrupt oligarchies that governed the provinces—the Chateau Clique in Lower Canada, the Family Compact in Upper Canada—and their political masters in London.

In Upper Canada, the rebels demanded "responsible government." They wanted real power to rest with an elected legislative assembly. The Upper Canadian rebels also wanted economic reform, believing—correctly—that current policies were designed to protect mercantilist interests. The rebels wanted instead increased immigration, greater access to capital, and more land opened up for agriculture (Careless, 1970; Norrie and Owram, 1996).

Though the movements in both Upper and Lower Canada were informed by liberal democratic ideals, inspired by the French and American revolutions (Rioux, 1978:49; Cook, 1995; Conway, 2004; Romney, 1999), a fundamental difference existed between the two rebellions. In contrast with Upper Canada, the rebellion in Lower Canada was not only inspired by demands for representative democracy, but also by nationalism (Conway, 2004:33–35). In consequence, the conflict in Lower Canada could only be more serious—and bloody.

In Lower Canada, the rebellion's leader was Louis-Joseph Papineau (1786–1871), a member of the new middle class and speaker of the Assembly. The rebellion occurred in several stages. In October 1837, Patriote leaders issued a "Declaration of the Rights of Man," based on the American declaration of 1776 (Ouellet, 1993:360). At St. Denis on November 23, 800 Patriotes defeated 200 British regulars. This was followed by a British victory two days later at St. Charles, then a massive British attack on the rebels at St. Eustache, north of Montreal, on December 14. Many of the rebels hid in the village church. The British, however, set the church alight and shot the rebels as they fled through the windows. Estimates of the number of Patriotes killed range from 58 to 100. The village of St. Eustache was razed. The fight continued into the countryside, where British irregulars left behind them a trail of scorched *habitant* homes, farms, and villages (Morton, 1997:37; Dickinson and Young, 2008:165; Conway, 2004:37).

In the wake of the Lower Canada rebellion, martial law was declared, the Canadian constitution suspended, and a new governor of British North America, Lord Durham (1792–1840), was named (Dickinson and Young, 2008:167). By now, Papineau had fled to the United States. The rebellion, however, soon flared anew.

A second uprising occurred in late November 1838, with its leader, a follower of Papineau, declaring Lower Canada a republic and issuing a "Proclamation of Independence." The uprising was soon put down, however. While a degree of leniency followed the first wave of rebellions in Lower Canada, no leniency was shown after the second rebellion. Twelve Patriotes were hanged and 58 deported to Australia's penal colonies, while 2 more were banished (Dickinson and Young, 2008:167; Conway, 2004:37; Wynn, 2012:204).

By contrast, the rebellion in Upper Canada was, in the words of historian Jack Granatstein (1996:29), a "small-bore affair." There, William Lyon Mackenzie (1795–1861)—publisher, editorialist, social critic, *and* grandfather to a later prime minister—led the rebellion. Since the 1820s, he had argued against the Family Compact and for democratic reform, to no avail. Finally, emboldened by events in Lower Canada—Mackenzie was in frequent contact with Papineau—the rebels took up arms in December 1837. On December 7, after a night of heated discussion at Montgomery's Tavern, 800 of Mackenzie's followers (mostly farmers, small-town tradesmen, and some professionals) marched up Yonge Street in Toronto. There, untrained militia recruited by Upper Canada's elite met them. Shots rang out. The rebellion soon ended. Mackenzie fled disguised as a woman to the United States—he would return 12 years later and be elected to the legislature—but two of his lieutenants died on the gallows. Ninety-two more of Mackenzie's followers were sent to the penal colonies, while hundreds more, disenchanted with the rebellion's outcome, eventually left for the United States. As in Lower Canada, a few cross-border skirmishes occurred in 1838, led by groups trying to liberate Canada from "the British yoke." In 1840, Mackenzie supporters also burned a British steamship at the Thousand Islands and blew up General Brock's monument at Queenston Heights. These events were mere sideshows, however. Upper Canada's rebellion was over (Morton, 1997:49; Dickinson and Young, 2008; Conway, 2004:32–33; Wynn, 2012).

Neither rebellion had widespread popular support. The movements were primarily middle class in origin (Morton, 1997; Ouellet, 1993; Trofimenkoff, 1993), no match for the power of the state and its allies. In Upper Canada, the rebels were easily tainted with the labels "American" and "republican" (Granatstein, 1996). In Lower Canada, the movement's avowed anticlericalism evinced even stronger condemnations from the Catholic Church (Trofimenkoff, 1993).

The rebels' final defeat in 1838 was decisive. French nationalism would not rise again with force until the 1960s (Cook, 1995). For Canada as a whole, defeat meant the throttling of liberal democracy (see Laxer, 1989; Trofimenkoff, 1993; Conway, 2004). Thereafter, conservatism, exercised both in the political-economic and religious realms, gained an increased hold on Canadian society.

Lord Durham and the Act of Union

The new governor, Lord Durham, spent only five months in Canada before resigning in anger. On his return to England, he produced his analysis of the rebellions, based on his short time in Canada, which included a 10-day steamboat trip and conversations with a few close acquaintances (G. Martin, 1993a:444). Durham's *Report on the Affairs of British North America* condemned the ruling oligarchy, the abuses of land granting, and Anglican privileges in the colonies, while also dealing with a host of other issues, from immigration to canal building (see Careless, 1970:195). It further made some of the most derogatory statements ever directed at the *Canadiens*, including this one, quoted in Colombo (1994:38):

> There can hardly be conceived a nationality more destitute of all that can invigorate and elevate a people, than that which is exhibited by the descendants of the French in Lower Canada, owing to their peculiar language and manners. They are a people with no history and no literature.

Finally, Durham's report included a particularly memorable paragraph (Colombo, 1994:38):

> I expected to find a contest between a government and a people: I found two nations warring in the bosom of a single state: I found a struggle, not of principles, but of races; and I perceived that it would be idle to attempt any amelioration of laws or institutions until we could first succeed in terminating the deadly animosity that now separates the inhabitants of Lower Canada into the hostile divisions of French and English.

Durham's analysis reflected European views of the time about the "necessary" relationship between state and nation (see the Introduction); as such, it is a textbook example of material reality being shaped to fit theory and of the problems of biases in conducting research (see Box 1.3). Theories have consequences, and in this case two significant consequences resulted from Durham's report.

Durham's report contained two major recommendations: first, that the British North American colonies be granted responsible government and, second, that Upper and Lower Canada be united (Careless, 1970:195). In effect, the sundering of the two colonies by the Constitution Act of 1791 would be reversed. There was now, however, an important difference. In 1791, the French had been in the majority; it was to protect the English minority

Box 1.3: Observer Bias: A Tale of Two Journeys

Lord Durham travelled through Upper and Lower Canada in 1838. Only a few years earlier (in 1830), Alexis de Tocqueville (1805–1859) journeyed to the United States. Both Lord Durham and Tocqueville were European aristocrats; both travelled in the respective countries for only a few months, yet the latter produced *Democracy in America*, still considered an accurate depiction of the United States' developing political culture, while the former's *Report* is viewed as biased and inaccurate. The result raises the question of why observer bias occurs and how it might be prevented.

Durham arrived with fixed notions of the situation in Lower Canada, and his informants were a relatively small number of the existing elite who supported his beliefs. By contrast, Tocqueville arrived in the United States to study that country's penal system, not U.S. society as a whole. As a result, he was relatively open to experiencing the new environment, and supplemented his observations by reading widely and interviewing a large number of Americans.

The tale of Durham and Tocqueville also raises the question of the proper distance researchers should have from the object of study. On the one hand, group members have an advantage over outsiders in understanding what is observed. On the other hand, insiders are sometimes too close to see what outsiders can observe.

that the colonies had been split. By 1840, however, the demographics had changed. Lower Canada still had the larger population, between 600,000 and 650,000, compared with Upper Canada's population of 450,000 (Dickinson and Young, 2008:183; also Conway, 2004). But virtually all of Upper Canada's population was anglophone, while approximately 150,000 people in Lower Canada were also of British heritage. Thus, the English could dominate in a united Canada. Moreover, Durham argued that English immigration should be strengthened to ensure over time the complete assimilation of the French, thereby blunting the nationalism that had fuelled the recent rebellions.

In 1840 the British government implemented much of Durham's report through the Act of Union, but what they did not implement was crucial. First, they denied outright responsible government, with the result that reformers in Upper Canada remained angry. Second, the union was not total. The Quebec Act's major provisions protecting French civil law, the rights of the Catholic Church, and local control of education remained extant. Even more importantly, the Act of Union meant that elected legislative assemblies in Canada East (Lower Canada) and Canada West (Upper Canada), each with 42 seats, would govern Canada (see Conway, 2004).

The seeds for further crisis, leading ultimately to Confederation in 1867, were thus sown. The French population would not—could not—be assimilated; indeed, the legislative structure actually gave the French minority power disproportionate to its numbers, power that they sensibly used, voting *en bloc*, to protect their interests. The English in Upper Canada, meanwhile, complained bitterly that they had cast off the oligarchic power of the Family Compact only to find themselves now dominated by Lower Canada and a French-speaking minority that was Catholic to boot (see Romney, 1999).

The rebellions of 1837–1838 had seen French Canada conquered a second time. Both Papineau's dream of an independent French republic and Durham's hope of French assimilation were equally chimerical. Nonetheless, the conflicts remained. It would take the forces of modernity, a major depression, two world wars, and the rise of a new intellectual class before Quebec nationalism would again rise, but rise it would, in unexpected ways, with consequences for conquered and conqueror alike.

Conclusion

New France gave Canada its name, its history, its founding myths (see Chapter 6), and one of its languages—according to Dufour (1990), its "heart." After 1840, however, the English increasingly put their stamp on the rest of Canada. A series of events symbolized the ongoing rejection of the French language and its near confinement to the province of Quebec: the hanging of Riel in 1885; the school acts adopted in several provinces, beginning with Manitoba in 1890; and, of course, the conscription crises of the two world wars.

Why does this matter? From the perspective of historical sociology, five later aspects of Canadian society derive, directly or indirectly, from these events. First, these events (beginning with the Conquest) help explain Canada's system of stratification until recent times, with those of English ethnic origin disproportionately occupying elite positions and people of French (and other) ethnic origins disproportionately occupying lower rungs (see Porter, 1965; Clement, 1975; Nakhaie, 1997). Second, they suggest why francophone Quebecers might feel a sense of grievance toward the rest of Canada (see Conway, 2004). Third, attention to historical and political contexts also sheds light on Quebec's continuing claims to linguistic, cultural, and religious distinctiveness.

A fourth, less obvious, consequence of this early history is that no "strong national myth" could cement Canadian federalism, as in the United States (Balthazar, 1997:45; see Part 2 of this text). In the words of political scientist Reg Whitaker (1987:23), "Nationalism as legitimation is a weak, derisory ploy in Canada." Any attempt by political demagogues to "fly the flag" has quickly run aground on ethnic divisions and the Canadian tendency, perhaps inborn, toward skepticism.

Finally, a fifth related consequence (which we shall explore further) involves the complex nature of Canadian federalism. Some of the Fathers of Confederation no doubt wanted to create a strong, centralized government, leaving the provinces with only meagre powers. Quebec's presence, however, as well as that of the smaller Maritime provinces, made this impossible. Canada's flexible and significantly decentralized system of powers and responsibilities—sometimes a benefit, sometimes not—is a product of efforts to solve real problems and conflicts among Canada's constituent communities.

To a degree, political institutions and cultural traditions before the 1950s restrained conflict between Canada's English and French communities. Where these might have proved insufficient to reduce conflict, social isolation provided additional restraint. But the world would not let the two communities go on this way. War and the relentless forces of modernity—capitalism, industrialism, and secularism—were about to throw the separate worlds together.

Key Terms

decapitation thesis
dominant ideology
mercantilism
power
social stratification
terrorism

Critical Thinking Questions

1. What are the similarities and differences between mercantilism and global capitalism today?
2. What are the processes by which social conflict between different groups emerges and is transformed over time?
3. Under what conditions are some means of power more effective than others?
4. Is it possible to overcome observer bias?
5. In what sense is nationalism always based on a myth?

Recommended Readings

Dickinson, John, and Brian Young. 2008. *A Short History of Quebec*, 4th ed. Montreal and Kingston: McGill-Queen's University Press.
This book provides an excellent social history of Quebec, from pre-European times up to the present.

Dufour, Christian. 1990. *A Canadian Challenge/Le défi québécois.* Halifax: Oolichan Books and the Institute for Research on Public Policy.
In a Weberian manner, this book allows anglophones to understand the world from the point of view of francophone Quebecers, while also showing the unrecognized influence that each community has had upon the other.

Manchester, William. 1992. *A World Lit Only by Fire: The Medieval Mind and the Renaissance.* Boston: Little, Brown.
This book brings to life, in a very readable way, Medieval Europe and shows how very different it was from the present day.

Moore, Christopher. 1997. *1867: How the Fathers Made a Deal.* Toronto: McClelland & Stewart.
This book tells the engaging story of how the Fathers of Confederation created Canada's first constitution.

Porter, John. 1965. *The Vertical Mosaic.* Toronto: University of Toronto Press.
Porter's book is a classic in sociology, detailing Canada's complex stratification system at the time and paving the way for subsequent studies.

Related Websites

Acadian-Cajun Genealogy, Culture, History, and Music Group
http://www.acadian.org/acadfounding.html
This Facebook group preserves and promotes the Acadian cultural heritage.

CanGenealogy
www.cangenealogy.com/quebec.html
Quebec's demographic history is among the best recorded anywhere. Cangenealogy has a list of sites for those interested in genealogical history.

Library and Archives Canada
www.collectionscanada.gc.ca
Extensive birth, marriage, death, and other records for Canada as a whole.

Canadian Society on Video

A License to Remember—Special Edition/Un certain souvenir—Édition spéciale. 2007. National Film Board of Canada, 121 minutes, 2 seconds.
Examines the meaning of the words on Quebec licence plates, *Je me souviens*, at the heart of Quebec history and society.

Canada: A People's History. 2000–2001. CBC, 17 episodes, 32 hours.
This 17-episode documentary television series, which first aired on the CBC, portrays the history of Canada. history.cbc.ca.

Canadian History Series. 1959–1961. National Film Board of Canada, 6 videos of roughly 28 minutes each.
The historically accurate videos deal with six individuals important to Confederation in 1867: Robert Baldwin, Lord Durham, Lord Elgin, Joseph Howe, William Lyon Mackenzie, and Louis-Jospeh Papineau.

CHAPTER 2

100 YEARS
OF SOLITUDES

English and French, we climb by a double flight of stairs toward the destinies reserved
for us on this continent, without knowing each other, without meeting each other, and
without even seeing each other, except on the landing of politics.
        —Pierre-Joseph-Olivier Chauveau, first Quebec premier after Confederation, 1876

He shall hang though every dog in Quebec howl in his favour.
                —Prime Minister Sir John A. Macdonald, refusing to pardon Riel, 1885

Society must take every means to prevent the emergence of a parallel power which defies
the elected power.
                —Prime Minister Pierre Trudeau, at the peak of the FLQ Crisis, 1970

Introduction

In the spring of 1955, Canadians were transfixed by television pictures of hundreds of
hockey fans rioting in the streets of Montreal to protest the suspension, for the rest of
the regular season and playoffs, of Maurice "Rocket" Richard (1921–2000). Store windows were smashed, cars overturned, and property looted, leading to the arrest of 37
adults and 4 juveniles. The Richard riot ended only when Richard went on radio and
television the next day to ask the rioters to stop.

We noted in the Introduction the importance of symbols to societies. In 1955, Quebec was on the verge of *La Revolution Tranquil*, the Quiet Revolution. In this context,
the Richard riot had little to do with hockey. Richard, the first player in NHL history to
score 50 goals in a regular season, was hero to a French-speaking population dominated
by an anglophone minority. For francophones, Richard's suspension was symbolic of this
unequal and discriminatory relationship. In turn, the riot was a symbolic protest against
what many Quebecers viewed as 200 years of subjugation and humiliation. As we will see
in this and subsequent chapters, however, symbols not only unite, they also divide. Indeed,
much of French-English conflict in Canada can be viewed as a clash of symbols.

This chapter provides a necessarily short account of Quebec during the period
between Confederation and the Second World War. It then provides a more detailed
account of the events, individuals, and ideas that transformed Quebec, leading to the
historic Quebec election of 1960 and the turbulent years of the Quiet Revolution, which
ended with the October Crisis of 1970, a moment when, once more, English-speaking
Canada watched transfixed by events on their television screens. Competing concepts of
nationalism are discussed.

English Expansion and the Isolation of Quebec

Confederation in 1867 recognized Quebec as distinct, with its own majority French-
Canadian population, Catholic religion, and civil law tradition, combined with

autonomous political powers. For many French-Canadians, the historic province on the shores of the St. Lawrence was their homeland. At the same time, significant French-Canadian communities existed outside Quebec, especially in New Brunswick, but also in Nova Scotia, Prince Edward Island, Ontario, and the western territories (Silver, 1997). Confederation partially disentangled issues of Quebec's governance from those of the other, majority-English provinces. Confederation did not, however, separate French and Catholic sensibilities from the issue of how their compatriots were treated in the other provinces, indeed, from the issue of respect.

Some French Quebecers in 1867 no doubt viewed diaspora French as "dead ducks," to use Parti Québécois leader René Lévesque's expression from the 1970s. In their minds, only Quebec could provide security for French language and culture. Nonetheless, French-Canadians in general also viewed Canada as a bargain between French and English. Yes, Quebec for all practical purposes would always be the citadel of French culture in Canada, but the rights of French Catholics outside Quebec were also to be respected. By 1900, a broader understanding that "the two races" were not to be compartmentalized but rather were to forge a new nation had emerged within French Canada (Silver, 1997). Henri Bourassa (1868–1952), grandson of Louis-Joseph Papineau, was a chief spokesperson for this "pan-Canadian" view (Rioux, 1993).

Not all French-Canadians held this view; even fewer English-Canadians did so. Alexander Muir's poem "The Maple Leaf Forever," written in the year of Confederation, says volumes about English Canada's view of the country just created:

In days of yore, from Britain's shore,
Wolfe the dauntless hero came,
And planted firm Britannia's flag,
On Canada's fair domain.

A hundred years of history had taught the English that the French could be neither defeated nor assimilated. However, the French could, it was believed, be contained. The French could have their separate language, religion, and civil laws, but only in Quebec. The rest of Canada would carry a distinctly British stamp.

These conflicting views of Confederation, and of the rights of minorities, inevitably met on the political landing. The rendezvous did not take long to occur. At Red River in the western territories in 1869, Canadian and American expansionism ran headlong into an established community of Métis (see chapters 6 and 9). Led by a young intellectual and visionary, Louis Riel (1844–1885), the Métis firmly rejected American efforts at annexation, but also demanded from the Canadian government full provincial status and protections for their French language and Catholic religion. The Conservative government of Prime Minister Sir John A. Macdonald (1815–1891) acceded to the demands. Thus, the Manitoba Act was passed in 1870, guaranteeing French-language rights in the legislature and schools, and the right to a Catholic education in the new province of Manitoba.

The battle for French and Catholic rights outside Quebec was not over, however. The social conflicts and political intrigues of 1869 were repeated again in 1885, this time against the wider canvas of the entire western territories. This time, the demands of Riel and the Métis, not to mention the concerns of Natives and non-Natives, were rejected. The "rebels" were hunted down and tried. Louis Riel was hanged amid outcries from French-Canadian politicians and the Quebec press, who were convinced that he would not have been executed had he not been French and Catholic.

Riel's hanging was a blow to both French-Canadian and Métis hopes on the Prairies. For French Quebecers, Riel's hanging symbolized their exclusion from the rest of Canada. Incensed by Prime Minister Macdonald's refusal to pardon Riel (see quotation, above), French Quebec thereafter generally refused to vote Conservative, the major exceptions being two landslide victories in 1958 and 1984, under John Diefenbaker (1895–1979) and Brian Mulroney (1939–), respectively (appendices 1 and 2). More than ever, French Quebecers retreated behind their provincial walls, where the Catholic Church and conservative political leaders urged them to remain (see Dufour, 1990; Rioux, 1993; Conway, 2004).

In the aftermath of 1885, immigrants quickly filled the West (see Chapter 6). In the early stages, many of these were from Ontario: English, Protestant, and often decidedly anti-Catholic. Soon they were a majority. In 1890, the English-speaking and Protestant legislature of Manitoba abolished Catholic separate schools and declared that French was no longer an official language (Careless, 1970; Conway, 2004). Declared unconstitutional by the Supreme Court in 1979, this legislative act nonetheless served its purpose: In the interim, French was reduced to a minority language in Manitoba. The legislature of the North-West Territories in 1892 passed similar language legislation that remains contested today (see Box 2.1). In 1912, Ontario eliminated French from its public education system. In 1916, Manitoba broke an agreement made with Sir Wilfrid Laurier (1841–1919) when he was prime minister and abolished French and any other language except English from its schools (Conway, 2004:48; Silver, 1997:244).

Throughout the 20th century, the minority status of French-Canadians and the political impotence of Quebec within Confederation were thus reinforced again and again. Symbolically, French-Canadians were "put in their place," that is, the place of a vanquished people. Canada was British.

The maintenance of British constitutional symbols, such as the monarchy and the Union Jack, was particularly grating to French-Canadians. For nationalists, such symbols were constant reminders of defeat. For pan-Canadianists, such symbols revealed English-Canadians as slavish colonials unable or unwilling to get on with the task of creating a new nation. Tensions heightened in 1903 with the Boer War, leading to Bourassa's break with the Laurier government. French-English conflict escalated into a full-blown political crisis during the First World War (see also Chapter 6).

Many French-Canadians viewed the First World War as not being Canada's fight, and were offended that English-Canadians had allowed themselves and the country to be dragged into the conflict. By contrast, many English-Canadians were still emotionally tied to the British Empire and could not understand the lack of a similar French-Canadian need to defend France. That the umbilical cord between French-Canadians

Box 2.1: The Case for Alberta as a Bilingual Province

In 2003, a 54-year-old truck driver, Gilles Caron, was ticketed for making an unsafe left turn and fined $54. He fought the ticket, wanting it and his hearing on the matter in French, but was denied under Alberta's 1988 Languages Act. That act states that "all Acts and regulations [in Alberta] may be enacted, printed and published in English only."

In 2008, a provincial court judge—after 89 days of hearings involving legal arguments and the testimony of several historical experts—threw out Caron's ticket. The judge ruled that bilingualism was an established part of Rupert's Land legislature and the Northwest Territories as early as 1845 and that bilingualism remained in force. In consequence, Alberta's Languages Act was unconstitutional and the ticket given to Caron invalid.

The Alberta government appealed this ruling. In 2009, a judge of the Court of Queen's Bench in Alberta sided with the government, ruling that historical documents and orders did not enshrine language rights in what became Alberta. In early 2014, the Alberta Court of Appeal upheld this ruling.

Caron rejects this finding. His lawyer, Robert Lepage, argues that French language rights were entrenched in the Royal Proclamation of 1869, which annexed western land and the Northwest Territories into Canada. In 1870, the Manitoba Act created that province and was specific about the legal right to legislative bilingualism for Manitobans. Lepage argues that the Manitoba Act still reaches beyond Manitoba's borders because that province's authority stretched into the Northwest Territories.

Justice Frans Slatter, of the Alberta Court of Appeal, rejected these historical arguments, however. In his ruling, Justice Slatter wrote, "Parliament knew full well how to entrench language rights, yet neither elected to do so in any constitutional document relating to what is now Alberta." Slatter wrote further that the 1905 Alberta Act, which founded the province, purposefully did not include French language rights. "Indeed its absence was discussed in Parliament at the time, and an amendment to add an equivalent provision was defeated by an overwhelming vote in the House of Commons."

Further complicating the issue is a Supreme Court of Canada decision made in 1988—the same year that Alberta's Languages Act was passed—that provinces have the power to determine their own language rights legislation.

At the time of writing, Caron has declared his intention to appeal the ruling to the Supreme Court of Canada.

What do you think? Should the legislatures and the laws of Alberta—and the rest of Canada—be recognized as formally bilingual? What would be the pros and cons of such a change?

Source: Ryan Cormier. 2014. "Alberta Court of Appeal Rules Provincial Laws Don't Have to Be Bilingual," *Edmonton Journal On-Line,* February 21 (www.edmontonjournal.com/Alberta+Court+Appeal+rules+provincial +laws+have+bilingual/9537105/story.html).

and France had been severed in 1763 entirely escaped most people in English Canada, who viewed French-Canadians *en masse* as disloyal, if not cowardly.

As the war dragged on, the need for fresh troops (and British demands that Canada "pull its weight") caused the Unionist government of Prime Minister Sir Robert Borden (1854–1937) to intensify its efforts at recruitment. These efforts were botched, and led in 1916 to anti-recruitment riots in several Quebec towns. Amid continued Quebec opposition, the next year Borden introduced the Military Conscription Bill, and called an election on the issue. Though many Canadians, farmers and labourers among them, opposed conscription, the election results revealed a particularly massive fissure between Quebec and the rest of Canada (see appendices 1 and 2). Borden's government won, but there were no French-Canadians from Quebec or Acadia among his MPs (Silver, 1997:248). The will of the English majority ruled over the French minority, and the Conscription Bill was passed. The riots resumed throughout Quebec (Careless, 1970; Conway, 2004).

In the end, only 60,000 men were actually drafted. A large number of French recruits—as many as 40 percent—did not report (Dickinson and Young, 2008:254). Few of the conscripts reached the front before the war ended. Bitterness lingered, however, between the French and English communities.

The Conscription Crisis of 1917 was reprised during the Second World War. In 1940, the Liberals, under Prime Minister William Lyon Mackenzie King, won re-election, partly on a promise made to Quebec that they would not bring in conscription. Two years later, however, as casualties again mounted, King sought political absolution from his promise through a national referendum. Since the promise had been made to them alone, French Quebecers viewed the matter as one that should have been resolved only with them, not all of Canada (Silver, 1997). Nonetheless, the referendum was held. The outcome was quite predictable: Once again, Quebec was isolated. Quebec voted 73 percent against releasing King from his promise, while the rest of Canada voted 80 percent in favour of the release and, thereby, conscription (Conway, 2004:54).

In the end, King's adroitness—some would say dithering—forestalled the sort of flare-up that had occurred in 1917. Though anti-conscription riots did occur in parts of Quebec, they were less intense than during the previous war (see Fraser, 1967:14). Most Quebecers understood that King had gone the extra mile in attempting to meet their objections to conscription.

For many French Quebecers, the hanging of Riel, Canada's ongoing British connection, the conscription crises, and the school controversies symbolized their minority status within Confederation. Too often, when conflicts arose, Quebec's views and interests were ignored. By the late 1940s, the idea of a pan-Canadian French and English Canada had all but retreated from Canada's political map. More than ever, Canada consisted of "two solitudes."

By then, however, the consequences of three historical world events were rapidly pushing the French and English communities together. The first two events were the world wars of 1914–1918 and 1939–1945. The third event was the intervening economic depression (see Chapter 6). All of these events had the consequence of enlarging and centralizing state power, the first two in making Canada a giant war factory, the third in creating the liberal welfare state (Rice and Prince, 2013). A further consequence was the emergence from the Second World War (in particular) of a new spirit of nationalism in English-speaking Canada. The stage was thus set for a clash over the nature of Canada and Quebec's place within it. These changes in English-speaking Canada cannot be understood, however, without reference to the profound social, economic, and, ultimately, political changes also occurring inside Quebec.

Social and Economic Change in Quebec, 1867–1960

Quebec's population grew from 1.36 million in 1881 to 2.36 million in 1921, then to 5.25 million in 1961. Its proportion of the Canadian population declined from 31.4 percent in 1881 to 26.8 percent in 1921, but rebounded to 28.8 percent by 1961 (see Table 0.1). In part, this decline during the middle period resulted from decreased birth rates. Quebec's birth rate fell from a pre-industrial high of 50 per 1,000 to 41.1 in 1884 and 1885 to 29.2 during the period from 1931 to 1935, when Quebec was rapidly industrializing (Dickinson and Young, 2008:202). Birth rates in rural areas remained higher than in urban areas, but high death rates, especially infant deaths, reduced overall population growth. During and after the Second World War, however, the birth rate once more rebounded—part of the broader Canadian phenomenon known as the baby boom (Chapter 7)—while life expectancy gradually increased.

The larger reason, however, for Quebec's relative decline in population during this period, compared with the rest of Canada, lay in immigration and emigration. The early 20th century witnessed massive European immigration into Canada, especially the West (see Chapter 6). At the same time, despite the exhortations of church leaders and politicians, many francophone people left the boundaries of Old Quebec. Fearful of their treatment elsewhere in Canada, but finding themselves unable to survive farm life economically, some were convinced to move into the Shield country north of the St. Lawrence. Thus began Quebec's period of northern expansion. Work in New England's lumber mills, however, proved a far greater attraction. Between 1840 and 1930, perhaps 900,000 Quebecers, along with many francophone people from Nova Scotia, moved (in particular) to the New England states (Cook, 1995:91; see also Dufour, 1990).

Of course, immigrants also came to Quebec. This was not a new occurrence. The potato famine of the 1840s, for example, saw the arrival in Quebec of large numbers of Irish, many of whom, as orphaned children, were welcomed into francophone families (Dufour, 1990). Immigration intensified during the period from 1911 to 1915, however, resulting in large and thriving Italian and Jewish communities arising in Montreal (Dickinson and Young, 2008:206). As in the rest of Canada, immigration declined during the two world wars and the intervening depression years. After 1945, however, as immigrants streamed into Canada, many again located in Quebec. Indeed, the proportion of immigrants to Canada settling in Quebec increased steadily, from 13.6 percent in 1946 to 23.7 percent in 1951 and remained at 23.6 percent in 1961 (GRES, 1997:97).

Nonetheless, Quebec remained about 80 percent francophone, while the actual number of anglophones declined and became more confined to the Montreal region.

These demographic changes were accompanied by other social and economic changes. For example, agriculture was still an important element of Quebec's economy in 1891, employing 45.5 percent of Quebec's labour force. Even then, however, Quebec was rapidly industrializing. Quebec's transition from a rural and pre-industrial society to an urban, industrial society intensified in the early 20th century, fuelled by the flow of foreign (mainly American) capital into Canada (see Chapter 6). By 1941, agriculture in Quebec employed only 19.3 percent of the workforce (Dickinson and Young, 2008:213). As noted, some of the "surplus" workers left Quebec. Many more, however, found employment in manufacturing (based on Quebec's abundant hydro power) and resource extraction (especially timber and mining).

The decline in rural Quebec was matched in both relative and absolute terms by growth in urban Quebec. In 1901, 36.1 percent of Quebec's population lived in urban areas; by 1931, the figure was 63.1 percent (Dickinson and Young, 2008:203). Montreal was the hub of much of this urban growth, spurred by the presence of the head offices for the Bank of Montreal, Sun Life, the Canadian National Railway, and the Canadian Pacific Railway. Other urban centres, many of them resource towns, sprang up across the province.

Again, however, the interrelated social and economic changes that Quebec experienced after Confederation and up until the end of the Second World War were not particularly unusual. Industrialization, urbanization, and assorted social changes occurred throughout Canada (see Chapter 6). What made Quebec's situation different was that the changes it experienced brought into sharp relief the social, political, and ideological structures that had arisen around the Conquest.

As we have seen, Quebec after 1760 was stratified along (among other things) ethnic lines. Whether an individual was French or English influenced his or her occupational status, class position, chances for social mobility, and even the town and neighbourhood in which he or she lived. Curiously, the arrangement "worked"—if that term can be used—after the years 1837 and 1838 precisely because French and English did live in separate worlds.

Industrialization and urbanization disrupted this arrangement, forcing French and English into renewed contact and conflict. For example, industrialization created a (largely) **francophone proletariat**. At work sites, francophone workers found themselves in regular conflict with their anglophone bosses. Class conflict merged with ethnic conflict, creating a dangerous mix that finally exploded at the company town of Asbestos in 1949 (Finkel, 2012:74). The Asbestos strike became a symbolic rallying point for opponents of the conservative government of Maurice Duplessis (1890–1959) and an economic structure that favoured anglophone-dominated corporations.

Likewise, industrialization, mass communication, and rising levels of literacy also gave rise to new occupations and professional groups. Quebec's new francophone middle class felt thwarted in its aspirations for social and economic advancement (Taylor, 1993:8–9; Rioux, 1993:82). Inevitably, these changes resulted in challenges to the old political order. These challenges came from trade unionists, progressive intellectuals (including some within the Catholic Church), and members of the new middle class and were directed first at replacing Duplessis's Union Nationale government, but the challengers also had the broader goal of changing Quebec's role within Confederation. The challengers were not homogeneous, however. In particular, each possessed a different ideological notion of Quebec's identity and its relation to the rest of Canada.

Ideology and Identity

What is ideology? **Ideology** is the set of assumptions, beliefs, explanations, values, and unexamined knowledge through which we come to understand reality (Marchak, 1988:1). As we have seen (Chapter 1), the dominant ideology tends to legitimize existing power relations; as Marx (1977a:236) stated, "The ruling ideas of each age have ever been the ideas of its ruling class."

Throughout the late 20th century, federalists and sovereigntists in Quebec argued strongly about Quebec nationalism and its future (see below). They agreed, however, on one thing: Quebec's past (Couture, 1998:48), in particular that Quebec had been governed, in the words of Rioux (1993), by an "ideology of conservation"—alternatively "conservative nationalism" or (reflecting the influence of the Catholic Church during this period) "**clerico-nationalism**" (Cook, 1995:91). After the rebellions of 1837–1838, they argued, Quebec had been in a 100-year "time warp," dominated by the Catholic Church, a bourgeois and anglophone business establishment, and an anti-democratic and authoritarian state, resulting in a reactionary and backward society (Trudeau, 1996).

Conservative nationalism stressed French Quebec's unique cultural heritage. The past and rural life was glorified. Engaging in business or seeking material rewards, by contrast, was denounced. So also were Quebecers warned against leaving their homeland, either for the United States (though many did so) or for Canada's opening West: There, the dragons of certain assimilation waited. Furthermore, French Quebecers were charged with an historic and sacred mission to defend and preserve their culture against the English, the last bastion of "true" Catholic France. (It was viewed as providential that Quebec had been saved from the radicalism and anticlericalism that had befallen the mother country after the French Revolution of 1789.) Large families were applauded. Catholic, French-speaking, agricultural, and traditional: These were the idealized traits, federalists and sovereigntists both agreed in the 1950s, that marked Quebec society in the second half of the 19th century and continued largely unchallenged until the end of the Second World War (Rioux, 1993).

There frequently is a kernel of truth in generalizations. The Catholic Church *did* grow more powerful after the failed rebellions, as was reflected in the Ultramontane movement, and continued to exercise considerable influence over Quebec society until the 1950s (Dickinson and Young, 2008). Anglophones *did* dominate Quebec's increasingly capitalist economy after 1880, especially its financial and manufacturing sectors. Quebec's political culture *was* strongly conservative, as represented by the Catholic priest, teacher, and historian Lionel-Adolphe Groulx (1878–1967), whose fierce nationalism also mixed with anti-secularism and, some argue, anti-Semitism. Its political system likewise *did* have anti-democratic and authoritarian aspects. Women, for example, did not get the vote until 1940, civil rights were sometimes abridged, and the state's coercive powers were frequently abused, particularly under the reign of Duplessis from 1936 to 1939 and again from 1944 to 1959 (see Black, 1977), against labour and in defence of private property (Dickinson and Young, 2008:292–296).

Nonetheless, dominant ideologies rarely go unchallenged. Recently, Couture (1998) has argued that pre-1960s Quebec was never entirely homogeneous. Equally important, he points out that Quebec was not much different from other Canadian provinces of the period. The Ultramontane movement had its counterpart in the Orange movement, which swept Ontario and much of the West (see also Saul, 1997:32). Into the 1960s, Canada as a whole was socially conservative and highly religious. With the exception of Saskatchewan after 1944 (see Chapter 6), Canadian governments at all levels were business-oriented and, on occasion, authoritarian. Likewise, the economic and social changes (such as urbanization and industrialization) occurring in Quebec during the 20th century were similar in broad terms to those in the other provinces. In short, while displaying some distinct features, Quebec historically was neither entirely monolithic nor dissimilar from much of the rest of Canada.

In the early 1950s, however, the dominance of conservative ideology in Quebec declined in the face of two other ideological views of Quebec's future.

The first of these ideologies was liberal, federalist, and anti-nationalist. Its leaders were Pierre Trudeau (1919–2000), a lawyer and political economist who rose to political prominence during the Asbestos strike, and Gérard Pelletier (1919–1997), a journalist, social activist, and long-time friend of Trudeau. They founded a radical magazine, *Cité libre*, in 1950 to articulate their vision of Quebec's future in Canada. The magazine denounced the insularity and conservatism of Quebec. Though Catholic, the editors also denounced the power of the Catholic Church. Finally, taking a stance that marked his later adult life, Trudeau also denounced Quebec nationalism—indeed, all forms of nationalism, new and old—as retrograde, a reversion to tribalism. Trudeau's vision of Quebec and Canada was essentially liberal, ostensibly valuing the individual over the collective (but see Couture, 1998). He and Pelletier argued that Quebec had all the powers it needed under the British North America Act. What was needed to address Quebec's rising demands was increased democracy within the province and greater power in Ottawa (McCall-Newman, 1982; Clarkson and McCall, 1990; Balthazar, 1993).

The second ideological strain challenging conservative Quebec was sovereigntist and nationalist. Quebec's intellectual class, especially historians, provided early impetus for the nationalist cause by reinterpreting the history of Quebec in light of neo-Marxist notions of class and colonial oppression. But other members of the new middle class, such as journalists, broadcasters, and teachers, were also prominent (Rioux, 1993; Cook, 1995). The old Quebec nationalism was cultural rather than political, largely unconcerned with economic development, based on a set of mainly Catholic values, inward looking and defensive, and rejecting of newcomers. By contrast, while the new nationalism shared with the old a belief in the French language and was perhaps even more dedicated to preserving the French fact in North America, it was otherwise opposed, even scornful, of Quebec's traditional culture.

Like the liberal anti-nationalists, the new nationalists favoured modernization and political reform. Unlike the liberals, however, the new nationalists were often stridently anticlerical and highly secular, and their reforms extended into the economy. Most importantly, the new nationalists argued that French culture could survive only if Quebec had the powers of an autonomous state (Balthazar, 1993; Taylor, 1993; Conway, 2004:60). These powers could be exercised within a loose federal arrangement, if not, however, within an independent country.

Embedded in this idea was an important transformation in identity. Prior to the Second World War, Canada's two identities, French-Canadian and English-Canadian, had existed (distantly) side by side. The war, however, fuelled a new sense of nationalism in English-speaking Canada and, by the close of the 1950s, fuelled increasing demands for an end to "hyphenated" Canadianism (see Chapter 6). In Quebec, however, these demands and the federal government's increasing encroachment into areas of provincial jurisdiction were viewed as threats. Quebec's long isolation and rejection by the rest of Canada produced, finally, an identity coincident with the new nationalism. The old nationalism identified with the French language and the Catholic faith; its people were *French-Canadian*. By contrast, the people of the new nationalism were Québécois (Webber, 1994:49).

Revolutions require not only symbols but ideological justifications and blueprints. Quebec's *Tremblay Report* of 1956 provided both of these. The report became a bible for the Quiet Revolution. In four volumes, it "gave ideological and statistical support to provincial autonomy and to the idea that the Quebec government was the primary defender of a threatened culture" (Dickinson and Young, 2008:296). In some ways profoundly traditional and nostalgic, the report nonetheless contained two ideas important to debates about Canada and Quebec ever since. First, the report gave voice to a belief already existing in Quebec that Confederation involved a pact between two equal peoples, French and English. Quebec was not "just one" of several provinces. Second, the *Tremblay Report* argued that Quebec was distinct from the other provinces and required continued jurisdictional autonomy in some areas into which the federal government was moving (Cook, 1995:162).

When Maurice Duplessis died in 1959, the last vestiges of conservative nationalism died with him. The Liberals, led by Jean Lesage (1912–1980), defeated Duplessis's Union Nationale government the next year. Quebec's Quiet Revolution had begun.

Clashing Nationalisms and Quiet Revolutions

Lesage's Liberal Party contained elements of both the new liberal and new nationalist factions. In time the marriage would break down. At first, however, the goals of replacing the Union Nationale and modernizing Quebec provided sufficient cement to hold the coalition together.

The Liberals, in their first mandate, moved to bring Quebec's public services (health, education, labour laws, social welfare) up to the level of the other provinces (Conway, 2004). Political changes were also made. The voting age was lowered from 21 to 18, new laws governing election expenses were passed, and patronage and gerrymandering were attacked. Much of English Canada applauded these steps. Two years later, however, Lesage won re-election using the slogan "*Maîtres chez nous*" ("Masters in our own house"). English Canada grew more wary.

In 1962 the Liberals called an election seeking a mandate to nationalize Quebec's private electric companies. The idea was that of René Lévesque (1922–1987), a former journalist and prominent television commentator, now Lesage's minister of natural resources. Like many Québécois, Lévesque believed Quebec's distinctiveness could be protected only if francophone Quebecers had control over the economy, a belief that in time caused him to leave the Liberal Party and to lead the Parti Québécois.

In the meantime, however, the Liberals created Hydro-Québec, which quickly became a symbol of Quebec nationalism. Other measures followed, such as the creation in 1965 of the Caisse de dépôt et placement du Québec, made responsible for Quebec's own pension plan. These actions were popular among Quebec francophones who saw in economic nationalism a means of addressing entrenched inequalities between themselves and the English minority. Quebec's English-dominated business community viewed these actions with alarm, however.

The fears of English-speaking Canadians within Quebec were matched by those of their counterparts outside the province, concerned that Quebec nationalism threatened their ideal of "One Canada." Few Canadians were yet travelling across their country; the Trans-Canada Highway was not formally opened until the summer of 1962. Television and radio provided a kind of link, but also reinforced regional and cultural divisions. Indeed, French television in Quebec after 1950 became a chief breeding ground for cultural nationalism (Balthazar, 1993). In consequence, Canadian nationalism exhibited what Rotstein (1978) described as **mapism**, the tendency of English-speaking Canadians to identify with the shape of Canada as learned in school by looking at the map, but to know nothing about the history or culture of their fellow citizens, especially those in Quebec. They knew only that Quebec was geographically at Canada's heart, and that Quebec nationalism now seemed to be a dagger pointed at that heart.

For most Quebecers, Canada outside Quebec also remained a mystery; more than a century of parochial education had ensured that. The new nationalists did not harbour any hatred toward English Canada. In the main, French Quebecers were simply indifferent to the rest of Canada.

For a few Quebec nationalists, however, the pace of social and political change was too slow. In the early 1960s, the Front de libération du Québec (FLQ) was formed for the sole purpose of taking Quebec out of Canada, by force if necessary. The FLQ and many of its sympathizers drew their revolutionary ideals from broader social currents of the time, in Canada and abroad. While in English Canada, anti-establishment politics focused upon opposition to the U.S., in Quebec the spirit of revolution focused on anglophone symbols and institutions and their supporters.

In the revolutionaries' view, Quebec was still a colony. In the blunt words of the nationalist writer Pierre Vallières (1971), francophone Quebecers were "White Niggers." They needed to be liberated.

In 1963, the FLQ began a terrorist campaign directed at symbols of English privilege and power. Banks were robbed, weapons were stolen, bombs exploded. The campaign began with the bombing of the Wolfe monument in Quebec City—what more symbolic target could there be? Over the next seven years the FLQ proceeded to other targets: McGill and Loyola universities; the Westmount district of Montreal; the Eaton's department store and the Montreal Stock Exchange; the RCMP and the Black Watch Regiment; a monument to Queen Victoria and the Queen's Printer. Six lives were lost. Some of the terrorists were caught, tried, convicted, and sentenced (Conway, 2004:64).

The FLQ's tactics never had strong support in Quebec; indeed, they were denounced. The bombings served a purpose, however, in garnering English-speaking Canada's attention. Thus began English-speaking Canada's education on Quebec and the history of French-English relations.

Commissions and the "Three Wise Men"

In the context of growing civil strife in Quebec and rising angst elsewhere, Liberal Prime Minister Lester Pearson (1897–1972) created the Royal Commission on Bilingualism and Biculturalism (Government of Canada, 1963) in 1963. In its preliminary report of 1965 and a final report, encompassing six books, the commission detailed the second-class status of francophones within Quebec and Canada's federal structures. In 1961, for example, unilingual anglophones had the highest average income in Quebec ($6,049), followed by bilingual anglophones ($5,929), bilingual francophones ($4,523), and finally unilingual francophones ($3,107) (Webber, 1994:45; see also Conway, 2004). Most of Quebec's private sector economy was owned by anglophone Canadians or non-Canadians. Francophones were similarly disadvantaged in the federal civil service, significantly underrepresented and concentrated in the lower tiers of administration. Both inside and outside Quebec, English was the language of work in the federal service. Francophone hospitals, schools, and universities were inferior to those of anglophones (see also Porter, 1965). In short, the pattern of social stratification in Quebec, set in motion by the Conquest, seemed largely unbroken 200 years later.

Even before the commission's final report, acting on its preliminary recommendations and spirit, the Pearson Liberals took several steps. There was never any intent that all of Canada could or should become a completely bilingual country. At the level of federal institutions, however, an intensive French- and English-language training program was instituted for civil servants. In keeping with its demands for greater control over internal economic affairs, Quebec was allowed to opt out of the Canada Pension Plan (Webber, 1994). And a new Canadian flag also was created (see Chapter 6), one that broke with Canada's long-standing fealty to Britain (Conway, 2004:66).

These measures had their critics, both among Quebec nationalists who viewed the commission as obscuring their demands, and some in English-speaking Canada who were unsympathetic to francophone demands for equality. Yet many English-speaking Canadians also accepted, even embraced, the administrative and linguistic changes.

More problematic was the commission's vision of Canada—specifically, the idea that Confederation involved a partnership of the French and English "nations." Very quickly, some academics, including the eminent historian Donald Creighton, denounced this **two nations theory** (a.k.a. **compact theory**) as revisionist (Creighton, 1970). For them, Canada was not a partnership between the French and the English, but rather a partnership of equal provinces (see Romney, 1999). In Weberian terms, French- and English-speaking Canadians had very different understandings of the basis of their relationship with the country. The resultant disagreement has continued to frame Canada-Quebec relations and constitutional debates into the present (see Chapter 4).

The federal Liberal party recruited three prominent Quebecers in an effort to win over the hearts and minds of francophone Quebecers: the aforementioned Pierre Trudeau and Gérard Pelletier, and a labour leader, Jean Marchand (1918–1988). Soon referred to as Quebec's "three wise men," Trudeau, Pelletier, and Marchand believed Quebec's demands for cultural protection could best be met by securing representation within Ottawa. For the Liberal Party, they also represented the resurrection of an old idea that Canada was the home of both English and French. In English Canada, however, another message was frequently understood: that Quebec's new ministers would stop the nationalist agitation and put Quebec back in its place.

The year 1967 was Canada's centennial. English-speaking Canada was optimistic, its cheery enthusiasm captured by Bobby Gimby's song "Canada." All Canada and much of the world seemed to congregate that summer in Montreal, home of the Man and His World exhibition, to celebrate. But France's president, Charles de Gaulle (1890–1970), came to Canada in July on a state visit. Steaming up the St. Lawrence on a French cruiser, he disembarked at Quebec City and proceeded by cavalcade to Montreal. There, overcome by the occasion, speaking from the balcony of city hall, de Gaulle shouted "*Vive le Québec libre!*" The Canadian government was not amused with this break in diplomatic protocol—Quebec and Quebecers did not, in its view, require liberation—and quickly insisted on de Gaulle's exit (see Clarkson and McCall, 1990:103–104). Nonetheless, for English-speaking Canadians the Quebec "problem" had reared its head once more.

In 1968, Pierre Trudeau succeeded Lester Pearson as leader of the Liberal Party and prime minister. As justice minister in the previous Cabinet, Trudeau had reformed Canada's divorce laws and made liberal amendments to Criminal Code laws on abortion and homosexuality (Clarkson and McCall, 1990:107). Now, in 1968, Canadians experienced "Trudeaumania" and became familiar for the first time with the word *charisma*, a term coined by Max Weber (1958:295), meaning *an extraordinary quality of a person, regardless of whether this quality is actual, alleged, or presumed.*

As prime minister, one of Trudeau's first acts was to bring in the policy of official bilingualism. Following in the footsteps of Henri Bourassa, Trudeau held a pan-Canadian vision of the country, one in which French and English were equal from sea to sea. Quebec nationalism, he believed, would wither as francophones came to feel at home in the rest of Canada. Two years later, however, the Canadian state and society faced a serious challenge from those in Quebec who believed Trudeau did not understand their demands and was selling the rest of Canada a false vision.

The October Crisis and Its Aftermath

On October 5, 1970, members of the FLQ kidnapped James Cross (1921–), a British trade commissioner. The terrorist cell quickly made seven demands in exchange for Cross's release. The Quebec and Canadian governments rejected all demands at first. They soon relented, however, granting one request: the broadcast and publication of the FLQ's manifesto.

Few Quebecers supported the FLQ's actions. Nonetheless, the manifesto, a broadly Marxist polemic laced with invective and dark humour, drew much applause. In its way, the FLQ touched on real frustrations and anger felt by francophones in the province.

Faced with unexpected public support within Quebec for the FLQ's position, the Quebec government declared on October 10 that no further concessions would be made to the kidnappers. A few hours later, the crisis escalated. Pierre Laporte (1921–1970), Quebec's labour minister, who had only months before nearly been elected provincial Liberal leader, was kidnapped by another FLQ cell acting independently.

René Lévesque, union leaders, and some others demanded negotiations with the FLQ for Cross's and Laporte's lives. Rejecting, however, the notion of a "parallel government," and thereby also invoking a classical definition of the state (see the Introduction), Pierre Trudeau ordered Canadian troops be positioned in Ottawa and the province of Quebec. On October 16, the federal government declared the War Measures Act (WMA). Under this act, all civil rights and liberties in Canada were technically suspended. Those suspected of criminal offences were arrested without charge and held without bail and without trial. The focus was upon Quebec and those suspected of being FLQ supporters, but the act's application was wider. Under the WMA, 465 FLQ "supporters" were arrested, 403 of whom were released without charge. Of the remainder, 32 were charged but not prosecuted, while 18 were convicted of minor offences (Conway, 2004:82–83).

The day after the WMA was declared, Laporte's kidnappers murdered him. The killing intensified feelings of fear and panic, both inside and outside Quebec. Support for the Trudeau government rose, especially in English-speaking Canada. Feelings were more mixed in Quebec, but many accepted the presence of tanks and the suspension of civil liberties without question.

Laporte's killers were eventually caught, tried, and convicted using regular police methods. Shortly thereafter, in early December, Cross was located and freed in return for his kidnappers' safe passage to Cuba. Over time, all of Cross's kidnappers voluntarily returned to Canada, where they too were tried, convicted, and sentenced (*Maclean's*, 2000).

Thus, the October Crisis—and the Quiet Revolution with it—came to an end. Today, the crisis and the imposition of the War Measures Act, though replaced in 1988 by the Emergencies Act, remain controversial (see Gagnon, 2000). Was invoking the

WMA necessary? Or was it an overreaction? What is the best way to protect civil society from threat? When is state coercion justified, and what are its limits?

In the short term, Trudeau's government was praised for its handling of the situation, while the use of violence to achieve sovereignty, never widely supported in Quebec, was thoroughly repudiated. Yet, if invoking the WMA was meant to render Quebecers fearful of pursuing nationalism, it utterly failed. Within a few years, support for Quebec nationalism among francophones was stronger than ever.

Conclusion

The story of Quebec in the 20th century is one of sociological change. These changes occurred early in the century, but became more obvious (especially to English-speaking Canada) after 1945. Still largely Catholic and conservative at war's end, Quebec only 25 years later was essentially secular and liberal. Birth rates fell remarkably and divorce rates rose. Likewise, sexual mores and social views changed, with Quebecers becoming more generally liberal in these matters than people elsewhere in North America.

Industrialization, long a fact in Quebec, also continued apace and expanded into the province's north, bringing Quebec society into increasing contact and conflict with its Native population, but economic development also remained uneven. After 1960, social stratification along French-English lines began lessening, and a new francophone bourgeoisie emerged. Rural-urban and gender differences remained, however.

At the same time, these changes were not dissimilar to changes elsewhere in Canadian society during this period. What made the changes occurring in Quebec particularly cogent was that they occurred against the historic backdrop of French-English relations starting with the Conquest. Moreover, Quebec's demands coincided with and reinforced changes occurring in English-speaking Canada's structure, beliefs, and identity. Sometimes, English-speaking Canada even changed in response to demands it *imagined* French Quebec had made (for example, bilingualism). Throughout the 1960s, Canada and Quebec danced together, each reacting to the other, tailoring their steps, measuring the other's performance. Yet, as the fall of 1970 ended, they were seemingly more separate than ever. Ironically, conflict increased between the French and English groups as the two communities became more functionally integrated and more similar as, to continue the metaphor, their steps became more synchronized. In 1970, no one could be certain how or when the dance would end.

Key Terms

charisma
clerico-nationalism
francophone proletariat
ideology

mapism
two nations theory (a.k.a. compact theory)

Critical Thinking Questions

1. In what ways did English expansion during the 19th and 20th centuries lead to both Quebec isolation and a strengthened nationalism in that province?
2. How might structural functionalists and conflict theorists view the political, economic, cultural, and social changes that occurred in Quebec during the 20th century?
3. Why is symbolism so important in shaping human relations?
4. In what ways do maps help or hinder our ideas about what is real?
5. Do individuals possess charisma, or is it something that their followers "read into" them?

Recommended Readings

Behiels, Michael D., and Matthew Hayday. 2011. *Contemporary Quebec: Selected Readings and Commentaries.* Montreal and Kingston: McGill-Queen's University Press.
This book is essential reading for understanding Quebec society both historically and the changes occurring since the Quiet Revolution.

Conway, John. 2004. *Debts to Pay: The Future of Federalism in Quebec.* 3rd ed. Toronto: James Lorimer & Company.
Written with passion, this book calls upon English-speaking Canada to discover its real history and thereby to understand the legitimate grievances of French-speaking Canada.

Gauvreau, Michael. 2005. *The Catholic Origins of Quebec's Quiet Revolution, 1931–1970.* Montreal and Kingston: McGill-Queen's University Press.
This book argues that debates and reforms within the Roman Catholic Church played a part in paving the way for the Quiet Revolution.

Romney, Paul. 1999. *Getting It Wrong: How Canadians Forgot Their Past and Imperilled Confederation.* Toronto: University of Toronto Press.
This book tells the story of how Confederation came about and holds lessons for Canadians today who seek constitutional reform.

Saul, John Ralston. 1997. *Reflections of a Siamese Twin: Canada at the End of the Twentieth Century.* Toronto: Penguin Books.
Almost a classic, Saul's book outlines the complicated relationship that has arisen between Canada's "two solitudes," creating the kind of society Canada has today.

Related Websites

CBC Digital Archives (October Crisis)
www.cbc.ca/archives/categories/politics/civil-unrest/the-october-crisis-civil-liberties-suspended/topic---the-october-crisis-civil-liberties-suspended.html
This archive contains numerous video clips of important events in Canadian history, including "October Crisis: Civil Liberties Suspended."

CBC Digital Archives (Richard Riot)
www.cbc.ca/archives/categories/sports/hockey/the-legendary-9-maurice-rocket-richard/the-1955-richard-riot.html
The archive also contains useful footage of the Richard riot.

Manitoba Metis Federation
www.mmf.mb.ca
This non-profit organization was founded in 1967 to give an independent voice to Métis people.

Canadian Society on Video

The Champions Series, Part One: Unlikely Warriors. 1978. National Film Board of Canada, 57 minutes, 27 seconds.
Examines the lives of Pierre Trudeau and René Lévesque from the early 1950s through to 1967, the year Lévesque left the Liberal Party and Trudeau became the federal minister of justice.

The Champions Series, Part Two: Trappings of Power. 1978. National Film Board of Canada, 55 minutes, 44 seconds.
Examines the period from 1967 to 1977, during which Pierre Trudeau won three federal elections, the October Crisis occurred, and the Parti Québécois under Rene Lévesque came to power.

The Great Resistance. 2008. National Film Board of Canada, 77 minutes, 22 seconds.
In the 1930s, in the throes of the Great Depression, the government relocated more than 80,000 citizens to found a new settlement in the virgin forests of Quebec's Abitibi region. After enduring back-breaking work to clear the land, however, many left, seeking a better life in the city or as labourers for the large corporations that came to exploit the North's valuable resources.

CHAPTER 3

THE
CONSTITUTIONAL
YEARS

The Magnificent Obsession
> —subtitle to Clarkson and McCall's 1990 examination
> of the Trudeau years and efforts at constitutional reform

Quebec constitutes, within Canada, a distinct society.
> —the Meech Lake Accord, 1987

The process of constitutional reform in Canada has been discredited.
—Quebec premier Robert Bourassa after the failure of the Meech Lake Accord, 1990

Introduction

Goa is a former Portuguese colony on India's western coast. In a country predominantly Hindu, Goa's population is largely Catholic, and much of its small population bears decidedly non-Indian names, like de Jesus. In other words, despite being surrounded by a dominant majority population, Goa, like Quebec, retains its distinct cultural identity.

One of this book's authors was travelling in Goa in the fall of 1976 when he heard that the separatist Parti Québécois (PQ), led by René Lévesque, had been elected to govern Quebec. Because he was a young, unilingual, and politically unaware Westerner, the significance of the event escaped him then. He remembers, however, two francophone Quebecers in their late twenties, also visiting Goa, who were elated by news of the PQ's victory and celebrated long into the night.

This chapter examines events in Quebec and the relationship between Canada and Quebec during the 20 years that followed the FLQ Crisis of 1970. As noted in the previous chapter, the FLQ crisis ended the Quiet Revolution in Quebec. Thereafter, nationalist and separatist impulses within the province took a less violent but, in the long term, potentially more lethal turn, alternating between efforts to reform Canada's Constitution and threats of referenda on Quebec's independence. The period ended with the failure of the Meech Lake Accord in 1990 and the referendum defeat of the Charlottetown Accord two years later, events whose aftershocks can still be felt today. The chapter begins with a discussion of sociology and its relationship to political constitutions.

Sociology and the Canadian Constitution

The events of the 1960s, culminating in the FLQ Crisis in 1970, set off a profound rethinking of Canada's Constitution. Sociology and sociologists played a major role in this rethinking. This should not surprise us. After all, one of sociology's main interests involves **social norms**, the more or less agreed-upon societal rules and expectations that specify ways of behaving in society.

Constitutions fall under a specific type of norm: **laws**. The term **constitution** refers "both to the institutions, practices, and principles that define and structure a system of government and to the written document that establishes or articulates such a system" (taken from Hemberger, 1993:189). A constitution defines a state's sphere of authority, the means of its governance, and the claims that may be made in the political realm, broadly defined and contested. More broadly, constitutions represent symbolically a statement of spirit or intent, for example, that "all people are created equal." Beginning with the American and French revolutions, constitutions arose as a means of formally specifying the relationship between individuals and groups and their relationship to the modern state, a chief interest of early sociologists such as Tönnies, Weber, and Durkheim (see the Introduction). Finally, while some constitutions are more easily changed than others, none are written in such a way that they can be changed at whim. Constitutions are meant to represent a more or less firm statement of a country's legal foundation. By comparison, the American Constitution is relatively "fixed" while the Canadian Consti- tution is sometimes referred to as a "rolling compromise." Beginning in the 1960s, the compromise picked up speed.

Until 1982, Canada's key constitutional document, of course, was the British North America (BNA) Act (later renamed the Constitution Act, 1867), creating the Domin- ion of Canada (Dunn, 1995) (see Chapter 5). Long before 1867, however, Canada's existence was structured by a series of constitutional acts: for example, the charter of the Hudson's Bay Company in 1670, the Royal Proclamation of 1763, the Quebec Act of 1774, the Constitution Act of 1791, and the Act of Union of 1841 (see Chapter 1). The BNA Act repealed some elements contained in these previous legal documents. Other commitments, however, remain in effect; for example, current Native land claims date from the Royal Proclamation Act (see Chapter 12).

The BNA Act was repeatedly altered after 1867 to meet changing conditions and demands. A partial list of these changes includes the various acts that incorporated the lands of the Hudson's Bay Company and the North-West Territories into Canada, made Manitoba, British Columbia, Alberta, and Saskatchewan provinces, established the Yukon Territory, and brought Newfoundland into Confederation.

Constitutional reform stalled, however, after the 1920s, even as the need for it became greater. The Statute of Westminster in 1931 declared Canada (along with Australia, New Zealand, and South Africa) sovereign and equal to Britain. Canada, however, declined at that time to take control over the Constitution because the federal and provincial governments could not agree on how the Constitution would be amended in future.

Why was the issue of an amending formula problematic? It was problematic because it dealt with issues of power between levels of government and between government and individual citizens. For example, would the federal government be constitution- ally able to make changes unilaterally? Or would provincial consent for constitutional changes be required? If so, how many provinces and would all provinces, large and small, be equal? If not provinces, would Canadian citizens have the ultimate say over constitutional changes through, for example, a Canada-wide referendum? How would the rights of smaller provinces and, in the case of Quebec, minorities be protected against the majority provinces or population? Would some elements of the Consti- tution be more easily changed than other elements? These were only some of the constitutional questions facing Canadian politicians after 1931. With no clear answers in sight, the Constitution remained "housed" in Britain, even as Canada symbolically distanced itself from Britain in other ways. (In 1950, for example, the British Privy Council ceased to be Canada's Supreme Court.)

Constitutional questions would not go away, however. Two issues with constitutional implications dominated federal-provincial relations in Canada during the 1950s. The first was the ongoing search for an amending formula. The second was fiscal relations between the two levels of government (Webber, 1994:93), a by-product of the federal government's control of revenues and the expansion of welfare state programs after 1945 (see Chapter 6). With the Quiet Revolution of the 1960s, a third issue was added to the mix: Quebec's historical relation to the rest of Canada. Was Canada a confederation of 10 equal provinces, or was it a bargain between 2 nations, French and English (Chapter 2)?

The events of the Quiet Revolution, culminating in the October Crisis of 1970, made obvious the necessity of resolving these issues. Quebec, however, was not the sole impetus for demands for constitutional change. In particular, the western provinces in the 1970s also demanded constitutional changes in two areas: first, "control over the taxing and marketing of natural resources" and, second, "reform of federal institutions, especially the Senate" (Webber, 1994:103) (see chapters 7 and 8). Quebec and many of Canada's "hinterland" provinces demanded *both* a greater devolution of federal powers and, concomitantly, more inclusion at the centre of federal decision making.

The Trudeau government's interpretation of Canada's "problem" was quite different. Among developed countries, Canada was significantly decentralized already. The problem was not an excess of power at the centre, but too much power in the regions. Giving in to Quebec's nationalist demands would only encourage more demands. Already other provinces were piggybacking on Quebec's demands, threatening further weakening of the Canadian state. The solution to Canada's problems, in Trudeau's eyes, lay in constitutional reforms that would bring Quebecers and Quebec into the "Canadian nation" (see Balthazar, 1997).

By 1971, the federal and provincial governments were seeking constitutional reform. At a federal-provincial meeting held in Victoria, the two levels of government appeared at last to have reached an accord on some principles for renewing Confederation. Quebec Premier Robert Bourassa (1933–1996) faced strong opposition from nationalists, unionists, business groups, and the media, however, upon his return to Quebec. These opponents feared the agreement would enhance federal authority while reducing Quebec to the status of just another province. Constitutional reform thus was put on hold. In the absence of a constitutional solution to Quebec's demands, new coalitions of social and political forces soon arose in Quebec, proffering different solutions to the Quebec-Canada "problem."

The Election of the Parti Québécois

On November 15, 1976, René Lévesque's Parti Québécois became Quebec's governing party, taking 71 of 110 seats and 42 percent of the popular vote (Conway, 2004:91). The election was a startling turnaround for the PQ, which in 1973 had won only six seats (though they won 30 percent of the vote) in losing to Bourassa's Liberals. Much of English Canada pan-icked. The business community was particularly stunned, fearing equally the PQ's avowed separatism—Levesque promised to hold a referendum on sovereignty sometime during his party's electoral mandate—and social democratic platform. What had happened?

In part, the PQ's election was the Liberal government's rejection. Bourassa's personal image had never fully recuperated from his handling of the FLQ crisis of 1970, when he was widely seen by francophone Quebecers as weak and ineffectual in defending their interests. More broadly, however, the PQ's election reflected a further evolution in Quebec society itself and in Quebec nationalism. By the 1970s, the economic changes undertaken during the Quiet Revolution were bearing fruit. New middle and entrepre-neurial classes were emerging, dominated by francophone Quebecers. Labour unions, long suppressed in Quebec, were also growing in power, and labour militancy was on the rise, exemplified in an extreme manner by workers' intentional destruction of the James Bay hydroelectric site in 1974. Quebec culture and arts, no longer insular or defensive, were also thriving. The PQ's positive message of creating a more autonomous, social democratic, and modern society appealed to a wide cross-section of francophones within the blue- and white-collar, intellectual, and cultural communities.

Like all Quebec political parties, going back to the previous century, the PQ was nationalist, but the PQ's nationalism was fundamentally different from that of previ-ous Quebec governments. First, reflecting changes among Quebecers themselves, the PQ's nationalism was more positive and future-oriented than in the past (Dufour, 1990; Thompson, 1995). Second, where Quebec governments in the past had defended the French "nation"—albeit with its obvious homeland in Quebec, still within Canada—the PQ rejected both the notion of allegiance to Canada and to a broader pan-Canadian French nation (Webber, 1994:101). For the PQ and many of its followers, there was only a Québécois nation, its interests represented by Quebec's quasi-state, on the verge of becoming a sovereign country. All that was needed to make Quebec sovereign was a decision by its people to assert their rights of self-determination.

Third, where the Union Nationale had been authoritarian and conservative, and the Liberals classically liberal, the PQ was unabashedly democratic socialist as reflected in several progressive policies enacted during its first term in office. Labour laws were amended, outlawing strikebreaking and adopting the Rand formula (see Chapter 7) for deducting union dues. Reflecting the strength of emergent feminism within the party, the rights of women also were extended (see Dickinson and Young, 2008). Finally, Que-bec's minimum wage became the highest in Canada, and the sales tax was removed on shoes, clothing, and furniture (Conway, 2004:96–97). The PQ's most important moves, however, were in defence of the French language.

The Language of Quebec Nationalism

Language is a central element of national identity as it represents continuity with the past and future (see Chapter 4). It is also central to much sociological thought. From a symbolic interaction perspective, for example, language is the chief vehicle for under-standing and expressing a group's history, beliefs, and values, but from a post-structural perspective, language and its putative efforts at defining a precise "meaning" are tied up with issues of power. Likewise, while structural functionalists view language as a means of facilitating mutual exchanges, conflict theorists view it as a contested terrain between the dominant culture and minority groups.

Until the Constitution Act of 1982, only the BNA Act of 1867 (later renamed the Constitution Act of 1867) dealt constitutionally with language, and then only in Sec-tion 133 and in a limited context. Section 133 states that either French or English can be used in the legislatures of Canada and Quebec and courts under their authority, and that records and journals of both Parliament and the Quebec legislature must be bilingual. Section 23 of the Manitoba Act of 1870 replicated the Quebec provisions of the BNA Act (Dunn, 1995:340–342), as did arrangements in the North-West Territories in 1874 (Cook, 1995:153).

The cultural wars of the 1890s and early 20th century, recounted in Chapter 3, saw English majorities abuse French language protections, however. Meanwhile, the major-ity French in Quebec found their social and cultural status gradually declining against the minority and unilingual anglophone population. In effect, where constitutional bilingualism existed, it provided greater protection for English speakers, minority or otherwise, than it did French speakers.

By the 1960s, survival of the French language and culture in Quebec was further threatened by a combination of declining birth rates and rapidly increasing immigra-tion into the province (Dickinson and Young, 2008; Fournier et al., 1997). Many of the new arrivals spoke neither French nor English. Surrounded by a North American sea of English, however, and experiencing the economic and social benefits of English within the province, most immigrants were choosing to speak English. Moreover, schools were pressed into the debate as immigrants demanded that their children receive education in English. For many francophones, their ancestral homeland and culture were once more under siege. Official bilingualism, enacted in 1969, did not address these fears. Indeed, official bilingualism was the answer to a question most francophone Quebecers had not asked, satisfying only Canadian nationalists outside the province. In 1968, vio-lence broke out in Montreal between francophone nationalists and immigrant Italians over language instruction in schools (Dickinson and Young, 2008:323–324; Thompson, 1995; Fournier et al., 1997).

The Bourassa government in 1974 attempted to deal with the issue through the Offi-cial Languages Act (Bill 22). Bill 22 made French Quebec's official language in certain key areas, such as business, labour, education, some professions, and public adminis-tration (Conway, 2004:92). It did not demand the exclusive use of French, however. Education matters, for example, were left largely untouched, with immigrant parents still able to enroll their children in English-language schools.

After its election, the Parti Québécois moved quickly to remove any ambiguity concern-ing the status of French in Quebec. The Charter of the French Language of 1977 (Bill 101) made French the province's official language and the "normal language of work, education, communications, and business." Bill 101 also restricted English instruction to those whose parents were educated in English in Quebec. (An exception was granted to Aboriginal peoples, especially in the case of Aboriginal languages.) Bill 101 further placed limits on bilingual signs and restricted the use of English in business and government (see Fournier et al., 1997:242–259; Dickinson and Young, 2008:324; Webber, 1994:100–101).

Anglophones within Quebec, many of whom had deep ancestral roots, felt themselves under attack. Their anger found support outside Quebec among English-speaking Canadians who could not understand the Quebec government's moves to make the province predominantly French at a time when they were (grudgingly) accepting bilingualism. Anger outside Quebec was aided and abetted by some English-Canadian politicians pandering to anti-French, anti-Quebec sentiment in search of cheap votes.

Supporters of Bill 101 pointed out, however, that its provisions dealt solely with Quebec's public and symbolic realms, not with cultural institutions (e.g., McGill University) or private interactions (Webber, 1994:101). They further pointed out the failure of governments elsewhere to protect and promote the French language (see Conway, 2004:93). However, few in English-speaking Canada listened to such arguments. Following the passage of Bill 101, Sun Life announced it was moving its headquarters from Montreal to Toronto. Other businesses soon followed. Many young anglophone Quebecers also left the province during this period (Morton, 1997).

By 1979, the Parti Québécois was entering the bottom half of its electoral mandate. It had been elected on a promise to hold a referendum on sovereignty that would make the Quebec state the political embodiment of that expression. Now time was running out to fulfill the promise. The stage was set for the 1980 referendum and one of the most compelling political rivalries of the late 20th century.

A Study in Personal Agency: The 1980 Referendum

One of sociology's ongoing central debates involves the relationship between individual behaviour and the constraints and imperatives of social structure. Do individuals really make a difference, or are we merely creations of our time and place? In a famous passage, Marx (1977b:300) once wrote that people "make their own history, but they do not make it just as they please, they do not make it under circumstances chosen by themselves, but under circumstances directly encountered, given, and transmitted from the past." The American sociologist C. Wright Mills (1961:6) viewed agency and structure as a meeting place for what he termed the **sociological imagination**, the ability "to grasp history and biography and the relations of the two within society." From this perspective, Pierre Trudeau and René Lévesque can be seen as products of prewar 1939 Quebec society and the political and ideological struggles of their time.[1] Yet each also influenced the shape and manner of those struggles (Cook, 1995:138).

Trudeau and Lévesque are often viewed as opposites: Trudeau the reasoned intellectual and committed federalist, Levesque the passionate "man of action" and Quebec nationalist. Certainly, their public styles were at odds (Clarkson and McCall, 1990:198–200), yet they were both children of the post–First World War French-Canadian bourgeoisie, had fought to end the Duplessis regime, and were social liberals dedicated to modernizing Quebec. Both believed in a "large role for the state in public affairs" (Chodos and Hamovitch, 1991:195). Moreover, each in his way represented a form of Quebec nationalism (see Dufour, 1990:81), Trudeau as passionately as Lévesque, Lévesque in as calculated a manner as Trudeau. In their time, each elicited mixed public responses. Loved by francophone Quebecers, loathed by their anglophone counterparts, Lévesque was at the same time both respected and feared in English-speaking Canada. For his part, Trudeau likewise was loathed and hated, admired and respected, often by the same people. (The late poet Irving Layton once wrote, "In Pierre Trudeau, Canada has at last produced a political leader worthy of assassination.") Yet Lévesque's death in 1987 resulted in a profound outpouring of grief in Quebec (Conway, 2004:128–129), while Trudeau's death in September 2000 was mourned by much of Canada, his funeral perhaps the largest attended and watched in Canadian history (*Maclean's*, 2000).

In 1979, Trudeau's and Levesque's visions of Quebec's relationship to Canada were on a collision course. Trudeau believed in a strong Quebec, but as a province among other provinces, within a bilingual Canada. As already noted, Trudeau held a pan-Canadian vision of a bilingual Canada, a vision with deep roots in Quebec (Chapter 2), but his idea of a strong central state was European while the notion of constitutionally equal provinces was American (see Dufour, 1990; Balthazar, 1997).

For many Quebecers, this vision of Canada was at odds with the historic reality of Quebec's relationship with the rest of Canada, going back at least to the Quebec Act of 1774. Perhaps worse, Trudeau's vision created a kind of straitjacket for constitutional change (Dufour, 1990). Many francophones supported Lévesque's vision of a strong Quebec with unique powers within a decentralized Canadian federation. By 1979, a sizable number of Quebecers believed the only option, if their nation could not be protected within Canada, was Quebec independence.

Lévesque's vision of the Canadian federation was neither radical nor recent. Debates about how centralized or decentralized Canada should be, or about jurisdictional responsibilities, had gone on since before Confederation and were a key aspect of discussion at Charlottetown and Quebec leading up to 1867 (Moore, 1997; Romney, 1999) (Chapter 5). Beginning with the Depression and the Second World War, however, Ottawa's role had increased in Quebec and Canada at large (Balthazar, 1997; Thompson, 1995). In the wake of Quebec's separatist threat, and faced with a stagnating economy in the 1970s, the Trudeau Liberal government attempted to reassert federal authority both politically and economically. These actions elicited hostility from Quebec, as well as other provinces, especially in the West (see Chapter 7). The stage was set for the constitutional conflict.

The Ottawa-Quebec, Trudeau-Lévesque showdown was briefly postponed by the Liberal Party's defeat in the 1979 federal election by the Progressive Conservatives, led by Joe Clark (1939–). A few months later, however, Clark's minority government was defeated and the Liberals, led by a rejuvenated Trudeau, returned to office in the subsequent election (see appendices 1 and 2). In the meantime, Lévesque's government had called for a sovereignty referendum to be held on May 20, 1980.

The debates and speeches leading up to the referendum vote were impassioned, occasionally nasty. Families were divided, friendships dissipated (Chodos and Hamovitch, 1991:193). In the end, 60 percent of Quebecers voted *No* in the referendum. Why did the first Quebec referendum turn out as it did?

In part, for older francophone Quebecers, the question represented a kind of "Sophie's choice" between two heritages, Canada and Quebec, and, for that matter, between two respected "sons," Trudeau and Lévesque. Many Quebecers in general also feared the economic consequences of sovereignty, a fear magnified by the *No* side throughout the campaign. But the reasons for the referendum's outcome were also reflected in the demographics of the voters. Quebec's anglophones and allophones, making up roughly 20 percent of the population, voted nearly en masse for the *No* side, meaning that francophone voters were split 50/50. In short, half of Quebec's large francophone population had publicly voiced their displeasure with their place in Canada's constitutional arrangements. Moreover, *Yes* supporters could take hope from the fact that the young and the educated among francophones had voted overwhelmingly in favour of sovereignty (Conway, 2004:110). The future seemed theirs to grasp.

The referendum outcome left *Yes* supporters with a sense of bitterness and gloom, feelings of "collective trauma," and a mood of "political exhaustion" (Chodos and Hamovitch, 1991:107). By contrast, for *No* supporters, the predominant feeling was one of relief (Conway, 2004). They understood too well that, in the words of Balthazar (1993), Quebecers had said *no* to sovereignty but had not said *yes* to Canada.

In the closing days of the referendum campaign, Trudeau repeated promises that if the *No* side won, he would work to revitalize Confederation (Clarkson and McCall, 1991:236–239; Conway, 2004). The vote was not likely swayed by these promises, vague in any case. The referendum was fought "on the ground" by individuals and groups on both sides of the debate. Nonetheless, Trudeau's pledge, repeated the day after the referendum, set the stage for the most substantial revision of Canada's Constitution since 1867.

The 1982 Canadian Constitution

Trudeau's statements before and immediately after the referendum were not clear, occasionally suggesting changes to federal institutions and a redistribution of powers. His only certain statement was that the patriated Constitution must contain a Charter of Rights and Freedoms. Such a charter had long been one of Trudeau's dreams. In February 1968, before announcing his run at the Liberal leadership, he had tabled a white paper in the House of Commons entitled "A Canadian Charter of Human Rights." Now, more than ever, he viewed the proposed charter as a means of ensuring the individual equality of all Canadians, especially against the "collective assaults of Quebec nationalism" (Conway, 2004:111).

By long-standing tradition, however, Quebec held a veto over constitutional changes. Quebec did not oppose per se the constitutional entrenchment of individual rights; after all,

Quebec had passed its own Charter of Human Rights and Freedoms in 1975 (see Fournier et al., 1997:260–267). Quebec nationalists, however, feared Trudeau's Charter could be used against Quebec's national interests, for example, in attacking Quebec's language laws.

Quebec's possible veto was not the Trudeau government's only problem. Many Conservative premiers also feared the Charter's application, believing that judicial activism would replace legislative supremacy. Several provinces also wanted changes in other areas. The western provinces wanted institutional reforms, notably dealing with the Senate. They also wanted clarification about provincial control over resources.

Finally, new political actors also appeared on the scene. Aboriginal Canadians, women's groups, and other social organizations also wanted input into constitutional changes.

In September 1980, the premiers and the federal government announced they had failed to agree on an amending formula. Not deterred, however, Trudeau announced his government's intention to proceed with unilaterally patriating the Constitution. A joint Commons-Senate committee held hearings throughout November and December on the proposed Charter of Rights and Freedoms.

In September 1981, however, Canada's Supreme Court ruled that, while the federal government could unilaterally patriate the Constitution, doing so "offended the federal spirit" (*Maclean's*, 2000; Clarkson and McCall, 1991). It was a strong judicial rebuke to Trudeau's plans. Thus, the federal government and provinces returned to talks in the fall of 1981.

As talks began that November, only the provinces of Ontario and New Brunswick supported the federal plans. The other premiers, known as the "gang of eight," posed a seemingly solid front, but the Trudeau government held a winning card. The public at large liked the idea of the Charter and wanted Canada's Constitution "brought home." In the negotiations that followed, the alliance of provincial premiers slowly began to crack. Equally important, Lévesque had agreed in the course of negotiations to give up Quebec's traditional constitutional veto. When the final agreement was reached on the Constitution, Lévesque stood alone, Quebec—in the eyes of nationalists—defenceless (Clarkson and McCall, 1991; Conway, 2004).

The new Canadian Constitution, proclaimed on April 17, 1982, has six parts (Government of Canada, 1982; Webber, 1994; Dunn, 1995). Part I deals with the Canadian Charter of Rights and Freedoms. These rights and freedoms include the fundamental freedoms of conscience, religion, thought, belief, opinion, expression, peaceful assembly, and association, as well as democratic, mobility, legal, equality, and language rights. Part I makes French and English the official languages of Canada. It further designates New Brunswick Canada's only officially bilingual province. The Charter of Rights and Freedoms, however, also includes a "notwithstanding" clause that allows provinces to opt out of a provision if they choose.

Part II of the Constitution Act, 1982, recognizes Aboriginal rights, including those existing by way of land claims, and formalizes the holding of conferences between first ministers and Aboriginal peoples (Chapter 11). Part III commits governments to promoting equal opportunities for all Canadians, reducing regional disparities, and providing essential public services. Part IV commits the government to holding two future constitutional conferences on Aboriginal peoples and the representatives of Yukon and the Northwest Territories, since held. Part V sets out a procedure for future amendments to the Constitution. Amendments may henceforth be made with the agreement of Parliament and seven provinces totalling 50 percent of the population. Part VI amends the British North America Act of 1867, renaming it the Constitution Act of 1867.

The Constitution's Aftermath

By and large, English-speaking Canadians were happy with the new Constitution. Gallup polls in May 1982 found strong support throughout Canada, and substantial, though not majority, support even in Quebec. Likewise, the political elite outside Quebec was also generally pleased with the new Constitution. Finally, the provinces outside Quebec also welcomed the act's clarification of provincial powers over natural resources—a key sticking point for provinces such as Alberta—and the insertion within the Charter of a "notwithstanding clause" that limited the Charter's application.

The PQ government and francophone nationalists in Quebec were embittered, however. For them, the promises of constitutional renewal had been hollow. Ottawa and the rest of the provinces had gotten what they wanted. What had Quebec gotten? Quebec had been "humiliated," "betrayed," "stabbed in the back." Quebec had lost its traditional veto, and now was constitutionally defenceless against Canada's anglophone majority. The Charter of Rights and Freedoms, it was feared, could and would be used to advance anglophone rights and attack French language laws. Thus, the Constitution Act of 1982, meant to heal the rifts of past years, became yet another source of Quebec grievances. Lévesque's government refused to put Quebec's signature on the Constitution and did not participate in the ceremonies marking the occasion.

Whether the PQ would ever have signed a constitutional agreement is a moot point. Trudeau, the provincial leaders, and most Canadians outside Quebec doubted that a government dedicated to separatism would ever have signed. Yet the referendum defeat had left the PQ with few options and Lévesque himself was viewed as a "soft" separatist.

In 1984, however, Lévesque's old nemesis, Trudeau, retired, and was soon replaced as Liberal leader by a former finance minister, John Turner (1929–). The Tories, meanwhile, also had a new leader, Brian Mulroney, a bilingual Quebecer and lawyer with strong ties to American business. When Mulroney promised Quebecers a deal that would allow them to sign the Constitution "with dignity," Lévesque and Quebec nationalists as a whole threw their support behind the Tories.

With Quebec support, the Mulroney Tories in 1984 routed the Liberals, taking 211 (of 282) seats, including 58 (of a possible 75) seats in Quebec (see appendices 1 and 2). It was the largest number of seats ever won by a federal party in Canada, reflecting the broad sweep of Mulroney's electoral coalition, which featured at its core western Canadian conservatives, pro-business advocates of free trade, and Quebec nationalists.

No sooner was the election over than Mulroney moved to make good his promise to Quebecers on constitutional reform. By the spring of 1987, informal discussions had proved sufficiently positive that a federal-provincial meeting was held at Meech Lake, a resort a few miles outside Ottawa. Much to everyone's surprise, that meeting ended in a formal agreement signed by the federal government and all the premiers. Five elements made up the Meech Lake Accord's proposed amendments to the Canadian Constitution (Balthazar, 1997:54). These elements were as follows:

- restoring and enshrining in the Constitution Quebec's historical veto;
- enshrining the convention that Quebec holds three of nine appointments to the Supreme Court;
- putting limits on federal spending in provincial jurisdictions;
- increasing powers over immigration; and
- recognizing Quebec as a **distinct society**.

Signing the Meech Lake Accord did not immediately change the Constitution, however. Both Mulroney and the premiers were required to take the accord back to the people, in the form of passage through their respective legislatures. The time frame for doing so was three years from the date when any one legislature passed the accord, failure by any legislature (federal or provincial) to do so resulting in the accord's rejection. Quebec passed the accord quickly. The clock hence began ticking on its acceptance by the various levels of government.

Opposition to the Meech Lake Accord was slow in mobilizing, in part because the impact of constitutional changes is not always apparent and such documents are far from easy (or enjoyable) reading. Slowly over the next few years, however, opposition mounted based on a mixture of ancient grievances and grudges, misconceptions, lofty but unmet expectations, and legitimate concerns. Three years after its signing, the accord collapsed, dividing Canada more than at any time since the FLQ crisis, and fuelling support for a second sovereignty referendum in 1995.

Of all the issues, what most brought down the Meech Lake Accord was a provision that would have recognized Quebec as a distinct society. Why was the notion of Quebec as a distinct society so controversial in 1990—and why would it likely be so again today?

Is Quebec a "Distinct Society"?

At least on the surface, few could seriously argue that culturally, Quebec is a province *comme les autres*, a difference reflected also in the distinctive focus of Quebec sociologists (see Box 3.1). Two measures of culture—language and religion—support this point.

Across Canada, the number of bilingual individuals has steadily grown since the early 1960s, today reaching 17.5 percent, with the highest rate observed in Quebec, followed by New Brunswick, though there has been a slight decline in recent years, possibly due to immigration from non-French-speaking countries (Lepage and Corbeil, 2013). But French remains the dominant language in Quebec; indeed, that province is the only domain in Canada and in North America

Box 3.1: Quebec Sociology and Quebec Society

Marcel Fournier argues that Quebec sociology developed over three particular periods: (1) a pioneering stage before 1939, when Quebec scholars focused on the province's ethnic particularity, often as a handicap or historicized artifact; (2) an institutional period between 1940 and 1969 when academic scholars, including many from the United States, examined the province's transition (according to a modernization theory) from a traditional to a modern society; and (3) the nationalization period of Quebec sociology, beginning in 1970 and continuing today, during which descriptions of Quebec as a "distinct society" or even "sociological nation" became *de rigueur*. His central argument is that sociological studies over the decades have made "significant contributions to the formation of national identity" within Quebec, contributing to such characteristics as race, ethnic, group, society, and nation.

What contributions might sociology make to your community?

Source: Marcel Fournier. 2001. "Quebec Sociology and Quebec Society: The Construction of a Collective Identity," *Canadian Journal of Sociology* 26(3):333–347.

in which the French language dominates, although New Brunswick is Canada's only officially bilingual province. Table 3.1 (below) shows that, in 2011, French was the mother tongue of nearly 80 percent of Quebecers, but less than 4 percent of people outside Quebec. On the other side, English was the mother tongue of only 7.7 percent of Quebecers in 2011, as it was in 2006, but was the mother tongue for 72 percent of Canadians outside of Quebec. In this sense, terming Canada a "bilingual country" is misleading. Canada is marked at the federal level by **institutional bilingualism**. At the level of everyday usage, however, **territorial bilingualism** predominates, much as it does in Belgium or Switzerland (Dunn, 1995:368–369). For francophones inside and outside of Quebec, the general pattern of decline plays into fears of assimilation.

If language remains a significant marker of cultural difference, religion historically has also played such a role. As indicated in Table 3.2, nearly 39 percent of Canadians in 2011 identified themselves as Roman Catholic while 28.5 percent identified themselves as belonging to another Christian religion. As with the French language, however, this figure is misleading. The largest majority of Roman Catholic identifiers are located within Quebec, with nearly 75 percent of people in that province describing themselves, at least nominally, as Roman Catholic. By contrast, only 28 percent of people outside Quebec identify themselves as Roman Catholic, while 34.7 percent of people adhere to another variant of Christian religion. Finally, one should note the joint processes of secularization and decline in identification with organized religion, with more than 27 percent of Canadians today stating an adherence to no religious faith. Indeed, the category "none" now makes up the third-largest category among Canadians' religious preferences.

Table 3.1: Population with English, French, or English and French Mother Tongue, Canada, Provinces, and Territories, and Canada Less Quebec, 2006 and 2011 (in Thousands and Percent)[1]

	2006						2011					
	English	%	French	%	Both	%	English	%	French	%	Both	%
Canada	**17,882.8**	**57.2**	**6,817.7**	**21.8**	**98.6**	**0.3**	**18,859.0**	**56.9**	**7,055.0**	**21.3**	**144.7**	**0.4**
Newfoundland & Labrador	488.4	97.6	1.9	0.4	0.3	0.1	497.6	97.6	2.5	0.5	0.5	0.1
Prince Edward Island	125.3	93.3	5.3	4.0	0.5	0.4	127.6	92.2	5.2	3.8	0.5	—
Nova Scotia	832.1	92.1	32.5	3.6	2.1	0.2	836.1	91.8	31.1	3.4	3.0	—
New Brunswick	463.2	64.4	233	32.4	4.5	0.6	479.9	64.9	233.5	31.6	6.6	—
Quebec	575.6	7.7	5,877.7	79.0	43.3	0.6	599.2	7.7	6,102.2	78.1	64.8	—
Ontario	8,230.7	68.4	488.8	4.1	32.7	0.3	8,677.0	68.2	493.3	3.8	46.6	—
Manitoba	838.4	74.0	44.0	3.9	2.6	0.2	870.0	72.9	42.1	3.5	3.8	0.3
Saskatchewan	811.7	85.1	16.1	1.7	1.1	0.1	860.5	84.5	16.3	1.6	1.7	—
Alberta	2,576.7	79.1	61.2	1.9	5.4	0.2	2,780.2	77.0	68.5	1.9	8.4	0.2
British Columbia	2,875.8	70.6	54.7	1.3	5.9	0.1	3,062.4	70.2	57.3	1.3	8.6	0.2
Yukon	25.7	84.9	1.1	3.7	0.1	0.4	28.1	83.4	1.5	4.4	0.1	0.3
Northwest Territories	31.5	76.8	1.0	2.4	—	0.1	31.3	76.3	1.1	2.7	0.1	0.2
Nunavut	7.8	26.5	0.4	1.3	—	0.1	8.9	28.0	0.4	1.3	—	—
Canada less Quebec	17,307.2	72.7	940.0	3.9	55.3	0.2	18,259.8	72.2	952.8	3.8	79.9	0.3

Note: 1. The 2006 data were calculated from the Mandatory Long Form Census while the 2011 data were calculated from the National Household Survey and so are not strictly comparable.

Sources: Adapted from Statistics Canada. 2006a. "Population by mother tongue, by province and territory, 2006 Census"; and Statistics Canada. 2011b. "Detailed Mother Tongue (232), Knowledge of Official Languages (5), Age Groups (17A) and Sex (3) for the Population Excluding Institutional Residents of Canada, Provinces, Territories, Census Metropolitan Areas and Census Agglomerations, 2011 Census," 2011 Census of Population. Statistics Canada Catalogue no. 98-314-XCB2011031. http://www12.statcan.ca/census-recensement/2011/dp-pd/tbt-tt/Rp-eng.cfm? Modified November 26, 2013.

Table 3.2: Population by Selected Religions, Canada, Provinces, and Territories, and Canada less Quebec, 2011 (in Percentage)[1]

	Roman Catholic[2]	Other Christian[3]	Buddhist	Hindu	Jewish	Muslim	None[4]	Other	Total
Canada	**38.7**	**28.5**	**1.1**	**1.5**	**1.0**	**3.2**	**23.9**	**2.0**	**99.9**
Newfoundland and Labrador	35.9	57.4	—	—	—	—	6.1	0.2	99.6
Prince Edward Island	43.1	41.6	—	—	—	—	14.6	—	99.3
Nova Scotia	32.9	43.4	0.2	0.2	0.2	1.0	21.9	0.2	100.0
New Brunswick	49.7	34.1	0.1	0.1	0.1	0.4	15.1	0.4	100.0
Quebec	74.6	7.6	0.7	0.4	1.1	3.1	12.1	0.3	99.9
Ontario	31.2	33.3	1.3	2.9	1.5	4.6	23.1	2.0	99.9
Manitoba	25.0	43.4	0.6	0.7	0.9	1.0	26.5	1.9	100.0
Saskatchewan	28.4	43.6	0.4	0.4	0.1	1.0	24.4	1.7	100.0
Alberta	23.8	36.5	1.2	1.0	0.3	3.2	31.6	2.4	100.0
British Columbia	15.0	29.7	2.1	1.1	0.5	1.8	44.1	5.7	100.0
Yukon	18.2	27.3	0.9	0.6	0.1	0.1	51.5	1.5	100.2
Northwest Territories	39.0	26.8	0.5	0.2	—	0.7	29.3	2.4	98.9
Nunavut	25.0	59.4	—	—	—	0.3	12.5	1.6	98.8
Canada less Quebec	28.0	34.7	1.3	1.8	1.0	3.2	27.1	2.5	99.6

Notes: 1. Some percentages may not add up to 100 due to rounding. 2. There are several varieties of Catholic, including Ukrainian Catholic, but those defining themselves as Roman Catholic make up 99.4 percent of this total. 3. Includes all "other" Christians. The other Christian category comprises primarily United Church (21.4 percent), Anglican (17.4 percent), Baptist (6.8 percent), Pentecostal (5.1 percent), Lutheran (5.1 percent), and Presbyterian (5.0 percent) adherents. 4. "None" includes agnostic, atheist, humanist, no religion, and no religious affiliation.

Source: Adapted from Statistics Canada. 2011c. "Religion (108), Immigrant Status and Period of Immigration (11), Age Groups (10) and Sex (3) for the Population in Private Households of Canada, Provinces, Territories, Census Metropolitan Areas and Census Agglomerations." *2011 National Household Survey* (www12.statcan.gc.ca/nhs-enm/2011/dp-pd/dt-td/Rp-eng.cfm?).

Clearly, Quebec is distinct from the rest of Canada in terms of both language and religion. Moreover, this distinctness is historically and constitutionally grounded. (Remember, for example, that the Quebec Act of 1774 granted Quebec control over language and religion, and a distinct legal system.) Most English-speaking Canadians, inside and outside of Quebec, acknowledge that the province of Quebec is distinct. Some even embrace Quebec's difference as a corner of their identity. So why did the notion of a "distinct society" lead to the failure of the Meech Lake Accord in 1990 and threaten Canada's survival?

Much of the furor revolved around the vagueness of society as a concept (Cook, 1995), previously discussed in the Introduction. For example, does the term mean that Quebec is distinct? Or does it refer to the francophone community within Quebec?

Opponents, like Pierre Trudeau, and the newly created Reform Party, led by Preston Manning (1942–), successfully argued that the Meech Lake Accord's "distinct society" clause went against the notion of equality of the provinces, granting Quebec powers or claims to a status not held by others (Denis, 1993; Harrison, 1995). They further argued that "distinct society" status implied something greater than mere difference: that it could be used later on by Quebec governments to leverage further demands for nationhood and, perhaps, separate statehood.

Interestingly, hard-line separatist factions in Quebec argued just the opposite. For them, Quebec was not merely a distinct society, but a sociological nation. The vapidity of "distinct society" was underlined by arguments that Canada was made up of "ten distinct societies" (see Bourgault, 1991:35). In this context, Denis (1993) argued that "distinct society" seemed merely a clever way of avoiding the "two nations" concept fundamental to many Quebecers' understanding of Canada.

At the more general level, the passions unleashed in English-speaking Canada by the notion of a "distinct society" can be traced to the fragility of Canadian identity itself. The author Joseph Conrad once wrote that underlying every great emotion is a great fear. What is English-speaking Canada's great fear? Just as Quebec's overarching fear has been assimilation into English Canada, Canada's fear has been a fatal embrace by the United States. For many Canadians, Quebec's assertions of difference and its refusal to unreservedly become Canadian nationalists threaten Canada's integrity. In the spring of 1990, English Canada's demands for uniformity, swelling in the aftermath of the recently signed Free Trade Agreement with the United States, ran up against Quebec's long-standing demands for respect and recognition of its differences.

The Failure of the Meech Lake and Charlottetown Accords

The Meech Lake Accord unravelled under increasing pressure in the spring of 1990. The unravelling occurred simultaneously from both the top and the bottom, attacked at one end by Trudeau, Manning, and the premiers of New Brunswick, Newfoundland, and Manitoba, and at the other end by popular grassroots elements (Conway, 2004:132).

In the end, despite last-minute efforts to save it, the accord died on the order paper, the three-year time frame for its ratification (June 23) having passed. An Aboriginal member of Manitoba's Legislative Assembly, Elijah Harper (1949–2013), delivered the decisive blow when he refused to allow that province's legislature to fast-track debate on the measure before time elapsed (see Chapter 11) (see Cohen, 1990; Conway, 2004).

The short- and long-term consequences of Meech Lake's failure were immense. Support for Quebec separatism increased (see Bourgault, 1991). The Bloc Québécois, formed in the spring of 1990 by a breakaway faction of Mulroney's government when it became apparent the accord would fail, received an immediate boost (Cornellier, 1995). Elsewhere, in the context of fear and anger, the fortunes of the western-based Reform Party also rose (Harrison, 1995). Three years later, the federal Tory party—its political coalition of westerners and Quebecers having evaporated—was dismembered, suffering the greatest electoral defeat by any government in Canadian history. In Quebec, the Tory limbs were torn off by the separatist Bloc, which, in a moment of supreme political irony, rose to the position of loyal Opposition to the victorious Liberals. The Reform Party led the slaughter in the West (see Appendix 1).

In the medium and longer terms, the failure to ratify the Meech Lake Accord left three principal concerns unresolved—(1) Quebec's role in Canada; (2) western Canada's growing sense of alienation; and (3) Aboriginal self-government (Meekison, 1993)—and with no clear means of resolution. Thus Canada entered a time of constitutional fumbling, culminating in an historical footnote known as the Charlottetown Accord.

The Charlottetown Accord arose out of a meeting of English Canada's nine premiers in July 1992. It was meant to appease the various parties who had opposed the Meech Lake Accord. The Charlottetown Accord gave widespread new powers to the provinces, while limiting those of the federal government. It further proposed entrenchment of Aboriginal rights and creation of a Triple-E (equal, elected, and effective) Senate. Finally, the Charlottetown Accord relegated the notion of "distinct society" to a newly proposed Canada clause, whereby its constitutional meaning would be constrained by commitments to "equality of the provinces" and "linguistic duality" (Conway, 2004:140). The new accord did not offer Quebec much. Nonetheless, Quebec Premier Robert Bourassa reluctantly accepted the agreement, with a few minor changes.

Like its predecessor, however, the Charlottetown Accord failed, defeated in a rare Canada-wide referendum, held on October 24, 1992. Why did the Charlottetown Accord fail? In part, after Meech Lake the chalice of constitutional reform was already poisoned. Charlottetown also failed in part because it was too unwieldy. It attempted to do too much, to address all issues, and to be all things to all people at the same time. In the end, the best thing that could be said about the referendum result was that the accord had been rejected throughout Canada, though the reasons for its rejection varied from person to person, and between Quebec and the other provinces.

The Charlottetown Accord's rejection thus ended, for a time, formal constitutional change in Canada. Many Canadians heaved a sigh of relief. Quebec's relationship with Canada, however, remained unresolved.

Conclusion

The history of societies, like that of individuals, is one of roads both taken and not taken. The failure of the Meech Lake Accord and its Charlottetown successor put an end to the era of formal constitutional change in Canada begun with the Quiet Revolution, but it did not end change. Canada was much different at the end of the constitutional years than it had been at the beginning, in part because of the Charter of Rights and Freedoms and promises made to Aboriginal peoples. But Canadians and Quebecers in 1992 also saw themselves differently from how they had in 1970. Meanwhile, new and different pressures for change were coming from forces beyond the political sphere and even beyond Canada's borders. The old issues were dying or being recast. In time, the old warriors themselves disappeared. Before then, however, one more battle was fought, one more reprise of the referendum wars.

Note

1. It is now known that Trudeau, in his youth, admired the corporatist (and fascist) regimes of Francisco Franco in Spain and Benito Mussolini in Italy (Nemni and Nemni, 2006). Trudeau's later conversion to liberalism shows that early socialization is reversible.

Key Terms

constitution
distinct society
institutional bilingualism
laws
social norms
sociological imagination
territorial bilingualism

Critical Thinking Questions

1. Why are constitutions important for understanding societies?
2. How might symbolic interaction theorists and post-structural theorists view the importance of language, particularly its ability to arouse strong emotions?
3. To what extent do individuals effect change? To what extent are they products of their time and place?
4. What did Joseph Conrad mean when he said that underlying every great emotion is a great fear?
5. From the perspective of counterfactual history, what might have happened had the Meech Lake Accord been enacted?

Recommended Readings

Clarkson, Stephen, and Christina McCall. 1990. *Trudeau and Our Times,* vol. 1: *The Magnificent Obsession.* Toronto: McClelland & Stewart.
This book is the definitive work on Pierre Trudeau's "obsession" with constitutional reform.

Cohen, Andrew. 1990. *A Deal Undone: The Making and Breaking of the Meech Lake Accord.* Vancouver: Douglas & McIntyre.
Cohen's book details the making and breaking of the Meech Lake Accord.

Gervais, Stéphan, Christopher Kirkey, and Jarrett Rudy. 2011. *Quebec Questions: Quebec Studies for the Twenty-First Century.* Don Mills, ON: Oxford University Press.
A good companion to Behiels and Hayday (2011), earlier mentioned, with especially useful discussions of memory, identity, citizenship, models of social and economic policy followed in Quebec, and the province's efforts at establishing a presence in the world community.

Harrison, Trevor. 1995. *Of Passionate Intensity: Right-Wing Populism and the Reform Party of Canada.* Toronto: University of Toronto Press.
This book examines the rise of the Reform Party in western Canada in 1987 and its impact in mobilizing opposition to the Meech Lake Accord and Quebec's demands more generally.

Mills, C. Wright. 1961. *The Sociological Imagination.* New York: Grove Press.
This book is essential reading for any beginning sociologist, outlining Mills's idea of the "sociological imagination."

Related Websites

Canadian Constitution Acts, 1867 to 1982
Department of Justice website: www.justice.gc.ca
The Consitution Act of 1982 fundamentally reshaped Canada. In the eyes of some, it also led to Quebec's increased isolation from the rest of Canada.

Official Bilingualism in Canada: History and Debates
www.mapleleafweb.com/features/official-bilingualism-canada
A useful summary of the history of bilingualism in Canada can be found on the Mapleleafweb.

Province of Quebec
www.gouv.qc.ca
The government of Quebec's website.

Canadian Society on Video

The Champions Series, Part Three: The Final Battle. 1986. National Film Board of Canada, 87 minutes, 2 seconds.
Examines the period from 1978 to 1986, including the divisive 1980 referendum on independence and the repatriation of the 1982 Constitution.

CHAPTER 4

THE RETURN
OF THE NATION

Canada suffers in many respects from the same ailments as Québec. In fact, Canadian nationalism is also in the process of congealing under the weight of myths and dogmas that are becoming obstacles to the country's evolution.

—journalist Alain Dubuc, LaFontaine-Baldwin Lecture, 2001

That this House recognize that the Québécois form a nation within a united Canada.

—motion passed by the House of Commons, November 27, 2006

We coexist by recognizing the volatility and not wanting to disturb it.

—John Wright, Ipsos Reid polling, 2008

Introduction

Since 1970, Quebec and Canada had held constitutional negotiations designed to address Quebec's grievances and resolve their different visions of the country. The defeat of the Meech Lake and Charlottetown accords removed constitutional change, at least for a time, as a means of doing so. What options now remained? Effectively, there seemed only two options: Either Quebec could accept the status quo and perhaps sign the current Constitution, or it could reject the status quo and push for independence.

This chapter begins with an examination of the 1995 Quebec referendum, through which the Parti Québécois government sought a mandate to pursue this second option; the House of Commons's recognition of Quebec as a nation in 2006; and events since. The chapter also examines sociological questions regarding individual and collective identity, the power exerted by symbols and metaphors in shaping group solidarity and conflict, and the issue of minority rights within a multicultural society. Finally, in anticipation of the book's next section, the issues of nation and state are reconsidered in the context of globalization and the threat posed by the United States to both the Québécois nation and English Canada.

A Near-Death Experience: The 1995 Quebec Referendum

On October 30, 1995, Quebecers once more voted in a referendum on sovereignty. Canadians watching on their televisions saw their country come within a few thousand votes of being fundamentally changed, perhaps disintegrating altogether.

The referendum was presaged by three major events. First, the separatist Bloc Québécois (BQ) elected 54 members to Parliament in the 1993 federal election, suggesting widespread support for independence within Quebec (Appendix 1). Second, the BQ's provincial counterpart, the Parti Québécois (PQ), led by Jacques Parizeau (1930–), won the Quebec provincial election in September 1994 with a commitment to pursue sovereignty. Third, the PQ tabled a draft bill on sovereignty, followed by public consultations throughout Quebec during the early part of 1995 (Balthazar, 1997; Conway, 2004).

It was clear from the beginning that the vote would be close. Polls conducted since the 1994 Quebec election showed support for sovereignty stable at 45 percent (Conway, 2004:201), a significant base upon which to build. Moreover, the sovereigntist camp believed the referendum question was sufficiently benign as to attract "soft" voters. By contrast, federalists were hamstrung by the fact that they appeared to have nothing concrete to offer Quebecers. The defeat of the Meech Lake Accord (Chapter 3) foreclosed the possibility of constitutional renewal, at least for a time. All that Canada's leaders could offer was the status quo, liberally sprinkled with threats, should the *Yes* side prevail (Conway, 2004:207).

As referendum day approached, many ordinary Canadians outside Quebec felt fearful, angry, bewildered, and powerless. On October 27, a unity rally was held at Canada Place in Montreal. The *No*-sponsored rally attracted between 30,000 and 150,000 people, many of them from outside the province, loudly declaring their love for Quebec. No doubt, these expressions of affection were sincere. But, as Balthazar (1997:58) notes, "Since those Canadians had nothing to offer but their words of love, they gave Quebecers the image of an all-inclusive Canada that did not allow for the recognition of Quebec's uniqueness."

Few televisions in Canada were silent on referendum night in 1995. In the end, nearly all of Quebec's eligible voters—90 percent, or 4.7 million people—cast ballots, the final result being that 50.6 percent voted *No* while 49.4 percent voted *Yes* (Morton, 1997:340). A swing of less than 30,000 votes would have changed the referendum's outcome (Young, 1998).

As in 1980, the 1995 referendum split not only Canada but also Quebec. The *Yes* side won strong support from francophones, about 60 percent of eligible francophone voters (compared with 50 percent in 1980). The *Yes* side also won strong support in Quebec City and rural Quebec, from middle-class and better-educated voters, and from union supporters. In contrast to 1980, the *Yes* side also received some support from business, though business in general remained on the sidelines of the sovereignty debate (Conway, 2004:205). Polls conducted prior to the referendum also suggested that sovereignty appealed especially to those aged 35 to 44, and to men slightly more than to women, though the gap had lessened (Trent, 1995). By contrast, the *No* side fashioned its close victory from about 40 percent of francophones and almost all anglophones and allophones, mostly located in Montreal (Fox, Andersen, and Dubonnet, 1999), not to mention northern Quebec's small but politically powerful Cree and Inuit peoples (Conway, 2004:210), thus opening up new and important ground for discussing the future of Aboriginal peoples within Canadian society (see Part 3).

Multiculturalism, Secularism, and Civic Nationalism

On referendum night in 1995, an obviously distraught Quebec Premier Parizeau remarked that the pro-sovereignty side had been defeated by "money and the ethnic vote" (quoted in Conway, 2004:208; see also Balthazar, 1997; Morton, 1997).

Reproached by colleagues and opponents alike for his divisive remarks, a remorseful Parizeau resigned the next day and was succeeded shortly thereafter as Quebec premier by Lucien Bouchard.

In broad statistical terms, Parizeau's observations leading to his resignation were correct. Francophones in Quebec *do* disproportionately favour sovereignty; non-francophones *do not* support it. His remarks, however, were divisive in singling out all members of Quebec's allophone community as being opposed to Quebec nationalism—indeed, being unpatriotic (Balthazar, 1997:59). As such, Parizeau's comments unearthed debates within Quebec and the Parti Québécois itself about who is a true Québécois, and the nature of Quebec nationalism.

As noted in Chapter 2, traditional Quebec nationalism was cultural and inward looking. It traced its ancestry through bloodlines to the original 10,000 *Canadiens* of the St. Lawrence. Old Quebec nationalism was anti-modern, tribal, and *Catholic*. Vestiges of it still exist today, expressed linguistically through descriptions of people as either *Québécois pur laine* (literally, "pure wool") or *Québécois de souche* ("later arrivals") (Ignatieff, 1993:172). This traditional form of nationalism dominated until after the Second World War.

But Quebec, like the rest of Canada, has changed a great deal since that time. The new nationalism that arose in the 1950s was modern, democratic, territorial, pluralistic, and secular, even if (as previously noted) most Quebecers still nominally declare themselves members of the Catholic faith. In theory, the new nationalism welcomes anyone living within Quebec's borders who is willing to accept the values of Quebec society. This is also the case in practice; most Quebecers today view their nationalism as civic, not ethnic (Ignatieff, 1993:169; also Smith, 1998). Nonetheless, the debate continues over who is a true Québécois.

An important element of this debate is the role of secularism. As already noted, the transformation from old to new nationalism in Quebec was tied to the decline of the Catholic Church's authority. Shortly after this transformation occurred, however, Quebec also began dealing—as did the rest of Canada—with the arrival of new immigrants, many from neither francophone nor anglophone countries, who still hold strong religious beliefs.

The concern expressed by many Quebec francophones is not simply whether new immigrants will support sovereignty (a specifically nationalist concern), but how immigrants can be successfully integrated into modern—and *secular*—Quebec society. These concerns always arise around specific incidents that take on larger symbolic meaning, such as a court ruling that a Sikh student could carry a kirpan (religious dagger) to school, and another instance in which a youth belonging to the Islamic faith wanted to wear a hijab (head scarf) while playing soccer, which was against league rules (see Maclure, 2011). Since the terrorist attacks on New York and Washington in 2001, much of the negative response by Quebecers has been directed at people identified as Arab or, more generally, Middle Eastern—a response, it must be noted, also seen in the rest of mainstream Canada and the United States.

In search of an answer to the perceived rise of cultural and religious divisions, in February 2007 the Quebec government established the Consultation Commission on

Accommodation Practices Related to Cultural Differences (Government of Quebec, 2008). The commission's mandate was to examine accommodation practices in Quebec; to examine similar experiences in other societies; to conduct extensive public consultations on the issue; and "to formulate recommendations to the government to ensure that accommodation practices conform to the values of Québec society as a pluralistic, democratic, egalitarian society" (Government of Quebec, 2008:7).

Co-chaired by a sociologist, Gérard Bouchard, and a liberal philosopher, Charles Taylor, the commission travelled throughout Quebec during the fall of 2007, garnering submissions on the question of **reasonable accommodation**—defined as "a form of arrangement or relaxation aimed at ensuring respect for the right of equality … which, following the strict application of an institutional standard, infringes on an individual's right to equality" (Government of Quebec, 2008:7)—of minority cultural and religious rights. In the end, the commission made 37 recommendations based on the notion not of multiculturalism but of "*interculturalisme*," what Saul (2008:147) describes as "the intercultural dovetailing relationship among four groups: the francophone majority, the anglophone minority, the Aboriginal minority, and *the cultural communities*, that is, the newcomers, with French as the central convening language of all four."

Among the commission's specific recommendations were greater cultural awareness, improved intercultural relations, better integration of migrants, and greater effort on the part of government and its institutions to deal with racism and inequality. Its broadest thrust, however, was to recommend Quebec's adoption of "open secularism" based on four principles: (1) the moral equality of persons; (2) freedom of conscience and religion; (3) separation of church and state; and (4) the state's neutrality with respect to religions and deep-seated secular convictions (Government of Quebec, 2008:45). The concept of open secularism was immediately contentious, however, seen by many Quebecers as being at odds with Quebec society as it had developed since the Quiet Revolution (Dickinson and Young, 2008:377). Not only had the province become more secular—**secularization** being a process that occurs when religion "progressively loses its relevance as a social and cultural framework for defining moral values and social conduct"—more fundamentally, Quebec's government since the 1960s had embraced a process of **laicization**, "by which the state deliberately distances itself from religion on an institutional level" (both quotes from Milot, 2011:125).

On November 7, 2013, the Parti Québécois government introduced a bill amending the Quebec Charter of Human Rights and Freedoms. The proposed Quebec Charter of Values, it was argued, would clarify the notion of reasonable accommodation. The bill, which (among other things) would have limited the use of conspicuous religious symbols by public employees and prevented the wearing of face coverings (e.g., hijabs) by anyone providing or receiving a state service, had wide support in Quebec among those who viewed the bill as a necessary defence of secular society. However, many others—including former premiers Jacques Parizeau and Lucien Bouchard—opposed the charter as xenophobic and racist. The bill died in the spring of 2014 with the PQ's electoral defeat at the hands of the provincial Liberals, led by Philippe Couillard (see *The Canadian Encyclopedia*, 2014).

Quebec's particular concern about the political power of religious institutions obviously has historical roots in the past role of the Roman Catholic Church in that province. Nonetheless, it is important to acknowledge that Quebec's anxieties, fears, and successes in accommodating cultural difference have their mirror in the rest of Canada. This is paradoxical, for Canada's mirror is in fact larger, embracing Quebec itself. Quebec's struggles to incorporate minority cultural differences within a framework of civic nationalism are a subset of Canada's struggle to fashion a coherent and cohesive national community that embraces three nations—the English, the French, and the Aboriginal—and an assortment of other ethnic groups (Saul, 1997, 2008).

The Sovereignty Question Today

How strong is the appeal of Quebec sovereignty today? Data gathered since 1995 are consistent on four points (Trent, 1995; Dubuc, 2001). First, the vast majority of Quebecers oppose holding another referendum. Second, few Quebecers believe a referendum on sovereignty would pass if held today. Third, support for sovereignty during "normal" periods averages about 42 percent (Leger Marketing, 2008). Support for sovereignty rises above this only when Quebecers feel attacked or rejected by English Canada, as during the Meech Lake crisis (earlier mentioned), or when the idea of sovereignty is presented in the abstract or its definition is unclear. And fourth, a large number of Quebecers hold the apparently contradictory belief that Quebec and Canada have reached an impasse *and* that federalism can be renewed.

Looked at another way, about a third of Quebecers are consistent federalists. Another third are hard-core *indépendantistes* who identify with the Quebec state. The remaining third of Quebecers are torn between choosing the Quebec nation or the country of Canada, a predicament captured in the oft-quoted joke of Quebec comedian Yvon Deschamps that "All we want is an independent Quebec within a strong and united Canada" (Colombo, 1994:224). It is on this third of Quebecers that the outcome of any future sovereignty referendum would hinge, should such a vote be held.

At the same time, most analysts agree that compared with the opinion in the 1960s and 1970s, sovereignty today invokes little passion in Quebec. Many observers view the 2014 Quebec provincial election, which saw the Liberal party elected, as a watershed. The party's leader, Phillipe Couillard, is considered the most unabashedly federalist premier in years. The Parti Québécois's defeat—coming on the heels of the 2011 federal election, which saw the Bloc Québécois's power reduced to less than a handful of seats (their losses attributed mainly to the gains of the New Democratic Party)—suggests that the political appeal of sovereignty is in decline. Why might this be the case? In part, the reason seems to be that many of the political, economic, and cultural grievances expressed during the Quiet Revolution have been addressed (Ignatieff, 1993).

Since the 1960s, francophones have used their political strength in Quebec, particularly, to make gains within Canada's political and labour sectors (Nakhaie, 1997). By contrast, while those of British background continue disproportionately to dominate elite positions within Canada, they do not do so unopposed; indeed, it can be argued that British Canada as a sociological construct no longer exists (Gwyn, 1996; Igartua, 2006). The object of francophone Canada's wrath—white Anglo-Saxon Protestant (WASP) Canada—is today largely an historical artifact, indeed, a myth.

Economically, French-Canadians in general, and francophone Quebecers in particular, no longer experience the second-place status relative to English-Canadians once identified by Porter (1965) and the Royal Commission on Bilingualism and Biculturalism (Government of Canada, 1963). Today, much of Quebec's bourgeoisie is francophone and, like the Canadian bourgeoisie at large, wedded to breaking down, rather than defending, national borders. By 1991, in Canada as a whole, workers of French ethnicity were actually earning significantly more than workers of British ethnicity (Lian and Matthews, 1998). And, while Quebec is not a "have" province economically, the circumstances of Quebecers as a whole have gradually improved since the 1960s. In November 2013, for example, the average before tax (gross) income of people in Quebec was $43,230 (calculated from Statistics Canada, 2014a). As shown in Table 4.1, the median income for all census families in Quebec in 2012 was $70,480, or about 94.6 percent of the Canadian median, ahead of the Atlantic provinces, though behind (sometimes significantly) many of the western and northern provinces and territories. (We will return to an interrogation of median and average incomes in Chapter 8.)

Quebec's success in stemming the cultural threat is harder to measure. Though the percentage of French-speaking people in Quebec has stabilized at roughly 80 percent (see Chapter 3), many francophone Quebecers remain "linguistically insecure" (Thompson, 1995:78; also Dickinson and Young, 2011). They particularly fear the impact of allophone immigrants to Quebec who might choose English rather than French as their adopted language, a fear that ties into concerns about cultural differences generally, as earlier discussed. Still, the level of insecurity concerning language is lower among younger Quebecers, who are used to the protections provided by Quebec's language laws. Moreover, recent census figures suggest that allophone immigrants today are actually strengthening the French language in Quebec by opting to adopt that language (Friesen and Peritz, 2012), an outcome strengthened by the provincial governments gaining greater control over immigration, allowing for the recruitment of immigrants from francophone countries.

Beyond Quebec, the world has also changed dramatically since the time of the Quiet Revolution. Liberation politics, drawn from Third World experiences and the writings of Frantz Fanon (1968) and Che Guevara (2003), have little appeal today. Few Quebecers, especially young people, see their province as colonized. In this time of increased global connectedness, as the world seems drawn closer and closer together by economics, technology, cultural exchanges, and trade deals, the very meaning of sovereignty seems unclear. (What would Quebec gain through sovereignty that it does not already possess?) Meanwhile, recent examples of ethnic nationalism gone wrong (e.g., in Yugoslavia and the Middle East) provide stinging counterpoints to the ideal of independence. (What would an independent Quebec lose?) Finally, many young Quebecers—not unlike young people elsewhere—increasingly see themselves as individual consumers

Table 4.1: Median Total Income, by Province and Territory (all census families),[1] 2008–2012; and Percentage of Canadian Median Total Income by Province and Territory, 2012[2]

	2008	2009	2010	2011	2012	Percentage of 2012 Canadian Median
Canada	**68,860**	**68,410**	**69,860**	**72,240**	**74,540**	**100.0**
Newfoundland and Labrador	59,320	60,290	62,580	67,200	70,900	95.1
Prince Edward Island	61,010	62,110	63,610	66,500	69,010	92.6
Nova Scotia	61,980	62,550	64,100	66,030	67,910	91.1
New Brunswick	59,790	60,670	62,150	63,930	65,910	88.4
Quebec	63,830	64,420	65,900	68,170	70,480	94.6
Ontario	70,910	69,790	71,540	73,290	74,890	100.5
Manitoba	64,530	65,550	66,530	68,710	70,750	94.9
Saskatchewan	69,800	70,790	72,650	77,300	80,010	107.3
Alberta	86,080	83,560	85,380	89,830	94,460	126.7
British Columbia	67,890	66,700	66,970	69,150	71,660	96.1
Yukon	85,070	84,640	86,930	91,090	94,460	126.7
Northwest Territories	98,530	98,300	101,010	105,560	106,710	143.2
Nunavut	58,590	60,160	62,680	65,280	65,530	87.9

Notes: 1. Census families include couple families, with or without children, and lone-parent families. 2. Percentages for 2012 calculated by authors.

Source: Statistics Canada (2014b). "Median Total Income, by Family Type, by Province and Territory (All Census Families)." *CANSIM*, Table 111-0009 (www.statcan.gc.ca/tables-tableaux/sum-som/l01/cst01/famil108a-eng.htm). Last modified July 23, 2014.

and mobile workers. Increasingly, sovereignty is a dream held mainly by the university educated 55 years and older (Hamilton, 2014).

At the same time, it would be a mistake to suggest that Quebec nationalism and the attendant possibility of separation have disappeared. For two centuries, English-speaking Canada has believed that this would be the case. Yet Quebec nationalism and the idea of an independent homeland have continued to stir within Quebec. Why is this the case? The answer lies in the fact that the issue of French-English, Quebec-Canada relations within the country cannot be addressed by material or even constitutional changes alone. The basis of the issue lies in such intangible, but immanently sociological, issues as self-identity, mutual respect, and the need for recognition.

Society, Nation, Modernity, and "Self"

Who are you? That is, what are the elements that shape who you are and speak to you and others of your "self"? This is a distinctly sociological question, one that emerged in the 19th century with modernity. Riesman and colleagues (1950), for example, observe that notions of individual identity make little sense in pre-modern, feudal societies, where ideas, norms, behaviours, expectations, and outcomes are fairly rigidly controlled by tradition. In the Middle Ages, no one would have sought to "find himself or herself," to use a popular phrase of the 1960s. People of that era were told directly and indirectly who they were from the time they were born. By contrast, in modern societies, individuals not only *seem* to be freer of social restraints, they are also expected to find and express their particular uniqueness.

What are the building blocks used in this construction? For Marx, writing in the mid-19th century, class was the primary factor in a person's identity kit; for Durkheim, occupation was central. For feminist scholars today, gender is a chief source of one's identity as well as one's world view, but other factors, such as religion, ethnicity, or education, may also provide salient materials informing an individual's self-identity. For people growing up in modern societies, the cache of materials from which to make a "self" is seemingly endless, drawn from television, the Internet, magazines, and so on.

Sociologists view this construction critically, however. First, individual and collective identities are mutually constructed. In a real sense, no one simply chooses an individual identity. Rather, an identity arises out of membership in a group (Tajfel and Turner, 1986). Second, both individual and collective identities are highly malleable (Cook, 1995:235). The importance of an identity may lessen over time for a person or group, or events may lead an individual or group to rediscover and reassert their roots. Third, individual identities are neither singular nor exclusive. A person may simultaneously see himself or herself as Italian, a doctor, a soccer player, a conservative, and gay or lesbian.

What does the issue of individual and collective identity have to do with Quebec and Canada? Simply this: Quebec's national culture, broadly conceived, provides many Quebecers with essential materials for their personal identities. Writing in 1951, André Laurendeau (1985) noted that "Except for the stateless (and even then!) every being carries the mark of a particular culture. The richer it is, the more it nourishes him [*sic*]."

This notion is at odds (at least on the surface) with dominant Western culture, where private and public spheres are viewed as separate, the individual is sacrosanct, and "the state and civil society are typically understood as facing off against each other" (White, 1997:22). Pierre Trudeau's denunciations of Quebec nationalism as tribal (Chapter 3) were rooted in a supposed separation of individual self and society (Couture, 1998), hence his desire to entrench the Charter of Rights and Freedoms in the 1982 Constitution as a means of protecting individuals from collective oppression.

Separating the spheres, however, is difficult, if not impossible. Note, for example, that Canada's Charter of Rights and Freedoms deals with both individual and collective rights (Cook, 1995:234). Likewise, the policies of official bilingualism and multiculturalism enacted by Trudeau similarly protect collective rights over language and culture (Webber, 1994; Couture, 1998).

It is therefore inaccurate to argue that a necessary opposition exists between the rights of the collective and those of individuals, represented by Quebec and English-speaking Canada, respectively. Repeated surveys show Quebecers have at least as much deep regard for individual rights as other Canadians. Indeed, Quebecers are generally quite liberal in their acceptance of individual differences regarding sexual orientation or marital status (Denis, 1993; also Dickinson and Young, 2008:348). At the same time, English-speaking Canadians also possess a sense of collective identity, albeit understated, as evidenced quickly if someone tells them they are "just like" Americans.

If the sociological (and political) problem between Quebec and Canada does not lie in an opposition between individual and collective rights, it is even less in an absolute separation of the French and English cultures. French and English identities (and others) in Canada include elements of each other (Dufour, 1990; Webber, 1994; Saul, 1997). Notes Dufour (1990:81), "Almost by definition, the Quebec identity comprises a more or less significant, more or less conscious, Canadian component." And again, "English is a deeply ambivalent and perturbing element of the Quebec identity" (1990:97). A majority of Quebecers (though less so among francophones) still see themselves simultaneously as Quebecers *and* as Canadians (see Smith, 1998), though the former generally takes precedence in their identity structures.

What, then, underlies the conflict? Simply that *the right of Quebecers to possess a distinct identity be recognized and respected by the rest of Canada* (Taylor, 1993; Coulombe, 1998).

There is an apparent paradox in this demand, for, as Taylor (1993) and Ignatieff (1993) note, Canada and Quebec have never been closer. Quebec was "more distinct" before the Quiet Revolution than it is today. Throughout Canada, regional differences in social factors and values have been lessening for decades (see Goyder, 1993; Baer, Grabb, and Johnston, 1993), a product of modernization. The paradox of diminishing differences and escalating demands for recognition is partly explained, however, if we consider globalization's impact upon states and nations (see the Introduction).

On the one hand, globalization has accelerated the process of homogenizing cultures. On the other hand, it has left many national groups feeling uneasy and compelled to overemphasize and protect remaining distinctions. The weakened capacity of states, especially multinational states such as Canada, to protect them, has further pressed national cultures to seek shelter in smaller units. In line with Daniel Bell's (1993:362) contention that national states today are both too big and too small to deal with important issues, supporters of sovereignty argue that an independent Quebec would be better able to adapt to the demands of the global marketplace (see Bourgault, 1991; Parti Québécois, 1994).

Such claims are debatable but ultimately beside the point. The question is this: Is it possible for English-speaking Canada to acknowledge Quebec's distinctness in a meaningful way; to grant recognition and respect for Québécois identity; and to give Quebec sufficient powers for its survival within Canada's existing state structures (see Taylor 1993; Denis, 1993; Coulombe, 1998)? Or—despite the recent lull in the conflict between the two nations—does the flow of history lead inexorably to Quebec sovereignty?

The Return of the National Question

Suddenly, in the fall of 2006, Canada caught up with its history and, one might argue, with sociology. In an act unimaginable only a few years before, on November 27, 2006, the Canadian House of Commons passed the following motion (by a vote of 266 to 16, the rest abstaining or absent): "That this House recognize that the Québécois form a nation within a united Canada."

How did this turn come about? And, to what extent, does it represent a "turn" in French-English relations? To unpack the meaning of the Commons' resolution, we need to briefly return to previous discussions.

We have seen that, depending on the time and place, since 1763 Canada's dominant anglophone elite have employed various policies (from coercion and subjugation, to isolation and subtle assimilation, to tentative efforts, beginning in the 1960s, at accommodation and recognition) of dealing with the smaller, but nonetheless significant and distinct francophone minority. The prevailing issue underlying these policies is that of the nation.

The Introduction noted the conflation of nation, state, country, and society. Canada is a textbook case of this conflation in practice. The "problem" with which Canada has struggled since its founding is in every sense a modern one: Can it survive as a country administered by a state that accommodates several nations within its territory? As noted in Chapter 1, Lord Durham's Eurocentric background led him to conclude that every nation must have a state, and that no state must have more than one nation, a situation that led to the failed Act of Union of 1841 and then to Confederation in 1867.

The years after 1867 saw the French "fact" in Canada largely isolated (but, thus, also strengthened) within Quebec, while the rest of Canada took on a decidedly English stamp. By the 1960s, arguments about the nature of Canada focused on whether it was a confederation of 10 provinces (of which Quebec was merely one) or a marriage of "two nations," with separatists in Quebec arguing for a third option: that the marriage be dissolved (Chapter 2).

The constitutional discussions of the 1970s and 1980s failed to resolve Quebec's place within Canada. Subsequent efforts to revise the Constitution also failed and even heightened the crisis. English-speaking Canada's rejection in 1990 of the Meech Lake

Accord, based primarily on the accord's recognition of Quebec as a "distinct society," increased many Quebecers' sense that they were not accepted by the rest of Canada; the result was a rise in support for sovereignty and the nearly successful vote for separation in 1995 (Chapter 3).

Fast-forward to the fall of 2006. Earlier that same year, the governing Liberal Party was defeated in a federal election by the Stephen Harper–led Conservative Party, a party rebuilt from the ruins of the former Progressive Conservative Party and Canadian Reform Conservative Alliance parties. In the course of the subsequent race to replace Paul Martin (1938–) as Liberal leader, one of the contenders, Michael Ignatieff (1947–) (see Chapter 8), suggested that Quebec be recognized as a "nation" in the Constitution. Though endorsed by the federal party's Quebec wing, the other Liberal candidates and much of English-Canada's media quickly denounced Ignatieff's proposal, which went against not only the Trudeau legacy of opposing Quebec nationalism in favour of a dual, pan-Canadian ideal, but went further than any previous constitutional effort, including the failed Meech Lake Accord, in recognizing Quebec's distinctiveness (Fidler, 2006).

Sensing an opportunity to divide the Liberal Party, however, the Bloc Québécois, which had elected 51 members in the 2006 election, proposed a parliamentary motion along the lines of Ignatieff's position that Quebec constituted a nation within Canada. Likewise, sensing the chance to build support in Quebec while blunting the Bloc Québécois motion, Prime Minister Stephen Harper (1959–) proposed the motion above, which the House of Commons subsequently adopted.

At first glance, the proposal appears to be a major step in recognizing Quebec's distinct identity, something that the Reform Party, of which Harper was a prominent member, had vehemently opposed two decades earlier.

Fidler (2006), however, argues that

> [T]he original Bloc motion, which had identified the "Québécois" as a nation, referred to them in English as "Quebeckers." That is, a territorial concept, encompassing everyone who inhabits Quebec irrespective of first language or ethnic origin. This is now the common definition of "Québécois" in Quebec. [Prime Minister] Harper's motion, in contrast, used the term "Québécois" in both French and English versions, an ethnic connotation implying that only those whose first language is French qualified as a "nation."

In short, the House of Commons motion recognized an ethnic definition of the nation, while the Bloc version recognized a civic definition of the nation tied to territory (see the Introduction).

Mere semantics? Perhaps. Linguistic meanings are slippery at the best of times, especially when moving between two languages. Nonetheless, Fidler raises important questions about the exact meaning of the House of Commons resolution. Quoting journalist Pierre Dubuc, Fidler argues that recognition of the Québécois nation is designed to prepare for the partition of Quebec should that province ever vote *Yes* to a referendum on sovereignty. That is, while the Québécois (francophone) nation might vote to separate, likewise the English-speaking areas could also vote to remain in Canada. Such a stance would be commensurate with that of previous Canadian governments, both Liberal and Conservative.

In short, the resolution passed by the House of Commons appears to thwart the Bloc Quebecois's motion by giving symbolic (but not constitutional) recognition to the Québécois nation, while simultaneously denying the territorial nationhood of Quebec with all its political implications. Likewise, while the Bloc version would have given particular power to the provincial state as representing and perhaps even constituting the Quebec nation and society, the House of Commons version reserved considerable political power for the Canadian state in this regard. Ultimately, was the House of Commons motion of 2006 too clever by half? Does it offer Quebecers the appearance of recognition, but provide something much less? Does it in consequence represent another failed opportunity to recognize Quebec's specific identity and needs?

How do Canadian people view Canada's "nations," not merely that of Quebec, but otherwise? A poll of 1,500 Canadians, conducted by Leger Marketing for the Association of Canadian Studies shortly before the vote on the House of Commons motion, found that 93 percent of those polled, both anglophone and francophone, agreed that Canada is a nation. When asked, however, if Quebecers are also a nation, only 38 percent of anglophone Canadians agreed, compared with 78 percent of francophone Canadians. The results suggest that anglophones are more likely to recognize ethnic definitions of nationhood, while francophones hold a more territorial or civic definition of nationhood. Moreover, while francophone Quebecers overwhelmingly believed that they constitute a nation, they also supported recognition of Aboriginal peoples and Acadians as nations (see Table 4.2).

Table 4.2: Percentage of Anglophone and Francophone Respondents Viewing Various Groups as Nations within Canada, 2006

Group	Anglophones	Francophones
Aboriginal peoples	65	79
Métis	45	59
Acadians	65	74
Quebecers	38	78

Source: Hubert Bauch. 2006. "Quebec 'Nation' Debate Divides French, English: Poll." *Montreal Gazette*, November 11 (www.canada.com/topics/news/national/story.html?id=23ba4837-5854-458d-b513-0c2d2d0b5ea3&k=50919).

Surveys conducted in the recent past suggest these different views have not changed. An online survey of 2,505 adults (including 932 Quebecers) conducted by Ipsos Reid in the summer of 2008, amid the celebrations of the 400th anniversary of the founding of Quebec City in 1608, found that 70 percent of Quebecers view themselves as "a nation within a united Canada," while only 36 percent of adults in the rest of Canada agree. Likewise, half of Quebecers subscribe to the "two nations" concept of Canada, compared with only one-third in the rest of Canada. Instead, more than 40 percent of those outside of Quebec see Canada as "a nation with one dominant culture and several equal minorities," a view held by only 20 percent of Quebecers (figures from the *Edmonton Journal*, 2008).

In short, Canada's French and English communities continue to view each other from quite different promontories.

Quebec "Solutions"—and Canada's Problem

In the aftermath of the events of 1995, successive federalist forces have adopted two strategies to counter the appeal of Quebec sovereignty. These strategies were referred to as "Plan A" and "Plan B" or, as Conway (2004:214–215) describes them, the carrot and the stick.

Plan A involved attempts to show Quebecers that Confederation works and perhaps, in time, to win Quebecers' hearts and minds. At the symbolic level, the House of Commons passed a motion one month after the referendum that recognized Quebec as a distinct society (Balthazar, 1997:59). Two years later, the premiers' Calgary Unity Declaration acknowledged the "unique character of Quebec society." At the more practical level, the federal government transferred administrative powers over immigration to Quebec; launched a series of programs, especially in higher education; promoted a national private French television network; and expanded French usage online. Finally, as in the past, the federal Liberal government of the day enticed federalist Quebecers such as Stéphane Dion and Pierre Pettigrew to Ottawa.

By contrast, Plan B involved a "tough love" approach to Quebec (Conway, 2004; Balthazar, 1997). Politically, the centrepiece of Plan B is Bill C-20 (the Clarity Act). Passed by the House of Commons in March 2000, the Clarity Act allows federal MPs to vote on both the clarity of the wording of any referendum question on sovereignty introduced by the Quebec National Assembly and the clarity of any victory in a referendum before beginning negotiations on Quebec sovereignty. In short, the Clarity Act renders a vote in favour of sovereignty in any future referendum null until debated and passed by the House of Commons. Quebec nationalists, and sovereigntists in particular, view the Clarity Act as an infringement on Quebecers' rights to self-determination and the jurisdiction of Quebec's National Assembly. The Clarity Act further suggests that Quebec's boundaries would be up for negotiation if Quebecers ever vote *Yes* to sovereignty, something that Fidler (2006) argues is repeated in the House of Commons' "nation" motion of 2006. For many Quebecers, Plan B repeats an all-too-familiar pattern of trying to coerce French Canada into accepting English Canada's rules for Confederation.

Even before the sovereignty vote, however, a third strategy, "Plan C," was being proposed in several quarters. Less discussed than either Plan A or Plan B, this strategy had as its aim a radical **decentralization** of Canada whereby Quebec's demands would be applied throughout the federation; that is, whatever powers Quebec obtained would be automatically given to every other province. In the words of Gordon Gibson (1994), a former Liberal and Social Credit politician and conservative policy adviser, Plan C would see Ottawa reduced to a "service centre," a relatively powerless clearing-house for functions residual to those of the provinces.

The idea of decentralization (or devolution) has been around for a long time and appeals to several distinct constituencies, albeit for different reasons. To rigid formalists, decentralization meets Quebec's demands while also maintaining a strict equality of the provinces. To provincial rights advocates, especially in western Canada, decentralization means a return to the division of powers written into the 1867 constitution, before the Great Depression and two world wars meant the growth of federal powers. To political leaderships in the "have" provinces, it means more money and power that need not be shared with other jurisdictions. To pro-business think tanks (such as the Fraser Institute) and corporations, decentralization means dealing with only one level of government— smaller and often more compliant—regarding, for example, environmental and labour regulations. To some mainstream economists, decentralization embraces the principle of **subsidiarity** that unless there is a valid reason to the contrary, state functions should be exercised by the lowest level of government (Courchene, 1997). Finally, in the years leading up to the financial crisis of 2007 and 2008, some viewed decentralization as an inevitable and perhaps even positive adaptation to globalization (Courchene, 1998; Resnick, 2000; Ibbitson, 2001) that might ultimately strengthen Canadian federalism through greater co-operation.

Decentralization also has critics, however. First, it is argued, Canada is already the world's most decentralized federation (Valaskakis and Fournier, 1995), a situation that slows responses to crises. Second, most Canadians still believe in a strong role for the federal government, particularly in areas of health and social policy. Further decentraliza-tion would result in large corporate interests playing regions and provinces against each other, endangering national standards and programs, such as medicare (Laxer and Har-rison, 1995). Third, the federal government provides one of the few "checks and balances" to provincial power, and vice versa (see Taylor, 1993), an equilibrium that decentralization would alter (Romanow, 2006). Fourth, as more power flows to the provinces, people's identification with Canada as a whole will lessen, threatening national unity.

Many of these same critics offer a different solution: **asymmetrical federalism** (Laxer, 1992; Taylor, 1993), or what could be termed "Plan D." Asymmetrical federalism begins from the premise that Quebec is not like the other provinces, that the needs of both Quebec and the other provinces are different, and that federalism cannot be practised in the manner of treating all provinces the same.

How would asymmetrical federalism work? Laxer (1992, 2002) and Webber (1994:230) suggest that Quebec be given constitutional powers over areas it views as necessary for preserving its national identity, while these same powers for Canadians elsewhere remain "housed" in Ottawa. In effect, Quebec would have more powers than the other provinces, but it would not have powers over the citizens of other provinces, nor would Quebecers have more powers than other Canadians. The change would require two sittings of the House of Commons: an all-Canada sitting, in which Quebec MPs would participate, and a separate sitting in which Quebec MPs would not participate, dealing with those areas delegated to the Quebec provincial government (see also Resnick, 1991).

In a more complex development of this argument, Resnick (2000) suggests Canada be reconfigured as a country with three tiers that include six provinces (the four Atlantic provinces, Manitoba, and Saskatchewan); three region-provinces with large populations and significant resources (Ontario, Alberta, and British Columbia); and one nation-province (Quebec). These changes could be combined with other political reforms, such as reform or abolition of the Senate, fixed electoral dates, and the replacement of Canada's first-past-the-post electoral system with proportional representation (Resnick, 2000; Conway, 2004:282).

Asymmetrical federalism also has its critics, however (see Cook, 1995:242–245; also Valaskakis and Fournier, 1995). First, such a change is politically unacceptable to the other provinces and most Canadians who subscribe to the formal equality of all provinces. Second, Canadian federalism is already asymmetrical in certain respects. Like decentralization, further asymmetry would weaken Canada's federal principle as other provinces quickly seek the same powers as Quebec. Third, by making the government in Quebec City more important to Quebecers, an action not wholly endorsed by many (especially anglophone) Quebecers themselves, the path could be set for further separatist agitation in that province.

Whether asymmetrical federalism could work is debatable. In any case, its program has little support outside of the academic community. By contrast, Plan C—decentralization—is supported by a number of powerful constituencies. In consequence, some observers suggest that after 1995, Canada embarked on a steady, slow, and largely invisible course of decentralization (see Gregg, 2005; Griffiths, 2008). Plans A and B got all the press, but Plan C had the greatest impact.

Gregg (2005) identifies decentralization's start with the 1995 federal budget. Canada was then dealing with a growing national debt. Canada's then–Liberal finance minister, Paul Martin, made deep cuts to the federal budget to deal with the problem. The cuts were particularly deep to shared-cost welfare-state programs (see chapters 7 and 8). In effect, the federal government opted out of paying its share for national programs that it had been instrumental in founding. But those who pay the piper get to call the tune; the provinces demanded more control over these programs. The province of Quebec saw the opportunity, suggests Gregg, to enlist the other provinces to join in calls for greater autonomy. The provincial premiers' demands also coincided with the impact of the free trade agreement (implemented in 1989) upon economic relations, which shifted traditional east-west exchanges to north-south exchanges, thus making the provinces less interdependent (see Courchene, 1998; see also Chapter 8). The effect of these changes was that, while the federal government over the next decade succeeded in eliminating its fiscal deficits and paying off much of the national debt, control over programs was increasingly delegated to the provinces. Decentralization, whether planned or not, became a *fait accompli*.

For critics of decentralization, the insistence of dealing with the "Quebec problem" through a rigid adherence to symmetrical powers poses the risk that Canada will not end with a bang—the cataclysmic result of Quebec's separation—but with a whimper: with the slow dismantling of Canada into a number of incoherent fiefdoms. In the words of former Saskatchewan premier Roy Romanow, "the soil has been tilled for the sprouting of views at odds with shared destiny, and today there is a palpable momentum toward decentralization, individualism, and privatization, all peddled as a means to forge a stronger nation" (Romanow, 2006:50).

Yet one does not exclude the other. The dissolution of all does not render impossible the separation of one. What if Quebec were to separate? What would it mean for Quebec and for the rest of Canada?

Thinking the Unthinkable: Separation

Countries, states, nations, and societies change. Though Canada's dissolution would astound and dismay much of the world—as Ignatieff (1993:147) remarks, "If federalism can't work in my Canada, it probably can't work anywhere"—no country is ordained to last forever.

What would Canada and Quebec look like if they separated? In descriptive terms, Canada would cover 8.4 million square kilometres, nearly 85 percent of its previous area, though the Atlantic provinces would be separated from Ontario (Young, 1995:9; Scowen, 1999), and the country would have a population of more than 27 million, roughly 50 percent of which would be located in Ontario. Quebec would cover 1.5 million square kilometres and have a population of about 8.2 million people (see Table 0.1 for these figures). The economies of both Canada and Quebec would still be large. For Canada, *sans* Quebec, the **gross domestic product** (GDP)—the total value of all goods and services produced by a country in a year—in 2012 was $1.462 trillion, while that of Quebec was nearly $358 billion (Statistics Canada, 2013c). Though Canada would fall from being the seventh-largest economy in the world, Quebec would still place 18th after separation (di Matteo, 2014). These figures, however, assume no massive transfers of land either way, no large movements of population, and no disruptions to either economy resulting from political unrest. These are big assumptions.

Setting aside the real possibility of violence (see Gibson, 1994; Monahan, 1995; Martin, 1999), with which authorities would have to deal, several key issues would need to be addressed immediately and would likely involve bitter negotiations. These issues would include territorial boundaries (Reid, 1992:37–66); the division of public assets and the national debt, a total of US$1.827 trillion in 2013 (World Bank, 2014a); and determination of citizenship (Bourgault, 1991; Scowen, 1999). A further key issue would be jurisdiction over and responsibility for Aboriginal peoples (Bourgault, 1991; Parti Québécois, 1994; Gibson, 1994; Conway, 2004; Scowen, 1999). These issues would only scratch the surface, however. Deeper questions would remain for the citizens of both new countries.

Canada and Quebec would both require new constitutions. Quebec could achieve this task more easily than Canada (Parti Québécois, 1994). By contrast, constitutional renewal in Canada would require far more actors and a fundamental rethinking of the country's purpose and structure. Despite arguments sometimes made by sovereigntists that Quebec could retain use of the Canadian dollar, it would in fact need to create its own currency, without which economic independence would be called into question.

Both countries would also have to refashion their international relations. Quebec's task in this case would likely be more difficult than Canada's, though successive Quebec governments have opened international offices and made important contacts. Quebec would seek a seat at the United Nations, and partnership in all agreements previously signed by Canada (Bourgault, 1991; Turp, 1993; Parti Québécois, 1994). Finally, both Canada and Quebec would need to consider their changed relationship with the United States.

By far, however, the most wrenching adjustment for people in both countries would be psychological. Only a minority of people within Quebec desire outright independence; most hold strong feelings of attachment for Canada. Outside of Quebec, while there is some anti-French, anti-Quebec sentiment, and in recent years a hefty dose of referendum fatigue (Scowen, 1999; see also Brimelow, 1986; Bercuson and Cooper, 1991), most Canadians want Quebec to remain within Canada—though, it must be noted, the level of irritation with Quebec's perceived "demands" increases as one moves westward, with a sizable minority of people on the prairies telling pollsters they would vote to remove Quebec from Canada if they had the chance (Berdahl and Gibbons, 2014:24).

A breakup would be difficult for both parties, though perhaps more so for English-speaking Canada. While Quebecers have had longer to prepare for the event and to define themselves as Québécois, English-speaking Canadians have not prepared themselves for such an eventuality. Their sense of identity includes Quebec, even if many—including western Canadidans—refuse to acknowledge this. The fact is that Quebec remains at the heart of most Canadians' psychological map of their country (as noted in Chapter 2).

Quebec and the "Other" Anglophone State

Bourgault (1991:24) notes that "In Quebec, pro-American feeling is probably stronger than in the rest of Canada." At first, this may seem curious, given the virulent antipathy between New France and the New England states in the years prior to the American Revolution (Chapter 1). After this time, however, Quebec's contacts with the United States gradually became more positive. The American Revolution's ideals appealed to Quebec's intellectual class and fuelled the rebellions of 1837 and 1838 (Conway, 2004). From Louis-Joseph Papineau to Louis Riel, French-Canadian "rebels" repeatedly sought safe haven across the border. Nor were they alone. Throughout the 19th and 20th centuries, francophone emigrants, too, chose the eastern United States over the Canadian West.

Meanwhile, American capital also streamed into the province, stimulating Quebec's industrialization (Chodos and Hamovitch, 1991). The fact that Prime Minister Brian Mulroney grew up in a Quebec town built by American investment and was president of an American branch plant before entering politics (Sawatsky, 1991) is symbolically significant.

The rise of English nationalism in the 1960s (Chapter 7) in counterpoint to Quebec nationalism further (unwittingly) pushed many Quebecers into the American embrace. Anglo-Canadian desires for a strong central government found little support among Quebecers, who viewed the concept of One Canada and the federal state with suspicion. Closer economic links with the United States were furthered by economic development after the Quiet Revolution, especially the expansion of hydroelectric power industry during the 1970s, and by the sovereigntist argument that less dependence upon Canada enhanced the separatist project. Thus was premised, in part, Quebec's support of the free trade agreement in the 1988 federal election, or so thought some of English-speaking Canada's nationalists (see Resnick and Latouche, 1990).

Like people everywhere, Quebecers are large consumers of American culture. Likewise, many Quebecers, including many of its elite, also spend considerable time in the U.S., especially Florida (Cook, 1995:229). For them, visits to the rest of Canada hold little attraction, though this sometimes changes once Quebecers have ventured into the other provinces.

Quebec's unconscious relationship with the United States raises interesting questions. As André Laurendeau (1985) argued, "the homogenizing influence of the United States put in question the very existence of both Canadian [French and English] cultures." Unlike English-speaking Canadians, few Quebecers seem concerned about this influence. Some have argued, however, that Quebec's distinct culture has survived against American influence precisely because of its protected place within Canadian Confederation (Dufour, 1990; Resnick, 1991; Valaskakis and Fournier, 1995). In this vein, Brunelle (1999) and Ramonet (2001) suggest that the sovereignty question has distracted Quebecers from examining the impact of neo-liberal globalization and Americanization upon Quebec society, and the problems it might face after separation. (One interesting sidelight to the American-led invasion of Iraq in March 2003 was the sudden rise of anti-American sentiment among Quebecers, who, of all Canadians, most opposed the war.)

Interestingly, a similar argument can be made regarding English-speaking Canada: that it has insufficiently valued the role of the French language and culture in differentiating Canada from the United States. Could either Quebec or Canada alone withstand the assimilating influences of the American giant for long? This question and others are addressed in Part 2.

Conclusion

Canada and Quebec have travelled a long way since 1960, let alone since 1763. Sometimes in conflict more often than in co-operation, each has shaped the other. Canada's institutions, its decentralized system of governance, its tolerance of cultural differences (not to be overstated), and much of its identity are built upon French foundations. For its part, Quebec—the territory in which the French "fact" was suppressed and contained, and therefore incubated—also contains a hidden English element. Together, Canada's French and English "nations" have withstood absorption into the United States and built, by nearly any standard, one of the best countries and societies on earth.

Canada, it is often said, is an experiment (Bernard, 1996; Conway, 2004; Saul, 1997). Is it possible to break the European model of nation *equals* state *equals* country *equals* society? Is it possible to conceive and create a state structure in which two nations—three, counting the Aboriginal peoples—exist harmoniously and prosper, housed within a single country? A society in which majority, minority, and individual differences are embraced and respected, and yet political and social coherence are maintained? This has long been Canada's challenge; it is the process of meeting this challenge that has defined Canada's unique identity in the world—a world that continues to watch, wondering whether the grand experiment will succeed.

Key Terms

asymmetrical federalism
decentralization
gross domestic product (GDP)
interculturalisme
laicization
reasonable accommodation
secularization
subsidiarity

Critical Thinking Questions

1. Is secularism a kind of modern "religion"?
2. Is it possible to differentiate between individual and collective identities?
3. Why do anglophone and francophone Canadians hold such differing views about the meaning of *nation*?
4. Why do many francophone Quebecers view the United States, another anglophone country, more positively than English-speaking Canada?
5. Does globalization increase or decrease the likelihood of independence movements in Quebec and elsewhere in the world? Why?

Recommended Readings

Courchene, Thomas. 1997. *The Nation State in a Global/Information Era: Policy Challenges*. Kingston: John Deutsch Institute for the Study of Economic Policy, Queen's University.
One of Canada's best-known economists, Courchene outlines in this book some of the difficulties faced by states in the era of globalization.

Griffiths, Rudyard. 2008. *We're Prying French and English Canada Apart*. Ottawa: The Dominion Institute.
Written by the head of Canada's Dominion Institute, this book argues that recent federal initiatives are tearing apart the country's historic relationship between French and English.

Igartua, Jose E. 2006. *The Other Quiet Revolution: National Identities in English Canada, 1945–1971*. Vancouver: UBC Press.
This book examines the enormous transformation that occurred in English-speaking Canada during Quebec's Quiet Revolution.

Ignatieff, Michael. 1993. *Blood and Belonging: Journeys into the New Nationalism*. Toronto: Penguin.
Ignatieff's book examines several nationalist movements, including Quebec's.

Riesman, David, with Reuel Denney and Nathan Glazer. 1950. *The Lonely Crowd: A Study of the Changing American Character*. New Haven, CT: Yale University Press.
Don't let the year of publication put you off. This book remains a classic examination of individualism and the construction of personal identity in modern society.

Related Websites

Bouchard-Taylor Commission Report
collections.banq.qc.ca/ark:/52327/bs1565996
In an effort to address perceived cultural and religious divisions, in February 2007 the Quebec government established the Consultation Commission on Accommodation Practices Related to Cultural Differences, otherwise known as the Bouchard-Taylor Commission.

CBC Digital Archives (1995 Sovereignty Referendum)
www.cbc.ca/archives/categories/politics/federal-politics/separation-anxiety-the-1995-quebec-referendum/topic---separation-anxiety-the-1995-quebec-referendum.html
A useful video clip dealing with the 1995 sovereignty referendum is *Separation Anxiety: The 1995 Quebec Referendum*.

Statistics Canada, "The Evolving Linguistic Portrait of Canada."
www12.statcan.ca/census-recensement/2006/as-sa/97-555/p13-eng.cfm
This website usefully traces changes in language usage in Canada.

Canadian Society on Video

The Black Sheep: Ten Years Later. 2003. National Film Board of Canada, 82 minutes.
In 1992, filmmaker Jacques Godbout made *The Black Sheep*, a film about rising discontent in Quebec after the failure of the Meech Lake Accord. This sequel deals with the new Quebec emerging today.

PART TWO

CANADA AND THE UNITED STATES

Part 1 of this book examined conflict and co-operation between Canada's French and English cultures, and how this relationship has shaped—often unwittingly—Canada's political, economic, and cultural landscape. Part 2 examines Canada's—especially English-speaking Canada's—equally complex, often troubled, and even ambivalent relationship with the United States.

The chapters that follow trace the political, economic, and cultural moments defining this relationship. Sometimes, such as during the development of the Canadian economy in the 19th century and during the administration of President Franklin Delano Roosevelt (1882–1945) in the 1930s, the United States has been considered a positive model for Canadian society. At other times, however, such as the turbulent period of the 1960s and the recent war on terrorism, the United States has been seen as a negative model. The result has been a relationship that, if traced, would show two ships occasionally running parallel, and occasionally tacking quite differently into the future.

These chapters do not focus solely on this external relationship, however. They also examine Canada's internal development and deal with such issues as regionalism, the evolution of corporate capitalism, and the development of the Canadian welfare state. Along the way, other changes in Canadian society are detailed, such as Canada's class structure, the role of women in Canadian society, and the country's immigration policy.

Finally, Part 2 examines the recent period of neo-liberal globalization and its impact upon Canada, from issues of free trade and market liberalization to the terrorist attacks upon New York and Washington in September 2001 and the subsequent wars in Afghanistan and Iraq.

CHAPTER 5

THE MAKING OF
ENGLISH CANADA

[T]he American continents, by the free and independent condition which they have assumed and maintain, are henceforth not to be considered as subjects for future colonization by any European power . . . . [W]e should consider any attempt on their part to extend their system to any portion of this hemisphere as dangerous to our peace and safety.
                              —US President James Monroe, Annual Message to Congress, 1823

It is our Manifest Destiny to overspread the continent allotted by Providence for the free development of our multiplying millions.
                                                                    —newspaper editor John O'Sullivan,
                                                    United States Magazine and Democratic Review, 1845

When the experiment of the "dominion" shall have failed—as fail it must—a process of peaceful absorption will give Canada her proper place in the great North American Republic.
                                              —publisher Horace Greeley, *New York Tribune*, 1867

Introduction

The phrase "the world's longest undefended border" is an overused metaphor to describe Canada's relationship with the United States. No Canadian prime minister, American president, or accompanying journalist leaves home without some variation on it. While the phrase is not entirely incorrect, it is historically misleading.

Canadians and Americans often forget that their mutual relationship began less cordially, with a war. The American Revolution spawned not only the United States but also Canada (Lipset, 1990). From that time until 1871, the threat of American invasion was real, and Canadians had frequent cause to anticipate war (Winks, 1998:3). Even later, until at least 1936, the American Department of Defense regularly updated invasion plans for Canada (Rudmin, 1993).

This chapter traces the development of English-speaking Canada from 1775, when the American Revolution began, until Confederation in 1867. The chapter concentrates on the troubled early history of relations between Canada and the United States and how events in the United States helped spawn the creation of Canada in 1867. Specifically, this chapter shows that Canadian society has developed socially, economically, and politically both for internal reasons and as a defensive response (see Aitken, 1959) to the American threat. Finally, the chapter begins the process of examining English Canada's struggles to define its identity.

The Birth of Two Nations

The American War of Independence, popularly known as the American Revolution, began at Lexington, Massachusetts, on April 18, 1775, and ended with the Treaty of Paris in 1783. Why did the American colonists revolt in 1775?

The American Declaration of Independence of 1776 (*Time*, 2013:521–522) provides a useful starting point for answering the question. Like all revolutionary tracts, the Declaration does not shy away from rhetoric: "The history of the present King of Great Britain is a history of repeated injuries and usurpations, all having in direct object the establishment of an absolute Tyranny over these States." The Declaration lists a series of specific complaints: the general suspension of natural and constitutional rights, unjust trials, press ganging, the denial of political representation, unlawful taxation, the prevention of trade, the growth of colonial bureaucracy, general harassment of the people, and the "quartering of large bodies of armed troops."

Many of these complaints were justified. The American colonists believed strongly that a paternalistic and authoritarian British monarch and his administration had breached constitutional rights guaranteed by the English Bill of Rights of 1689.

Taxation was a particularly vexing issue. From the late 17th century on, the English Crown and Parliament had imposed a series of taxes on the colonies. After 1763, taxation—until then, purely regulatory in nature—became a means of generating revenues (Hofstadter, 1958:3–4). The colonists were unaccustomed to paying revenue-raising taxes and, in any case, viewed them as potentially ruinous. The colonists also believed that the taxes had been imposed without their consent, given either directly or indirectly, through the will of Parliament (Hofstadter et al., 1957:42).

The British viewed taxation differently. "The empire was expensive; costly wars had been fought to acquire and defend it; still more money would have to be laid out in the future to garrison it" (Hofstadter, 1958:3). In short, it was time for the colonists to shoulder their fair share of state expenses.

Though frequently the tax measures were withdrawn under protest, or otherwise circumvented by the industrious colonists (see James, 1997), taxes were certainly a major sore point leading up to the revolution. Anti-tax protests were common. In several instances, such as in Boston in 1770, there was violence between British troops and civilians. These confrontations invited further repressive measures. Troops were posted, and dissenters were dealt with harshly.

Nonetheless, as James (1997:107–109) notes, "Americans in 1774 enjoyed considerable freedom," including a free press, rights of assembly, and the right to travel. Indeed, these freedoms provided much of the basis for the revolution's success. While the issues listed in the Declaration were important, they were not intractable before 1775. There was little support for independence, even less for war (Zinn, 1995:76).

The reasons for this lack of support are easy to discern. The American Revolution was less a nationalist fight against foreign oppression than a family squabble. Nine-tenths of the colonies' 2.5 million people were of British descent (James, 1997:101), many of them "excessively proud of their Britishness" (James, 1997:100). At least a third of the American colonists were staunch Loyalists to the Crown, while another third were probably neutral throughout the conflict (Zinn, 1995:76). Many of the colonists were not sure why they were fighting (Hofstadter, 1958).

Why, then, did the American colonies revolt? Ironically, the general answer is that the conclusion of the war with France in 1763 removed a major threat to the colonies. In simple terms, the British Empire had outlived its usefulness. But this explanation only provides a context, not a substantive cause for the revolution.

More to the point, the consequences of managing the peace created enormous and unexpected conflicts between the British and certain colonists, especially in New England (see Orchard, 1998). The colonies that would become Canada were integrally involved in these disputes. Two sections of the Declaration of Independence make clear this connection (*Time*, 2013:521). One of the two sections reads as follows:

> For abolishing the free System of English Laws in a neighboring Province, establishing therein an Arbitrary government, and enlarging its Boundaries so as to render it at once an example and fit instrument for introducing the same absolute rule into these Colonies.

The second important section of the Declaration reads,

> He [the King] has excited domestic insurrections amongst us, and has endeavoured to bring on the inhabitants of our frontiers, the merciless Indian Savages, whose known rule of warfare is an undistinguished destruction of all ages, sexes and conditions.

The reference in both quoted sections is to the Quebec Act of 1774. That act, as we have seen (in Chapter 1), restored to the French-Canadians and the Catholic Church certain privileges removed in 1763 by the Royal Proclamation Act. The resurrection of French Catholicism in North America provoked hysterical alarm among the overwhelmingly Protestant colonists whose memories of sectarian conflict were fresh. James (1997:105) notes that, in early 1775, "the New England backwoods buzzed with rumours that Popery was about to be imposed." Among the colonists, papal fears alone might have seemed sufficiently provocative. But the Quebec Act also extended the boundaries of Quebec into the Ohio-Mississippi Indian Territory, thereby limiting the expansionist ambitions of American agrarians, investors, and land speculators (among them George Washington, Thomas Jefferson, and Benjamin Franklin) (see Orchard, 1998:14).

Why did the British extend Quebec's boundaries? In part, they did so under pressure from merchants in the Montreal-based fur trade (Innis, 1962:176). But the British also extended the boundaries in hopes of reasserting control over lands designated in the Royal Proclamation Act of 1763 as specifically "reserved" for the Indians: the lands west of the Appalachian Mountains (see Chapter 11). The expansion-minded colonists had consistently ignored the Royal Proclamation Act, resulting in renewed conflict with the Indians of the Ohio Valley. The British meant, through the Quebec Act, to curtail settlement in the volatile region. In the minds of the colonists, however, the Quebec Act had merely incited further conflict with the Indians, whom the colonists hated and wanted removed from the territory, hence the Declaration's hostile statements quoted above.

The Quebec Act was passed in the summer of 1774. Shortly after, in September 1774, a Continental Congress was convened to devise a slate of measures in retaliation to the Quebec Act (James, 1997:105). Events thereafter continued apace. The revolution's first volleys were fired only days before the Quebec Act was to have come into effect on May 1, 1775.

The war dragged on for six years. It was fought by unconventional means by untrained colonists and conventional means by the trained British troops. Long periods of idleness and boredom were punctuated by brief battles of horrific savagery on both sides.

In June 1775, the Americans launched a two-pronged attack on Canada. One American army went along Lake Champlain and captured Montreal, forcing Governor Guy Carleton (1724–1808) to flee to Quebec City. A second American army landed in Maine and proceeded to the shores of the St. Lawrence, where both armies then joined in an assault upon Quebec City. The siege failed the following May, however, when a flotilla of British troops arrived, causing the American forces to withdraw (Conway, 2004; James, 1997; Orchard, 1998).

Thereafter, the war never seriously threatened Canadian territory. Nonetheless, the American colonists believed throughout the conflict that Canada would soon join them in open revolt. The invasion of Canada in 1775, for example, was "advertised as a war of liberation" (James, 1997:113). When the American Articles of Confederation were written in 1777, a special Canada provision (article 11) was even included:

> Canada, according to this confederation, and joining in the measures of the United States, shall be admitted into, and entitled to all the advantages of this Union: but no other colony shall be admitted into the same unless such admission be agreed to by nine states.

The idea that Canada might join the rebellion was not entirely far-fetched. The people in Nova Scotia, linked by trade and family connections to the New England states, briefly considered joining the cause (Winks, 1998:3). Likewise, many within Montreal's English-speaking business class supported the revolutionary cause (Morton, 1997). The larger French-Canadian community—clergy, seigneurs, and merchants alike—remained neutral, however, an outcome the British had hoped the Quebec Act would secure.

Which side would emerge victorious was not quite certain until 1778, when France, ever desirous of revenge upon Britain for losses suffered in 1763, joined the conflict. With French assistance in the form of both troops and a naval blockade, the Americans won the last great battle of the war at Yorktown, Virginia, in October 1781 (Hofstadter et al., 1957:108–109; Zinn, 1995:79).

The Treaty of Paris saw England recognize American independence. The treaty further set America's borders at the Mississippi River on the west, the 31st parallel (just above Florida) in the south, and the Great Lakes in the north. The treaty also acknowledged American rights to Newfoundland's fisheries. England, however, retained joint privileges with America in navigating the Mississippi. The Americans further agreed to compensate British creditors for private debts owed them and to recommend that individual states restore Loyalist property (Hofstadter et al., 1957:109–110).

In 1783 many Americans viewed Canada as a natural extension of their colonies, and wanted to remove British influence entirely from the continent. The United States, however, was not strong enough, politically or militarily, to press such demands

(Horsman, 1993). Moreover, at least some Americans may have viewed a continuing British presence in North America, for all its drawbacks, as a kind of bulwark against possible French and Spanish expansion (James, 1997:119). For these reasons, Canada remained standing, but it was a Canada quickly changing, a Canada that soon faced renewed threats from its youthful American neighbour.

The War of 1812

The Treaty of Paris did not end disputes between Britain and its former American colonies. A major source of conflict was ended with the signing in 1794 of Jay's Treaty, which saw Britain evacuate the forts it had maintained in the Ohio Valley in defence of Montreal's fur interests (Horsman, 1993:297). Setting a pattern that would repeat itself again in 1814 (the Treaty of Ghent) and in 1846 (the Oregon Treaty), trade—and good relations—with the United States was far more important to Britain than trade with Canada. The interests of Montreal's fur traders, and Canada generally, were expendable.

Still, irritants remained and were heightened after 1793 by the outbreak of yet another war between Britain and France. In their zeal to defeat the French (this time in the person of Napoleon), the British began seizing American ships that traded with France, arresting escaped British seamen, and pressing American seamen into Royal service (Berton, 1980; Horsman, 1993). Understandably, Americans viewed Britain as not only harming American trade but also breaching American neutrality and sovereignty (Bowler, 1993). America's still fragile honour was at stake (Horsman, 1993:279).

Once more, the Aboriginal peoples also featured prominently among American complaints. The British, it was alleged, were encouraging their Indian allies, led by the Shawnee Chief Tecumseh (1768–1813) (see Chapter 9), to attack American settlers (Bowler, 1993:298; Hofstadter, 1958:227; Berton, 1980; Morton, 1997; Granatstein, 1996).

As such "provocations" mounted, war fever gripped the United States. During the American congressional debates of 1811 and 1812, legitimate complaints gave way once again to calls that Canada must be liberated. Finally, in June 1812, President James Madison declared the beginning of a second War of Independence (Morton, 1997:42).

As before, many Americans believed Canada would be an easy conquest. Former president Thomas Jefferson stated confidently that "The acquisition of Canada this year . . . will be a mere matter of marching" (Colombo, 1994:29).

As in 1775, such confidence was well placed. In 1812, there were only half a million people in British North America, compared with 7.5 million in the American states (Morton, 1997:33). Moreover, two-thirds of Upper Canada's population were newly arrived Americans (Bowler, 1993:302), largely indifferent to the war. The British themselves were occupied in fighting Napoleon. In short, the War of 1812 seemed like one that Britain's colonists could not win.

The War of 1812 was fought almost entirely in Upper Canada, though it strayed occasionally into Lower Canada, spawned a few memorable sea battles, and touched off a mini-boom in maritime smuggling (Bowler, 1993). Along Upper Canada's main front, the war began in a gentlemanly fashion, continuing indifferently at times—along the invisible border, truck, trade, and personal contacts continued, largely unabated—but became more savage as time progressed (Berton, 1980). In April 1813, the Americans sacked and burned York (now Toronto). In revenge, in August 1814, British forces captured and burned the U.S. Capitol building and the presidential mansion at Washington.

In the end, a combination of three things saved Canada from American takeover: American military ineptness, French and Indian support at key moments, and the end of the Napoleonic Wars in Europe, which freed regular British troops to come to Canada (Berton, 1980:27; Morton, 1997:42; Horsman, 1993).

The Treaty of Ghent in 1814 formally ended the war. The pre-existing borders were restored; the problems that began the war were forgotten or soon disappeared. In the words of historian Desmond Morton (1997:43), "The war changed no boundaries, brought no reparations, avenged no wrongs." The Battle of Waterloo and Napoleon's subsequent banishment to St. Helena ended Britain's need to seize ships and impress seamen. The severely weakened Aboriginal tribes were no longer a threat—if they ever had been—to Americans and the American government's expansionist desires.

The War of 1812 gave English Canada its first heroes: Major-General Sir Isaac Brock (1769–1812) and Chief Tecumseh, who both died in battle, as well Lieutenant Colonel Charles-Michel d'Irumberry de Salaberry (1778–1829) and Laura Secord (1775–1868) (Morton, 1997; Bowler, 1993; Orchard, 1998). The war also strengthened British resolve to protect its North American colonies. It further solidified the alliance of the French, English, and Aboriginal peoples, who had fought side by side against the Americans, though the Aboriginals received the least reward for their sacrifices (see Chapter 9). Most importantly, however, the War of 1812 took on the status of a founding myth around which English Canada forged the beginnings of its distinct identity.

The Making of English-Canadian Identity

We have briefly to reacquaint ourselves with the Loyalists (Chapter 1), especially those 10,000 or so who settled in Canada and caused its division in 1791. Canadians' first impressions were not favourable. Contemporaries used the words "quarrelsome" and "bitter" to describe them. It is time, however, to revisit the Loyalists and ask: Who were they? And, more importantly: What became of them?

To the first question: The Americans portrayed the Loyalists as an "elite of Anglican clergy, bureaucrats, and merchants living off government favours" (Dickinson and Young, 2008:69), an image the Loyalists themselves later encouraged. The image was incorrect, however. The Loyalists were not fundamentally different from the Americans who stayed behind. Most were subsistence farmers, disproportionately young, often poor and illiterate. While most were recent immigrants from Britain, the Loyalists also included various other religious and ethnic minorities (Dickinson and Young, 2008:69; Brown, 1993:244, 247; Granatstein, 1996:15). They also included approximately 3,000 escaped Black slaves, who settled in Nova Scotia, and almost 2,000 Iroquois, who settled north of the Great Lakes, where the city of Brantford today commemorates the name of their leader, Joseph Brant (Wynn, 2012:212–214).

The American Revolution did not merely create two nations; it also created two myths. Not *all* Americans were democrats; not *all* Loyalists were monarchists. Most people on both sides were indifferent, confused, and scared, caught up in events beyond their control (see Granatstein, 1996:13). Yet the Loyalists quickly began to believe their own myths, which brings us to the second question: What became of them? A couple of quotations will point us toward an answer.

The first is taken second-hand from Christian Dufour (1990:54), who cites a Canadian history text used in English-Canadian high schools in the 1930s as it concludes the episode of the American invasion of 1812: "Once again, the American invaders were repelled, as in 1776, as in 1690." But, asks Dufour, "How can the British Canada that drove back the Americans in 1812 be linked to the New France that stood up to the English in 1690?" Put another way, who were the "Americans" in 1690? They were, of course, the English. (The specific date 1690 refers to a famous incident in which Governor General Louis Frontenac defeated the invading army of the Bostonian Sir William Phips.)

The second quotation is from historian P.B. Waite, recalling his days as a schoolboy in Belleville, Ontario, in the early 1930s. In the quotation, Waite (1997:13) remembers situating his identity within Canada's history:

> We mapped the voyages of Champlain, of La Salle . . . . We rejoiced in the story of Phips' demand . . . and Frontenac's reply . . . . Thus did we English-*Canadiens* fight the Americans and their British allies. And we continued to be *Canadiens* . . . .
>
>   Then suddenly, oddly, sharply we became English. It was something of a wrench. Wolfe had laid siege to Quebec in the summer of 1759 and all that summer we stayed with Montcalm fighting off the British. Then, early on the morning of 13 September 1759, we changed sides. We crossed the St. Lawrence with Wolfe and the British in the dark, silent boats, we fought with the British regulars on the Plains of Abraham; and though we mourned both Montcalm and Wolfe, by the time of Montcalm's death the next morning we were already on our way at last to being English-Canadians.

What became of the Loyalists? Upon their arrival, they were defeated and humiliated, indeed, not unlike the French they found in the new land. But they found in the French something of particular value: The French had an identity, one ready-made for appropriation, an identity, moreover, shaped by being the first anti-Americans. Thus, the Loyalists became *Canadiens* and Canadians became (by Loyalist definition and thereafter) anti-Americans.

Of course, we cannot lay the whole weight of appropriation upon the Loyalists. In most provinces, the Loyalists soon found themselves a minority (they never were a majority in Quebec). The sole exception was New Brunswick. Even there, however, after 1812 the Loyalists found themselves engulfed by other immigrants. In 1812, only one-fifth of Upper Canada's population of 100,000 was Loyalist in origin (Brown, 1993:247; see also Wynn, 2012). Nonetheless, the Loyalists' myth of rejecting American takeover and their incorporation of French Canada into their identity structure began the process of forging in English Canada a distinctive identity (Brown, 1993; Granatstein, 1996). After 1812, the people of British North America at last had something in common: British and French, Aboriginal and Black alike, they were *not* Americans.

The Monroe Doctrine, Manifest Destiny, and American Exceptionalism

The Treaty of Ghent did not end tensions between the United States and Britain's North American colonies. Conflict was blunted, it is true, by the signing in 1817 of the Rush-Bagot Convention, which prohibited large warships on the Great Lakes, and by the 1818 Convention, which clarified somewhat international boundary lines. The existing line was extended westward from the Lake of the Woods to the Rocky Mountains along the 49th parallel (Careless, 1970:134–135).

American expansion continued unabated, however, fuelled by the demands of a growing population (9.6 million people in 1820) (*Time*, 2013:575) and a changing economy. But American expansion also invoked as its justification the notion of "liberating" land and people from the foreign and colonial yoke, even when the people involved did not want to be liberated and viewed the United States as an aggressor, a justifiction and response sadly not without its recent echoes. Thus, President James Monroe, in his message to Congress in December 1823, introduced what become known as the **Monroe Doctrine** (see opening quotation above), which declares that the Americas are to be free of foreign influence and that the United States will act to prevent such influence. American expansion also was justified by the notion of **manifest destiny**, a term coined in 1845 by John O'Sullivan, which held that the new country was divinely ordained with a special mission to cover North America (see quotation above). In turn, such beliefs paved the way for what is often termed **American exceptionalism**, the belief held by many Americans that the United States cannot be judged by the same standards as other countries (see Chapter 8).

The United States expanded steadily across the continent throughout the first half of the 19th century. The process was always similar. American trade with and exploration of new territories was soon followed by immigration. Soon the American land speculators, merchants, and settlers would complain about the actions of local government officials (usually Spanish in origin); then they would lobby Washington to intervene. Covert aid would follow. In time, the existing government would be dethroned (sometimes with the help of American troops), the populace would "ask" to be annexed, and the United States would oblige. Thus, Florida was seized from Spain in 1819; Texas, after years of internal intrigue inspired by the American government, was also seized from Spain in 1845; and New Mexico and California, following an American-provoked war, were annexed from Mexico in 1848 (Hofstadter et al., 1957:181–182, 279–281; Orchard, 1998:32–33). The annexation from Mexico doubled the size of the United States, not incidentally, on the eve of the California gold rush.

Canada was not immune from American intrigues and claims. War nearly erupted in the 1820s after Maine's governor declared New Brunswick's timberlands part of the state and ordered U.S. troops to seize the territory (Orchard, 1998:30). In a prelude to the Mexican wars, in 1844 the United States also claimed, by dint of biblical injunctions, the Oregon territory. The dispute was settled in 1846, again under threat of war, on grounds favourable to the Americans. In 1859, the so-called Pig War erupted over the San Juan Islands in Puget Sound, ending in 1873 with the United States gaining sole ownership of the islands (Lower, 1983:66–88, and 75). Also by the 1850s, Americans settled in the Red River Valley were actively pressing for the United States to annex that territory.

In these ventures, the biggest losers were the Aboriginal peoples (see Chapter 9), who were vilified, pacified, assimilated, and often hunted down, sometimes to extinction. Before becoming American president in 1832, Andrew Jackson (1767–1845) earned a well-deserved reputation for savagery directed at Aboriginal peoples, terrorizing and killing them by the thousands before taking more than two million acres in northern Alabama (Wright, 1993:211–212). Another future president, Abraham Lincoln (1809–1865), while sympathetic to the situation of Blacks, thought the Indian people unredeemable and, as a young man, fought briefly in the vicious Illinois Black Hawk War of the 1830s.

By 1853, the United States had nearly achieved its present territorial size. Alaska was added in 1867 and Hawaii in 1898. The only territory in North America unincorporated into the United States was what the French author Voltaire once called "a few acres of snow": Canada (quoted in Colombo, 1994:18).

The Political Economy of British North America, 1800–1866

To the unreflecting eye, the British colonies in 1800 must still have seemed not much more than a frozen wasteland. The combined population of the five British North American provinces in 1805 was about 360,000. Of this total, about 230,000 resided in Lower Canada, 46,000 in Upper Canada, 54,000 in Nova Scotia, 25,000 in New Brunswick, and 5,000 or so in Prince Edward Island (Careless, 1970:122; Norrie and Owram, 1996:84, 119; Dickinson and Young, 2008). Newfoundland's total population in 1805 was just short of 20,000, but this number included a large number of semi-permanent residents engaged in the seasonal fisheries (see Norrie and Owram, 1996:75).

The end of the Napoleonic Wars, however, saw Britain hit by a depression and rising unemployment. Thus, after 1815 the colonies—except Newfoundland, which itself entered a period of stagnation until the 1850s (see Norrie and Owram, 1996)—experienced a massive wave of immigration that lasted four decades. Between 1815 and 1850, nearly 800,000 immigrants, mainly British, arrived in Canada: "discharged soldiers and half-pay officers from Wellington's armies, Irish weavers and paupers, Scottish artisans and dispossessed crofters, English country labourers and factory workers" (Careless, 1970:147).

Few British immigrants remained permanently in Lower Canada. Those who did settled mainly in the Eastern Townships and the growing cities of Montreal and Quebec.

Elsewhere, however, British immigration left a permanent mark. Scottish immigration especially filled Nova Scotia, competing with the settled Loyalists and pre-Loyalist New Englanders, and Prince Edward Island, while the Irish, especially after the 1840s, filled New Brunswick (Careless, 1970:148).

Immigration effects were felt most, however, in Upper Canada. There, British immigration rose steadily after 1820, dropped in the mid-1830s due to cholera and the province's political troubles, then rose again sharply during the 1840s. Though all elements of British society—"English, Welsh, Lowland and Highland Scots and Catholic and Ulster Irish" (Careless, 1970:149)—arrived, it was perhaps the Irish who left the greatest impression. Driven from their homeland by poverty, overcrowding, and, finally, the potato famine, the Irish soon found employment building canals and, later, the railways (Morton, 1997:54; also Pentland, 1991; Norrie and Owram, 1996).

American immigration to the British colonies generally declined during this period due to westward American expansion. A sole exception to this pattern was the relatively large influx into the Maritimes and Upper Canada of American Blacks escaping slavery during the 20 years leading up to that country's Civil War (see below). By 1861, there were about 60,000 Blacks in British North America (Winks, 1998:8; also Kelly, 1997).

As a consequence of immigration and births, British North America's population by 1851 had grown to more than 2.4 million; by 1861, 3.2 million. Upper Canada now had the largest population—nearly 1.4 million—followed by Lower Canada (1.1 million), Nova Scotia (331,000), New Brunswick (252,000), and Prince Edward Island (81,000) (see Table 0.1).

Immigration to the colonies, however, began declining in the early 1850s, and by the 1860s was actually outpaced by people leaving Canada. Indeed, from 1851 to 1901, while 1.9 million people entered Canada, 2.2 million left, primarily for the United States (McKie, 1994:26).

The British colonies' problem in attracting and retaining people was simple: Their economies were unable to compete with the expanding and rapidly industrializing neighbour to the south. Though economic development occurred, the British colonies generally lacked investment capital; their transportation systems were substandard and internally not integrated; and their separate economies exhibited many of the instabilities characteristic of staple-based, export-driven economies.

Newfoundland, for example, remained an imperial outpost, not even a colony, until 1824. And, though the granting of responsible government in 1855 coincided with a period of growth lasting until the mid-1880s, its economy remained dangerously one-dimensional. In 1858, 89 percent of Newfoundland's labour force worked in the fishery, a statistic that remained relatively constant over the next decade, indicating a single-industry dependence that would sink the Newfoundland economy two decades later (Norrie and Owram, 1996:78–79, 350–351).

The situation elsewhere in the colonies was less bleak but still no cause for optimism. The American Revolution had spurred a short-lived economic boom. Nova Scotia's timber industry developed around producing pine masts for the British navy; shipbuilding, formerly concentrated around local markets, also grew to service trade with the West

Indies; and internal markets, especially for agricultural products, arose around the province's increased population, inspired in part by Loyalist immigration. Subsequently, the Napoleonic Wars produced a second Maritime boom, as Britain increased its colonial imports. The fisheries remained important, but now forestry also developed in New Brunswick and spurred forward economic linkages: sawmills and (especially) shipbuilding. By 1860, the Maritimes were one of the world's premier shipbuilding centres. Other important industries that developed included Nova Scotia's trade in coal and agricultural produce (Norrie and Owram, 1996:79–80, 86).

The years, especially after 1815, were not kind to Lower Canada. The fur industry entered a period of decline following the signing of Jay's Treaty in 1794 and left the St. Lawrence Valley altogether following the merger, in 1821, of the North West Company with the Hudson's Bay Company. Wheat became a major export item to Britain and the West Indies during the late 18th century, but early the next century it too entered a period of permanent decline occasioned by recurrent crop failures (see Trofimenkoff, 1993:384) and increasing competition from Upper Canada (see below).

These losses were partially offset by other sources of economic growth, notably timber (Norrie and Owram, 1996) and power generation. Also, the two major urban centres of Quebec City and Montreal increased in size and importance, the former economy based on shipping, the military, and services; the latter on industry and finance. But much of the province remained rural—indeed, became even more disproportionately so during the century (see Chapter 2)—and underdeveloped, while the benefits of industrialization went almost entirely to the anglophone bourgeoisie.

By contrast, Upper Canada's situation grew decidedly more hopeful as the 19th century progressed. The province was at first economically dependent on British administrative expenditures in the form of direct handouts: subsidies and claims to Loyalists, and military and civil construction. In the words of Norrie and Owram (1996:123), "the British government subsidized the initial stages of settlement in Upper Canada." The arrival of the "late Loyalists" (Americans newly arrived in the early 1800s) and of British immigrants after 1820 provided both labourers and consumers. Local domestic markets developed and the timber industry grew. But wheat was Ontario's real story.

Small amounts of wheat were already being shipped down the St. Lawrence as early as 1794 (Norrie and Owram, 1996:124). During the War of 1812, however, wheat became a major export to Britain. Though wheat sales declined after the war, a new market was soon found in Lower Canada, then later again in Britain and the United States. Wheat exports from Upper Canada rose by 500 percent during the 1840s and then doubled again, peaking in 1861 (McCallum, 1991:11).

The importance of wheat to Upper Canada's economy cannot be overestimated. In 1820, more than 95 percent of the province's population was still rural (Norrie and Owram, 1996:126). Locally produced wheat thus fed Upper Canada's population without resort to imports. Capital acquired through exports of surplus wheat, especially after 1840, later fuelled industrial development (McCallum, 1991).

Instances of economic development and diversification aside, in the mid-1850s the British colonies were marked by uneven development and export dependency. Nova

Scotia's export trade was spread among the other British North American colonies, the United States, and the West Indies. New Brunswick's export trade was heavily tied to Britain. Prince Edward Island's export trade was moderately tied to the other colonies. The Province of Canada's economy was based on agricultural and forestry exports, primarily to the United States. All of the colonies imported a larger percentage of their manufactured goods (Norrie and Owram, 1996:91).

The colonies' resultant economic instability fuelled ongoing political demands, particularly from the Province of Canada's business class, for either annexation by the United States or (at the very least) a reciprocity agreement with the U.S. that would ensure stable markets. In 1854, they got their wish.

Understanding how the Reciprocity Treaty of 1854 came about requires a brief discussion of changes in economic thinking that had occurred since the 18th century. As the reader will remember (Chapter 1), Canada was founded primarily as a mercantilist adventure. Two centuries later, however, mercantilism was under increasing attack. Adam Smith (1723–1790) launched the first attack in his classic text *The Wealth of Nations*, which, fittingly, came out in 1776, the same year as the American Declaration of Independence. The latter stated a liberal interpretation of political freedom. Smith's text similarly argued for a liberal interpretation of economic freedom.

Smith directed three specific arguments against mercantilism. First, he argued that free trade among countries was mutually beneficial. Second, he argued that trade enhanced specialization in production, leading to increased efficiency. And third, Smith denounced mercantilism on the basis of the "collusive relationship" it encouraged between governments and the merchant classes (La Haye, 1993:535).

Smith's arguments found fertile ground in Britain during the American Revolution. Many British already viewed the colonies as expensive to maintain, administratively and militarily. Now they were a political headache as well.

The outbreak of the Napoleonic Wars in 1793 brought mercantilism a temporary reprieve as Britain became dependent upon its colonies for food and materials, for example, Maritime fish and timber. After 1814, however, Smith's ideas—now augmented by those of a young economist, David Ricardo (1772–1823)—gained momentum. Slowly at first, then with greater alacrity, mercantilism's regulatory walls collapsed. In 1833, Britain abolished colonial slavery, thus creating "free labour." "Free trade" followed in the 1840s with the repeal of timber duties, the Navigation Acts, and the Corn Laws (Norrie and Owram, 1996:173). Britain's policy of preferential trade with the North American colonies ceased after 1846.

Free trade made perfect sense from the British point of view. Britain, after all, was the first modern industrialized capitalist country. Moreover, it was still a great empire possessing the world's most powerful fleet.

Elsewhere, including the United States, Smith's and Ricardo's ideas had far less appeal (Laxer, 1989; Watkins, 1991) (see Chapter 6). The ending of free trade–protected markets was viewed with especial fear in Britain's North American colonies. How did this affect the security of the colonies' exports? The panic climaxed in April 1849.

The Canadian government had been moved the previous year from Kingston to Montreal, the site of Canada's business establishment. In 1849, the Reform government of Baldwin-Lafontaine passed a bill compensating Patriotes and innocent victims of the rebellions of 1837 and 1838 (see Chapter 1) for losses suffered during the conflict. Montreal's English business class, already feeling abandoned by the British government's adoption of free trade and fearing a recession, stormed and burned the new Parliament buildings, and threatened the Governor General, Lord Elgin (1811–1863) (Careless, 1970:203; Morton, 1997:56–57). A manifesto circulated in favour of annexation to the United States. In Chatham, New Brunswick, meanwhile, inhabitants "marched through the streets on July 4, 1849, firing pistols in the air and singing 'Yankee Doodle'" (Wynn, 2012:199–200).

Annexation was not very popular anywhere. Within weeks, talk of joining the United States subsided. Nonetheless, many in the colonies remained concerned about securing access to the large American market. The Reciprocity Treaty of 1854 was the result. The treaty came into effect in 1855 and lasted until 1866, when the United States terminated it. Specifically, the treaty eliminated the tariff on natural products, including fish.

The signing of the Reciprocity Treaty blunted Montreal merchants' demands for annexation (Winks, 1998:4). The following decade witnessed rapid economic growth throughout the British colonies (Aitken, 1959). This period featured the increased economic integration of the St. Lawrence lowlands, the extension of the agricultural area of southern Ontario, the beginning of manufacturing in Ontario and Quebec, and the development of a railway from the Detroit River to the Atlantic seaboard.

How responsible was the Reciprocity Treaty for this period of prosperity? The question is not easily answered. On balance, however, reciprocity seems to have increased the overall volume of trade between the two countries and specifically to have benefited British North American trade in wheat, oats, and flour (Norrie and Owram, 1996:184–185; see also Careless, 1970; Laxer, 1989).

By the 1860s, some business and political leaders in the United States had turned against the agreement, believing—with some justification—that Canada had gotten the better of the deal. Ultimately, however, the Reciprocity Treaty collapsed for reasons other than economic.

Canada and the American Civil War

As the debate over the Meech Lake Accord and "distinct society" heated up in 1989, Reform Party leader Preston Manning repeatedly borrowed American President Abraham Lincoln's phrase warning of the perils of a "house divided" (see Harrison, 1995:173). In the overheated aftermath of the 1995 Quebec referendum, parallels between Canada's situation and events leading up to the American Civil War in 1861 were again advanced (McPherson, 1998). The discerning of Canadian parallels, or parables, in the American Civil War was not new. The war was very much on the minds of Canadian politicians in 1864 as they began deliberations on Confederation.

The American Civil War (1861–1865) previewed wars soon to come, introducing trench warfare, advanced weaponry (for example, the Gatling gun), and calculated terrorism against civilians. To this day, the number of Union and Confederate deaths during the American Civil War (563,000) is larger than the number of American deaths in any other war (*Time*, 2013:572). As in later wars, a modern invention—the camera— "brought home" the Civil War to those far removed, including the people of British North America.

British North America was affected by events in the United States even before the war began. In the months leading up to the conflict, some American officials suggested that a war with Britain over Canada might prove a useful diversion and unite the squabbling states. Other Union officials argued that, in the event of losing the South, the conquest of Canada would make for an adequate replacement (Morton, 1997:61; Winks, 1998; see also Marquis, 2000).

In the beginning, many people in the British colonies—where, despite history, slavery had been formally abolished in 1833 (see Box 5.1)—supported the North, believing that the war was intended to abolish slavery (Winks, 1998). As the war went on, however, sympathies in the colonies became more conflicted. It became apparent that ending slavery was incidental to the Union's crusade. The war's first purpose was to save the Union (Hofstadter, 1958). The South's argument that individual states had voluntarily entered into a Confederacy in 1776 and therefore retained the right of self-determination, including the right of exit, struck a more responsive chord in the British colonies than did the North's federalist alternative.

Inevitably, the British colonies also found themselves caught up in the war's actual dynamics. To the North's displeasure, the British continued to trade with the South. The South also used the British colonies as a staging ground for raids against the Union, both by land and sea (Winks, 1998; Marquis, 2000). In retaliation, and much to British annoyance, northern forces also breached the Canadian border in pursuit of the rebels. Throughout the American Civil War, many in Canada feared, and some in the Confederacy actively hoped, that Britain would be dragged into war with the Union (Winks, 1998).

Nor did fears lessen with the conflict's end. British and colonial officials noted the United States had a battle-tested army of 2.3 million men, nearly equal to the entire population of the province of Canada (Martin, 1993b:560), which now could be turned north. Facing the American army was a regular military force of little more than 19,000 (Winks, 1998:282) and perhaps another 10,000 militia. Elaborate plans concerning Canada's defence were made and discussed throughout 1864 and1865 (see Winks, 1998:351–352). These plans became more urgent when Irish raiders, known as the Fenians, invaded Canada (with tacit American support) in 1866 (McCue, 1999).

Most British officials, including Prime Minister William Gladstone (1809–1898), accepted the obvious: Canada ultimately was not defensible against American attack. So, to avoid provocation, in 1871 Britain removed all its troops from Canadian soil. But the American Civil War, and the threats of invasion that followed, provided the psychological context (Martin, 1993b:559) for getting on with a task long debated: Confederation (see also Winks, 1998:379; Moore, 1997).

Box 5.1: Slavery in Canada

The 2014 Academy Award–winning film *Twelve Years A Slave* highlights, in stark fashion, the horrors of slavery in the United States. Few Canadians realize, however, that Canada has its own history of slavery—and not only as a refuge for African-Americans escaping that country via the Underground Railroad. Citizens in New France held Black slaves as early as 1629 and, by 1671, were acquiring Amerindian slaves, though the practice did not begin in earnest until two decades later and was only formally legalized in 1709. Marcel Trudel's (2013:256) empirical study, based on existing records, shows that the slave population of New France over two centuries was at least 4,185 (comprising 2,683 native Amerindians; 1,443 Blacks; and 59 "others"), a significant number, though low compared to the slave count in English colonies to the south. The slave owners came from every walk of life: professionals, tradespeople, merchants—even the clergy.

Taken more broadly, a complete history of slavery in Canada would include "the revolt of Celtic slaves against their Viking masters on Baffin Island" in 997; the intertribal slave-trade among Aboriginal peoples on the Pacific coast and Eastern Woodlands; the European, especially Portuguese, trade in Aboriginal slaves on the east coast; the capture as slaves of White Europeans by Aboriginal tribes; the French seizure (under Louis XIV) of Huguenots as galley slaves; and even the taking into bondage of Newfoundland sailors by Barbary pirates in the early 17th century (Tombs, 2013:11–12).

Britain's passage of the Slavery Abolition Act in 1833 formally ended the practice of slavery throughout the British Empire. By this time, however, slavery had all but ended throughout Canada, as the result of moral and economic arguments in favour of wage labour.

Sources: Trudel, Marcel. 2013. *Canada's Forgotten Slaves: Two Hundred Years of Bondage.* Translated by G. Tombs. Montreal: Véhicule Press; and Tombs, George. 2013. "Translator's Preface." In *Canada's Forgotten Slaves: Two Hundred Years of Bondage*, edited by M. Trudel. Montreal: Véhicule Press.

Confederation

Confederation in 1867 was intended to address three problems. First, Confederation was meant to provide an "effective defence" against the threat of American invasion. (The fact that such a defence was no more possible after Confederation than before is incidental.) Second, Confederation was meant to create an economic union. Economic union was made necessary by the American government's suspension of the Reciprocity Treaty in 1866 in response to British support for the South during the Civil War. Third, Confederation was meant to deal with French-English political instability in the Province of Canada, where 12 governments had fallen in 15 years (see Moore, 1997; Romney, 1999).

Confederation began as a discussion of Maritime union at Charlottetown, Prince Edward Island, in June 1864. Almost immediately, however, these discussions expanded to include plans for a broader union of all British North America. A follow-up meeting at Quebec City in October that same year drafted the union's essential features. The Quebec Resolutions were then taken back to the individual colonial legislatures for debate and ratification (see Careless, 1970:243–249; Norrie and Owram, 1996:207–209; Moore, 1997; Silver, 1997; Romney, 1999).

Confederation's blueprints, and the British North America (BNA) Act of 1867, which legally constituted the federation, drew heavily from "British precedent and practice" (Norrie and Owram, 1996:210), including an elected federal Parliament and a system of jurisprudence based on the British model. Also, the British monarch remained the formal head of state, and the highest court for judicial appeals remained in London. But Confederation also drew upon practices already employed in the Province of Canada and the American model.

From the Province of Canada was adopted the idea of tariffs, an important element of the National Policy soon devised (see Chapter 6). Likewise, many of the Dominion's banking regulations copied legislation developed in the Province of Canada (Norrie and Owram, 1996:211).

From the American model came the idea of the Senate. Like the American Senate, which represents individual states (Hofstadter, 1958:76–77), the Canadian Senate was meant to represent the provinces (Moore, 1997:108–109). Unlike American senators, however, Canadian senators were not to be elected. Why not? The reason, in part, was that the Canadian Senate was also modelled on the British House of Lords, and, in part, that an appointed Senate left obvious opportunities for patronage, a current criticism. But the Fathers of Confederation additionally feared that elected senators would possess legitimacy equal to the elected members of Parliament—the "House of the People"—while threatening the principle of "one person, one vote" (see Moore, 1997:108; Romney, 1999).

The Fathers of Confederation also discerned in the American experience, specifically the recent Civil War, an object lesson (Winks, 1998) on the perils of decentralized government. Here, however, the perceived lesson could only be partially applied (Moore, 1997; Silver, 1997; Romney, 1999). Certainly, Sir John A. Macdonald desired to construct a strong central government, but this was not possible. Neither the Maritime provinces nor (especially) Quebec would accept a strongly centralized federation.

The result was a Confederation in which jurisdictional powers were divided between the federal government and the provinces. The federal government was given powers over national defence, postal services, the census and statistics, currency and banking, navigation and shipping, fisheries, criminal law, the regulation of trade and commerce, weights and measures, bankruptcy and insolvency, and taxation. Provincial governments were given powers over two areas of minimal importance at the time, but hugely important later on, health and education, as well as generally local matters, such as property and civil rights, civil law, municipal governments, licences, and the chartering of companies, as well as direct taxation for government costs. All residual powers lay with the federal government. Finally, the federal government was further charged with the responsibility of ensuring equitable fiscal assistance to all the provinces to meet their constitutional functions (Careless, 1970:254–255; Norrie and Owram, 1996:209–210).

There was no great outcry of public support in 1867 for Confederation; in some quarters there was significant opposition. Newfoundland and Prince Edward Island rejected Confederation (Careless, 1970:246; Norrie and Owram, 1996:208), while New Brunswick and Nova Scotia were only slowly brought on side (Careless, 1970; Moore, 1997). In Canada East, opposition remained high despite the implicit and explicit promises of the Conservatives and their leader, George Cartier, that Confederation offered the French a sovereign homeland within a federated state (see Silver, 1997; Romney, 1999). Only Canada West—festering under the Act of Union, demanding separation from entanglements with Canada East and a system of "Rep by Pop," its gaze fixed on westward expansion—greeted Confederation with something like passion.

Thus, on July 1, 1867, the Dominion of Canada was proclaimed, made up of four provinces: New Brunswick, Nova Scotia, Quebec (formerly Canada East), and Ontario (formerly Canada West). The new country covered 370,045 square miles (958,416.5 square kilometres), a tenth of British North America, and housed roughly 4 million people—mainly French and English, Catholic and assorted flavours of Protestant. Small clusters of minority populations were growing, however, presaging Canada's multi-ethnic mix of the next century.

Montreal, the site of trade and finance, was the country's largest city, with more than 100,000 people, followed by Quebec City (59,699), Toronto (56,092), Halifax (29,582), and Saint John (28,805) (Morton, 1997:12–19), but the majority of people still lived and worked on rural farms and in small villages.

A significant manufacturing base was developing (Laxer, 1989), but most manufactured goods were still imported, and staple exports (fish, wheat, and trees) still ruled Canada's economy (Norrie and Owram, 1996:208). Indeed, the new Dominion remained largely pre-industrial, even pre-capitalist. Probably few people realized immediately that they had become subjects of a new country. Even fewer Aboriginal peoples of the West and the North knew that they too would soon be absorbed into something called Canada (see chapters 9 and 10).

Conclusion

English Canada was born as a fragment cast off by the American Revolution. The United States became English Canada's "Other," a place of attraction, mystery, awe, and fear. Where few differences marked the Loyalists from other Americans in 1775, war, politics, and economics erected borders that, in time, took on a cultural and psychological reality. Separate histories make separate peoples: Attempts to unite East and West Germans after the Cold War provide a contemporary example.

Confederation made concrete the idea of Canada. Shortly thereafter, American efforts at conquering Canada militarily ceased almost entirely. As Governor General Vincent Massey (1887–1967) later noted, "the disparity of population has made armaments for one country futile and for the other superfluous." Yet Canada's future remained uncertain beside the American behemoth that, on the shores of the 20th century, was flexing its muscles. Much remained to be done if the new country was to thrive.

Key Terms

American exceptionalism
manifest destiny
Monroe Doctrine

Critical Thinking Questions

1. How might North America look different today had the American colonies not revolted in 1775?
2. Why did the notion of manifest destiny arise in the United States and what is its continued impact today?
3. Why did Canada expand more slowly than the United States?
4. Why did beliefs in free trade arise in England?
5. In light of how the Canadian Senate was originally conceived, how would you deal with more recent controversies about its role?

Recommended Readings

Berton, Pierre. 1980. *The Invasion of Canada, 1812–1813*. Toronto: McClelland & Stewart. Written by one of Canada's great popularizers of history, this book details the events of the somewhat ambiguous War of 1812.

Granatstein, Jack. 1996. *Yankee Go Home? Canadians and Anti-Americanism*. Toronto: HarperCollins.
This book examines the history of anti-Americanism in Canada.

Norrie, Ken, and Douglas Owram. 1996. *The History of the Canadian Economy*. 2nd ed. Toronto: Harcourt Brace and Company, Canada.
This book details the economic history of Canadian development, from resource extraction to industrialization.

Winks, Robin. 1998. *The Civil War Years: Canada and the United States*. 4th ed. Montreal and Kingston: McGill-Queen's University Press.
Winks examines the complex relationship between Canada and the United States during the latter's civil war, 1861–1865.

Zinn, Howard. 1996. *A People's History of the United States 1492–Present*. New York: Harper Perennial.
One of the United States' best-known radical historians, Zinn provides an historical account of that country's development significantly at odds with conventional narratives.

Related Websites

Historica Canada: Black History Canada
www.blackhistorycanada.ca
A web archive of information on Canada's Black community.

Library and Archives Canada: Confederation
www.collectionscanada.gc.ca/confederation/index-e.html
Library and Archives Canada holds Canada's national collection of books, historical documents, government records, photos, films, maps, music, and so on. The archives contain valuable documents on Confederation.

Library and Archives Canada: Reciprocity Treaty, 1854
www.collectionscanada.gc.ca/confederation/023001-7101-e.html
The archives also contain the full text of the Reciprocity Agreement of 1854.

Canadian Society on Video

Canada: A People's History, "Episode 5: A Question of Loyalties." 2000. Canadian Broadcasting Corporation, 120 minutes.
Covers the period from 1775 to 1815 and deals with the arrival of the United Empire Loyalists during the American Revolution and the American invasion of Canada in 1812.

Canada: A People's History, "Episode 8: The Great Enterprise." 2000. Canadian Broadcasting Corporation, 120 minutes.
Covers the period from 1850 to 1867 and the events leading to Confederation.

CHAPTER 6

ENGLISH CANADA
IN TRANSITION

We often say that we fear no invasion from the south, but the armies of the south have already crossed the border. American enterprise, American capital, is taking rapid possession of our mines and our water-power, our oil areas and our timber limits.

—Sara Jeannette Duncan, *The Imperialist*, 1904

I am for [reciprocity] because I hope to see the day when the American flag will float over every square foot of the British North American possessions clear to the North Pole.

—Champ Clark, speaker of the U.S. House of Representatives, 1911

The Dominion of Canada is part of the sisterhood of the British Empire. I give you assurance that the people of the United States will not stand idly by if domination of Canadian soil is threatened by any other Empire.

—U.S. President Franklin Delano Roosevelt, Queen's University, Kingston, 1938

Introduction

Despite Confederation, immediately after 1867 Canada faced two great challenges: constructing a viable national economy and securing the western region from American advances. Between 1867 and 1905, two internal wars were fought, the economy was transformed, immigrants entered the country in droves, and five new provinces joined the Dominion: Manitoba (1870), British Columbia (1871), Prince Edward Island (1873), and Saskatchewan and Alberta (both 1905). Over the following 40 years, Canada fought in two world wars and suffered through a major economic depression. Canada also changed structurally. Corporate capitalism took hold, mass consumerism flourished, and class conflict intensified. Canada became more urbanized. Women entered the workforce as never before. Slowly, a fledgling sense of Canadian nationalism began emerging from the broad shadows cast by Britain and the United States. This chapter examines these and other events, ending with the Second World War.

The "American System" and the National Policy

Confederation in 1867 was meant in part to deal with Canada's recurrent economic problems and the threat of American expansion (Chapter 5), but the new nation still faced the question of what specific policy to adopt to meet these goals.

Looking around the world today, models of economic and social development are dominated by "globalization," based on economic liberalism and free trade. In the 19th century, however, several models competed. The British system, with ideas similar to current neo-liberalism—a belief in free markets and limited state involvement in the economy (see Chapter 8)—provided one model, but outside of England it was widely rejected. A European system of economic development existed, based on activist government policies, investment banks, and technical education (Watkins, 1991), but it was largely unknown and culturally distant from the Canadian experience. A third model, however, known as the American system, existed next door and was therefore more familiar to Canadian business and political leaders.

The American system employed three elements: (1) high tariffs to protect domestic manufacturers, therefore making it cheaper to buy domestically than to import products, a policy often referred to as **import substitution**; (2) expanded transportation systems (especially railways), built through federal contracts and guaranteed loans to private operators, and designed to bring products to market; and (3) immigration to supply domestic markets (Hofstadter, 1958:250; also Laxer, 1989; Watkins, 1991). In 1878, the Conservative government of Sir John A. Macdonald ran on a platform of economic development based on the American system, naming it the National Policy.

The National Policy's specific elements were not new to Canada. Tariffs, for example, were already an established tradition in Upper and Lower Canada by the time of Confederation. Thus, in 1879, tariffs were raised from 17.5 percent to 29 percent on a host of manufactured and agricultural goods, and in 1887 they were raised again, especially on iron, steel, farm machinery, and textiles (Norrie and Owram, 1996:249). Likewise, railway construction was by then another Canadian tradition going back to the boom years of 1850 to 1859 (Norrie and Owram, 1996:191). What was fundamentally different about the National Policy, compared with previous economic policies, was its broader aim of nation building, specifically incorporating the western territories into Canada.

Canadian politicians, and the people of Ontario specifically, had long viewed the lands west to the Pacific as theirs to occupy. By the 1860s, however, competing notions of manifest destiny were evident along the 49th parallel. In British Columbia, 30,000 people were attracted to the Fraser Valley and Cariboo regions by the discovery of gold in 1857 (Norrie and Owram, 1996:213; see also Easterbrook and Aitken, 1988). Many of these immigrants were Americans, veterans of the recent California boom, who began pressing for annexation to the United States (see Morton, 1997).

Similar pressures were exerted at Red River (later Winnipeg). Between 1850 and 1860, the population of Minnesota, just south of Manitoba, increased by 2,730 percent (Winks, 1998:4). As arable land filled up, Americans pushed further northward into the Red River area, where in 1869 they too pressed for statehood. Caught between the Canadian and American visions for the West were the Aboriginals and Métis (see Chapter 9). In both cases, Sir John A. Macdonald's vision won out, aided by the use of force in Manitoba and the Territories and the promise of a railway in British Columbia.

Between the two newest provinces lay the vast North-West Territories. The Territories had long been the Hudson's Bay Company's preserve. Especially after its merger with the rival North West Company in 1821, the entire region, including British Columbia, had fallen under the company's control. By the 1860s, however, the fur trade was dying and the West was coveted by Canadian politicians, for whom the National Policy was already a gleam in the eye, not to mention Americans with their own plans for the Territories.

In 1870, the Hudson's Bay Company formally transferred the Territories to Canada, and settlement of the western region slowly began. Immigrants first settled in the "postage stamp" province of Manitoba, so-called because of its shape. When the best land was taken, later settlers pushed further westward into the Territories. In 1883, however, land prices soared, the Canadian Pacific Railway faced bankruptcy, and immigration stopped (see Morton, 1997). The word *secession* was voiced in British Columbia (Conway, 2014).

The times were especially hard on the West's Aboriginal and Métis people. The buffalo were disappearing, the fur trade no longer provided a secure living, and unscrupulous traders were wreaking havoc on the people. In 1885, rebellion in the Territories provided the Canadian government with justification to send in troops (see Chapter 9). The long-promised rail link to British Columbia was completed in time to facilitate their arrival.

Thus, by 1885, Canada had expanded to fill the top shelf of North America from sea to sea. The National Policy's alleged economic benefits, however, had yet to be realized: Public debt was rising, markets were failing, and immigration was stalled. Why was the National Policy slow in delivering expected results?

Several factors limited Canada's economic takeoff. First, beginning roughly in 1873 and lasting for six years, the increasingly integrated world economy entered a prolonged slump that reduced demand for Canadian commodities and hindered the necessary flow of investment capital into Canada (Hobsbawm, 1995:86–87; Lairson and Skidmore, 1997; Saul, 1969). Second, the National Policy depended upon the development of western agricultural land, specifically for wheat exports. But development of the Canadian West could not proceed until the more productive lands of the American West were "used up" (Morton, 1997) and new strains of wheat were developed to meet the Canadian Prairies' harsh climate and short growing season (Norrie and Owram, 1996:227; also Laxer, 1989). Third, public debt acquired throughout the early 19th century meant that after 1867 the Canadian government employed private interests to build railways by granting them monopoly rights and free land (Laxer, 1989). The companies, however, restricted railway construction to areas of profitability and limited land development to keep prices high, with the result that the massive immigration necessary to make the National Policy viable never occurred.

By 1890, the mood in Canada was sour. Many felt the National Policy had failed. Demands were renewed for a reciprocity treaty with the United States; some called for outright annexation.

The federal election of 1891 was held in this context of uncertainty. The Liberal Party under Sir Wilfrid Laurier ran on a platform of unrestricted reciprocity with the United States (Morton, 1997; also Norrie and Owram, 1996). By contrast, the Conservatives under Macdonald appealed to anti-American and pro-British sentiments (see Granatstein, 1996) in successfully arguing that free trade would inevitably lead to Canada's political annexation, and won.

Canada's first free trade election occurred just as the world economy was rebounding. After 1896, investment capital was freed up and circulated throughout the world at an unprecedented rate (Dunning, 1983). Internationally, consumer demand increased, while production also expanded in the wake of the second industrial revolution (Norrie and Owram, 1996:223).

At last, the National Policy had its desired result. Fuelled by the Yukon gold rush (see Chapter 10), increased mining in the Canadian Shield, the development of the newsprint industry, and large-scale hydroelectric developments on the Great Lakes and the St. Lawrence, between 1900 and 1913 Canada (especially southern Ontario) experienced its second economic boom (Aitken, 1959). While Canada's real gross national product (GNP) grew at a compound rate of only 2.38 percent during the period from 1870 to 1896, between 1896 and 1913 it grew at a rate of 6.48 percent (Norrie and Owram, 1996:218).

Integral to this growth was a change in Canada's labour market. Though still dependent upon primary sector employment (for example, resource extraction industries such as agriculture, mining, and forestry), employment in the secondary sector (manufacturing, construction, and the like) also grew under the National Policy, as did employment in the tertiary or service sector, where the commodities exchanged have no tangible form (e.g., teaching, retail trade, hotels, and finance). By 1891, 49 percent of Canada's labour force worked in primary industry, 20 percent in secondary industry, and 31 percent in the service sector.

But the benefits of economic growth were unevenly shared: Aboriginal peoples were particularly left out (see Part 3), but others outside the industrialized region of southern Ontario soon also felt the sting of colonization.

Regions and Regionalism

Sociological concepts, such as class and gender, condition the way we see social relations. Within Canada, the concept of region is particularly persuasive as the lens through which Canadian society is often viewed. Such an emphasis is not misplaced, even if the definition of *region*, like so many concepts, and a host of terms that stem from it, is unclear (see Box 6.1).

Regional (and subregional) divisions already existed at Canada's inception. Quebec and Ontario are obvious examples, with different cultures, histories, and economies, but there were also differences among Canada's three Maritime provinces of Prince Edward Island, Nova Scotia, and New Brunswick, and between the people of this region and the two larger provinces, over issues of political control and economic development.

Nova Scotia provides a useful example. Important early on for its geopolitical and military position on the Atlantic coast, by 1867 Nova Scotia was a major economic player with a diversified economy that sported the building of ships and the manufacture of steel, glass, and rope. At the same time, however, the businesses were small, often family affairs. Moreover, they were not well integrated into the British North American economy, instead remaining dependent upon exports to Britain. In consequence, much of the province's business and political elite opposed joining Canada, fearing that Confederation would negatively impact the region's (and their) prosperity, a fear that proved correct in the years after 1885, as the direction of economic flows changed to benefit Ontario's larger manufacturing sector. In effect, Nova Scotia and

Box 6.1: What Is a Region?

A **region** is a territory defined physiologically, geographically, climatically, culturally, politically, or economically. This definition is not as straightforward as it seems, however. Even using the same definition, two people may recognize different regional boundaries. Thus, regions do not exist as physical things. Rather, they are "read into" the landscape, socially constructed (as symbolic interaction theory argues), and then reified (see the Introduction).

The concept of **regional differences** refers to observable variations between two or more regions. For example, the West Coast is wet, while the Prairie provinces are dry. Likewise, Ontario is home to much of Canada's manufacturing, while Alberta is a major producer of oil.

Regionalism refers to an individual's personal identification with a region. In this sense, regionalism provides a sense of who we are, much as nationalism does.

Regional alienation refers to a sense of grievance based on the belief that regional differences are not "natural" but result from the actions of individuals or groups residing outside the region.

Sources: Brodie, Janine. 1990. *The Political Economy of Canadian Regionalism.* Toronto: Harcourt Brace Jovanovich; Westfall, William. 1993. "On the Concept of Region in Canadian History and Literature." In *A Passion for Identity: An Introduction to Canadian Studies,* edited by D. Taras, B. Rasporich, and E. Mandel. Scarborough, ON: Nelson Canada; and Wonders, William. 1993. "Canadian Regions and Regionalism: National Enrichment or National Disintegration?" In *A Passion for Identity: An Introduction to Canadian Studies,* edited by D. Taras, B. Rasporich, and E. Mandel.

much of the Maritime region exchanged its status as a colony of Britain for that of being a colony of central Canada.

Canada's fourth Atlantic province, Newfoundland, provides another example. Sparsely populated and less economically diversified than Nova Scotia, economic development in Newfoundland nonetheless increased into the late 19th century, built upon the inshore fisheries and the port city of St. John's. As in Nova Scotia, however, the island experienced a major downturn after 1880 as the importance of the island on shipping routes declined.

Each of these regions faced developmental problems common to the rest of Canada, and responded with similar policies. Economically, they were geographically far from markets, hence subsidies and other inducements were given to private developers to build transportation systems (roads, railways, and canals). As the Atlantic provinces also lacked investment generally, generous inducements were given to companies to settle in these areas. Likewise, land was opened up cheaply to encourage immigration.

Often, however, people in these regions found that development was uneven and centred on a single commodity—the fishery in Newfoundland, for example—resulting in recurrent cycles of boom and bust (Norrie and Owram, 1996). (Amid the Great Depression and facing bankruptcy in 1933, the Newfoundland legislature voted to suspend its operations and reverted to a Crown colony of Britain in the following year.) In turn, economic instability often resulted in political unrest, with its own distinctive regional characteristics (Clark et al., 1975; Brym and Sacouman, 1979). This unrest has had national consequences. As many scholars have pointed out, Canada does not have a national economy, nor even national policies of development, but instead regional policies that too often pit one region against another (see Clement and Williams, 1989; Laxer, 1991), a situation no more evident than in the history of western Canada.

Immigration and the West

Pre-Confederation, in 1861, 3.2 million people lived in British North America. Canada's population stood at only 4.8 million (Table 0.1) 30 years later. By contrast, the population of the United States during this period rose from 31.4 million to nearly 63 million (*Time*, 2013:675). Nature and geography, mercantilist policies, and American competition held Canada's population growth at bay. Indeed, so unattractive was Canada relative to its southern neighbour during the 50-year period from 1851 to 1901 that only 1.9 million people entered Canada while 2.2 million left, most of them for the United States (McKie, 1994:26).

By 1896, however, the American West was virtually filled and the depression over. In Ottawa, administrators fervently pursued immigrants. By 1900, the West's Aboriginal peoples had largely been pushed aside (see Chapter 9). Now the prohibitive land regulations (Laxer, 1989) were changed, the railways were forced to open up land for settlement, and irrigation construction was proceeded with, especially in the arid region known as the Palliser Triangle (see Norrie and Owram, 1996:227). Above all, Canadian immigration was promoted as never before. The result was the largest influx of immigrants in Canadian history. Nearly 2 million immigrants entered Canada between 1901 and 1911 (McKie, 1994:28; Hall, 1977); another 375,756 arrived in 1912, and 400,870 more in 1913 (see Table 6.1).

The immigrants came primarily from three main areas: the United States, Great Britain, and Europe. Of these groups, the first two were viewed as particularly desirable. American immigrants had capital, goods, and Prairie farm experience, and they could "fit in" ethnically into Canada. Thus, the number of American immigrants to Canada increased from 2,400 in 1897 to 12,000 in 1899. Between 1902 and 1905, 40,000 to 50,000 Americans annually entered Canada (Hall, 1977:70). For their part, British immigrants, with the exception of the Irish, were viewed as loyal to the Crown. The immigration boom attracted large numbers of people from the rural areas of England and Scotland. By 1901, however, the great wave of British immigration, fuelled in the early 19th century by a population boom in the Old Country, was declining. Thus, Canadian immigration officials hesitantly expanded their search for immigrants beyond the traditional Anglo countries, into northern and eastern Europe.

Table 6.1: Immigration to Canada 1852–2012

Year	Immigrants	Year	Immigrants	Year	Immigrants	Year	Immigrants	Year	Immigrants	Year	Immigrants
1852	29,307	1880	38,505	1908	143,326	1936	11,643	1964	112,606	1992	254,790
1853	29,464	1881	47,991	1909	173,694	1937	15,101	1965	146,758	1993	256,641
1854	37,263	1882	112,458	1910	286,839	1938	17,244	1966	194,743	1994	224,385
1855	25,296	1883	133,624	1911	331,288	1939	16,994	1967	222,876	1995	212,865
1856	22,544	1884	103,824	1912	375,756	1940	11,324	1968	183,974	1996	226,071
1857	33,854	1885	79,169	1913	400,870	1941	9,329	1969	161,531	1997	216,035
1858	12,339	1886	69,152	1914	150,484	1942	7,576	1970	147,713	1998	174,195
1859	6,300	1887	84,526	1915	36,665	1943	8,504	1971	121,900	1999	189,951
1860	6,276	1888	88,766	1916	55,914	1944	12,801	1972	122,006	2000	227,456
1861	13,589	1889	44,543	1917	72,910	1945	22,722	1973	184,200	2001	250,637
1862	18,294	1890	75,067	1918	41,845	1946	71,719	1974	218,465	2002	229,048
1863	21,000	1891	82,165	1919	107,698	1947	64,127	1975	187,881	2003	221,349
1864	24,779	1892	30,996	1920	13,824	1948	125,414	1976	149,429	2004	235,823
1865	18,958	1893	29,633	1921	91,728	1949	95,217	1977	114,914	2005	262,242
1866	11,427	1894	20,829	1922	64,224	1950	73,912	1978	86,313	2006	251,640
1867	10,666	1895	18,790	1923	133,729	1951	194,391	1979	112,093	2007	236,753
1868	12,765	1896	16,835	1924	124,164	1952	164,498	1980	143,140	2008	247,247
1869	18,630	1897	21,716	1925	84,907	1953	168,868	1981	128,642	2009	252,172
1870	24,706	1898	31,900	1926	135,982	1954	154,227	1982	121,179	2010	280,689
1871	27,773	1899	44,543	1927	158,886	1955	109,946	1983	89,192	2011	248,748
1872	36,758	1900	41,681	1928	166,783	1956	164,857	1984	88,276	2012	257,887

1873	50,050	1901	55,747	1929	164,993	1957	282,164	1985	84,346
1874	39,373	1902	89,102	1930	104,806	1958	124,851	1986	99,353
1875	27,382	1903	138,660	1931	27,530	1959	106,928	1987	152,084
1876	25,633	1904	131,252	1932	20,591	1960	104,111	1988	161,588
1877	27,028	1905	141,465	1933	14,382	1961	71,689	1989	191,555
1878	29,807	1906	211,653	1934	12,476	1962	74,586	1990	216,452
1879	40,492	1907	272,409	1935	11,277	1963	93,151	1991	232,806

Sources: Citizenship and Immigration Canada. 1996. *Citizenship and Immigration Statistics 1996*: Cat. no. MP22-1/1996. Ottawa: Citizenship and Immigration; and Government of Canada. 2013. *Facts and Figures 2012—Immigration Overview: Permanent and Temporary Residents* (www.cic.gc.ca/english/resources/statistics/facts2012/permanent/01.asp). Modified August 7, 2013.

Certain ethnic groups, however, remained restricted from entering Canada. These groups included "Negroes," "Orientals" (including East Indians), "Galicians" (meaning eastern Europeans), Italians, and Jews, whom, it was argued, were urban people who could not adjust to the demands of Prairie life and who, in any case, would not fit into Canadian culture. In the case of the Chinese, government policies were explicitly racist. Good enough to be employed as cheap labour in building the railways, and later in British Columbia's mines and forestry industry (Morton, 1997:122), Chinese immigrants were not considered good enough, however, to become citizens. The first of several "head taxes" was enacted on the Chinese in 1885 to prevent workers from being able to afford to bring over family members (Hall, 1977:78).

Immigration moved in waves across the Prairies, leaving distinctive cultural traces that remain today in every province. Between 1871 and 1891, Manitoba's population increased from 25,000 to 153,000, rising to 461,000 by 1911 (see Table 0.1). The early days saw Anglo farmers and expatriate elements of Ontario's upper class settle in southern Manitoba (Lower, 1983:195), though a sizable Icelandic contingent also moved to Manitoba in 1873, settling north of Winnipeg. Later European immigrants who arrived, finding the best land already taken, settled in the north and west of the province, while Anglo-Americans moved into the southwest (Widdis, 1997). But these waves of immigrants to Manitoba were not only ethnically distinct. Over time, they also transformed Manitoba's class structure and political culture. By the start of the First World War, Winnipeg had developed a strong working-class culture, the product of British and Eastern European immigrants, paving the way for the strike of 1919 (see below) (Wiseman, 2007).

The combined population of the entire Territories in 1871 was about 48,000 (not including Aboriginal peoples). By 1901, Saskatchewan's population alone had risen to 91,000, while that of Alberta stood at 73,000. Ten years later, these provinces' populations had risen to 492,000 and 374,000, respectively (see Table 0.1). Before the turn of the century, there were significant francophone populations in Saskatchewan's north and southwest. Like western Manitoba, however, the early 20th century saw Saskatchewan settled by the second wave of Anglo and European immigrants, not to mention (in the province's southwest) American immigrants (see Wiseman, 2007; Widdis, 1997).

Alberta, too, at the turn of the century had a large francophone population, located mainly in the northeast. In the late 19th century, however, Anglo-American immigrants moved into southern Alberta, bringing with them populist notions of direct democracy, as well as strong beliefs in possessive individualism (Harrison, 2000). American influence in the south was further strengthened after the discovery in 1914 of oil at Turner Valley, a harbinger of events to come. But other ethnic groups also arrived. The mining communities of the southern Crowsnest Pass, for example, filled with southern (especially Italian) and eastern Europeans, while the province's north similarly experienced an influx of central and eastern Europeans.

British Columbia's population growth was slower, but steadier. Approximately 36,000 people (not including Aboriginals) lived in BC at Confederation in 1871, rising to 179,000 by 1901 and 393,000 by 1911. Much of this non-Aboriginal population was English and Scottish in origin, via Canada's Atlantic region; others were American. In the early stages, settlement was tied to the coastline and Vancouver Island. Later, settlers spread inland, along paths set by the railways. These late arrivals, employed in construction and resource extraction, brought a distinctive working-class consciousness (see Robin, 1993). At the same time, sizable numbers of Chinese and Japanese immigrants also came.

There were other distinctive populations throughout the West who were unable or unwilling to be "fitted" easily into the dominant British mould. Black communities developed early on, for example, in Breton, Alberta, and around Maidstone, Saskatchewan. Catholic, and Anglican and other Protestant religious orders dominated Canadian religious and cultural life. Nonetheless, some persecuted religious minorities also found a home in the West. With the moral and financial support of Count Leo Tolstoy, some 7,400 Doukhobors arrived in Canada between December 1898 and April 1899, settling near Yorkton and Prince Albert, Saskatchewan (Mayes, 1999). Other religious minorities—Mennonites in southern Manitoba, Hutterites throughout western Manitoba and southern Alberta, and Mormons in southern Alberta—also arrived.

National concern focused on how best to assimilate the "new Canadians" whom James S. Woodsworth (1874–1942), a Methodist minister and later first leader of the Co-operative Commonwealth Federation, in 1909 called the "strangers within our gates" (Woodsworth, 1909/1972). Outside Quebec, Canada's immigration and other policies (e.g., education) at the time enforced **Anglo-conformity**—the requirement that subordinate group members express outward compliance with the values and practices of the dominant British group—and reflected broad public sentiment and fears of social discord.

In the early 1900s, "Canadians were more provincial than cosmopolitan, more openly biased than politically correct, and each social grouping more protective of its niche in society" (Lyon, 1998:26). Small differences, even the neighbourhood one lived in, were magnified in importance. There was a recognized pecking order even within the British "tribes": Scots and English on top, Irish Catholics on the bottom.

In extreme cases during the period from 1901 to 1911, **racism** (the belief that one racial category is innately superior or inferior to another) and **xenophobia** (the fear of what is strange) resulted in anti-immigrant riots in several cities (see Palmer, 1982). Anti-Oriental riots broke out in Vancouver during the recession year of 1907 (Whitaker, 1991), for example. In most cases, however, public reaction took the form of occupational or social exclusion, or snickering at the new immigrants' "exotic" and "peculiar" lifestyles. Groups kept to their own turf. Finally, we should keep in mind the well-meaning, if often paternalistic, efforts of many individuals, voluntary agencies, and church groups who assisted the new immigrants' adjustment to Canadian life.

The immigration boom ended in 1913. That year, more than 400,000 immigrants landed on Canada's shores. But the world economy was slowing down, and the war that followed ended immigration almost entirely. In 1914, only 150,484 immigrants entered Canada, and the number declined further during the war years (see Table 6.1, above).

The wartime decline in immigration was presaged in May 1914 by the arrival in Vancouver harbour of a former collier ship, the *Komagata Maru*. Immigration officials met the ship, which carried 376 East Indians, mainly Sikhs, and refused the migrants entry. The ship was held in port for two months, its passengers detained while a Canadian warship kept watch. Finally, 21 of the migrants were allowed to disembark. The rest, however, returned to India on the ship. Arriving there in September, they were greeted by British gunfire. Eighteen died (Jensen, 1988).

Between Two Empires

Why did many in English Canada view new immigrants as such threats during this period? First, English Canada in 1900 certainly was parochial and ethnocentric. Second, however, English-Canadians remained anxious over the country's future. As we have seen, Canada's hesitant economic development after 1867 raised questions not only about the National Policy but Confederation generally. While some, such as the liberal historian and journalist Goldwin Smith, positively embraced the idea (see Smith, 1891/1971), many others feared annexation by the United States.

A group of eminent intellectuals argued for strengthened ties to the British Empire. These "Canadian imperialists"—among them novelist Sara Jeannette Duncan, Presbyterian minister and educator George Monro Grant, humorist and political economist Stephen Leacock, and educator Sir George Robert Parkin—idealized the Loyalist legacy, especially elitism and anti-Americanism. Nostalgic for a simpler life and opposed to the raw materialism, industrialism, and urbanism represented by the United States (Cook, 1995), the imperialists saw Canada as having a kind of religious "mission" on earth (Berger, 1976; Romney, 1999).

Canadian imperialism and its organizations had some successes in pressuring the Canadian government to increase ties with the Crown. In 1897, Prime Minister Sir Wilfrid Laurier re-established preferential trade with Britain (Norrie and Owram, 1996:249). In 1899, to the chagrin of his French-Canadian supporters, Laurier also sent Canadian soldiers overseas to fight alongside Britain in the Boer War (Miller, 1999).

After 1900, however, the United States' economic influence upon Canada steadily increased while that of Britain waned. Trade and investment figures highlight this trend.

Throughout the late 19th century, Canada's trade with the United States and Britain steadfastly shifted toward the former. While British import and export trade with Canada continued to grow during this period, its overall importance to the Canadian economy declined relative to that of the United States. By 1891, Canadian imports from the United States surpassed those from Britain and thereafter never looked back. Export trade took longer to shift, picking up additional steam during the First World War as Canadian industry met British wartime demand. By 1921, however, Canadian exports to the United States, like imports, also surpassed those to Britain (Marchildon, 1995; see also Alford, 1996:38–39).

This shift in trade was, in part, reflected in the amount and form of British and American investment in Canada. Canadian economic development historically has relied upon massive amounts of foreign capital. The boom after 1896 involved especially huge investments, with foreign capital flows into Canada increasing from 2.1 percent of GNP in 1897 to a high of 17.7 percent in 1912 (Norrie and Owram, 1996:241). Until 1922, Britain was Canada's chief source of investment capital. That year, however, American investment totalled $2.6 billion (50 percent of total foreign investment), compared with $2.5 billion (47 percent) from the U.K. (Norrie and Owram, 1996:324; also Marchildon, 1995; Li, 1996). Thereafter, American investment in Canada, both in actual dollars and as a percentage of foreign capital, was never overtaken.

There was also an important difference between American and British foreign investment. Foreign investment takes two forms: portfolio investment (e.g., long-term investments, such as bonds and loans) and direct investment (the actual ownership of productive property). British investment took predominantly the portfolio form. By contrast, American investments abroad were predominantly direct in nature. In Canada, direct investment involved buying up Canadian resources and firms or establishing branch plants. This meant, in practice, that American capital had greater control than British capital over the Canadian economy as a whole, but especially in certain areas of the economy—automobiles, newsprint, metals, and petroleum—that would become important in the 20th century. The increasing number of American firms in Canada also helps explain the rising level of exports to, and imports from, the United States: American firms were trading with themselves.

As always, Canada's need for capital and the prospect of jobs were balanced against the fears of American control leading to annexation (see the Sara Jeannette Duncan quotation at the beginning of this chapter). These fears reached a symbolic climax in 1911.

In 1910, Laurier became the first Canadian prime minister to visit western Canada. There, he heard repeated complaints from farmers regarding the National Policy's tariffs. Remembering his defeat in 1891, but still dedicated to the liberal notion of open markets, Laurier's government worked out a limited reciprocity agreement with the United States (Norrie and Owram, 1996:250). Laurier believed the Conservatives under Sir Robert Borden would not seriously oppose the agreement, as they had for years held out hopes of gaining a similar agreement.

The American House of Representatives and Senate gave the agreement swift passage, but the outspoken remarks of several congressmen that the agreement would hasten Canada's annexation (see Champ Clark quotation at the beginning of this chapter) soon became front-page news in Canada. The election that followed saw Laurier's Liberals defeated by a potent mixture of fear, anti-Americanism, and protectionism (see Granatstein, 1996; Orchard, 1998; Norrie and Owram, 1996). The issue of free trade hence disappeared from public debate, revived only in the late 1980s by the Conservative government of Brian Mulroney (Chapter 7).

Outside of Quebec, Canada in 1914 remained decidedly British, but American economic, cultural, and geopolitical influence over Canada was gradually increasing. The war that followed reinforced this emerging pattern.

A World Interrupted: Canada and the First World War

In 1914, years of political posturing, unbridled jingoism, and imperial competition resulted in war. Estimates for the number of people killed in the First World

War (1914–1918) range between 8.5 and 16 million; the number of wounded is estimated at more than 21 million (Stearns, 1975:277–278). Russia's casualties were the greatest, made even greater by the revolution and the famines that followed, but Germany, France, and Britain also suffered enormous costs, including in effect the wasting of an entire generation. Many who returned bore wounds that were not always obvious. In strictly monetary terms, the total direct costs of the war were $180 billion, the indirect costs $151 billion, substantial amounts for the time (Langer, 1948:951).

Canadian wartime losses amounted to 60,661 Canadian troops dead, among them a host of "war poets," such as John McCrae. Another 1,600 people were killed (6,000 more wounded) at Halifax harbour on December 6, 1917, when an ammunition ship collided with a freighter, exploding with the force of an atomic bomb and destroying much of Halifax. The year following war's end saw nearly as many Canadians die as a result of a worldwide influenza epidemic, caused indirectly by the war.

European places like Ypres, Passchendaele, and Vimy Ridge entered Canada's history, while a small number of individuals—mainly "air aces" like Billy Bishop, William Barker, and A. Roy Brown—became household names for a time. Small towns and villages throughout Canada erected monuments to the dead that still stand, augmented later by more names from other wars. Some towns were named after the battles (such as Vimy, Alberta); however, Berlin, Ontario (founded by people of German ancestry who were now afraid to admit their heritage), was renamed in 1916 after a British war hero, Field Marshal Lord Kitchener, who had died at sea.

Beyond the obvious losses of men, money, and material, the war had several major impacts on Canada, some more immediate than others.

First, the war altered Canada's position relative to other powers within the international state system. The Russian, German, Austro-Hungarian, and Turkish empires were destroyed; the British Empire was hobbled. By contrast, the United States, already the world's leading economy in 1914 (Norrie and Owram, 1996:223), ended the war as the world's leading creditor country (Palmer, with Colton, 1957:691), second only to Britain as the world's chief direct investor (Dunning, 1983), and in military matters an increasingly formidable power. A series of invasions and military coups after 1898, underpinned by the Monroe Doctrine, had ensured that, in the Americas especially, the United States reigned largely unopposed (Zinn, 1995:399).

Second, the war discredited old institutions and traditional authorities, especially in Europe but also in Canada, paving the way for the rise of new political ideologies and parties during the 1920s and 1930s. Third, at the same time, the role of the state in Canadian society (as elsewhere) expanded. Canadian government spending on goods and services, for example, rose from 10 percent of GDP in 1913 to 14.5 percent of GDP in 1914 and remained at that level throughout the war (Norrie and Owram, 1996:300). The bureaucratic infrastructure of government also expanded, notably through the introduction of the Pension Act of 1919, which provided disability pensions for returning soldiers and which, in turn, gave impetus to later federal intervention in social policy (Rice and Prince, 2013:209). On the revenue side, the Canadian government introduced business and personal income taxes, a temporary wartime measure that soon became a permanent part of Canada's fiscal landscape.

Fourth, the First World War accelerated in all countries a series of social changes. Women, for example, entered the labour force in larger numbers, finding work, especially in the growing public bureaucracies (Lowe, 1987). As in most combatant countries, women in Canada also gained the vote (in 1918). (The previous year, Louise McKinney [1868–1931] had been elected to the Alberta legislature, becoming the first woman to hold such an office in the British Empire.) But there were other social changes, notably the continued decline in rural population and the growth of cities (see below), a gradual shift from primary production to secondary manufacturing and services, and the expansion of wage labour.

Fifth, as noted earlier (Chapter 2), the Conscription Crisis became part of the panoply of grievances dividing the French and English in Canada. Sixth, as also noted earlier, the war slowed immigration to Canada—indeed, killing off many who might have come—thus cutting off an important leg of Canada's National Policy.

Finally, the war also sparked in English Canada a fragile sense of independent nationalism. In 1914, Canada was still very much a British colony. Britain's declaration of war on August 4 meant that Canada was itself immediately at war, its troops under British command. By 1918, however, there was a distinct Canadian Corps led by Canadian officers. Canada's separate signing of the Treaty of Versailles in 1919 and garnering of a seat in the newly founded League of Nations further symbolized the country's growing independence from Britain.

Canada, 1919–1929

The troops returning in 1919 were greeted with high unemployment, rising inflation, declining wages, and mounting anxiety. In Winnipeg in the spring of 1919, a dispute between labourers in the metal and building trades and management over collective bargaining rights, wages, and working conditions escalated into a general strike of 24,000 workers that lasted 40 days. The strike encouraged sympathy strikes (particularly in the West) involving another 88,000 workers. It ended on June 25, amid lingering images of the RCMP on horseback charging into a crowd of strikers at the corner of Portage and Main—causing 30 casualties and at least 1 death—and of federal troops occupying the streets of Winnipeg (Conway, 2014:86–88).

There was also anxiety in rural Canada, especially in the West. Mass immigration between 1901 and 1911 (see above) had transformed the Prairie landscape and, in less than two decades, had led to Ontario being supplanted as Canada's wheat-growing region (see Morton, 2000:28; Norrie and Owram, 1996:233). This transformation came at a cost, however.

The West, reliant upon a single commodity, was particularly at the mercy of world markets. When wheat prices collapsed at the end of the war, Canada's agrarians revolted at the ballot box. The United Farmers of Ontario were elected in 1919. Subsequently, the United Farmers of Alberta gained office in 1921, and the United Farmers of Manitoba in 1922. Meanwhile, at the federal level, in 1921 the newly founded National Progressive Party elected 65 MPs, the most successful showing by a federal "third party" until the Reform Party in the 1990s (see Chapter 8). Among the Progressives was the first woman to be elected to Canada's Parliament, Agnes Macphail (1890–1954).

Why the widespread discontent following the war? The explanation lies in a series of social and economic trends that, beginning in the early 20th century, were rapidly transforming Canadian society.

Think for a moment about life in mid-19th-century Canada. Family and community were the focal point around which people's lives revolved. People, other than arriving immigrants, travelled little in their lifetime. Much of Canada was still rural (80 percent in 1871). The family was still the site of production and consumption, gender roles were largely fixed, markets were mainly local, and few people were full-time wage labourers. Well into the late 19th century, small, paternalistic, family-operated businesses—what Marx termed the "petite bourgeoisie"—dominated the Canadian economy, while family farms were the norm.

After 1900, however, a new form of capitalism emerged: corporate capitalism. Moving beyond the limitations of either petit bourgeois or mercantile or industrial capitalism, corporate capitalism (sometimes also termed "monopoly capitalism") is large-scale, highly capitalized, centralized, and non-competitive (Heron and Storey, 1986; Li, 1996). Between 1900 and 1920, for example, the number of manufacturing units in Canada fell from 76,000 to 22,000 (Li, 1996:16; also Morton, 2000:29). Similarly, the number of Canadian banks went from 36 in 1900 to 22 in 1914 to 10 in 1928 (Li, 1996:20). Canada was quickly transformed from a society of petite bourgeoise agrarians and nascent small-time industrialists into one in which large-scale manufacturing (especially in the automobile industry) and services began playing an increasingly large role. At the same time, industrialization and economic development were unevenly distributed, and thus increased regional divisions within Canada.

The rise of corporate capitalism had particular impact in shaping Canada's labour market. Demand for labour grew. Thus, the number and percentage of wage labourers in the overall labour force grew rapidly (see Li, 1996:34). As in the past, labour demand was met in part by new immigrants, but immigration during the 1920s did not recover to prewar levels. Instead, labour demand was met largely through natural population growth, rural migration—hence, in part, the agrarian revolts of 1919 to 1922—and a still largely untapped source: women.

The period leading up to the 1920s saw increasing numbers of women entering the workforce. Between 1911 and 1921, the participation rate for women aged 14 to 65 rose from 16.6 percent to 19.9 percent, compared with a rise from 82 percent to 89.7 percent for men in that age group during the same period. By 1931, the participation rate of women in the labour force was 23 percent, compared with 87.2 percent for men (calculated from Denton, 1983). Women's jobs, however, were mostly in the low-paying clerical occupations that arose in the burgeoning bureaucracies of the state and corporations (Lowe, 1987; Krahn, Lowe, and Hughes, 2015).

The situation of women was changing at the political level, too. In 1929, five women—Irene Parlby, Louise McKinney, Henrietta Muir Edwards, Emily Murphy, and Nellie McClung—won an especially important legal battle when the Judicial Committee of the Privy Council in Britain (then Canada's highest court) overturned an earlier ruling by the Supreme Court of Canada and declared that women were "persons" under the law and therefore could hold public office (Bellamy and Irving, 1981).

Meanwhile, corporate capitalism was also changing Canada's workplaces and workplace relations in important ways. This period saw the introduction of new forms of organization to the workplace. Bureaucratic principles and management techniques based on Frederick Taylor's principles of scientific management were introduced into factories and soon also into white-collar work. These organizational forms increased managerial control over workers and deskilled workers in the name of efficiency and higher profits, but also increased worker alienation and labour conflict (Krahn et al., 2015).

In the long run, concentrated capitalism also meant concentrated labour, resulting in the rise of trade and industrial unions. In the short run, however, these changes led to growing alienation and intensified class conflict, as evidenced in Winnipeg.

Technology, the war, the increasing role of the state, and the rise of corporate capitalism changed Canada in other ways during this period. Canada gradually became more urbanized. In 1901, 63 percent of Canadians still lived in rural areas. By 1921, however, a nearly equal number of Canadians lived in urban and rural areas (see Table 6.2), with the urban population remaining consistently higher than the rural population since 1931. Canada's urbanization had begun.

In 1901, Montreal (population 328,172) and Toronto (population 209,892) were still Canada's largest cities. The next largest city was Quebec City, with 68,840 people. Over the next 10 years, however, Winnipeg grew from 42,340 to 136,035 people, while Vancouver's population increased from 29,432 to 120,847. By 1921, Hamilton and Ottawa also exceeded 100,000 people, joined in 1931 by Quebec City (see Norrie and Owram, 1996:334).

Mass consumption became a reality in the 1920s (Bell, 1996:66; Robbins, 2014). The automobile was the chief symbol of this new consumer society. Cars had been around for decades; by the 1920s, however, mass production technology, low cost, and easy credit made it possible for more people to own cars. The number of cars registered in Canada increased from 275,000 in 1918 to 1.9 million in 1929 (Norrie and Owram, 1996:327), a growth rate far outstripping even the United States (see Hofstadter et al., 1957:642).

By the 1920s, British influence, though still strong, was waning; the pull of American culture was increasing. Many of Canada's corporations were American-owned. Faintly, however, a more independent Canadian culture was stirring within English-speaking Canada, spearheaded by artists such as Emily Carr and the Group of Seven. Prints of these artists' paintings soon appeared in banks and magazines across the country, promoting images of their land that few Canadians had actually seen.

The first half of the 1920s in Canada, as elsewhere, began with a recession. By contrast, the years between 1925 and 1929 were a time of prosperity, marked by illegal gin, Charleston-dancing flappers, Model T Fords, and jazz. Then, suddenly, the prosperity ended.

Table 6.2: Canadian Rural and Urban Population, 1851–2011 (in thousands and percentage)

Year	Total Population	Urban	Rural	Urban (%)	Rural (%)
1851	2,436,297	318,079	2,118,218	13	87
1861	3,229,633	527,220	2,702,413	16	84
1871	3,737,257	722,343	3,014,914	19	81
1881	4,381,256	1,109,507	3,271,749	25	75
1891	4,932,206	1,537,098	3,395,108	31	69
1901	5,418,663	2,023,364	3,395,299	37	63
1911	7,221,662	3,276,812	3,944,850	45	55
1921	8,800,249	4,353,428	4,446,821	49	51
1931	10,376,379	5,572,058	4,804,321	54	46
1941	11,506,655	6,252,416	5,254,239	54	46
1951	14,009,429	8,628,253	5,381,176	62	38
1956	16,080,791	10,714,855	5,365,936	67	33
1961	18,238,247	12,700,390	5,537,857	70	30
1966	20,014,880	14,726,759	5,288,121	74	26
1971	21,568,305	16,410,785	5,157,520	76	24
1976	22,992,595	17,366,970	5,625,625	76	24
1981	24,343,177	18,435,923	5,907,254	76	24
1986	25,309,330	19,352,080	5,957,250	76	24
1991	27,296,856	20,906,872	6,389,984	77	23
1996	28,846,758	22,461,207	6,385,551	78	22
2001	30,007,094	23,908,211	6,098,883	80	20
2006	31,612,897	25,350,743	6,262,154	80	20
2011[1]	33,476,688	27,147,274	6,329,414	81	19

Note: 1. Starting with the 2011 Census, the term population centre replaces the term urban area. For more information, please see Statistics Canada's note titled "From Urban Areas to Population Centres," available at www.statcan.gc.ca/subjects-sujets/standard-norme/sgc-cgt/notice-avis/sgc-cgt-06-eng.htm. This note explains the new terminology and classification of population centres. The rural population from 1981 to 2011 refers to persons living outside centres with a population of 1,000 *and* outside areas with 400 persons per square kilometre. Previous to 1981, the definitions differed slightly, but consistently referred to populations outside centres with a population of 1,000.

Sources: Statistics Canada. 2011d. "Population, Urban and Rural, by Province and Territory (Canada)." Ottawa: Statistics Canada (www.statcan.gc.ca/tables-tableaux/sum-som/l01/cst01/demo62a-eng.htm). Modified February 4, 2011.

The Depression Years, 1929–1939

In October 1929, the New York stock market crashed. Stock values on the New York Stock Exchange alone fell by 40 percent (Palmer, with Colton, 1957:780), and 10 percent of private wealth vanished, virtually overnight (Norrie and Owram, 1996:296). Despite repeated statements by government officials in Canada, the United States, and elsewhere that the economy was sound, the crisis soon spread. As industrial and financial capital collapsed, production fell and unemployment rose, resulting in more uncertainty, a further decline in consumption, and yet more layoffs throughout the industrialized, capitalist world.

During the Depression's worst period (1932–1933), the **unemployment rate**—generally calculated as the number of people out of work and actively looking for work divided by the total number of labour force participants, including the unemployed (Krahn et al., 2015:67)—reached 23 percent in Britain and Belgium, 24 percent in Sweden, 27 percent in the United States, 29 percent in Austria, 31 percent in Norway, 32 percent in Denmark, and no less than 44 percent in Germany (all rates from Hobsbawm, 1995:90–93). Canadian unemployment rose officially from 3 percent in 1929 to between 25 and 30 percent in 1933, the peak year (Rice and Prince, 2013:53). How much these official statistics underestimate the problem is open to question, however.

Canada suffered uniquely in the Depression because, first, its economy was export dependent; second, its range of exports was small and lacked diversification; and third, its chief export market was the United States, a country that became highly protectionist during the Depression (Norrie and Owram, 1996:354). Canada's economy was insufficiently developed, self-contained, and integrated to withstand the shocks. In consequence, during the period from 1929 to 1933, Canadian industrial production fell by 50 percent, exports by 67 percent, and construction by 90 percent (Rice and Prince, 2013:53).

Within Canada, the Depression hit the West hardest. The region's economy was particularly dependent on wheat for export. Additionally, much of the West experienced a long, harsh drought. The worst hit area was southwest Saskatchewan, resulting in an estimated quarter of a million people abandoning their farms during the 1930s (Berton, 1991:291). However, for the Maritimes, in semi-permanent recession since the 1880s, and many Aboriginal reserves that were often outside the capitalist market system, the Depression hardly seemed a change.

The Depression halted, even reversed for a time, years of social change in Canada. Barter, for example, partially replaced the money economy. Cars morphed into horse-drawn carriages, nicknamed (after Prime Minister R. B. Bennett [1870–1947]) "Bennett buggies." The process of urbanization slowed. Immigration to Canada all but ended; indeed, for the first time since the 19th century, more people left Canada than entered (McKie, 1994). Most Canadians did not mind, however. Anti-immigrant sentiment in the 1930s was high. The Canadian government took special steps to halt the entry of people viewed as communist agitators and "troublemakers," or people who were deemed to not fit in. In a replay of the *Komagata Maru* incident, in 1939 the Canadian government refused the disembarkment of 907 Jews aboard the liner *St. Louis*, resulting in their return to Europe and, ultimately, to Nazi Germany's death camps (Abella and Troper, 1982; Whitaker, 1991).

The Depression damaged Canada's social fabric. Crime rates rose. The year 1931 witnessed an "unprecedented wave of bank holdups" (Berton, 1991:88). Fuelled by Prohibition south of the border, booze became a growth industry throughout Canada, from the Maritime ports to the cities of southern Ontario to the Crowsnest Pass region of Alberta. Suicide rates climbed while birth rates, already dropping in the 1920s, declined further to 3.0 per 1,000 in 1936 and 2.8 per 1,000 in 1941 (see Li, 1996:155), figures not seen again until the 1960s. In the 1930s, few people wanted to have children, not knowing if they could care for them.

Yet Canadians' sense of being part of a larger society also expanded during the Depression. Some young Canadians experienced the country first-hand, hopping freight cars and travelling from community to community in search of work (Berton, 1991). Others learned about Canada and the world at large through the cinema, though in the main the silver screen provided not access to, but an escape from, reality. By contrast, radio played a major role in incorporating Canadians into society. Bennett's government recognized in the early 1930s the importance of radio in nation building and so created the Canadian Radio Broadcasting Commission. Radio manufactured an "imaginary collective," creating and sharing common experiences for Canadians from coast to coast, and related to a host of events, from Foster Hewitt's hockey broadcasts, to disasters both real and fake (e.g., *The War of the Worlds* broadcast), to human interest stories (e.g., the Dionne quintuplets).

Bennett's Conservative government expanded the role of the state in other ways, notably through the creation of the Bank of Canada and the Wheat Board. In areas of economic and social concern during the early years of the Depression, however, Bennett followed the policies of his American counterpart, President Herbert Hoover (1874–1964), in steadfastly arguing that governments could not—*should* not—do anything to interfere in the economy. In both countries, problems of the poor, the hungry, and the unemployed were thrown back on local authorities and charities. The role of governments was to balance budgets, protect private property, and maintain social order.

In Canada as in the United States (Zinn, 1995), there were strikes and protests by workers throughout the decade. The state did not hesitate to use coercive force to deal with them. At Estevan, Saskatchewan, in 1931, low wages, poor living conditions, and unsympathetic management led to a confrontation between striking mine workers and police in which three strikers were killed, eleven more injured, and five policemen sent to hospital (Berton, 1991:126–127).

As the Depression continued, Canadian governments grew increasingly wary of worker unrest—the mining town of Blairmore, Alberta, twice elected a communist town council in the mid-1930s, which promptly erected Karl Marx Park—and took further steps to curtail political agitation. One such step involved setting up work camps for the unemployed in remote rural areas. Before being shut down in 1936, Canada's relief camps housed 170,248 men and provided 10.2 million worker-days of relief

(Howard, 1999:2408), but the food was poor and predictable, the clothing of army issue and distinctly prison-like, and camp control was authoritarian and punitive (Berton, 1991:176). The camps became breeding grounds of hopelessness and anger.

In June 1935, 1,500 young men of various racial and ethnic backgrounds, refugees from the British Columbia camps, set off from the Vancouver waterfront by train, headed for Ottawa, picking up supporters along the way. They were forcibly halted at Regina, however, on Dominion Day. Under orders from Prime Minister Bennett, the RCMP and local police moved into an unsuspecting crowd of 1,500 people on Regina's Market Square to arrest the trek leaders. A panic ensued. By the time it was over, 12 trekkers and 5 Regina citizens were hospitalized for gunshot wounds, 39 RCMP officers had been hospitalized for injuries (none from gunfire), and 1 plainclothes detective lay dead. Over 100 people were arrested. Twenty-eight went to trial; eight were eventually convicted and sent to jail (see Berton, 1991).

In the main, unrest in Canada during the Depression paled in comparison with other countries where strikes, protests, civil violence, and state repression were daily news. Still, it was a time of serious political unrest. Both communism and fascism gained converts in Canada. The authorities treated communists, or those suspected of being communists, far more harshly than fascist sympathizers, who garnered at least tacit support from some members of Canada's political, business, and religious elite (see Robin, 1991; Berton, 1991:22).

Two less politically extreme alternatives to communism and fascism arose in western Canada. Like the agrarian parties of the early 1920s, both were **populist** parties; that is, parties built around mass political movements—and mobilized around symbols and traditions congruent with the popular culture—that express a group's sense of threat, which arises from powerful "outside" elements and is directed at the group's perceived "peoplehood."

In Saskatchewan, the Co-operative Commonwealth Federation (CCF), built around a broad coalition of farmers, labourers, religious activists (mainly Protestants), and university-trained intellectuals (mainly economists), melded traditional Prairie populism with democratic socialism. Its leader was James S. Woodsworth (see above), a former Methodist minister who had been among those arrested in the 1919 Winnipeg Strike and later elected to the House of Commons as a National Progressive in 1921. In 1944, another minister, Tommy Douglas (1904–1986), led the CCF to success in Saskatchewan, bringing to power the first socialist government in North America. In 1961, the CCF became the New Democratic Party (Lipset, 1968a; also Conway, 2014) (see Chapter 7).

In Alberta, Reverend William Aberhart (1878–1943), a radio evangelist, adopted the economic ideas of a British engineer, Colonel Douglas, in founding the Social Credit Party. In 1935, Aberhart's party was elected, defeating the tired and scandal-ridden United Farmers of Alberta. Broadly supported by farmers and workers alike (E. Bell, 1993), the party at first mixed populist rhetoric and evangelical zeal, demanding protection against bankruptcy, unemployment insurance, and public health care. Following a series of legislative setbacks, Aberhart's death in 1943, and the discovery of oil in the late 1940s, however, Social Credit became a fairly conventional conservative party opposed to government intervention in the economy (Finkel, 1989).

Government policies in Canada in the 1930s were shaped by events in the United States. In 1932, Franklin Delano Roosevelt was elected president. Soon Canadians as well as Americans were hearing Roosevelt over the still-new medium of radio. Canadians liked what they heard. Like Canada, the United States was faced with massive unemployment, civil unrest, and populist agitation. Unlike Bennett, Roosevelt offered solutions to the crisis, embarking on a series of economic and social reforms between 1933 and 1938 that protected farmers, regulated banking, gave relief to the unemployed, extended labour rights, and fuelled the economy through public works projects (Langer, 1948:1053–1056; Hofstadter et al., 1957:650–675; Zinn, 1995:382–384).

Facing political pressures, in 1934 Bennett's government launched its own version of Roosevelt's "New Deal": unemployment insurance, minimum wages, legislation dealing with hours of work, marketing legislation, and laws against price-fixing (Langer, 1948:1060; Morton, 1997:205–206). The reforms came too late, however, to save Bennett's government from defeat in 1935 at the hands of William Lyon Mackenzie King's Liberals.

Under King, as under Bennett, the state's role in building Canada grew stronger. The Canadian Radio Broadcasting Commission became the Canadian Broadcasting Corporation, and government-owned Trans-Canada Air Lines was launched (Morton, 1997:207). The economy, however, continued to languish. After a short period of recovery, both Canada and the United States entered recession again in 1937. Labour and civil unrest continued. A strike in 1937 by General Motors' workers in Oshawa, Ontario, over poor wages and union recognition led to violence. Meanwhile, ties to the United States grew, symbolized by the signing of a limited reciprocity agreement in 1935, King's almost fawning relationship with Roosevelt, and the latter's comments at Queen's University in 1938, pledging American support in the event of war (Martin, 1982).

Canada and the Second World War

On September 1, 1939, at the end of what English poet W. H. Auden once referred to as a "low, dishonest decade," Germany invaded Poland. Within days, much of the world, except the United States and the Soviet Union, was at war.

It is impossible to overstate the war's human devastation. Hobsbawm (1995:43) notes that the "losses are literally incalculable" because many of those killed were civilians and "much of the worst killing took place in regions, or at times, when nobody was in a position to count . . . ." Gilbert (1991:746) estimates the total of civilian and military deaths for China, Japan, the Soviet Union, Germany, Poland, and Yugoslavia, and assorted Jewish populations within Europe to be "in excess of forty-six million," suggesting that the total figure for all countries is at least 50 million deaths (Keegan, 1990), and perhaps much more.

More than a million Canadian men and women (out of a total population of only 11 million) joined the army, navy, or air force during the Second World War. In total, 42,042 Canadian military personnel were killed and 53,145 wounded. Canada's financial expenditures rose from $118 million in 1939–1940 to $4.5 billion in 1943–1944 (Stacey and Hillmer, 1999:2552). Public debt rose from $5 billion in 1939 to $18 billion by 1945 (Norrie and Owram, 1996:378), resulting in a net federal public debt of nearly 107 percent of GNP in 1946–1947 (Chorney, 1989:43).

Journalist Blair Fraser (1967:14) later wrote, "The most that could be said was that World War II had done less damage to the fabric of the nation than World War I did." The lasting effects of the Conscription Crisis of the Second World War were less—no "gaping wound," merely "a bruise." There were "no jobless veterans begging or rioting in the streets," no "counterpart of the Winnipeg General strike," though a strike at Windsor in 1945 proved significant for labour relations. Canada's liberal self-image, however, did take a beating for its treatment of ethnic minorities, notably the expulsion and internment of men, women, and children of Japanese extraction.

Yet there were also positive gains. Dragged from their towns and farms, many Canadians saw their own country for the first time; many also gained a sense of their own and Canada's place internationally. Likewise, skills were developed that paid dividends in the post-war years.

The Canadian economy benefited as a whole. The war dragged Canada and the world out of the Depression and set off Canada's third great period of economic growth, a period that continued into the early 1960s (Aitken, 1959). Enormous investments in economic infrastructure had turned Canada into a gigantic armaments factory, producing thousands of aircraft, tanks, anti-aircraft guns, tracked vehicles, and machine guns (James, 1997:509). These plants were soon refitted to meet peacetime consumer demand. Likewise, Canada ended the war with a huge and disciplined navy and the world's fourth-largest merchant marine, important to export trade. At the same time, however, Canada's military and economy were more integrated than ever into the American orbit.

Conclusion

Within a few short decades of Confederation, the world of 1867 had ceased to exist except in memory and old photographs. The basic contours of Canadian society in the second half of the 20th century were forged by events during this early period in Canada, up to the end of the Second World War; the after-effects continue into the 21st century.

First, the United States clearly arose as successor to the British Empire, both internationally and in its influence upon Canada. In the words of Innis (1956), Canada had gone from colony to nation to colony. In this context, new notions of English-Canadian nationalism arose with consequences seen 20 years later (Chapter 7).

Second, English Canada's culture changed during this period, largely as a result of mass immigration in the first decade of the 20th century, to be resumed after 1945. Thus was set in motion a further decline of English dominance, the distinctive pattern of ethnicity that marks Canadian provinces, and the enactment of Canada's policy of multiculturalism.

Third, corporate capitalism largely replaced petit bourgeois capitalism. No elements of Canadian society, from family size to social values to urban growth, were left unmarked by this event. By the end of the Second World War, the vast majority of Canadians, including large numbers of women, had become part of the paid labour force.

Fourth, the state gradually came to play a larger role in the lives of Canadians. The crumbling of traditional society and its institutions, accelerated by the wars and the Depression, resulted in the deepening and centralizing of state policies, evidenced particularly in the nascent welfare state. More than ever, state and civil society became inseparable.

Canada, in 1945, seemed a land of promise. On its outskirts, however, lay new perils to Canadian identity, harmony, sovereignty, and peace. The next chapter examines Canada's efforts to wend its way through the post-war world's uncertain waters.

Key Terms

Anglo-conformity
import substitution
populist
racism
region
regional alienation
regional differences
regionalism
unemployment rate
xenophobia

Critical Thinking Questions

1. Why did Canada not adopt the European model of economic development after 1867?
2. In what ways did corporate capitalism benefit from the major wars and other social disasters of the 20th century?
3. Is unemployment a "natural" phenomenon or is it socially produced?
4. In what sense is it possible to think of the First and Second World Wars as one long war?
5. In what ways did the Second World War bring Canada closer into the American economic, social, and political orbit?

Recommended Readings

Brodie, Janine. 1990. *The Political Economy of Canadian Regionalism*. Toronto: Harcourt Brace Jovanovich Canada.
Brodie's book explores the different meanings of regionalism while also tying it to political development.

Finkel, Alvin. 1989. *The Social Credit Phenomenon in Alberta*. Toronto: University of Toronto Press.
This book provides a social and historical account of the rise of the Social Credit Party in Alberta in the 1930s.

Krahn, Harvey, Graham Lowe, and Karen Hughes. 2015. *Work, Industry, and Canadian Society*. 7th ed. Toronto: Nelson.
In its seventh edition, this is the definitive text on work and industry in Canada.

Laxer, Gordon. 1989. *Open for Business: The Roots of Foreign Ownership in Canada*. Toronto: Oxford University Press.
Winner of the 1991 John Porter Award for best book published in sociology, this book examines empirically the social and political relationships underlying economic development.

Robin, Martin. 1991. *Shades of Right: Nativist and Fascist Politics in Canada, 1920–1940*. Toronto: University of Toronto Press.
Robin's book details the little-known rise of nativist and fascist movements in Canada during the 1930s.

Related Websites

Bank of Canada
www.bankofcanada.ca/en/about/history.html
Amid the Great Depression, the Bank of Canada was created in 1934 by an act of Parliament as a means of stabilizing Canada's monetary system. This is a history of the bank.

Canadian War Museum
www.warmuseum.ca/splash.html
Located in Ottawa, the Canadian War Museum is Canada's national museum of military history.

Museum for Human Rights
museumforhumanrights.ca
Though criticized in some quarters for its selectivity, the museum (located in Winnipeg) provides an important venue for highlighting the important issue of human rights.

Canadian Society on Video

Between Two Wars. 1987. National Film Board of Canada, 87 minutes, 8 seconds.
Three films cover the period from the end of the First World War to the onset of the Second World War: *The Good, Bright Days* (1919–1927), from the Armistice of 1918

to the economic boom of the late 1920s (28 minutes, 55 seconds); *Sunshine and Eclipse* (1927–1934), from the end of the boom to the onset of the Great Depression (28 minutes, 57 seconds); and *Twilight of an Era* (1934–1939), the years leading up to war in Europe (29 minutes, 3 seconds).

On Strike: The Winnipeg General Strike, 1919. 1991. National Film Board of Canada, 19 minutes, 46 seconds.
The dramatic story of the Winnipeg General Strike in 1919 as told through the recollections of the men and women who were there.

Reckoning: The Political Economy of Canada, "Part 1: Riding the Tornado." 1986. National Film Board of Canada, 57 minutes, 22 seconds.
Do not let its date dissuade you: This video explains the phenomenon of boom and bust cycles related to staples-driven economies better than any video produced since.

CHAPTER 7

FROM COLONY
TO NATION—
TO COLONY?

There are two ways to conquer a country—one is by force of arms; the other is by taking control of its economy.

—American Secretary of State John Foster Dulles in the 1950s

Living with you is in some ways like sleeping with an elephant. No matter how friendly or temperate the beast, one is affected by every twitch and grunt.

—Prime Minister Pierre Trudeau to the National Press Club in Washington, 1969

We built a country east and west and north. We built it on an infrastructure that deliberately resisted the continental pressure of the United States. For 120 years we've done it. With one signature of a pen, you've reversed that, thrown us into the north-south influence of the United States and will reduce us, I am sure, to a colony of the United States, because when the economic levers go the political independence is sure to follow.

—Liberal Opposition Leader John Turner, 1988 free trade debate

Please be serious.

—Prime Minister Brian Mulroney's response to Turner

Introduction

The end of the Second World War stimulated in Canada an unprecedented, albeit uneven, period of economic expansion and social and political transformation. Increased demands for skilled labour were ultimately met by immigration and the increased workforce presence of women. Birth rates soared, before resuming in 1956 a longer trend of decline (Li, 1996:70), and family forms changed. The modern welfare state evolved, underpinning a compromise between labour and capital. And, on April 1, 1949, Newfoundland joined Confederation, though some Newfoundlanders to this day claim they annexed Canada.

Meanwhile, abroad, the hot menace of fascism was replaced by the Cold War. Anti-communist hysteria gripped the United States and soon found its way across the border. At the Bretton Woods conference held in 1944, Western countries, led by the United States, designed an economic regime meant to rebuild and stabilize the post-war world and—not incidentally—pave the way for orderly capitalist expansion. Key institutions of this plan included the International Monetary Fund (IMF) and the World Bank (also known as the International Bank for Reconstruction and Development). The General Agreement on Tariffs and Trade (GATT), formed to negotiate tariff reductions and the removal of other trade barriers, joined these institutions in the early 1950s (Lairson and Skidmore, 1997). Politically, the international post-war era also saw the creation of the United Nations, successor to the failed prewar League of Nations.

Consumption flourished throughout the next decade, underpinned by continued strong economic growth. Suburban Canada was born, aided by the ubiquitous presence of automobiles. Television invaded family living rooms and bedrooms, creating a more-or-less mass media culture.

In Canada, the prosperous 1950s gave way in the early 1960s to renewed concerns of American control. In the context of growing American defeats abroad and social discord at home, and in contraposition to Quebec's demands for sovereignty, a new nationalism arose in English-speaking Canada. In the 1970s, English-Canadian nationalism paved the way for a further expansion of state involvement in the economy and society, referred to as "Canadianization." By the 1980s, however, debt and internal divisions hobbled the Canadian state, setting the stage for the adoption of free trade and a new developmental paradigm more generally: neo-liberalism.

This chapter traces the key events and changes that occurred in Canadian society between the end of the Second World War and the fateful Canadian election of 1988.

Canada and the United States in the Cold War Era

In 1945, Canada's 12 million people seemed enviably blessed. The country had a large public debt, but also ample resources much in world demand: steel, timber, wheat, and oil, for example. It also had an established industrial and state infrastructure. Abroad, Canada's chief economic competitors lay in ruins. Reconstruction in Europe and the subsequent Korean conflict (1950–1953) fuelled demand for Canadian resources. Meanwhile, at home, a large reservoir of consumer power was ready to be unleashed (Norrie and Owram, 1996). The result was generally high economic growth throughout the 1950s, yet the new prosperity also hid real political, economic, and cultural dangers.

To the north, across the Arctic waters, lay the Soviet Union, which only months before had been a staunch ally. Now it was suddenly the enemy. The period was highlighted by the case of Igor Gouzenko, a Soviet embassy clerk who in September 1945 defected with documents revealing Soviet espionage in Canada (Finkel, 2012). As in the United States, anti-communist hysteria soon became a staple of Canadian political and cultural life.

To the south lay a more subtle threat, however. The United States ended the Second World War as the globe's lone superpower, possessor of the world's strongest economy and a large battle-hardened military. The United States alone also had the atomic bomb, a fact quickly interpreted by several American politicians and religious figures as symbolizing America's divinely chosen status among countries (Ungar, 1991).

More than ever, in 1945 Canada fell under America's sway. Following a secret meeting between Canada's Prime Minister King and U.S. President Roosevelt at Ogdensburg in 1942, the two countries' militaries became strategically linked. These links became more formal in 1949, when Canada became part of the newly formed North Atlantic Treaty Organization (NATO), an anti-communist self-defence bloc headed by the United States. In the 1960s, Canada also became the United States' northern partner in a continental defence pact, the North American Air Defense Command (NORAD).

Economically, wartime production had stimulated Canada's growth but had also increased links with the United States. After the war, American companies began buying up Canada's redundant war factories and retooling them for civilian use. Much the same occurred regarding Canadian resources. In 1952, American President Harry Truman (1884–1972) released the Paley Report (Roberts, 1998). The report, issued as the Cold War heated up, suggested Canada's resource wealth made it a potential economic rival to the United States. The report argued further that the American government should do everything in its power to secure Canadian raw materials, especially uranium, in the service of defending the United States.

America's cultural presence in Canada also grew during and after the war through cinema and radio, and increased again in the 1950s with the rise of television. The fact that a disproportionate number of Canadians found employment in movies and television, both in front of the camera and behind the scenes as writers, technicians, and directors, did not change the impact. The productions were generically American, meant to be sold first into the United States' larger market, then resold abroad to foreigners, including Canadians, who were increasingly entranced by that empire's technology, power, and wealth.

But the American presence in Canada was also increasingly demographic and social. Construction of the Alaska Highway during the Second World War (see Chapter 10) was completed almost entirely with American labour and investment, and the development of large-scale oil production in Alberta after 1947 resulted in a further influx of American money, personnel, and expertise (House, 1978; Richards and Pratt, 1979). Calgary quickly became the Houston of the North, and an ethos of rugged individualism slowly replaced the settler traditions of co-operation and community. In the long term, the development of Alberta's oil industry set the stage for interprovincial rivalry and federal-provincial hostility, while furthering a continental approach to development at odds with the tenets of the old National Policy.

Internationally, the immediate post-war period saw the start of the divvying up of the world between state communism, represented by the Soviet Union, and corporate capitalism, represented by the United States. During the early period, the final dismantling of colonialism provided opportunities for both superpowers to expand into new territories, notably the Middle East, Africa, and, especially following the French retreat from Vietnam in the late 1950s, Asia. Both the Soviet Union and the United States took measures to secure their strategic borders and expand their influence throughout this period and after. The Soviet Union invaded Hungary in 1956, Czechoslovakia in 1968, and Afghanistan in 1979. Similarly, the United States, acting on the Monroe Doctrine (Chapter 5), continued a long policy after the 1950s of threatening, destabilizing, and sometimes invading sovereign countries throughout the Americas. Occasionally, as during the Cuban missile crisis in 1963, the boundaries of American and Soviet interests intersected, bringing the world close to nuclear war. For Canada, finding its way in this bipolar world was a task not easily accomplished.

There was one notable similarity, however, between communist and capitalist countries: the continued growth of the state. This was no less true in the case of Canada.

From State to "Welfare State"

Far from being a nation-state or even a multinational state, Canada may best be described as a state-nation (see the Introduction). That is, the state often came first, and then set about constructing the institutions of nationhood. In the course of this construction, Canadian society was also changed in particular ways.

The Hudson's Bay Company was a kind of prototype for early Canadian development, with other corporations following (for example, the Canadian Pacific Railway). From building railways and canals to building defensive fortifications, to the pacification of the West by the North-West Mounted Police to pave the way for immigrants, the Canadian state (including, to a lesser degree, the provinces) acted as chief architect, administrator, and banker. Until the 1930s, much of this involvement was minimalist and remained tied directly or indirectly to furthering private capital accumulation. Slowly, however, the state's involvement in Canadian society entered broader areas of nation building (such as CBC Radio) and social policy.

To a degree, the state's initially minimalist role in Canadian society in 1867 is understandable, given that Canada was a small, still largely pre-capitalist and pre-industrial country. Thereafter, however, the Canadian state and society expanded together. Five periods mark this expansion, transformation, and later retrenchment (see Rice and Prince, 2013). The first period occurred between 1867 and 1914, during Canada's initial industrialization and expansion. The second period occurred between the start of the First World War and the end of the post-war boom, from 1914 to 1929, during which corporate capitalism took hold and Canada urbanized (see Li, 1996). The third period, from 1929 to 1945, began with the Depression and ended with the close of the Second World War. The fourth period, with which we are primarily concerned here, began in 1945 and continued roughly to 1973 (Rice and Prince, 2013:208), at which time the structural basis of the post-war welfare state came into question, leading to the fifth stage, marked by the retreat of the state under neo-liberal globalization (see Chapter 8).

Each period saw a gradual shift in government functions in areas of social policy. Rice and Prince (2013:56–57) note that responsibility for social welfare changed over time in five important ways. First, responsibility shifted from the private to the state sector. Second, responsibility shifted from lower to higher levels (that is, from municipalities to the provinces or the federal government). Third, the administration and provision of services became more centralized and under the auspices of professional authorities. Fourth, there was a move in policy approaches from remedial to preventive policies.

A fifth related, but gradual, change saw a shift from particularistic to more universal policies, though this was never extensive and has in recent years been curtailed (Chapter 8). The Pension Act of 1919 was Canada's first universal program in the sense that it was provided to all returning soldiers without resort to a means test. A further move toward standardization and universality occurred with the federal government's introduction of the Old Age Pensions Act in 1927.

In Canada, as elsewhere in the industrialized West, the greatest public expansion into social programs, however, occurred after the Second World War (see Turner, 1981; Rice and Prince, 2013). Influential in this regard were the ideas of British economist John Maynard Keynes (1883–1946), who argued that the state had a role in ensuring economic and, hence, political stability. With full employment as the goal, counter-cyclical measures to ward off market fluctuations became a standard feature of post-war government planning. In the context of the Cold War, such interventions also proved useful in showing that capitalism could be responsive not only to market demands but also to human needs.

As in other countries, the war enlarged, centralized, and strengthened the Canadian state, increasing its capacity to act. Important models for action were garnered from President Roosevelt's New Deal administration in the United States (Chapter 6) and from the Beveridge Report produced in Britain. Within Canada, the Royal Commission on Dominion-Provincial Relations (Rowell-Sirois Commission) in 1940 and the federal government's Advisory Committee on Post-war Reconstruction (the Marsh Report) in 1943 provided similar blueprints for reshaping Canada's system of social security.

Pressures for political change came from a variety of sources, particularly unions, social activists, progressive think tanks (such as the League for Social Reconstruction), and the CCF (see Chapter 6). In 1940, these pressures resulted in King's government bringing in Canada's first Unemployment Insurance Act. This was followed in 1944 with the introduction of the Family Allowances Act, a universal program that (at the time) substantially assisted young families in raising their children and, not unintentionally, also encouraged Canada's birth rate.

These tentative steps at reshaping Canada's social security system were nothing compared with what followed, however. Health care provides a specific example of this process of state expansion.

The post-war period saw the Canadian federal government set up a system of national health grants (1948). This was followed in the 1950s by the Old Age Security Act (1951), the expansion of government assistance under the Unemployment Insurance Act (1956), and the passing of the Hospital Insurance and Diagnostic Act (1957), which introduced federal cost-sharing to pay for provincial hospital insurance. In 1965, the compulsory Canada Pension Plan and Quebec Pension Plan were introduced. The following year, the Guaranteed Income Supplement Plan and Canada Assistance Plan were created, and medicare (a system of public health insurance) was introduced with the passage of the Medical Care Act (see Li, 1996:84–85).

Together, programs such as health care, education, unemployment insurance, social allowance, and others make up what is often referred to as the Canadian "welfare state." What are they and what do welfare states do?

Briefly, the term **welfare state**, often referred to in Canada and the United States as the Keynesian welfare state (KWS) after John Maynard Keynes, refers to a system of state provision of people's social needs outside private markets. Unlike regular commodities that are bought and sold, social needs are de-commodified and provided as a right of citizenship (Esping-Andersen, 1990).

In practical terms, the post-war KWS resulted from a compromise between capital and labour. Labour accepted owners' right to a profit and to make decisions regarding company matters. In return, capital (that is, owners and managers) accepted labour's right to organize and bargain. The state, meanwhile, provided the legal, political, and often financial resources underpinning this compromise. During the Depression and the Second World War, for example, Canada experienced a series of bitter strikes (Roberts, 1998:7). In 1944, however, the Canadian government passed legislation granting private sector workers the right to organize, to bargain collectively, and to strike (Panitch and Swartz, 1988). This and similar labour legislation and decisions (such as unemployment insurance and the Rand Formula, which requires the deduction of union dues from paycheques even if an employee in a unionized workplace does not want to belong to the union) introduced a period of relative harmony to labour relations. In effect, the state set the rules for Canada's post-war form of capital accumulation, but in doing so, the state also shaped, more broadly, the contours of Canadian society.

The state's greater role in Canadian society after the Second World War was not restricted, however, to areas of health and social security. The late 1960s also saw the state—both federal and provincial—finance a rapid expansion of post-secondary education (Wanner, 1999). Between 1971 and 2001, the percentage of Canadians 15 years of age and older with some post-secondary education rose from 17.1 to 35.6, while the percentage of those with university education climbed from 4.8 to 15.4 (look ahead to Table 12.5). By 2010, 24.8 percent of Canadians in the labour force had a university degree, while 35 percent had a post-secondary certificate or degree (City of Toronto, 2014).

The state also became more concerned with issues of nation building, social inequality, and social justice. Especially worth noting in regard to these are the Royal Commission on Bilingualism and Biculturalism, also known as the Dunton-Laurendeau Commission (Chapter 2); the Hawthorn Report into Canada's Aboriginal peoples (see Chapter 11); and the Royal Commission on the Status of Women in Canada, also known as the Bird Commission. Echoing the call of U.S. President Lyndon Johnson (1908–1973) for a war on poverty, similar efforts were made in Canada, highlighted by a massive government study (Mincome, 1973–1980) into the efficacy of a guaranteed annual income (see Hum, 1983), in which many sociologists (including one of this text's authors) played a small role.

How does Canada's welfare state compare with that in other countries? Though neoliberal policies have placed enormous pressures on all welfare states (see Chapter 8), three broad types of welfare states can still be discerned (Esping-Andersen, 1990; Wahl, 2011): (1) conservative welfare states, such as Austria, France, Germany, and Italy; (2) social democratic welfare states, such as Sweden, Norway, and Denmark; and (3) liberal democratic welfare states, such as the United States and Australia (see also Olsen, 2002). Of these, social democratic welfare states have high taxes, but also extensive and universal social programs, while liberal democratic welfare states have low taxes, few social programs, and programs that are means-tested, that is, not available to all. Conservative welfare states fall somewhere in between, with moderate to high taxes and fairly extensive programs, but ones that often are designed to maintain traditional class and gender hierarchies.

Canada's welfare state is primarily of the liberal kind, emphasizing means-testing, modest levels of social transfers, belief in individualism, faith in markets, and protection of private profits (Li, 1996; Rice and Prince, 2013:4). At the same time, however, Canada's welfare state has embraced some conservative elements (e.g., an emphasis upon maintaining the traditional family and gender roles) and social democratic elements (e.g., social equality and, albeit limited, universality) (see Baker, 1996; Finkel, 2012; Rice and Prince, 2013). As many feminist theorists have noted, none of these existing models adequately deals with the problem of poverty for many women, insofar as their situation results from barriers to full participation in the labour force. That is, while decommodification is not unimportant to issues of equality, it does not address the real inequalities resulting from a stratified labour market (see Olsen, 2002).

By European standards, Canada's welfare state programs historically have not been generous or extensive and appear so only when compared with that of the United States (see Finkel, 2012; Olsen, 2002), and this generosity has declined over time, as we will explore in the next chapter. Closely tied to the rise and fall of Canada's welfare state during the post-war years were also material, cultural, and ideological changes in the role of women.

Women in the Changing Canadian Society

As the Second World War began, women at last had formal political power, but little actual political, economic, or social power. The war started the process of changing this.

Economically, while many women remained to work the farms left behind by men fighting overseas, many others were pressed into non-traditional occupations, such as welding in wartime factories or taking on higher administrative roles in the growing public service. Fears that the end of war would result in mass unemployment proved unwarranted. Indeed, the demand for skilled labour increased (see below) and women now ably filled this demand.

Of course, some women did return to the home and to unpaid labour to raise families; the post-war baby boom was about to start. But a large number of women, single and otherwise, remained in the workplace—though only casually and often shunted to the service end of the labour market—attracted both by the social and economic opportunities. Moreover, the period after 1945 saw an intensification of consumerism that could be met only by families with one-and-a-half (if not two) salaries.

To a degree, women's increasing participation in Canada's labour force mirrored that of women in other countries. Participation was more intense in Canada, however, and increased even more after 1960. Between 1960 and 1975, female labour force participation rose from 28 percent to 45 percent, increasing again over the next decades to nearly 63 percent in 2008 (Krahn et al., 2015:68). In turn, these changes in the female participation rate set off a series of unintended consequences for fertility rates, family structures, gender roles, family and individual finances, and public services, such as the need for child care. After 1975, for example, dual-income families, rather than single-income families, became the Canadian norm.

Other interrelated factors, besides labour economics and increased consumerism, were changing the situation of women, however. The idea of greater individual freedom took hold in Canadian society as elsewhere. Likewise, the 1950s saw a loosening of cultural prescriptions for male and female gender roles and behaviours, which were sometimes reflected, and sometimes not, in Hollywood films. Technological advances in the 1960s—notably, the contraceptive pill—further changed sexual behaviours and gender relationships. In turn, and over time, these things also began changing family structures. Divorce rates rose while, despite the incidence of the baby boom, the average family size declined.

Underlying the changing status of women in Canada (and elsewhere) was also a transformative change in the dominant ideology brought about by feminism. Though far from a unified ideology, the rise of feminism has been broadly viewed as involving three stages or waves. First-wave feminism, beginning in the mid-19th century, sought—largely with success—to gain for women equal property rights and the right to vote. The 1960s brought second-wave feminism, inspired by writers such as Simone de Beauvoir, Kate Millett, and Germaine Greer. Whereas the attention of first-wave feminists had been upon political institutions, second-wave feminists, many of whom had been involved in student protest movements, concentrated on establishing women's organizations from below, in civil society (Brym, 2014:455). Third-wave feminism, begun in the 1990s, critiqued the position of women belonging to ethnic minorities and the dominance of middle-class White women within the feminist movement (Morrow, 1994:18).

As in the previous century, those in dominant positions—but also many in Canada at large, including some women—often opposed feminist demands for greater equality. In the mid-1970s, a backlash against the gains made by women began building, finding its political champions in the 1980s and 1990s in a series of New Right political parties and movements. The complaints of these parties and their supporters were not just economic but more often cultural; that is, women's demands (and gains) upset Canada's patriarchy (see the Introduction) and, more broadly, what Hiller (1987) termed the **symbolic order**, that is, the set of values, beliefs, and behaviours that lend predictability to our everyday surroundings. (One ironic measure of feminism's success, however, was the growing reluctance of many younger women, having not experienced the earlier struggles and wary of some stereotypes, to self-identify themselves as feminists.) More often than not, after the 1970s, these fears were focused not only on the feminist movement but also on Canada's changing ethnic and racial profile.

Labour Markets, Immigration, and Multiculturalism

Canada's KWS, like that of other countries, was predicated on a prosperous national economy and full employment, since employed workers could pay taxes and would not draw upon social security. At the macro level, Canada's finances to pay for these expanded programs remained particularly dependent, however, upon the export of raw resources. Meanwhile, Canada's economy after the Second World War also underwent a substantial transformation.

Most especially, Canada experienced continued change in its labour market with jobs in the secondary and service industries coming to dominate. As you will recall (Chapter 6), in 1891, 49 percent of Canada's labour force still worked in primary industry, compared with 20 percent in secondary industry, and 31 percent in the service sector. By 1951, however, 31 percent of Canada's labour force worked in the secondary sector, of which the auto industry was key, while 47 percent were employed in services (Krahn et al., 2015:75).

The following decades saw a further growth in Canada's service industries, while the other sectors declined in relative importance to the economy. At the same time, however, the service sector itself became increasingly polarized between jobs in an upper tier (employing well-paid and well-educated people, often "symbolic analysts" able to manipulate data and other information) and a lower tier (frequently employing the young or very old, often marginalized, at low wages in such things as the fast-food, retail, and hostelry industries). By 2012, the service sector employed 77.9 percent of working Canadians, while the secondary sector employed 18.2 percent, and primary industries only 3.9 percent (Krahn et al., 2015:75, 79).

Immediately after the Second World War, however, Canada experienced a heightened demand for labour, especially skilled labour. Some of this demand was met by returning veterans, whom the government retrained under generous financial terms. Women (as noted above) also played a large role in filling demand, especially in the growing service industry (Lowe, 1987; Li, 1996:149). Canadian industry's demand for labour after the Second World War was inexhaustible, however. Immigration to Canada had virtually ceased during the Depression and subsequent war years (see Table 6.1). Now the Canadian government once more opened the immigration door to let in new workers.

At first glance, Canada's post-war immigration policy seems remarkably similar to that during earlier periods of economic expansion (see Chapter 6), especially in favouring immigrants from Britain and Western Europe, but there were important differences. While British immigrants at first remained favoured, there were fewer people from that country who wished to come. Also, throughout the 1950s, Canada faced increased competition from Australia and the United States for a shrinking pool of labour, especially skilled labour. Thus, Canadian policy gradually stretched to allow more immigrants from non-traditional source countries, first eastern and southern Europeans (especially those escaping communism), and later people from Asia, Africa, and the Caribbean. Changes in the Immigration Act of 1967, which saw the introduction of a point system, furthered this transition. Before this time, race and ethnicity were explicit criteria for entry. After this time, immigration and labour market needs became more closely aligned. The criteria for entry shifted first to educational qualifications, then (by the 1980s) to financial and class (that is, business) qualifications (Harrison, 1996). Table 7.1 compares the birthplaces of immigrants over three periods, beginning with the period before 1971, up to 2011. In the earliest period, slightly more than 78 percent of immigrants came from Europe, especially northern and southern Europe. Between 1971 and 1990, however, this percentage dropped to just under 30, and during the most recent period constituted the birthplace for just over 16 percent of immigrants. By contrast, the proportion of immigrants from Asia has grown steadily, and made up nearly 60 percent of immigrants in the period from 1991 to 2011, with especially high numbers of arrival from eastern and southern Asia. But Canada has also experienced a steady, if less spectacular, growth in immigration from Africa and the rest of the Americas in recent decades.

While immigration after 1945 was influenced by the need for skilled workers, after 1960 broader social factors also became influential. Notable among these was the introduction of the birth control pill in the early 1960s, which led to a rapid decline in Canada's birth rate. By the 1970s, some policy-makers feared that Canada's working-age population might one day be insufficient to pay for the expanding services required for an aging population. Immigration thus became tied not only directly to economic needs but also to the growing fiscal requirements of the welfare state (see Li, 1996).

The changes to Canada's immigration policy were particularly noticeable in some major cities (Toronto, Montreal, Vancouver), where sizable ethnic communities arose as the result of **chain migration**, the tendency of new immigrants to settle in areas already populated by members of their cultural community. The result has been the continued prominence of British ancestry within the East Coast's population, declining generally as one travels westward; the continuance of French ancestry in Quebec (see Part 1); the prominence of people of middle and eastern European heritage on the Prairies; and the larger presence of people of Asian ancestry on the West Coast. Note, in Table 7.2, for example, the relatively large proportion of all immigrants to Newfoundland and Labrador who come from Europe (42 percent), especially northern Europe (primarily the United Kingdom at 30 percent) and, similarly, the large proportion of immigrants to British Columbia who arrive from Asia (58.5 percent).

But ethnic identification in Canada is also increasingly mixed. While a large proportion of Canadians continue to have either British or French ancestry, in many instances these are not exclusive of other heritages, and this blend of heritages also crosses provincial borders, making it inaccurate to summarily categorize any province as, for example, "British."

In 1969, Canada adopted the policy of official bilingualism in response to the rise of Quebec nationalism (Chapter 2). Many people accepted (albeit some grudgingly) the need for two official languages to bind the country together and address the demands of Quebec's sizable francophone population. The notion of two official cultures, however, was received more skeptically by Canadians, particularly visible minorities and Aboriginals. The result was Canada's adoption two years later of a policy of **multiculturalism**, whereby no culture is officially privileged over another.

Multiculturalism today is an official mainstay of Canadian identity. Supporters of the policy contend that Canada is leading the way in becoming a post-modern society, and that the country's ability to manage cultural differences adds to its strength economically, culturally, and politically (Adams, 2007). The policy also has critics, however. In the eyes of some, multiculturalism merely hides the continuing reality of an ethnic

Table 7.1: Immigrant Population by Place of Birth and Period of Immigration (Total and Percentage) [1]

Place of Birth	Total Immigrant Population		Period of Immigration					
	Number	%	Pre-1971	%	1971–1990	%	1991–2011	%
Total	6,775,765	100.0	1,261,060	100.0	1,820,660	100.0	3,694,040	100.0
In Canada	2,220	—	520	—	780	—	915	—
Outside Canada	6,773,550	100.0	1,260,540	100.0	1,819,885	100.0	3,693,120	100.0
Americas	1,058,010	15.6	132,365	10.5	399,030	21.9	526,625	14.3
North America	263,760	3.9	63,640	5.0	80,120	4.4	111,000	2.8
Central America	151,630	2.2	3,925	0.3	54,440	3.0	93,260	2.5
Caribbean and Bermuda	351,430	5.2	47,530	3.8	152,945	8.4	150,960	4.1
South America	291,090	4.3	17,230	1.4	102,520	5.6	171,340	4.6
Europe	2,127,785	31.4	987,855	78.3	535,730	29.4	604,200	16.4
Western Europe	397,440	5.9	221,945	17.6	72,135	4.0	103,350	2.8
Eastern Europe	501,620	7.4	97,390	7.7	116,315	6.4	287,915	7.8
Northern Europe	602,120	8.9	318,680	25.3	185,120	10.2	98,310	2.7
Southern Europe	626,570	9.2	349,815	27.7	162,150	8.9	114,605	3.1
Africa	492,025	7.3	24,530	1.9	107,605	5.9	359,880	9.7
Western Africa	76,070	1.1	725	—	10,710	0.6	64,635	1.7
Eastern Africa	154,590	2.3	3,605	0.3	55,580	3.1	95,410	2.6

Northern Africa	186,745	2.8	15,560	1.2	24,905	1.4	146,280	4.0
Central Africa	32,640	0.5	460	—	2,975	0.2	29,205	0.8
Southern Africa	41,955	0.6	4,180	0.3	13,430	0.7	24,350	0.7
Asia	3,041,100	44.9	106,795	8.5	757,180	41.6	2,177,135	58.9
West Central Asia and the Middle East	455,940	6.7	14,805	1.2	99,710	5.5	341,425	9.2
Eastern Asia	962,560	14.2	47,395	3.8	225,595	12.4	689,595	18.7
Southeast Asia	729,800	10.8	14,965	1.2	257,740	14.2	457,095	12.4
Southern Asia	892,760	13.2	29,620	2.3	174,130	9.6	689,010	18.7
Oceania	54,530	0.8	8,915	0.7	20,335	1.1	25,285	0.7
Other[2]	700	—	170	—	120	—	350	—

Notes: 1. Differences within regional totals and between regional totals and Canadian totals due to rounding. 2. Includes all populations not identified elsewhere (n.i.e.) by region.

Source: Adapted from Statistics Canada. 2011e. "Citizenship (5), Place of Birth (236), Immigrant Status and Period of Immigration (11), Age Groups (10) and Sex (3) for the Population in Private Households of Canada, Provinces, Territories, Census Metropolitan Areas and Census Agglomerations, 2011 National Household Survey." Ottawa: Statistics Canada (data. gc.ca/data/en/dataset/20381917-0a55-45ca-9f66-330135ce3267). Modified March 4, 2014.

Table 7.2: Canadian Immigrant Population, by Place of Birth and Province/Territory of Residence, 2011 (in Percentage)

Place of Birth	Canada	NL	PE	NS	NB	QC	ON	MB	SK	AB	BC	YT	NT	NU
Americas	15.6	21.0	23.0	22.8	35.3	22.8	16.0	16.6	13.5	13.4	8.8	16.5	12.7	20.3
North America	3.9	17.3	18.7	17.2	28.9	2.8	3.2	4.0	7.3	4.8	4.9	13.2	7.8	9.8
Central America	2.2	0.4	1.3	0.8	1.0	3.6	1.8	5.6	2.3	3.1	1.6	1.6	1.6	1.6
Caribbean and Bermuda	5.2	1.5	1.6	2.8	2.7	9.9	6.3	2.3	1.5	1.8	0.8	0.3	1.9	5.7
South America	4.3	1.6	1.6	2.1	2.8	6.5	4.8	4.7	2.5	3.6	1.6	1.6	1.6	3.3
Europe	31.4	42.0	35.7	42.5	36.0	31.0	33.4	31.2	30.0	27.7	27.1	47.0	27.4	33.3
Western Europe	5.9	5.8	10.9	10.0	11.0	10.0	4.3	8.3	6.9	6.6	5.9	20.1	7.3	5.7
Eastern Europe	7.4	3.6	2.4	4.2	3.0	7.8	8.2	9.0	7.3	7.2	4.8	6.4	5.0	5.7
Northern Europe	8.9	30.2	19.2	25.1	19.7	1.8	9.0	7.8	12.1	10.2	12.5	18.1	11.6	19.5
Southern Europe	9.2	2.4	3.2	3.2	2.4	11.4	11.9	6.1	3.7	3.7	3.9	1.5	3.5	2.4
Africa	7.3	8.3	1.8	5.6	5.7	18.6	5.4	6.1	7.0	8.7	3.1	2.9	16.3	8.9

Western Africa	1.1	1.5	0.8	0.9	1.3	2.1	1.1	1.3	1.2	1.5	0.2	0.0	1.4	2.4
Eastern Africa	2.3	2.7	0.4	1.9	1.4	2.0	2.3	2.6	3.0	4.2	1.4	0.4	10.6	2.4
Northern Africa	2.8	1.8	0.2	1.9	1.6	12.6	1.2	1.2	1.1	1.6	0.4	0.0	3.3	1.6
Central Africa	0.5	0.4	0.0	0.2	0.7	1.8	0.3	0.5	0.3	0.4	—	0.0	0.0	0.0
Southern Africa	0.6	2.0	0.3	0.7	0.6	0.1	0.5	0.5	1.3	1.0	1.1	2.0	1.4	1.6
Asia	44.9	27.4	39.2	28.1	21.9	27.5	44.8	45.7	48.5	48.8	58.5	27.0	42.5	35.0
West Central Asia and the Middle East	6.7	4.2	7.6	12.0	2.8	9.7	7.2	3.1	4.3	5.3	4.3	0.3	4.9	2.4
Eastern Asia	14.2	8.8	24.6	6.5	10.0	5.9	12.7	6.2	9.3	12.9	28.3	5.5	7.8	6.5
Southeast Asia	10.8	3.4	2.7	4.4	4.7	7.0	9.1	27.8	23.8	17.1	12.6	18.4	26.2	17.9
Southern Asia	13.2	11.0	4.4	5.2	4.3	4.9	15.8	8.5	11.1	13.5	13.3	2.9	3.6	8.9
Oceania	0.8	1.3	0.3	0.9	0.6	0.1	0.3	0.4	1.0	1.4	2.5	6.3	0.9	0.0
Other[1]	—	0.0	0.0	0.0	0.0	—	—	0.0	0.0	—	—	0.0	0.0	0.0

Notes: 1. Includes all populations not identified elsewhere (n.i.e.) by region.

Source: Adapted from Statistics Canada. 2011e. "Citizenship (5), Place of Birth (236), Immigrant Status and Period of Immigration (11), Age Groups (10) and Sex (3) for the Population in Private Households of Canada, Provinces, Territories, Census Metropolitan Areas and Census Agglomerations, 2011 National Household Survey." Ottawa: Statistics Canada (data.gc.ca/data/en/dataset/20381917-0a55-45ca-9f66-330135cc3267). Modified March 4, 2014.

hierarchy in Canada. Others see it as an expensive and destructive policy that encourages people to retain past identities and live in ethnic quarters of Canadian cities rather than forge together a common sense of being Canadian (Bissoondath, 1994). It may also undermine universalist social policies as groups call for particularistic programs to meet their unique needs (Rice and Prince, 2013).

The impact of the "new ethnics" upon Canadian identity was not particularly evident in the 1960s. Nonetheless, a new sense of identity was already emerging in English-speaking Canada.

The Rise of English-Canadian Nationalism

After the Second World War, English-speaking Canada remained very British. It was not until the Canadian Citizenship Act of 1946, for example, that "Canadian citizens" existed. Before that time, Canadians were British subjects, and many—at least those outside Quebec—were quite content to hold British passports.

Into the mid-1960s, Canadian culture outside of Quebec also remained decidedly British. At a time when there were only two television channels (CBC and CTV), a large number of British programs competed with American shows to fill the airwaves. Comedy shows such as *Monty Python's Flying Circus* and English adventure shows such as *Danger Man* and *The Avengers* were standard viewing for many English-speaking Canadians growing up.

Canada's British ties were weakening, however. Economically, bilateral trade between Canada and Britain declined sharply after the Second World War, replaced by trade with the United States (see Marchildon, 1995; Norrie and Owram, 1996). Politically, Canada's ties to the throne were also eroding. In 1951, for example, Canada's Supreme Court replaced Britain's Privy Council as Canada's last court of appeal, setting the stage for Canada's later dropping of other British symbols.

Britain's declining role in Canadian life reflected not only cultural and ethnic changes, brought about by immigration, but also a growing pride and confidence among Canadians themselves. Success in the war caused English-Canadians as a whole to become less parochial and to slough off some of their colonial anxieties. Many wanted Canada to take a greater and more independent role among the victorious states. Thus, after 1945 Canada proudly gained membership in the United Nations, NATO, and other international organizations. Likewise, it participated in the Korean conflict (1950–1953) and took a leading role in settling the 1956 Suez conflict, for which Lester Pearson (prior to becoming prime minister) won the Nobel Peace Prize. But each of these actions also reflected a growing policy convergence with the United States. Thus, as Canada drew away from Britain's embrace, it also found itself increasingly under America's blanket.

In short, by the late 1950s, English-speaking Canada was seeking a new vision of itself, an identity. The result was the rise of English-Canadian nationalism, often referred to as Canadianization. English-Canadian nationalism was not supported by all elements. Business generally disliked or feared nationalism in any form. Francophones viewed English-Canadian nationalism as merely a new variation on assimilation. Regional elements often feared federal intrusions into their areas of jurisdiction (Finkel, 2012:157–159). Nonetheless, a sizable portion of English Canada's population favoured the heightened nationalism of the time.

The new nationalism was not of one type, however. Some forms expressed nostalgia over the loss of things British (especially the replacement of the Union Jack by the Maple Leaf flag in 1965). Some variations were defensive, a response to the rise of Quebec nationalism or to the increased influence of the United States. Others were frankly imperialist, as when Prime Minister John Diefenbaker invoked his vision of the Canadian North in the 1958 election (see Chapter 10). The new nationalism that gripped English-speaking Canada came in different forms, manifesting itself politically, culturally, and economically.

Politically, English-Canadian nationalism can be divided into formal and popular politics. At the formal level, after 1950, Canadian prime ministers found themselves in a series of delicate skirmishes with their American counterparts. Until Roosevelt, most American presidents had ignored Canada. Canada was viewed as an extension of the United States, a place of eccentric country cousins. In the context of the Cold War, however, the United States demanded particular obedience from its allies, beginning with Canada. Thus, the Diefenbaker administration's (1957–1963) efforts at an independent defence policy, not to mention encouraging trade with Fidel Castro's Cuba and Communist China, aroused particular antagonism. President John F. Kennedy (1917–1963) had called Prime Minister Diefenbaker an "SOB" and gave encouragement and strategic support to successful Liberal efforts to unseat Diefenbaker in the 1963 Canadian election. Relations between Prime Minister Pearson and President Johnson (following John F. Kennedy's assassination) proved no better, however. Quickly, Canada found itself at odds with the United States over the war in Vietnam and trade policy, especially the 1965 Auto Pact (see Martin, 1982; Norrie and Owram, 1996). Pearson, like Diefenbaker before and Trudeau after, learned the truth of the axiom that states do not have friends, they have interests. Increasingly, the interests of Canada and the United States were diverging.

English-Canadian nationalism manifested itself politically at the popular level. In keeping with the times internationally, many of these expressions were anti-American and directed at American imperialism in Vietnam and elsewhere, themes often picked up on Canadian campuses (see Box 7.1). But there was also widespread revulsion directed at "the American way of life" in general, as reflected nightly on American television. Race riots and the killings of civil rights workers and politicians provided an ample "negative model" for Canadians and for between 70,000 and 125,000 American draft dodgers and deserters (Finkel, 2012:154; Rodgers, 2014) who wanted to build a better society in North America.

English-Canadian nationalism was also cultural. In 1951, the Massey Commission outlined the need for Canada to develop its own cultural institutions and distinctly Canadian voice. The commission's report focused on high culture and drew little initial response, official or otherwise (see Morton, 1997). Eventually, however,

Box 7.1: The Canadianization Movement in Sociology

Canadianization at large found its mirror in English Canada's universities and colleges beginning in the late 1960s. The immediate catalyst for a nationalist response was the hiring at Canadian institutions of higher learning of a large number of foreign-trained (often American-born) academics to meet the demands of a growing student population. Nationalists sought to bring a Canadian perspective to research and teaching in the academy. Among those involved in the Canadianization movement were a number of sociologists, students, and the Canadian Anthropology and Sociology Association.

Canadianization benefited sociology in at least two ways. First, it led to an increase in Canadian curricula and content being taught. A survey of five disciplines (French, history, political science, economics, and sociology and anthropology) at six universities (Dalhousie, Montreal, Carleton, Alberta, Simon Fraser, and UBC) shows that the number of undergraduate full-time course equivalents with Canadian content increased by 108 percent between 1970–1971 and 1980–1981, with a particularly large increase in sociology and anthropology (Steele and Mathews, 2006:494–495).

Second, Canadianization also impacted the education of sociologists within Canada. In 1970, only 17.5 percent of full-time sociologists in Canada had received their highest degree in Canada, compared with 63.4 percent who received their degree in the United States. By 1980, these percentages had changed to 29.2 percent and 53.2 percent, respectively. In 2005, 52.3 percent of full-time Canadian sociologists had received their highest degree in Canada, while 31 percent had received their highest degree in the United States (Gingras and Warren, 2006:513).

The Canadianization movement raises several questions, however. Is a national perspective necessary to understanding sociology? Or are sociological insights inherently universal? Even more intriguing: Is there a need for a revitalized Canadianization movement in sociology today?

What do you think?

Sources: Steele, James, and Robin Mathews. 2006. "Canadianization Revisited: A Comment on Cormier's 'The Canadianization Movement in Context.'" *The Canadian Journal of Sociology* 31(4):491–508; Gingras, Yves, and Jean-Philippe Warren. 2006. "A British Connection: A Quantitative Analysis of the Changing Relations between American, British, and Canadian Sociologists." *The Canadian Journal of Sociology* 31(4):509–522.

such institutions as the Canada Council for the Arts, the National Film Board of Canada, and Telefilm Canada were formed to encourage Canadian culture. Whether these institutions were responsible for the spread of cultural nationalism or not is debatable. Nonetheless, except in the area of television and film, which remained largely overwhelmed by American capital and technology, a distinctively Canadian cultural industry slowly emerged in English Canada. In the area of literature, the 1950s and 1960s saw the rise to prominence of a host of writers, including Pierre Berton, Leonard Cohen, Robertson Davies, Timothy Findley, and Margaret Laurence.

(A few intellectuals, notably Marshall McLuhan, also became international cultural icons.) Other writers, many of them women (such as Margaret Atwood, Alice Munro, and Carol Shields), followed in the 1970s, joined more recently by Yann Martel, Lisa Moore, Michael Ondaatje and Rohinton Mistry, pointing also to Canada's increasingly multicultural nature.

There had long been a Canadian popular music scene, stretching from jazz to pop to country. Except at the local and regional level, however, much of it was derivative of American music. Canada's climb aboard the rock-and-roll bandwagon of the 1950s continued this trend. But the late 1960s saw Canadian music also take a nationalistic turn, assisted by the creation of the Canadian Radio and Television Commission, which legislated Canadian content. Groups such as The Band (headed by Robbie Robertson) became internationally known, as did individual artists such as Neil Young and Joni Mitchell. More importantly, each also remained distinctively Canadian, as often evidenced in their lyrics, setting the stage for bands such as The Tragically Hip in the 1990s and Arcade Fire later on. In keeping with the times, the music of this period sometimes took on an overtly political, often anti-American tenor, as in the words to The Guess Who's "American Woman" and Gordon Lightfoot's "Black Day in July" (about the Detroit riots), continued today in the music, lyrics, and activism of the Portage la Prairie band Propagandhi.

Economic Nationalism, or the Uses of Good Theory

Among the subgenres of nationalism, however, economic nationalism was arguably the most influential. After years of growth, in the late 1950s the Canadian economy entered a recession (Norrie and Owram, 1996). In this context, a number of influential Canadians—led by political economist Melville Watkins (1963), conservative philosopher George Grant (2005), and Liberal finance minister Walter Gordon (1966)—asked (each in his own way) why Canada continued to be "the world's richest underdeveloped country" (Levitt, 1970:25). In particular, many noted that Canada's declining economic performance coincided with increased foreign, mainly American, control of the economy. Were the two events related? For economic nationalists, the answer was a definite *yes*.

Keynes once remarked that there is nothing so practical as a good theory. But good theory arises out of the need to understand real issues. The economic nationalism of the 1960s arose out of genuine concerns over Canada's future; in turn, it provided impetus for a renaissance of investigation into the roots of Canada's economic, political, and social development (see Laxer, 1991), a renaissance that ultimately had practical impacts upon Canadian policy.

At least initially, these studies took their inspiration from the work of the Canadian economic historian Harold Innis (1894–1952). Innis's **staples theory** argued that Canada's founding as a hinterland producer of raw exports for world markets curtailed normal economic and political development, resulting in it being prone to being caught in a staples trap. The nature of the trap was that, while staple products (such as cod, furs, trees, and wheat) were often seductively profitable in the short term, their prices were inherently unstable and subject to boom and bust. In Innis's view, an economy built upon raw resources alone did not develop the forward and backward linkages and social structure characteristic of a fully developed economy (see Innis, 1995).

Staples theory, based on the historical relationship between the metropolis and the hinterland, bears some relationship to **dependency theory**, which emphasizes the unequal relationship between the core and periphery in the world capitalist system set in motion by early colonialism (see Frank, 1975), though the latter also utilizes a Marxian class analysis. Dependency theory did not fit the Canadian situation well, however. After all, by the 1960s, many parts of Canada were heavily industrialized, while residing uneasily with pockets of underdevelopment. Moreover, the benefits of industrialization were—as now—unevenly distributed by gender, race, ethnicity, and region (see Panitch, 1977; Laxer, 1991; Clement, 1997). Hence, the years following the late 1960s saw a "new" tradition of political economy that took analyses of Canadian dependency in different explanatory directions.

Some scholars used **elite theory** to explain Canada's development. Naylor (1975), for example, went back in history to argue that merchants who were concentrated in export industries, especially the fur trade, had conspired against industrial capitalists to hinder economic development (the merchants against industry thesis). Clement (1975), meanwhile, argued that a troika of elites continued to dominate the Canadian economy: a parasite elite (foreign owners and managers), an indigenous elite (Canadian owners and managers), and a comprador elite (Canadians managing companies in Canada for foreign firms).

Others, however, used **class theory** to explain the trajectory of Canadian development. Panitch (1981), for example, argued that, ironically, the relative power of Canada's proletariat during the country's initial stage of industrialization development (1870–1910) hindered capitalism's accumulation of surplus. By contrast, Laxer (1989) argued that Canada had been a successful late industrializing country, but had fallen back into dependency due to the political weakness of its agrarian class during this period, which had prevented Canada from adopting the kind of policies (low taxes, easy credit, the targeted construction of railways, and a robust defence policy) that worked successfully in similar countries, notably Sweden.

Many of these studies focused particularly on the impact of the National Policy in Canada's economic development. You will recall that the National Policy's use of tariffs was meant to encourage manufacturing within Canada (Chapter 6). As intended, a number of American branch plants moved to Canada in the early part of the 20th century to feed the Canadian market and also to gain preferential entry at that time into other Commonwealth countries, especially Britain. In the short term, the economy boomed. Employment in new industries soared, out-migration decreased, and banks made profits. The long-term impacts, however, were less rosy.

Economic nationalists pointed out several problems that accompanied these branch plants (see Laxer, 1991). First, company profits were unavailable for further domestic investment. Finkel (2012:161) notes that in the 1960s, dividends to American owners exceeded American investment in Canada. American profits, alternatively, were often used to buy up more Canadian companies. Second, branch plants tended to obtain materials and personnel in the home country. Thus, Canada lost the backward and forward linkages, or "multiplier effects," necessary to develop the economy fully. Third, the branch plants were not sources of innovation. Statistics showed Canadian companies invested little in research and development. Instead, Canadian branch plants produced copies of American (or other foreign) products for the local market, a pattern known as the miniature replica effect (Finkel, 2012:163; Levitt, 1970).

Ultimately, economic nationalists also saw the issue in broader political terms. American Secretary of State John Foster Dulles (1888–1959) had once opined that there are two ways to conquer a country: by force of arms or by taking over its economy (Laxer, 1995:229). The economic nationalists took Dulles at his word, arguing no country could remain politically sovereign for long with an economy controlled by a foreign power. But adopting a national strategy faced a seemingly obdurate problem: the fact that national solutions often gave rise to regional interests and conflicts (see Chapter 6's discussion of regionalism).

The New West

No region of Canada changed more than the West after 1945. The changes were particularly apparent in Alberta and British Columbia, which experienced enormous population growth and industrialization. But all the western provinces changed in important ways, and influenced Canada as they did.

In 1941, the populations of the four western provinces were roughly equivalent, ranging from a low of 730,000 in Manitoba to a high of 896,000 in Saskatchewan. By 1971, however, a shift westward was already evident. British Columbia's population had tripled to 2.2 million and Alberta's population had doubled to 1.6 million, both surpassing Manitoba (under 1 million) and Saskatchewan (932,000). Looking ahead 40 more years, the population changes in the most westerly provinces become even more startling. By 2011, nearly 4.5 million people resided in British Columbia and nearly 3.8 million in Alberta. By contrast, Manitoba's population had stabilized at around 1.5 million, while Saskatchewan's population, even in the midst of growing prosperity, remained at just over 1 million (see Table 0.1). Today, more than 30 percent of Canadians live in the four western provinces.

These population changes do not tell the whole story. Like the rest of the country, after the war, western Canada experienced rapid urbanization (see Driedger, 1991; see also Chapter 6). This occurred even in Manitoba and Saskatchewan. Winnipeg, for example, grew from 412,000 people in 1956 to 667,000 in 1996. During the same period, Regina's population went from nearly 90,000 to 193,000, while Saskatoon's population increased from 73,000 to 219,000. The greatest urban growth, however, occurred in British Columbia and Alberta. Between 1956 and 1996, Vancouver's population nearly tripled, from 665,000 to more than 1.8 million people. Victoria's population also increased rapidly, from 134,000 to 303,000. In Alberta during this period, Edmonton's population expanded from nearly 255,000 to 862,000, while Calgary's population climbed from 201,000 to nearly 822,000. These figures alone do not tell the tale, however, for many smaller cities and suburbs of larger cities were also spawned during this period. In consequence, the urban centres within areas such as the Vancouver mainland and that between Edmonton and Calgary became largely contiguous.

Today, much of Canada's population (both east and west) is urbanized, with 33 census metropolitan areas (CMA). (A CMA is an area consisting of one or more adjacent municipalities situated around an urban core of at least 100,000 people.) As shown in Table 7.3, 9 of these 33 CMAs are now located west of Ontario; indeed, the West has three of the six largest areas—Vancouver, Calgary, and Edmonton—with Calgary having the fastest population growth rate between 2001 and 2013 (43.4 percent), while the lowest rates of population growth for the 33 CMAs occurred in Ontario.

Western Canada's population changed in other ways. Settled by massive immigration in the early 20th century, the West had always been culturally, religiously, and ethnically diverse, but this diversity was often suppressed in the name of Anglo-conformity (Chapter 6). After the 1970s, however, as multiculturalism became Canadian government policy, the West allowed its diversity to emerge more fully (see above discussion of multiculturalism).

Underlying these population shifts were fundamental economic changes. The Prairie region was originally opened up for agricultural development (Chapter 6). As noted above, changes in the farm economy throughout the 20th century resulted in a reduction in Canada's agricultural labour force overall. In 1951, 15.6 percent of Canada's workforce as a whole was employed in agriculture. By 1971, this had fallen to 5.6 percent. By 1991, the proportion of the Canadian workforce employed in agriculture had dropped to 3.6 percent (Li, 1996:45), and is less than 2 percent today. This drop has been less pronounced, though unevenly, on the Prairies, especially Manitoba and Saskatchewan (Krahn et al., 2015:111). Overall, however, there has been a steady move to large corporate farming. Yet, while it remains a big part of the Prairie economy and continues to reflect (albeit nostalgically) the cultural history of the West, agriculture—like ranching—is largely a corporate exercise. Economies of scale and the high costs of farm technology have put the farm beyond the reach of families.

The decades after 1945 saw a steady westward shift of population as new industries emerged. Though each province developed somewhat distinctly, economic growth, large or small, in all the western provinces shared certain characteristics. First, it was invariably government-led. Local capital was often scarce, while private, exogenous capital was reluctant to invest in what often seemed tenuous opportunities for profit. Thus, eastern and (more often) foreign capital and expertise were welcomed in under favourable conditions set by the provincial governments. The 1970s, in particular, saw every western government, of every political stripe, engage in what was termed **province-building**: an activist approach to economic development on the part of provincial governments.

Second, economic growth in all the western provinces focused on megaprojects, especially in the North (see Chapter 10). Hydroelectricity in Manitoba, potash and uranium in Saskatchewan, tar sands in Alberta, and hydroelectricity and forestry in British

Table 7.3: Population of Canada's 33 Census Metropolitan Areas (in Thousands) 2001, 2011, and 2013 (Projected), and Percentage Change 2001–2013

	2001	2011	2013[2]	Percentage Increase (2001–2013)[3]
Toronto	4,682.9	5,769.8	5,959.5	27.3
Montreal[1]	3,451.0	3,885.7	3,981.8	15.4
Vancouver	1,987.0	2,373.0	2,443.3	23.0
Calgary[1]	951.5	1,264.5	1,364.8	43.4
Ottawa–Gatineau[1]	1,067.8	1,270.2	1,305.2	22.2
Edmonton	937.8	1,206.0	1,289.6	37.5
Quebec[1]	686.6	776.8	791.9	15.3
Winnipeg[1]	676.6	746.1	771.2	14.0
Hamilton	662.4	742.5	758.1	14.4
Kitchener-Cambridge-Waterloo	414.3	493.0	504.3	21.7
London[1]	435.6	489.5	498.6	14.5
Halifax	359.2	402.4	408.7	13.8
St. Catharine–Niagara	377.0	402.6	405.0	7.4
Oshawa	296.3	367.3	380.0	28.2
Victoria	311.9	352.1	357.3	14.6
Windsor	307.9	328.3	333.1	8.2
Saskatoon	225.9	270.2	292.6	29.5
Regina	192.8	217.7	232.1	20.4
Sherbrooke[1]	176.0	204.7	210.0	19.3
St. John's	172.9	202.5	208.4	20.5
Barrie	148.5	192.8	197.8	33.2
Kelowna	147.7	183.5	186.3	26.1
Abbotsford-Mission	147.4	174.3	177.5	20.4
Kingston	146.8	164.5	167.2	13.9
Greater Sudbury/Grand Sudbury	155.6	165.3	165.5	6.4
Saguenay	154.9	159.4	160.2	3.4
Trois-Rivières	137.5	153.2	155.0	12.7
Guelph	117.3	145.6	150.3	28.1
Moncton[1]	118.7	140.2	144.9	22.1
Brantford[1]	118.1	139.4	141.3	19.6
Saint John	122.7	128.6	127.9	4.2
Thunder Bay	122.0	125.0	125.1	2.5
Peterborough[1]	110.9	122.2	123.1	11.0

Notes: 1. Figures for 2001 adjusted because of boundary change. 2. Population estimates for 2013 are for July 1. They are based on 2011 Census counts adjusted for census net under-coverage and incompletely enumerated Indian reserves. They are also based on the 2011 Standard Geographical Classification. 3. Percentage change 2001–2013 calculated by authors.

Sources: Adjusted figures for 2001 taken from Statistics Canada. 2007a. *Canada Year Book 2007.* Ottawa: Statistics Canada, 386; data for 2011 and 2013 taken from Statistics Canada. 2014c. "Population of Census Metropolitan Areas." Ottawa: Statistics Canada (www.statcan.gc.ca/tables-tableaux/sum-som/l01/cst01/demo05a-eng.htm). Modified May 30, 2014.

Columbia became the hallmarks of economic development in the West. In classically liberal and typically Canadian fashion, the belief was that these projects would create the capital necessary to diversify the economy and break the cycle of boom and bust so common in the West. Often, however, it meant putting the provinces' eggs in one or two baskets. Too frequently, when the world price of the particular commodity collapsed, individuals and governments, who had backstopped the projects with huge amounts of public capital, were left holding the empty bag. People either sat out the downturn or moved on. No region in Canada better fit Harold Innis's description of a "staples trap" than did the West (Watkins, 1963; Drache, 1995).

Third, and finally, economic development in the West invariably involved the exploitation of each province's northern region. Flin Flon in Manitoba, Uranium City in Saskatchewan, and Fort McMurray in Alberta are but a few examples. The result sometimes was the building of temporary resource towns that disappeared in time (such as, again, Uranium City). But the impacts of the changes were always permanent, especially for the Aboriginal peoples living in those areas. In Canada, as elsewhere around the world, the forces of modernity and capitalism displaced the old ways of living (see Chapter 10).

Population shifts and economic growth brought other political and social changes. In the mid-1960s, Porter (1965) noted that Canada's elite were largely British, represented "old money," were highly interrelated through business, political, school, and even marital ties, and were located primarily in central Canada. His findings were generally validated a few years later by Clement (1975), who traced the corporate interlocks underlying the power of this insular elite.

The emergent power of the new West challenged this elite structure (Richards and Pratt, 1979). Throughout the West, but particularly in Alberta, a new regional elite arose, demanding its say in how Confederation should be run. The shift of Sun Life from Montreal to Calgary in the 1970s, followed by the establishment of other financial institutions and corporate head offices in that city, was not merely symbolic. It represented a genuine shift in power—especially corporate power—within Canada, led by Calgary's oil and gas industry (see Chapter 8).

The changes in Canada's West did not come without challenges. The increased power of provinces led to provincial identification replacing regional identification (Gibbins, 1979; see also Chapter 8). In some communities, cultural and ethnic diversity created tensions. Expansion into the North disrupted Aboriginal communities in particular, and created social problems (see Chapter 10). At the same time, economic development did not always lead to security. From the 1970s on, the West's economy continued to experience waves of boom and bust.

Finally, the changes also heightened traditional tensions between western Canada and the other provinces and the federal government over the structure of Confederation. By the 1970s, many in the West, like others in the past, were coming to view the Canadian government as alien and unsympathetic to their views. They resented the "imposition," as they saw it, of policies such as bilingualism and metrification. They believed that Canadian institutions had an eastern bias, and that "national" policies, in general, meant central Canadian policies. Thus, the late 1970s and early 1980s saw the rise throughout western Canada, but especially in Alberta, of a number of western separatist movements (Pratt and Stevenson, 1981). Later, in 1987, regional alienation combined with right-wing populism to found first the Reform Party (Harrison, 1995), and later the Canadian Alliance Party (Harrison, 2002), on the way to re-fashioning the federal Conservative Party in the early 2000s. In short, the re-emergence of regional alienation, as much a staple of western Canada as wheat, became a central feature of Canadian society in the years following the 1970s.

The Economic Crisis of the Canadian State

Taken as a whole, the period from 1945 until the 1990s was a time of spectacular economic growth for Canada. Canada's gross domestic product (GDP) in 1947, for example, was $91.7 billion (constant dollars). By 1992, GDP had grown to $560 billion. Even accounting for the impact of population growth on GDP, the average Canadian in 1992 was three times better off economically than in 1947 (Norrie and Owram, 1996:398).

These figures are misleading, however. For Canada, the period can be broken into two halves, the first signalling the prosperous times of an economic "long wave," the second a period of economic decline (Watkins, 1997). But the recession of the early 1970s was not Canada's alone. Every country in the Western industrial world experienced rising unemployment and increased government debt during this period. In Canada after the early 1970s, personal and corporate bankruptcies skyrocketed, while the annual unemployment rate (see Chapter 6) rose steadily, changing also from a temporary or occasional situation to one more long-term and chronic. In this context of rising demands but falling revenues, federal and provincial government deficits and debt also spiked. Canada's massive federal debt as a percentage of gross domestic product following the Second World War had declined steadily during the prosperous years. Thereafter, however, it began to rise alarmingly during the 1980s and early 1990s, with interest payments on the debt eating up a growing proportion of revenues (Li, 1996:89). Canada's federal debt peaked in 1997, then steadily declined as a result of severe budget cuts and renewed prosperity throughout the 1990s and early 2000s, before rising again in recent years (see Chapter 8).

What led during this period to the fiscal crisis faced by Western governments and the Canadian government in particular? First, new technologies were displacing workers; hence the rising unemployment that lowered demand for goods and services, while also reducing tax revenues just as state expenditures increased for unemployment insurance and welfare. For Canada, these new technologies cut into jobs in both the primary and secondary sectors. Second, in a preview of globalization (Chapter 8), transnational corporations began shifting finance capital and production to low-wage countries, at the same time avoiding taxation or pressuring governments to lower corporate taxes (Li, 1996:156–157). In all countries, these factors combined to weaken the full employment policies upon which the welfare state relied.

Also exacerbating the economic recession of the early 1970s, however, were the economic circumstances surrounding a single commodity: oil. Since the beginning of the second industrial revolution, and particularly with the advent of the automobile, oil and natural gas had increased in prominence and power as commodities. Their worldwide importance became quite apparent in 1973 when, following the Yom Kippur War, the Organization of Petroleum Exporting Countries (OPEC) announced it was limiting supply and increasing the price of oil. The OPEC crisis, as it became known, awakened Americans to the fact their country was no longer capable of ensuring a stable and low-priced oil supply. Hence, discussions began on exploration of previously untapped areas under American control, such as Alaska, and means of securing stable supplies from reliable sources, such as Canada.

On the surface, the crisis should have provided a unique opportunity for Canadian development. With large untapped reserves of oil and natural gas, Canada would seem to have been in an ideal position to take advantage of the escalating market price, but Canada was not.

First, 75 percent of Canada's petroleum and natural gas in 1973 were under foreign control, 58 percent under American control (Li, 1996:24–25; see also Fossum, 1997). Canada might be the home of large oil and gas reserves, but Canadians had no right of first call on them. Second, while the governments of producing provinces could do quite well from rising prices that translated into increased royalties, non-producing provinces faced only rising costs. The crisis thus pitted the oil-producing provinces, especially Alberta, against the manufacturing provinces of central Canada, with the federal government caught in the middle. But the problem was not merely political. In Canada, as elsewhere, rising oil prices provoked a worldwide phenomenon known as **stagflation**: the simultaneous occurrence of a declining economy and increasing unemployment with rising inflation.

Finally, Canada's fiscal crisis beginning in the 1970s was particularized by its relationship to the United States. In the late 1960s, facing increased competition from the rebuilt economies of Japan and Germany, and in the midst of the widely unpopular Vietnam War, the United States found itself suffering a negative balance of trade with most countries, including Canada. As economic times worsened, the United States government resorted to a time-worn measure: It adopted a series of protectionist measures to buffer American workers, consumers, and companies against the outside world. In 1972, President Richard Nixon (1913–1994) came to Canada bearing news that while the two countries might be good friends, there was no special relationship between them. The United States was going to pursue its own agenda, and Canada should feel free to do the same (Martin, 1982).

As an exporting country, with the United States as its major market, Canada was rightly concerned about American protectionism. In 1968, 24 percent of Canada's GDP resulted from exports, a figure six times larger than that of the United States. Moreover, 60 percent of Canada's trade was with its southern neighbour (Finkel, 2012:159–160). Given the American actions and Canada's own declining economic prospects, what was the Canadian government to do?

The Rise and Fall of Canadianization, 1972–1982

In the early 1970s, in the context of Quebec separatism, the federal Liberal government of Pierre Trudeau began taking steps to increase the role of central government, politically and symbolically, in the lives of Canadians (Chapter 3). The economic crisis of the same period, in conjunction with the federal election of 1972, which saw the Liberals reduced to a minority government propped up by the left-wing New Democratic Party (Appendix 1), likewise gave the federal government impetus to strengthen its role in the economy. For the Liberal Party, it was a remarkable turnaround. Over many years, the Liberals had developed a solid reputation as pro-business, pro–free trade, and pro-continentalist. Yet, during the next decade (1972–1982), the Trudeau government instituted a series of measures designed both to increase the role of government in the economy and to patriate the economy, in much the same way that the Constitution was brought home from Britain in 1982. Later than the Canadianization of some other parts of society, the government began efforts to Canadianize the economy.

These efforts manifested themselves in several ways, including creation of the Foreign Investment Review Agency (FIRA), designed to oversee foreign takeovers of Canadian companies. Given the specific nature of the economic crisis, however, the heart of Canadianization was a series of measures dealing with oil and gas.

One of these measures was the creation of Petro-Canada in 1975. Today, Petro-Canada is a large private company with retail outlets spread across the country, no different from ESSO or Shell. (In March 2009, the company merged with Suncor.) Petro-Canada's original mandate was very different, however. The federal government originally created it as a Crown corporation for the purpose of exploring and developing oil reserves, mapping out the number of existing reserves in Canada, and generally providing the government with a window on the oil industry.

Canadianization of the economy was a logical extension of the wave of English-Canadian nationalism that swept the country in the 1960s. Certainly, many of the actions taken by the federal Liberals had considerable public support, though this varied from region to region. People in Ontario were the most supportive, while most opposed were people in Quebec and the western provinces, especially Alberta. Many Quebecers, separatist or not, viewed the strengthening of the federal government as threatening their "national" interests. Equally, many in western Canada viewed with suspicion the efforts of the federal Liberals, who had little parliamentary representation in their region. More broadly, many westerners saw this Canadian nationalism as a veil disguising central Canadian interests opposed to their own.

The return of the federal Liberals to power in 1980, following the brief rule of Joe Clark's Progressive Conservative government (see Chapter 3), saw the Liberals resurrect efforts to rebuild the central powers of the Canadian state. Thus, a new Constitution was enacted in 1982. Meanwhile, on the economic front, and in the wake of the Iranian Revolution in 1979, which sparked a second major world oil crisis, the Liberals introduced the National Energy Program (NEP) (Fossum, 1997).

The NEP had five purposes. First, it was intended, through a series of taxes on the oil industry, to increase federal revenues with which to deal with the growing debt. Second, the NEP was meant to keep Canadian energy prices below world levels, smoothing out the impact of rising prices between producing and consuming provinces. (At the same time, it also placed a floor on prices should they suddenly drop, thereby protecting producing provinces.) Third, the NEP was designed to foster Canadian ownership of oil and gas through a series of monetary incentives. Fourth, the program was meant to encourage exploration in the Canada lands (such as in the North, particularly the Beaufort Sea), therefore increasing energy self-sufficiency. Finally, the NEP also was explicitly meant to promote energy conservation (Finkel, 2012; Fossum, 1997).

The National Energy Program was the pinnacle of Canadianization. In retrospect, many of its goals (such as its restrictions on foreign ownership and efforts at self-sufficiency) seem modest, the measures it proposed standard elsewhere. However, by 1982, the NEP was dead, though not formally buried by the subsequent Progressive Conservative government of Brian Mulroney until 1986. Why did the NEP fail?

First, the NEP was based on pricing projections that failed to materialize (Fossum, 1997). As members of the OPEC cartel began cheating on oil production, the price rapidly declined, throwing economies once more into turmoil and ruining the revenue hopes of both the federal government and the oil-producing provinces.

Second, the NEP, and Canadianization in general, ran afoul of the newly elected administration of Ronald Reagan (1911–2004) in the United States. Reagan's electoral campaign in 1980 was based on a promise to the American people to make that country "strong" again. Economically, he promised to make the United States self-sufficient and, further, to use the power of the state to open doors for American free enterprise and business. Implementation of the NEP resulted in a series of hostile letters to the Canadian government written by high-level individuals in the Reagan administration, warning of retaliation for Canadian actions that harmed American business interests (Clarkson, 1985).

Third, competing interests and internal fractures within Canada itself undermined Canadianization. These conflicts were not limited to the federal-provincial or inter-provincial level, although these were important. For obvious reasons, American-owned businesses in Canada, including many in western Canada's oil and gas industry, opposed Canadianization. But large private corporations in general opposed Canadianization both on theoretical grounds (they did not like government regulation in general) and because they increasingly favoured open borders for capital.

Today, the NEP remains controversial; in Alberta, it is mythic. From the point of view of its detractors, the NEP was an unconstitutional intrusion on provincial jurisdiction that stole millions of dollars from the Alberta treasury and led to a subsequent recession (1981–1982). NEP supporters, however, argue that the program was a legitimate effort by the Canadian government to carve out an economic policy independent of the United States, and they suggest that the policy is unfairly blamed for a downturn that hit all oil-producing regions, including Texas and Oklahoma.

Regardless of the relative merits of these arguments, the fact is that the political and economic failure of Canadianization left the Liberal government, and the Canadian state more broadly, without an economic blueprint for managing the country. Sir John

A. Macdonald's National Policy (Chapter 6) of 100 years earlier had led to Canada's industrialization. Its modern equivalent, Canadianization, had attempted to resurrect the role of activist government in shaping the country for the late 20th century. The policy was now in tatters. What path should Canada take?

Adopting Free Trade

Two items headed the Conservative government's agenda when it took office in 1984: a new constitutional arrangement with Quebec that eventually led to the Meech Lake Accord (Chapter 3) and a new economic policy for Canada. In seeking the latter, Mulroney had to look no further than a study recently commissioned by the defeated Liberals.

The failure of Canadianization led the Liberal Party to set up the Royal Commission on the Economic Union and Development Prospects for Canada in late 1982. The commission's final report, published in 1985, concluded that the Canadian economy needed less government involvement, that businesses and workers in Canada were insufficiently competitive, and that the only solution was greater reliance upon market forces. The report advocated a policy of free trade with the United States to achieve these changes.

To understand fully the significance of this recommendation, one has to go back into Canadian history. The option of free trade with the United States had always been there; indeed, the Reciprocity Treaty of 1854–1866 (see Chapter 6) was a form of managed free trade (Norrie and Owram, 1996). After 1867, and particularly after the formulation of the National Policy in 1879, Canadian economic, political, and social development had been nurtured along an east-west grid. But the idea of free trade with the United States persisted, pursued by the Liberal Party and certain supporters, especially western farmers. In the elections of both 1891 and 1911, Sir Wilfrid Laurier's Liberals campaigned on a platform of unrestricted trade with the United States, losing on both occasions to the Tories, the first time to Sir John A. Macdonald, the second time to Sir Robert Borden (Appendix 1). Thereafter, the topic of free trade largely disappeared from sight. Free trade was the ideological plaything of a few academics and "continentalists," those who saw Canada's future within a greater North American whole.

In 1988, the vast majority of Canadians still viewed free trade as a threat to Canadian sovereignty, but two important elements within Canadian society supported the initiative (see Doern and Tomlin, 1991). First, Canadian business, represented by the Business Council on National Issues (since renamed the Canadian Council of Chief Executives) lobbied hard for free trade, in part because much of Canada's business class was already heavily integrated with its American counterparts and in part because it believed such a deal would ensure Canadian access to American markets for export goods and investment capital. Second, several provinces, notably Quebec and Alberta, also supported free trade, the former because its then separatist government believed free trade would loosen that province's dependence upon the rest of Canada and pave the way for sovereignty (see Chapter 3), the latter because it saw free trade as preventing future federal initiatives such as the National Energy Program.

Additionally, Canada faced enormous political and ideological pressures from outside its borders, especially from the United States. The elections of Ronald Reagan as American president in 1980 and of Margaret Thatcher (1925–2013) as British prime minister the year before gave political heft to policies favouring minimal government intervention and the pursuit of free trade.

The 1988 election was highly polarized, comparable only to the conscription election of 1917 (Chapter 2). In the end, though, by a narrow margin (only 43 percent of voters voted for the PCs), Mulroney's Tories won a majority of seats (see Appendix 1). The free trade agreement was ratified. Almost immediately, the newly elected administration of George H. W. Bush in Washington began pushing for a broader continental agreement that would include Mexico. The United States—militarily, politically, and economically powerful, but resource poor—was poised to access the resources of its two closest neighbours. In the late 20th century, North America quickly emerged as one large trading bloc, with its headquarters in the United States, to compete against other trading blocs that began emerging in Europe and Asia.

Nor was the move to closer ties reversed with the election in 1993 of a new Canadian government. In 1993, the victorious Liberal Party, which only five years earlier had denounced free trade, under new leader Jean Chrétien signed the North American Free Trade Agreement (NAFTA) Accord, bringing together the economies of Canada, the United States, and Mexico. The years that followed saw Canada pursue further economic ties with the United States, while that country spearheaded efforts for global free trade through agreements such as the Multilateral Agreement on Investments. For Canadians, the tepid nationalism of the Trudeau era was quickly swept away.

Conclusion

Post-war Canada was built upon an expanding and prosperous economy and a set of welfare state programs to assist the social adjustments necessary to such an economy. These changes in turn resulted in different social arrangements and the emergence of a distinctive English-Canadian identity. Nationalism was the result.

The fiscal crisis beginning in the mid-1970s challenged this vision of Canada. Canadianization was a response to this crisis. In many ways, it was an attempt to create a modern-day National Policy. These efforts crashed, however, against internal regional divisions and pressures exerted by the United States and its business allies. The failure of Canadianization left Canadian politicians and policy-makers without a clear direction for the country. Much of Canada's political and economic elite sought refuge in closer ties to the United States. The Free Trade Agreement was emblematic of this pursuit.

The future does not unfold as a straight or predictable line, however. Few in 1988 could have guessed that the Cold War was about to end, replaced by a new era marked by neo-liberal globalization, economic uncertainty, and war—an era with particular consequences for Canada, which would raise renewed questions about Canada's relationship with the United States and the world.

Key Terms

chain migration
class theory
dependency theory
elite theory
multiculturalism
province-building
stagflation
staples theory
symbolic order
welfare state (a.k.a. Keynesian welfare state)

Critical Thinking Questions

1. Why do you think Canada's welfare state developed in the way that it did during the 20th century?
2. In what ways do changes in family structure and the economy impact upon each other?
3. To what extent can Canada still be described as having a British culture?
4. Does Canada have a national economy or a regional economy?
5. How important is culture to national identity?

Recommended Readings

Clarkson, Stephen. 1985. *Canada and the Reagan Challenge*. Toronto: Lorimer.
Using official documents, Clarkson details the coercive actions of the American government of President Ronald Reagan in attempting to alter the Canadian government's economic policy in the early 1980s.

Doern, B., and B. W. Tomlin. 1991. *Faith and Fear: The Free Trade Story*. Toronto: Stoddart.
This book is an essential primer for understanding Canada's adoption of free trade after 1988.

Olsen, Gregg. 2002. *The Politics of the Wefare State: Canada, Sweden, and the United States*. Oxford: Oxford University Press.
This book compares the different welfare states of Canada, Sweden, and the United States, explaining the variations according to theories in political sociology.

Rice, James, and Michael Prince. 2013. *Changing Politics of Canadian Social Policy*. 2nd ed. Toronto: University of Toronto Press.
This book examines the relationship between politics and social policy in Canada, beginning in the 20th century and up to recently, with an emphasis on the types of programs delivered, who delivered them, and what level of government was involved.

Rodgers, Kathleen. 2014. *Welcome to Resisterville: American Dissidents in British Columbia*. Vancouver: UBC Press.
Rodgers's book examines a little-known part of Canadian cultural history, the arrival of American draft-dodgers during the Vietnam War and the cultural relationship between the resisters and other minority groups in the interior of British Columbia.

Related Websites

Department of Finance Canada
www.fin.gc.ca
This ministry develops policies and provides advice to the government regarding the economy.

Canadian Radio-television and Telecommunications Commission
www.crtc.gc.ca
This commission was established by Parliament in 1968, with the role of supervising and regulating Canadian broadcasting and telecommunication.

CBC Digital Archives
www.cbc.ca/archives/categories/economy-business/trade-agreements/canada-us-free-trade-agreement/topic-canada-us-free-trade-agreement.html
This site contains 15 video clips and 1 radio clip dealing with the Canada-U.S. Free Trade Agreement.

Canadian Society on Video

America, Love It or Leave It. 1991. Alioli Associates Ltd., 50 minutes.
Examines the exodus of 125,000 American political refugees to Canada during the Vietnam War and their impact upon Canada.

Reckoning: The Political Economy of Canada, "Part 4: In Bed with an Elephant." 1986. National Film Board of Canada, 59 minutes, 48 seconds.
Describes the often difficult relationship between Canadian prime ministers and American presidents.

CHAPTER 8

CANADA IN A
NEO-LIBERAL
WORLD

New World Order

> —term used by U.S. president George H. W. Bush on the occasion
> of the signing of the North American Free Trade Agreement, 1993

A number of neoliberal societies, including the United States, have become addicted to violence.

> —Henry Giroux, 2014

This, without a doubt, is neoliberalism's single most damaging legacy: the realization of its bleak vision has isolated us enough from one another that it became possible to convince us that we are not just incapable of self-preservation but fundamentally not worth saving.

> — Naomi Klein, 2014

Introduction

The global economic order after 1945 can be divided into two major eras. The first period was the Keynesian era, stretching from the end of the Second World War until the OPEC crisis of 1973. The second is neo-liberal era, of which Canada's signing of the Free Trade Agreement in 1989 played a major part. Since that time, a number of regional free trade agreements have been signed throughout the world between the developed countries and many former Third World states.

Situated within the rise of neo-liberal globalization and its attendant conflicts, this chapter examines the political, economic, social, and ideological changes in Canada since the adoption of free trade. Among the issues specifically examined are questions of employment, social stratification, and Canadian values. More broadly, however, the chapter examines pressures for further political, economic, social, and military integration into a new form of empire at whose heart resides the United States. The chapter begins with a discussion of neo-liberal globalization.

Neo-Liberal Globalization

Thesis and Antithesis

The Free Trade Agreement of 1989 was enlarged in 1994 under the North American Free Trade Agreement that brought Mexico into the Canada-U.S. economic partnership. These agreements were followed by several other bilateral or regional trade agreements with Chile and Israel (both in 1997), Costa Rica (2002), and Peru and the European Free Trade Association (both in 2009) (Foreign Affairs, Trade and Development Canada, 2013). Since the election of a majority Conservative government in 2011 (see Appendix 1), Canada—in the words of economist Jim Stanford—has "accelerated its quest for new free trade agreements," with as many as 17 more currently being negotiated (Stanford, 2014). At least two of these are extremely large and significant: the Canada–European Union Comprehensive Economic and Trade Agreement (CETA) and the Trans-Pacific Partnership Trade Agreement (TPPTA), both of which—in contrast to the FTA in 1988—few Canadians know anything about because they were crafted in secret and the details have not been released.

Free trade agreements are only part of broader efforts begun in the late 1970s by Western governments (led by the United States), conservative think tanks, and business leaders to remake the world according to a set of liberal political and economic principles based on the ideas of Adam Smith and David Ricardo, and often referred to as **neo-liberalism**—defined as an ideological belief in the efficacy of free markets, limited government, and private property. Proponents of neo-liberal globalization make several assertions.

First, they claim that everyone, consumers and producers alike, benefit in time from free (unregulated) and open trade. Consumers have access to a wider variety of goods and services at lower prices, and resources are used in a more efficient manner than would otherwise occur under protectionist policies. And while those at the top of the economic ladder become wealthier, everyone below also benefits from a larger economic pie and the gradual trickling down of wealth to the bottom. Second, proponents argue that economic freedom is necessary in order to have political freedom and an expansion of human rights. Third, they argue that global economic integration is inevitable, part of the natural history of progress. The words of Britain's then–prime minister Margaret Thatcher, "There is no alternative" (or TINA), quickly became, as post-structural theorists might observe, a discursive means of eliminating debate. Finally, at a philosophical level, neo-liberal proponents assert the primacy of the individual over the group or society (see Giroux, 2014); as Thatcher also famously remarked, "There is no such thing as society," a statement inherently antagonistic of sociology (see Box 8.1). We will return to the cultural implications of neo-liberalism later in this chapter.

Opponents of economic globalization dispute these arguments. They note that the world's wealthiest countries became wealthy not through free trade but through protectionist policies (see Chapter 6). They further argue that, as neo-liberalism has proceeded, the economic situation of many countries and individuals has declined while that of the wealthiest has more than prospered (see Piketty, 2014). For example, there were 1,584 billionaires in the world in 2014 (*Forbes*, 2014), and an Oxfam report notes that the world's 85 wealthiest people possessed as much wealth ($1.7 trillion) as the world's poorest 3.5 billion people (i.e., half the world's population) (Fuentes-Nieva and Galasso, 2014).

Opponents of neo-liberal globalization further argue that rising inequality has resulted in increased social and political conflict, whether in the Middle East, Africa, South America, or even within the boundaries of the core capitalist countries themselves. Indeed, opponents contend that neo-liberal globalization is merely an updated name for a pattern of global exploitation that began with mercantilism (Chapter 1), then morphed into colonialism (see Chapter 9), and now in its neo-colonial variant

Box 8.1: Neo-Liberalism's Challenge to Sociology

In April 2013, while discussing a recently foiled terrorist plot, Prime Minister Stephen Harper told the House of Commons that it was no time to "commit sociology" (Heath, 2013)—a remark that quickly raised eyebrows (and also led to a large number of t-shirts bearing a picture of the prime minister and the phrase being sold at the Victoria meetings of the Canadian Sociology Association that summer). Then, in August 2014, in rejecting calls for a national inquiry into the murder of Tina Fontaine, a 15-year-old Aboriginal girl (one of over a thousand murdered and missing Aboriginal women), the prime minister stated that Fontaine's murder was a crime that should not be viewed as a "sociological phenomenon." In a narrow sense, as some editorialists quickly noted, the prime minister was correct: Murdering someone is a crime. As Kaye and Béland (2014) noted, however, "crime is a social phenomenon shaped by powerful historical and social forces," and without taking these into account, one cannot adequately frame a public policy response.

The prime minister's comments echo a neo-liberal understanding of human behaviour that rests solely on the individual. This understanding, as Frances Fox Piven—one of the world's best-known and most influential sociologists—has noted, is fundamentally at odds with sociology:

> Although we were slow to recognize it, Thatcher and the neoliberal project she championed declared war on the basic tenets of the sociological enterprise. To be sure, we also study individuals and families, but the sociological enterprise rejects the radical individualism of Thatcher and the personal responsibility [of neo-liberalism]. Our distinctive preoccupation is with the social environments that shape individual and family life. (2007:13–14)

Piven's response to the challenge is a call for sociologists to take a critical stance regarding political and economic trends, adding that "The early 21st century is reproducing the turmoil of the 19th century, and it is also reviving the moral and political concerns that animated some of the best sociological work in the past" (2007:15).

What do you think? Is it possible to merge radical individualism with sociology? And what do you think should be the stance of sociologists in the world? Should sociologists merely "interpret the world" or should they, as Marx argued, work to change it?

Sources: Heath, Joseph. 2013. "In Defence of Sociology." *Ottawa Citizen*, April 30; Kaye, Julie, and Daniel Béland. 2014. "Stephen Harper's Dangerous Refusal to 'Commit Sociology.'" *Toronto Star*, August 22 (www.thestar.com/opinion/commentary/2014/08/22/stephen_harpers_dangerous_refusal_to_commit_sociology.html); and Piven, Frances Fox. 2007. "The Neoliberal Challenge." *Contexts* 6(3):13–15.

holds countries and their peoples hostage through trade agreements and debt in which states themselves are complicit (Sassan, 2001; Mann, 2008). From this perspective, the "freedom" lauded by neo-liberals is that of the wealthy to exploit the poor and weak, unhindered by concerns for democracy, equality, and justice.

Yet even its opponents admit that the era of neo-liberal globalization that began in the late 20th century differs in some significant respects from past periods of capitalist expansion. First, in many instances neo-liberal globalization has involved a genuine transfer of productive forces from the industrialized North to the underdeveloped South, with consequences for class structures and living conditions both within underdeveloped and developed countries. Second, where capitalist globalization in the past often resulted in intensified conflict between competing capitalist classes and their patron states (as in the First World War), neo-liberal globalization has been marked by a growing convergence of capitalist interests across borders—indeed, an international capitalist class (Carroll, 2010).

The Three Periods of Neo-Liberal Globalization

The neo-liberal era can be divided into three relatively distinct periods by decade: (1) ascendancy (the late 1970s and 1980s), (2) triumph (the 1990s), and (3) crisis (the 2000s to present).

The ascendancy period began with the crisis of Keynesianism in the 1970s, followed by the elections of British Prime Minister Thatcher in 1979 and American President Reagan in 1980. Both Thatcher and Reagan avidly promoted neo-liberal policies such as the privatization of public services, the deregulation of finance capital, attacks on the power of unions, the lowering of personal and corporate taxes, and the shrinking of the post-war Keynesian welfare state. The signing of the Canada-U.S. FTA in 1989 provided a symbolic capstone to the era, launching neo-liberalism's next stage.

Unlike this first period, during which neo-liberal policies were contained largely within Britain, the United States, and the other Anglo-democracies, including Canada, neo-liberalism's period of triumph saw these policies actively promoted globally. The period was marked symbolically by the collapse of the Soviet Union in 1991, the historic importance of this event captured by American President George H. W. Bush (1924–) in heralding a "New World Order." Lacking an ideological and military adversary, the United States quickly emerged as the "uni-polar" centre of world power. American politicians, economists, and bureaucrats proclaimed neo-liberalism's victory, also known as the "Washington Consensus."

Faced with soaring debts and struggling economies throughout the 1980s and early 1990s, many governments adopted neo-liberal solutions. In the early 1980s for example, Mexico turned its back on decades of autonomous development and later (in 1993) signed the North American Free Trade Agreement with Canada and the United States. Other Latin American countries, such as Argentina, followed suit. Nor was the impact of neo-liberal ideology upon states confined to the underdeveloped world. European countries, including the social democratic welfare states of Scandinavia (see Chapter 7), also felt pressured to accept the supremacy of market ideology.

Neo-liberalism's good times soon ended, however. A serious recession in the early 1990s had nearly faded from memory when Thailand's currency (the baht) collapsed in 1997. This event should have been a minor event in the overall scheme of things. Instead, the collapse of the baht set off a chain reaction of economic tur-moil that continued through Japan, South Korea, and Indonesia, then (in August 1998) northward to Russia, and finally across the Pacific to Brazil, decimating as it went the emergent middle class in multiple countries and causing several govern-ments to threaten to default on their loans. In stark fashion, the events of 1997 and 1998 pointed out a major peril of globalized capitalism: that economic crises could no longer be isolated to a single country or region. The problem was made worse by the fact that the organizations set up at the end of the Second World War to manage orderly capitalism (i.e., the International Monetary Fund, the World Trade Organization, and the World Bank) had failed miserably; indeed, their active role in deregulating capital flows exacerbated the crisis and increased inequities across classes, genders, and ethnicities, both within and between the developed and under-developed worlds, resulting in social and political unrest (see Bello, 2002:4–6). As the crisis unfolded, governments (especially in Central and South America) began defaulting on loans and not co-operating with the IMF, setting the stage, in the years that followed, for several governments in that region to revert to more state-interventionist policies, breaking away from the laissez-faire American model.

Economic and socio-political instability were not the only problems facing neo-liberalism as the 1990s came to a close, however. Nature itself began asserting the limits of economic globalization through a dramatic shift in weather patterns, the concomitant rise of new diseases and micro-organisms, resource depletion, and global warming (see Harrison, 2005; also see Chapter 10). Again drawing attention to the perils of interconnectedness, evolutionary bio-geographer Jared Diamond (2005:23) remarked, "[g]lobalization makes it impossible for modern societies to collapse in isolation.... For the first time in history, we face the risk of a global decline."

Inevitably, the instability was also social and political. In *The Great Transformation*, originally published in 1944 as the Second World War was nearing an end, political economist Karl Polanyi (1944/2001) argued that the economy was necessarily embed-ded in society. Efforts to deregulate the economy, in the fashion of neo-liberalism, had been tried once before—beginning in the late 19th century—only to result in what he termed a **double movement**. Polanyi argued that as the first movement—that of unregulated markets—proceeded, causing enormous social hardships (e.g., homeless-ness, unemployment, poverty), a second (double or counter) movement inevitably arose, comprising individuals, communities, and citizens who protected themselves by drawing inward. The form of protection they chose varied. Protest parties and unions were one form; fascism, communism, and authoritarianism in general were another. In Polanyi's estimation, the Second World War resulted directly from a social and political breakdown occasioned by deregulated markets.

As Polanyi would have predicted, the late 1990s witnessed an array of double move-ments arise throughout the world in opposition to neo-liberal globalization, bringing together a cross-section of global society: workers, students, intellectuals, social activ-ists, Aboriginal peoples, and others. Drawn from both the global North and South, the protests represented a host of causes, including peace, the environment, and justice.

Ironically, computer technologies (especially the Internet), which had fostered capitalist expansion, became a chief means by which mass opposition also was mobilized.

Arthur Schlesinger Jr., an historian and former special assistant to U.S. President Kennedy, aptly described the growing sense of disorder heralding the new millennium that beckoned:

> The world today is torn in opposite directions. Globalization is in the saddle and rides mankind, but at the same time drives people to seek refuge from its powerful forces beyond their comprehension . . . . The faster the world integrates, the more people will huddle in their religious or ethnic or tribal enclaves. (1997:10)

Nothing could quite prepare the world for the events to come, however.

The War on Terrorism

9/11

On September 11, 2001, 19 terrorists aligned with an extreme Islamic fundamentalist group known as Al-Qaeda crashed two passenger planes into New York's World Trade Center, killing roughly 2,800 people. Another plane was flown into the Pentagon in Washington, resulting in the loss of nearly 200 more lives. Though the actual number of people killed was relatively small, the attacks had long-term importance in world history. As the perpetrators had planned, the attacks pierced the American myth of invincibility, shocking America's collective psyche, and bringing home to some the fact that in the 21st century terrorism had gone global (Keohane, 2002). In Orwellian fashion, the attacks also gave rise to authoritarian impulses both at home and abroad.

Within the United States, fear provided the basis for greater state powers and the disciplining of the population, who surrendered long-held rights in the name of security (Wolf, 2007). Likewise, dissent was stifled (see Chomsky, 2001). The mainstream media silenced itself and was complicit as an unthinking agent of the state (see Gonzalez, 2001). Critics lost their jobs; members of minority groups were sometimes attacked. Some critics warned of creeping authoritarianism, if not fascism, in the land of the free (Wolf, 2007; Hedges, 2009, 2010).

Abroad, the United States, still using the discourse of liberal democracy, began exercising its global authority more openly than ever. While Americans do not typically think of themselves as the citizens of an imperial state, and American politicians, for political reasons, shy away from describing their country in terms of empire, several scholars after 9/11 began describing the United States as just that (see Ferguson, 2004; Johnson, 2006; Mann, 2008).

Given geographic proximity, the United States made a series of specific demands of Canada (see Clarkson, 2002a, 2002b). Militarily, these demands included the creation of a military zone around North America under American command and control. Politically, the U.S. demanded that Canada adopt American immigration policies and common security practices. The U.S. also changed the entry requirements for everyone, including Canadians, entering or even flying over the country. Neo-liberal theorists had long envisioned a borderless world (see Ohmae, 1990); suddenly, however, borders once again mattered (Laxer, 2004).

Canada's Unexpected War: Afghanistan

The United States' demands on Canada and other countries escalated in late 2001, when the U.S. and a loose coalition of allies invaded Afghanistan, where many members of Al-Qaeda and its leadership resided. That conflict quickly resulted in Afghanistan's Taliban government being defeated and the Al-Qaeda terrorists being killed, imprisoned, or on the run, retreating primarily across the Pakistan border,[1] where Canada was obliged to join the mission under Article 5 of the Treaty of Washington, which states that an attack upon any NATO country is an attack upon all (Stein and Lang, 2007:10–11).

Article 5 aside, why and how did Canada get involved in the Afghanistan mission? Certainly, Canada and Canadians wanted to show support for the United States after 9/11. But how? And why Afghanistan? Three reasons were paramount. First, the federal Liberal government in 2001 wanted Canada to have a larger presence on the world stage, and saw the Afghan mission as fitting within Canada's post-1960s efforts in international peacekeeping and reconstruction. Second, the mission had widespread support among much of Canada's military establishment, which wanted Canada to pursue a more "muscular" role in the world and believed that war was necessary in order to turn Canadian troops into real combat soldiers. Third, involvement in the Afghanistan mission was a trade-off for not participating in the then-looming Iraq War, which the United States formally launched in spring 2003. The Afghan mission appeared the "safer" engagement at the time.

Canada's formal involvement began in December 2001; it ended just over 12 years later, on March 12, 2014, when the maple leaf flag was lowered at NATO headquarters in Kabul, Afghanistan's capital (CTV, 2014). The military mission began with much bellicosity and bravura but gradually morphed into what Stein and Lang (2007) have termed the "unexpected war." The sheer brutality of war (Smith, 2013), combined with a growing sense among much of the West's political and military elite that the war was unwinnable by military means (Margolis, 2008; Milne, 2008) and the inevitable tally of military casualties, gradually eroded public support. The final official count was 158 Canadian soldiers and 1 diplomat killed during the mission's duration (2001–2014), though there were also several civilian deaths. These numbers, however, do not count the injured—nearly 2,000—or the 160 military suicides that occurred in the period from 2004 to 2014 among soldiers suffering, primarily, the effects of post-traumatic stress disorder (PTSD) (Kilpatrick, 2014). Nor do they include the estimated 3,273 Afghan civilians killed directly by U.S. and NATO air strikes between 2006 and 2008 (Milne, 2008).

Besides the human toll, the financial costs of war also rose. Mid-way through Canada's involvement, Canada's Parliamentary Budget Officer (2008) estimated the Afghan mission would cost the country between $13.9 billion and $18.1 billion by 2011, or about $1,500 for every household in the country. Siebert (2014) has since argued that the $18 billion figure is the correct total, though not a final one: Canada has also committed to providing financial support for security and development into 2017.

Canada's role in the Afghan conflict ended not with a bang but a whimper. The war—like so many modern conflicts—quickly faded from television screens, replaced by yet another conflict whose complexities and purpose was hard to fathom, even for the most skilled observer.

Iraq: The Senseless War

In September 2002, the release by the administration of President George W. Bush (1946–) of its new National Security Strategy was central to the emerging post-9/11 international political framework (Government of the United States, 2002). The document, popularly called the Bush Doctrine, argues that the terrorist attacks made the principle of launching war purely in retaliation (that is, for defensive purposes) inoperative. Instead, the document states that the United States will in future attack in pre-emptive fashion any country it believes may possess, or may seek to possess, weapons dangerous to the U.S. The Bush Doctrine further argues that, because the threat to American interests is now worldwide, the United States is justified in taking military actions anywhere. (For this reason, some see the Bush Doctrine as an extension of the Monroe Doctrine, discussed in Chapter 5.) Finally, the Bush Doctrine proposes as its aim that no country in the future will be allowed to compete militarily with the United States.

Beyond the immediate demands placed on Canada, the 9/11 attacks, and the U.S. response to them, had major impacts on Canada. After months of debate at the United Nations, which attempted collectively to implement a peaceful way of disarming Iraq, the United States, Britain, and a handful of smaller countries (most of them financially indentured to the U.S.) broke with the UN and invaded Iraq in March 2003. The formal war was quickly over, but peace did not come; instead, the next few years witnessed the outbreak of sectarian violence and the deaths of tens of thousands of Iraqi civilians and occupying troops. The war's primary justification—that Iraq had "weapons of mass destruction"—soon proved a fabrication. (No rational person believed the other argument: that Iraq had been involved in the 9/11 attacks.)

Canada's decision not to join the subsequent American-led invasion of Iraq proved a good one, but at the time was contentious. Canada's Liberal government, headed by Jean Chrétien, viewed the mission as foolhardy and unjustified; it was also unpopular at home, being especially opposed by Quebecers. Canada's decision, however, was opposed by powerful forces, including the U.S. administration of President Bush and many political leaders in Canada, among them Alberta's Premier Ralph Klein (1942–2013) and then–federal Conservative Opposition leader Stephen Harper. Likewise, most of Canada's corporate community disagreed with staying out of the Iraq conflict, fearing that doing so invited American economic reprisals. In the end, no reprisals came, but Canada did experience an onslaught of anti-Canadianism from right-wing talk radio and television commentators (Harrison, 2007).

The exact body count for the Iraq and Afghan wars after 9/11 is somewhat unclear. The number of U.S. military deaths is about 6,800, with an almost equal number of contract workers killed, but these figures do not include suicides or those wounded (Costs of War, 2014a); nor does it include the estimated half million Iraqis, mainly civilians, killed since the invasion in 2003 (Vergano, 2013) or the 21,000 Afghan civilians killed in that country (Costs of War, 2014b). In the end, the wars to "liberate" Iraq and defeat terrorism in Afghanistan succeeded in neither. Instead, both countries remained consumed by sectarian violence and disorder. Iraq's instability, in particular, spilled over into other countries.

Then, just as it seemed that the world situation could not get worse, the Great Recession—the most serious challenge to global capitalism since the 1930s—began, bringing down long-established financial institutions and leading to massive job layoffs throughout North America and Europe. War made money for some but, in the larger picture, was a further unsustainable drag on the world economy.

In this paired context of war and recession, the United States in 2008 elected its first African-American president, Barack Obama (1961–). His election reflected growing divisions within the American people, along partisan and socio-demographic lines, over the money and American lives spent in fighting the wars—wars that, moreover, seemed increasingly without purpose and led by a governing political class, representing both parties, whose acumen and integrity was now questioned. With its expensive and sophisticated weaponry, the United States could win the war, but it could not win the peace.

President Obama slowly began withdrawing troops from the assorted war zones, the authority of the American Empire carried instead by drones firing from safe distances and guided via satellite. But instability throughout the Middle East increased. Starting in Tunisia in early 2010, protests and popular revolts erupted throughout the region, fuelled by cellphone technology and demands for democracy. But neither democracy nor peace came; instead, the Middle East descended into warfare along nearly the entire length and breadth of its borders, fuelled by ancient sectarian grievances, geopolitical interests, and an endless supply of lethal weapons provided by assorted Western governments and Russia. In 2014, a new militant group, the Islamic State of Iraq and Syria (ISIS) emerged out of the chaos. Claiming religious authority over all "true" Muslims and declaring its intention to restore a caliphate incorporating much of the land currently part of Syria, Jordan, Israel, Cyprus, and southern Turkey (*Wall Street Journal*, 2014), ISIS began seizing large chunks of Iraq and Syria. In this conflict, as in Libya in 2011, and as in Afghanistan before that, Canada played a small combat role, supplying planes for targeted bombing missions.

Wars change societies, and Canada is no exception (see Chapter 6). Many critics believe the Afghan conflict and the War(s) on Terrorism generally have fundamentally changed Canada. Author and political activist Murray Dobbin (2008) argues that the endless conflicts since 2001 have not only integrated Canada more tightly into the

American Empire, through defence and security policies, but have also militarized Canada's values and culture. Others argue that this change has been intentional on the part of the Conservative administration of Prime Minister Harper: that the government has used war to "rebrand" Canada as a military nation with a "glorious" military past (McKay and Swift, 2012) and to valorize the role of the warrior in opposition to the "peacekeeper" image established during previous Liberal regimes (Richler, 2012). Still others contend that the wars have led, as in the United States, to increased state power in the form of heightened security; restrictions on free speech, even at universities (Turk and Manson, 2007); and the use of practices, such as "rendition," that threaten civil liberties.

Are these arguments correct? Is Canada today, at a deep level, a more militarized nation than it was before September 2001? There is evidence to suggest this may not be the case. For example, while Canada's military budget grew substantially in the years after 9/11 (Staples and Robinson, 2008), it has declined to more traditional levels since. In 2009, Canadian military expenditures were 1.4 percent of the GDP, but had dropped to one percent by 2013. By contrast, military expenditures in the U.S. were 4.6 percent of the GDP in 2009 and slipped only gradually to 3.8 percent in 2013 (World Bank, 2014b; see also Johnson, 2006:139–140). And, while Canada's military industry is not small—in 2010–2011 alone, Canada's 20 largest military contractors obtained orders of more than $3.3 billion (Epps, 2011)—it does not seem as functionally enmeshed in Canadian society as does its counterpart in the United States, once described by the American sociologist C. W. Mills (1956) and later (famously) termed by President Dwight D. Eisenhower (1890–1969) the **military-industrial complex** (Kurth, 1993).

Canada's Economy Today

As we have seen, neo-liberalism was already in some difficulty when the 9/11 attacks were launched. Amid the going chaos of war, the world in late 2007 entered into the worst economic crisis since the 1930s. The immediate cause of the Great Recession was a mortgage crisis in the United States, as large numbers of buyers defaulted on their house payments. Quickly, however, the crisis reverberated around the world, bringing down banks and other financial institutions that had given the buyers easy credit. In turn, credit markets seized up, making it harder for businesses to borrow money, resulting in businesses laying off workers. Unemployed workers and consumers who were already in substantial debt began buying fewer goods and services, leading to even more business layoffs. In short, Depression-era economics (see Galbraith, 1997) returned with a vengeance. To deal with the crisis, Western governments, including Canada's, bailed out many of the world's corporations and financial institutions to the tune of $20 trillion (McNally, 2010; Panitch and Gindin, 2012). In effect, private debt became public debt that has since been paid for by public sector layoffs, reduced public services, and the privatization of public companies.

Today, Canadians find themselves living in a much more conflicted and unpredictable world than it was when the new millennium began. What have the twin crises of war and recession meant for Canada's economy? To this question we turn, examining arguments made in 1988 to anchor neo-liberalism's impact upon Canada.

In 1988, free trade supporters argued the agreement would increase both Canadian exports (and cross-border trade in general) and jobs; secure access to American markets; and encourage efficiency, making the Canadian economy better able to compete in world markets. Have these things occurred?

Exports and Imports

Even before the adoption of free trade, north-south trade with the United States was increasing in every region of Canada. Free trade only hastened this trend. By the early 2000s, 87 percent of Canada's exports were going to the United States (Grunwald, 2002). As Table 8.1 shows, trade in absolute terms has continued to grow between the two countries; indeed, Canada since the adoption of free trade in 1989 has had a positive balance of trade with the U.S. However, much of this positive balance is the result of crude petroleum exports (Villarreal and Fergusson, 2014) (discussed below). In 2013, $358.7 billion in goods and services were exported to the U.S., compared with imports of $313.4 billion. But the percentage of exports going from Canada to the U.S. has declined (74.8 percent in 2013), in part due to increased trade with other countries. In short, Canada's trade options are today more diversified.

Nonetheless, U.S. trade remains very important to Canada; the reverse is not quite the case, however. Based on the trade in goods only, Canada-U.S. trade made up only 16.5 percent of all American foreign trade in August 2013, with exports to Canada making up 19.2 percent of all U.S. exports, and imports from Canada making up only 14.7 percent of all goods coming into that country (United States Census Bureau, 2013). In short, the U.S. remains more important to the Canadian economy than Canada is to the American economy with one notable exception: petroleum (see discussion below).

Employment

Increased integration of North American production after 1988 meant significant restructuring of Canada's labour markets, especially the manufacturing sector. It is estimated that, between 1988 and 1994, 334,000 manufacturing jobs were lost (Hemispheric Social Alliance, 2003), mostly in Ontario. Free trade supporters, however, argued that, in the long run, more and better paying jobs would be created in Canada (Lipsey, 2000); and, indeed, job growth in Canada grew over the two decades between the adoption of free trade and the Great Recession that began in 2007. Table 8.2 provides labour force statistics for Canada and the Canadian provinces for 2013.

Note the generally higher levels of participation and employment as one moves from Canada's East Coast to the West. This trend is primarily the result of growth in Canada's resource-extraction industries. These job shifts are also gendered, to a degree, with rates of unemployed men being higher than those of unemployed women in the East, and only beginning to catch up once one crosses into Ontario. More broadly, four years after the recession ended, the unemployment rate for both men and women remained quite high (7.5 percent and 6.6 percent, respectively).

Even before the recent recession, opponents of neo-liberalism were leery of job creation and unemployment numbers, instead asking questions about what kinds of jobs were being produced in Canada. Such opponents suggest that far too many of these jobs have been part-time, insecure, and low paying, part of a trend toward non-standard employment (Krahn et al., 2015). Especially among young people, a new form of social class has emerged defined by work insecurity (see discussion of social stratification below).

Secure Access to American Markets

Ending American protectionism was one of Canada's chief aims in pursuing free trade in 1988. The Mulroney government insisted that the FTA's dispute settlement mechanism would protect Canadian businesses from arbitrary barriers being erected by the American state. Economist Richard Lipsey (2000) argues that the dispute resolution mechanism has worked well, and that Canada would have been much worse off during the economically turbulent 1990s without it. Writing for the C. D. Howe Institute, Macrory (2002) argued (at the time) that since NAFTA, Canada and Mexico had been "subject to far fewer AD [anti-dumping] and CVD [countervailing duty] investigations and orders by the United States than … other countries, proportionate to trade volume."

For critics, however, such a tepid defence of NAFTA's benefits points to the fact that the United States did not give up, under the FTA (or NAFTA), its right to make laws restricting trade with Canada. (American trade negotiators in 1988 emphasized the same point.) Indeed, critics argue the United States has continued to invoke trade restrictions on a host of things, including softwood lumber, uranium, beer, magnesium, steel, pigs, sugar, peanut butter, tobacco, milk, and paper (Dyck, 1998:92–93). A continuing dispute over U.S. efforts to impose country of origin labels on meat products has recently led Canadian officials to threaten a retaliatory use of duties on U.S. imports (*Globe and Mail*, 2014). In short, free trade has not ended trade irritants between the two countries.

Efficiency and Global Competitiveness

Free trade supporters argued in 1988 that the agreement would prepare Canadians to compete in the emerging global economy. Canadian businesses would have to become more entrepreneurial and efficient; workers would be forced to become more productive. A Statistics Canada report (Baldwin and Gu, 2004) suggested that Canada's manufacturing sector did become more productive as a consequence of trade liberalization after 1988 through specializing, innovating, and learning how to compete.

Gross domestic product (GDP) provides one means of assessing Canada's increased productivity. Stanford's (2006:168) comparison of Canada, the United States, and Mexico—the three NAFTA signatories—suggested that GDP in Canada and the United States actually dropped in the period of the FTA (1989–1994), but increased for all three countries, even over their pre-FTA levels, during the period from 1994 to

Table 8.1: Canadian Imports, Exports, and Trade Balance, by Country or Country Grouping, $ Billions, Percentage, and Percentage Change, 2003–2013

	2003	2004	2005	2006	2007	2008	2009	2010	2011	2012	2013	Percentage 2013	Percentage Change 2003–2013
Exports	**399.1**	**429.0**	**450.1**	**453.7**	**463.0**	**487.30**	**367.2**	**404.0**	**456.8**	**462.5**	**479.4**	**100.0**	**20.1**
United States, including Puerto Rico and Virgin Islands	329.0	350.6	368.4	361.4	356.1	368.90	270.1	295.1	329.9	338.4	358.7	74.8	9.0
Japan	9.8	9.8	10.2	10.3	10.0	117.6	8.8	9.8	11.3	10.8	11.0	2.3	12.2
United Kingdom	7.7	9.4	9.4	11.3	14.2	14.2	12.9	17.0	19.4	19.8	14.8	3.1	92.2
European Union excluding the United Kingdom[1]	16.4	17.5	18.6	20.9	24.2	25.4	18.8	20.2	23.0	21.1	20.4	4.3	24.4
Other OECD[2]	12.7	14.2	14.5	16.8	19.7	21.1	16.6	17.9	20.5	18.5	18.7	3.9	47.2
Other countries	23.5	27.5	29.1	33.1	39.0	47.3	40.0	44.0	52.6	53.8	55.9	11.7	137.9
Imports	**342.7**	**363.2**	**387.8**	**404.3**	**415.0**	**442.8**	**374.0**	**413.7**	**456.1**	**474.5**	**486.7**	**100.0**	**42.0**
United States, including Puerto Rico and Virgin Islands	240.4	250.0	259.3	265.0	269.8	280.7	236.1	259.9	281.5	296.5	313.4	64.4	30.4
Japan	10.6	10.1	11.2	11.9	12.0	11.7	9.3	10.1	9.4	10.8	9.6	2.0	-9.4
United Kingdom	9.2	9.5	9.1	9.5	9.9	11.2	8.5	9.6	10.6	8.3	7.5	1.5	-18.5

European Union excluding the United Kingdom[1]	26.0	27.0	29.5	32.5	32.4	35.4	30.3	30.9	35.2	36.3	37.8	7.8	45.4
Other OECD[2]	22.3	24.3	23.7	25.0	27.4	6.2	26.0	28.8	32.7	36.0	36.0	7.4	61.4
Other countries	36.8	44.3	54.4	61.6	65.9	76.4	63.7	74.4	86.7	86.7	82.4	16.9	123.9
Balance (Exports/Imports)	**56.4**	**65.8**	**62.3**	**49.5**	**48**	**46.7**	**-6.8**	**-9.7**	**0.8**	**-12.0**	**-7.3**	**—**	**-112.9**
United States, including Puerto Rico and Virgin Islands	88.6	100.5	109.1	96.4	86.3	89	34.0	35.2	48.5	42	45.3	—	-48.9
Japan	-0.1	0	-1.0	-1.5	-2.0	0.2	-0.5	-0.3	2.0	n/a	1.4	—	1500.0
United Kingdom	-1.5	0	0.3	1.7	4.2	3	4.4	7.4	8.8	11.5	7.2	—	580.0
European Union excluding the United Kingdom[1]	-9.6	-9.5	-10.8	-11.6	-8.2	-10.0	-11.6	-10.6	-12.2	-15.2	-17.4	—	-81.25
Other OECD[2]	-6.9	-8.1	-10.0	-6.9	-5.3	-6.3	-9.4	-11.0	-12.2	-17.5	-17.2	—	-149.3
Other countries	-13.3	-16.8	-25.4	-28.6	-27.0	-29.1	-23.7	-30.4	-34.1	-33.0	-26.6	—	-100.0

Notes: 1. The European Union includes Austria, Belgium, Bulgaria, Cyprus, Czech Republic, Denmark, Estonia, Finland, France, Germany, Greece, Hungary, Ireland, Italy, Latvia, Lithuania, Luxembourg, Malta, Netherlands, Poland, Portugal, Romania, Slovakia, Slovenia, Spain, and Sweden. 2. Other countries in the Organisation for Economic Co-operation and Development (OECD) include Australia, Chile, Iceland, Israel, Mexico, New Zealand, Norway, South Korea, Switzerland, and Turkey.

Sources: For 2003–2007, Statistics Canada. 2008. "Imports, Exports, and Trade Balance of Goods on a Balance-of-Payments Basis, by Country or Country Grouping"; for 2008–2013, Statistics Canada. 2014d. "Imports, Exports, and Trade Balance of Goods on a Balance-of-Payments Basis, by Country or Country Grouping." (www.statcan.gc.ca/tables-tableaux/ sum-som/l01/cst01/gblec02a-eng.htm). Modified September 4, 2014. Percentages calculated by the authors.

Table 8.2: Labour Force Participation, Employment and Unemployment, Levels and Rates, by Province and Sex, 2013

	Total Labour Force Population (in thousands)	Participation Rate (%), Men	Participation Rate (%), Women	Unemployment Rate (%), Men	Unemployment Rate (%), Women	Employment Rate (%), Men	Employment Rate (%), Women
Canada	**19,079.3**	**71.1**	**62.1**	**7.5**	**6.6**	**65.8**	**58.0**
Newfoundland and Labrador	262.8	65.4	57.2	12.7	10.0	57.0	51.5
Prince Edward Island	83.7	73.2	65.7	13.1	9.8	63.6	59.2
Nova Scotia	498.9	67.2	60.8	10.5	7.6	60.2	56.2
New Brunswick	392.0	67.4	59.3	12.7	8.0	58.9	54.5
Quebec	4,365.1	69.5	61.0	8.3	6.8	63.7	56.9
Ontario	7,440.8	70.8	62.2	7.9	7.1	63.7	56.9
Manitoba	669.0	74.2	63.3	5.5	5.2	70.2	60.0
Saskatchewan	578.3	76.0	64.1	3.8	4.2	73.1	61.4
Alberta	2,318.2	79.1	66.8	4.7	4.5	75.4	63.8
British Columbia	2,470.5	67.7	60.6	6.7	6.4	63.2	56.7

Source: Statistics Canada. 2014a. "Labour Force, Employment and Unemployment, Levels and Rates, by Province, 2013." (www.statcan.gc.ca/tables-tableaux/sum-som/l01/cst01/labor07a-eng.htm). Modified January 10, 2014.

2003. GDP is a controversial measure, however. Because it is a measurement of the total value of goods and services produced in a country during a given period, GDP typically goes up not only during good times but also during wars or immediately after a disaster, such as an earthquake, as rebuilding starts. In this sense, GDP says nothing about the quality of life being lived. It also says nothing about how much you can buy with the money you earn. For this reason, many economists and sociologists turn to purchasing power measures.

By these measures, Canadians still lag behind their U.S. counterparts. In 1990, Canada's gross national income per capita, calculated based on purchasing power parity (PPP) was $29,231, roughly 80 percent of American incomes. In 2013, Canadian incomes based on PPP were $41,887, or still 80 percent of American incomes (all figures in constant 2011 dollars) (World Bank, 2014c).

Opponents also dispute the economic efficiency arguments of free trade supporters. A decade after the signing of the FTA, Jackson (1999) argued that free trade had not brought the investments in research and development that might prepare Canada for the new knowledge economy. As we have seen (Table 8.1), Canadian trade is today more diverse than it was in the early 1990s, but critics note that, more than ever, Canada's economy is dependent upon the export of raw (staple) resources. This brings us back to an important debate.

As previously noted (Chapter 7), staples can be a source of great wealth when the world economy is booming, as it did during the recent heyday of globalization (the 1990s and early 2000s). Then, the newly emerging economies, in Asia particularly, came calling for Canadian minerals, forestry products, agricultural products, and petroleum. A report by Statistics Canada (2007b) in late 2007 noted that Canada's economy, as in the past, was being driven by commodity prices, though Canadians had become less "hewers of wood and drawers of water" than "conveyers of crude and moilers of metals." But, as earlier noted, the boom has come at a cost. While the demand for commodities has boosted the economies of western Canada and the Atlantic region, especially Newfoundland and Labrador, the manufacturing sector in central Canada has declined. Is Canada once more becoming a victim of the "staples trap," this time based on petroleum production instead of furs?

Energy Superpower or Petro-Colony?

Petroleum, you will have observed, is not just like any other resource. Next to water, it is today the world's most important resource; one, you will also recall (Chapter 7), that led to the controversial introduction of the National Energy Policy in the early 1980s, arousing passionate anger among many western Canadians and those in the corporate community until it was finally abandoned by the federal government. Since 1988, Canada's petroleum industry has boomed, not only in Alberta, but also in Saskatchewan and, with the discovery of offshore reserves, Newfoundland and Labrador and Nova Scotia, not to mention the North (see Chapter 10). The development of Canada's petroleum industry is controversial, however. In this section, we will examine both the economics and the economic, political, and social implications of petroleum production.

Canada's petroleum industry been lauded by many business leaders, economists, and politicians. Canada's oil and gas reserves, and the United States' (and the world's) seemingly insatiable demand for them, would appear to put Canada in the driver's seat, justifying a declaration once made by Prime Minister Harper that Canada is a rising "energy superpower." But several critics have pointed to the industry's dark side and the perils that an overreliance upon petroleum might pose for Canada's economy.

How large is Canada's petroleum industry? According to the Canadian Association for Petroleum Producers (CAPP), Canada is today the world's third-largest natural gas producer, the fifth-largest crude oil producer, and the fifth-largest energy producer. In 2013, Canada produced 1.38 million barrels per day of conventional oil, but Canada exported 2.55 million barrels per day of crude oil, concentrates, pentane, and other petroleum products (including conventional and non-conventional oil). Given that Canada's consumption of conventional oil was 1.5 million barrels, this meant that Canada also imported 0.6 million barrels (CAPP, 2014), which went mainly to the East Coast.

In short, much of Canada's energy production is exported. According to Statistics Canada (2013d), "Canada exported 73.5% of its crude oil production in 2012, 56.3% of its marketable natural gas, and 23.3% of its refined petroleum products." Nearly all of Canada's petroleum exports go to one country: the United States. The United States Energy Information Administration (2014) states that total petroleum imports from Canada during the first six months of 2014 averaged 3.26 million barrels per day, compared with 1.35 million barrels per day from the next larger supplier, Saudi Arabia.

Today there are a series of pipelines connecting Canada's North (well beyond the Athabasca oil sands) to refineries in California, Texas, and the American East Coast, with many more planned by 2030 (Laxer and Dillon, 2008:25; see also Laxer, 2010). The planned pipelines include the Northern Gateway pipeline (to take crude oil from Alberta to the Pacific coast), the Keystone XL pipeline (to take raw bitumen from Alberta's oil sands to the U.S. Gulf coast for processing), and the Energy East pipeline (to take crude oil from Alberta and Saskatchewan to eastern Canada). These proposed pipelines have led to serious conflicts between governments, corporations, environmentalists, and Aboriginal peoples, among others.

Pipeline supporters argue, first, that oil gives Canada a comparative advantage over other non-producing countries, and that Canada must exploit this advantage now or the chance will be lost. Second, they argue the petroleum industry creates a large number of direct and indirect jobs, as well as taxes and royalties that go into government revenues to pay for important services. Enbridge claims, for example, that its Northern Gateway proposal will create 63,000 person-year jobs during the construction phase and 1,146 full-time jobs thereafter (Lee, 2012:12). Average wages in the oil and gas sector are roughly $130,000 per year, while many skilled workers in the oil patch make considerably more (Healing, 2014). Third, proponents of the industry contend that, amid worldwide geopolitical instability, Canada is a reliable and "ethical" producer of oil compared with many other countries, such as Iraq, Iran, or Venezuela (Levant, 2011).

Critics of the petroleum industry approach these issues in a variety of ways. Many object on purely economic grounds. They argue, for example, that Canada's energy resources (e.g., the Keystone XL pipeline project) have been developed too quickly, leading to inflation, and that insufficient attention has been given to adding value to the resources so that better, long-term jobs are retained in Canada. Critics also dispute the alleged number of jobs the pipelines would create. Lee (2012:12) contends that the numbers given by Enbridge (above) are highly inflated; in fact, the Northern Gateway project would create only 1,850 jobs over the first 3 years and only a handful of permanent jobs afterwards.

Yet others argue the economics of oil and gas production make it increasingly unattractive. For example, years ago, the energy of 1 barrel of oil was required in order to get 99 barrels out of the ground, but by the 1970s, the ratio was 1 to 25. Today, the ratio in the oil sands and similar fields is about one barrel of oil for every three to five barrels produced (Mason, 2014). In short, producing the energy upon which the world relies is becoming uneconomical (see Nikiforuk, 2012). Finally, the volatility of oil prices is an invitation to the kind of "boom and bust" economy that staples theorists have long warned about (see Drache, 1995).

While not ignoring economic arguments altogether, other critics contend that Canada and Canadians absorb the real environmental and health costs of development. In the Alberta oil sands area, for example, local residents, many of them Aboriginals, disproportionately shoulder these costs—a point that questions the idea of "ethical" production (see Marsden, 2007; Nikiforuk, 2010, 2012; see also Chapter 10). More broadly, critics argue that the market price of oil and gas does not reflect its true cost, and that the real costs of production have been passed on to individuals, families, communities, and even the ecosystem; they are **externalities** (see Klein, 2014).

Finally, Laxer and Dillon (2008:9) argue that Canada, far from being an energy power, is in fact an "energy colony." Why is this the case? The answer, they suggest, is found in a section of NAFTA called the proportionality clause. This clause prohibits Canada from decreasing the proportion of oil and gas exports relative to its total supply for the most recent three-year period, even if Canadians experience shortages, a situation that new pipelines to the U.S. will only potentially worsen as this proportion continues to increase (Laxer and Dillon, 2008). Proportionality also works against Canadian efforts at energy conservation and efforts to protect the environment by slowing the pace of development. Laxer (2010) argues that the proportionality clause means the United States has first dibs on Canadian oil and natural gas, over and above the needs of Canadians, and will do so until the resources have been used up. The only way around this situation, he contends, is a renegotiation of the clause.

These concerns about petroleum development are only part, however, of what critics argue is a growing dependency in the Canadian economy that threatens Canada's future as a sovereign, democratic society.

Political Sovereignty and the Drive for "Deep Integration"

Free trade supporters view questions of ownership and fears of a loss of political sovereignty as red herrings. They argue that markets are neutral and that companies respond solely to consumer demand. By contrast, free trade opponents in 1988 and today argue that it deliberately removes democratic control of the economy from citizens, placing important decisions in the hands of companies, investment dealers, and shareholders who may have little concern for Canada.

What is the level of foreign ownership in Canada today? Has this level changed since 1988? And if so, how? A Statistics Canada study conducted by Baldwin and Gallatly (2005) argued that foreign ownership or control of key sectors of the economy peaked in the 1960s, declined in the 1970s during the period of Canadianization (particularly due to the Foreign Investment Review Agency), but had returned to mid-1960 levels. Foreign control was especially noticeable, the report concluded, in the manufacturing sector where, in 1999, foreign firms controlled 52.7 percent of all exports and employed 31.7 percent of all workers in manufacturing, although this was before the recent recession, during which manufacturing took a major hit.

The push to further "marketize" Canada's resources has been led by the corporate community. Headed by the Canadian Council of Chief Executives (formerly the Business Council on National Issues)—made up of Canada's largest 150 companies and pro-business think tanks like the C. D. Howe Institute, the Fraser Institute, and the Conference Board of Canada—corporate Canada has repeatedly called for Canada's "deep integration" into the North American economy. An ongoing series of papers (termed *The Border Papers*) published by the C. D. Howe Institute, for example, have called for such things as a common North American tariff and integrated energy, environmental, and regulatory policies (see Dymond and Hart, 2003; Bradley and Watkins, 2003; Hufbauer and Schott, 2004). In the words of Dymond and Hart (2003:1), "The time has come to achieve a seamless border with our neighbour, embraced within a new agreement implementing rules, procedures, and institutions consonant with the reality of ever-deepening, mutually beneficial crossborder integration."

As in the past, corporate leaders and their supporters argue the economic merits of "getting inside the American tent," but who would primarily benefit? Might there be other costs? Campbell and Finn (2006:11) place the push for deep integration within a deeper political and social context:

> The big business push for deeper integration policies has been driven by fear, in the 1980s by the fear of increased U.S. protectionism, and since 9/11 by the fear of security-related border disruptions. But it has also been driven by the goal of harmonizing Canadian policies, regulations, and institutions with those of a more "business-friendly" America, reducing the significance of the border, and foreclosing the ability of any future Canadian government to return to the interventionist policies of the 1960s and 1970s. It is a way to smuggle a corporate agenda, unpopular with most Canadians, through the back door.

Is Canada becoming more tightly integrated into the United States? Is Canada losing control of its destiny? Clarkson (2008) argues that, nearly two decades after NAFTA, Canada, the United States, and Mexico still operate separately, but there have been significant changes. Notably, he argues (2008:461–470) that there is a deepened asymmetry among the three countries, with the United States dominant; that the U.S. exercises growing hegemony over its other partners, but that both Canada and Mexico also retain "substantial residual autonomy" over their affairs—if they choose to use it. NAFTA, says Clarkson, was meant by its negotiators "to bring down political barriers to trade and investment," but not to fashion the institutions that would further social integration (2008:459), that is, to create a *society*.

Canadian nationalists may take some solace from Clarkson's conclusion that formal social and political integration into the American Empire is not yet on the horizon. Nonetheless, might tighter economic integration still pose problems for a united, coherent Canada?

Canada is not an easy place to govern. As the economic historian Harold Innis argued years ago, Canada does not have a single, national economy, but rather several regional economies that trade with the United States; Courchene (1998) notes that free trade resulted in a shift from east-west to north-south trade, though interprovincial trade is still the norm. Politically, also, Canada's system of federal-provincial powers is designed to be fractious and to often follow the regional divides found in the various economies; the last several federal elections have pointed out the regional nature of Canadian politics (see Appendix 2), though these results may also reflect problems in the country's first-passed-the-post electoral system.

What finally tied these regional economies together as a nation—a society—was a network of transport systems, communication systems, and social programs (such as medicare), many of them arising after 1945, that facilitated positive and ongoing interactions between people within and across the provinces and territories. In short, becoming and remaining a country meant that Canada also had to become a unified *society*. But this did not just happen. Might tighter integration with the U.S., even short of a formal merger, lead to Canada's internal fragmentation?

Some, such as business commentator Diane Francis (2013)—like the liberal elites of the 19th century who saw Canada as destined to join the United States (see Chapter 5)—welcome the notion of a merger of the two countries. But most view concerns over Canadian independence to be overstated (see Ibbitson, 2009). They argue that Canadians possess distinct beliefs and values, and a strong identity that will not only fend off American influence, but will also continue to bind the country together.

Political and Social Value Orientations

We previously examined the notion of ideology in relation to the development of modern Quebec (Chapter 2). Here we want to ask, What are Canada's dominant ideological strains? How do these strains differ from those of the United States? How have they shaped Canadian values and beliefs? And have Canadian values and beliefs changed during the time of neo-liberal dominance?

The American political sociologist Seymour Martin Lipset (1968b, 1986, 1990, 1996) argues that Canadian political values fall between those of the United States and Great Britain, such that, by contrast with the United States, Canadians are more elitist (hierarchical), conformist, statist, collectivist, and particularist (group-oriented) (Lipset, 1996).

Lipset's thesis is contentious. First, recent scholarship suggests that the American revolutionary leaders were republican individualists, not liberal individualists; the colonial masses believed in "local communalism," not rugged non-conformity; and, in many ways, there was little to distinguish the revolutionaries from the Loyalists (Grabb, Baer, and Curtis, 1999; Grabb, 2000). Second, Lipset's emphasis upon the revolution as a founding moment ignores perhaps more important events in American history, notably the Civil War (Chapter 5), while his discussion of Canada often ignores the influence of French culture. Third, Lipset's thesis lacks a dynamic element, thus freezing both countries in time.

Nonetheless, Lipset's depiction of Canada's dominant ideological strain may be accurate for a certain period of time. Research suggests that the War of 1812 and the failed rebellions of 1837 and 1838 reinforced conservative elements in English-speaking Canada. (Quebec, as we have seen, had its own particular forces shaping a similar conservatism there.) The 19th-century form of English-Canadian conservatism was of a particular type, referred to as Toryism.

In *Lament for a Nation*, Canadian philosopher George Grant (2005) chronicled the importance of Toryism to Canada, arguing that it had been an ideological bulwark against Canada's absorption into the American Empire. Like its British counterpart, English-Canadian Toryism was monarchist, lauded tradition and order, and believed in a natural order of things that extended across class, race, religion, and gender. In its better moments, this latter belief in a natural social hierarchy was balanced by a deep sense of *noblesse oblige* toward those less fortunate, something that, when forged with socialism, gave support to the development of a more extensive welfare state in Canada than is found in the United States (Horowitz, 1966).

In Grant's view (2005), however, certain characteristics also distinguished Canadian Toryism from its British forebear. First, Canadian Toryism was staunchly anti-American, thus the Tory party's opposition to free trade in both 1891 and 1911. Second, the Canadian Tory tradition also espoused a particularly strong belief in a positive role for the state both in the economy and in society at large, hence Macdonald's formulation of the National Policy (Chapter 6) and R. B. Bennett's creation of the Canadian Radio Broadcasting Commission in 1932, which led to the founding of the Canadian Broadcasting Corporation four years later.

By the 1960s, however, Grant viewed the Tory tradition in eclipse due to Britain's fading presence in Canadian life and the growing dominance of liberal ideals in Canada and much of the world, as promoted by the United States through the economy and new media technologies. For Grant, the end of Toryism meant the end of economic nationalism in Canada, with Canada's ultimate demise the result. Both the Liberal and

Progressive Conservative parties would henceforth become "liberal" parties supporting continental integration into the larger United States.

Lament for a Nation is a seminal book in Canadian thought, but it is not without problems. Notably, in lauding Canada's British traditions, Grant largely ignores the significant contributions of other peoples to the construction of Canada and Canadian identity, a point emphasized by recent scholars.

Resnick (2005:89), for example, argues that Canada is essentially a European country, composed of its "European historical connections, a North American geographical setting, multiple national identities, robust social programs, multicultural practices, increasingly secular values, and a multilateral outlook on international affairs," to which he adds one last element setting Canadian political culture off from that of the United States: self-doubt.

Saul (2008), however, refutes Resnick's European depiction of Canada, instead arguing that Canada is in fact an Aboriginal nation (see Chapter 12) that thrives on complexity and nuance. In fact, Saul contends the United States is the far more European country, with its relatively fixed notions of nation and state.

Finally, Michael Ignatieff (2009)—Harvard scholar, briefly leader of the federal Liberal Party, and George Grant's nephew—contends that his uncle had it all wrong. Ignatieff argues that Grant misunderstood the importance and endurance of differences between Canadians and Americans regarding such issues as freedom and collective rights, and that he ignored the role of Aboriginal and Métis peoples and Quebec. Ignatieff further chides Grant for having given up on Canada at the very moment (1965) when Canada was engaged in a major transformation of itself—strengthening the welfare state, adopting a new flag, embracing bilingualism, becoming multicultural, and patriating the Canadian Constitution with a Charter of Rights and Freedoms. Finally, he notes that the period of neo-liberal globalization—of capitalism on the march—has also witnessed the rebirth of nationalism everywhere, including Canada.

Surveys conducted throughout the 1990s and 2000s provide evidence that Canadians, in general, hold quite distinct value orientations from those of their American counterparts. Nevitte (1996:10–18) and Adams (1998, 2003) contend that, compared with Americans, Canadians tend to be

- less deferential to authority,
- less conformist,
- less formally religious,
- less characterized by a traditional work ethic,
- less accepting of violence,
- more desirous of personal autonomy,
- more individualistic,
- more hedonistic,
- more relaxed, and
- more suspicious of big business.

In short, both theory and evidence suggest that Canada is a distinct society on the North American continent. It should be noted, however, that the distinctness of these value orientations is mitigated by such sociological factors as class, gender, ethnicity, religion, and region. Recent scholarship, for example, has described North America as comprising four value regions: a liberal Quebec; the rest of Canada; a very conservative American South; and the rest of the United States, with both Quebec and the American South drawing their respective national partners closer to their particular value orientations and away from cross-border similarities (Grabb and Curtis, 2005). More importantly, such studies suggest that while some Canadian and American values have converged over time, others have diverged. Perhaps especially startling is the suggestion made by some researchers that Canadians today are more likely than Americans to believe in and experience the American Dream of individual opportunity (Adams, 1998, 2003; Hood, 2008).

A joint survey between Nanos research and the State University of New York at Buffalo, conducted in August 2014, suggests some evidence for the divergence thesis. The survey questioned 1,000 Canadians and an equal number of Americans. The results suggest that the peoples on opposite sides of the border are in fact drifting apart on issues of border co-operation, security, and fighting terrorism (Nanos, 2014).

Culture, the Corporate Media, and Canadian Identity

For critics of free trade, culture was a specific concern in 1988. Free trade proponents said at the time that culture was not open to negotiation. Nonetheless, the United States, home to Hollywood production and many of the world's largest music and magazine industries, has since repeatedly pressured Canada to drop "protectionist" policies toward its cultural industries. From a neo-liberal perspective, culture is just another commodity, indeed, simply another industry. An Industry Canada report (2014) states that the cultural industries (including publishing, motion picture and sound recording, broadcasting, Internet, telecommunications, and data processing) produced $51.4 billion in value in 2012. But from a nationalist perspective, American culture is a threat to Canada possessing a distinct identity, as well as, in the specific case of some Hollywood movies, even state propaganda (Gardner, 2002).

A similar debate involves Canada's media. Canada has the least-competitive media landscape among G8 countries, with four large corporations dominating: Quebecor, Bell Media, Rogers Communications, and the Canadian Broadcasting Corporation. For neo-liberals, this is not a problematic situation. Media ownership is a matter of personal (or corporate) interest. Moreover, from the viewpoint of efficiency, new technologies have created the basis for concentration and convergence across a range of media (e.g., print, television, Internet, and radio). Others, however, have noted that corporate concentration raises concerns that touch on important issues for Canadian society, including democracy:

While corporate convergence can be beneficial to companies, there are potential undesirable consequences, including: a reduction in competition; increased barriers to entry for new companies; the further commercialization of the media; and the treatment of audiences as consumers rather than citizens. The substantial costs of corporate mergers have also led converged companies to seek profits through cost-cutting rather than increased investment in communication services.

Corporate convergence also prompts concerns about the quality of corporate journalism, such as: the role of the media in democratic societies to provide objective information and analysis to an informed citizenry; the independence of journalists; the range of voices and diversity of viewpoints on current events; coverage of local issues; and conflicts of interest between properties owned by the same company. (Gasher, 2014)

Ultimately, the debate may come down to whether one believes Canada has a national culture and, if so, one worth preserving. Pevere and Dymond (1996) have argued persuasively that Canada does not in fact have a national culture; that, rather, the essence of "Canadian" culture arises from its regions. Canada's proximity to the United States allows many of its artists to mirror American culture and therefore to do very well in that marketplace. (Shania Twain and Nickelback provide two examples.) Such artists can "pass" as generically American. By contrast, regional artists (Great Big Sea) and films (*My Winnipeg* or *The Necessities of Life*), or those artists whose content remains too resolutely Canadian (The Tragically Hip) are not as easily sold in the United States. They are "too Canadian." Likewise, one may note the region-specific nature of such acclaimed television shows as *Corner Gas* and *Republic of Doyle*.

What role such cultural artefacts play in Canadian identity is not entirely certain, yet many Canadians do appear to acknowledge and value the distinctive products of Canadian culture and to include them in their identity kits.

Social Cohesion: Social Stratification and Inequality

Models of Social Stratification

In recent decades, as several societies have witnessed increased conflict, many sociologists have returned to the age-old question asked by structural functionalists (Introduction): What holds societies together? One such sociologist, Robert Putnam (see Putnam, 2000), has coined the term **social capital**, defined as a positive combination of interaction, reciprocity, and trust that bonds people to their communities (see Krahn et al., 2009). In turn, social capital is facilitated by a high degree of **social cohesion**, defined as the bonding effect of society that arises spontaneously out of individuals willingly interacting in order to achieve collective goals. Social cohesion is enhanced when there is a relative equality of income and life chances, while high social and economic equality, in turn, lead to a better economy (see Osberg, 2003).

We previously examined social stratification in early Canada (Chapter 1). The question of social stratification is important to again examine here, given neo-liberalism's belief in "trickle-down" economics and a minimalist role for the state in reducing social inequalities. What is the nature of Canada's social stratification system today after nearly 30 years of neo-liberal policies? To what extent are the life chances of Canadian citizens more or less equal?

There are two major paradigms for thinking about social stratification and inequality in society. The first employs the neo-Marxist notion of class, updated to reflect the complexity of modern labour markets and especially the rise of managers and technical experts since Marx's time. The second, termed a measure of **socio-economic status** or SES, combines education, occupation, and income in a composite index (see Box 8.2).

Box 8.2: Neo-Marxist and Socio-Economic Status (SES) Models of Class

Neo-Marxist[1]	SES Model
Capitalist classes	Upper upper
Grand bourgeoisie	Lower upper
Small employers	Upper middle
Petite bourgeoisie	Lower middle
New middle classes	Upper lower
Managers and supervisors	Lower lower
Expert and semi-credentialed workers	
Proletarians	
Underclass	

Note: 1. Capitalists own the means of production in varying degrees, but may or may not purchase labour. The managerial and supervisory members of the new middle class may have discretionary control over capital and command labour. All members of this class exercise some degree of job autonomy. The proletarians neither own nor control the means of production, do not command labour, and have no assets in the labour market but their labour.

Sources: Adapted from Eric Olin Wright. 1985. *Classes*. London: Verso.; Murray Knuttila. 2002. *Introducing Sociology: A Critical Perspective*. Toronto: Oxford University Press.

There are similarities between Marxian class and SES measures of class. Occupation as measured by the SES model, for example, is a reasonable proxy for class in the Marxian sense, but there are also clear theoretical and ideological differences in the manner in which each describes systems of social stratification in modern, capitalist societies. First, there is a structural relationship among Marxist classes, especially between (as Marx saw it) the two chief antagonists, the capitalist class (or bourgeoisie) and the workers (or proletariat). There is no such relationship between any of the strata described in the SES model; these are merely continuous statistical categories. Second, and related to the first point, people move through life in the Marxist model as members of a group, with the potential of becoming conscious of this affiliation (that is, a **social class**), and acting politically upon this knowledge. By contrast, in the SES model people are placed in a category on the basis of their individual credentials, a fact that suggests the essentially liberal basis of this model and its further congruence with functionalist explanations of social inequality (see the Introduction). Third, whereas the Marxian model implies a relatively closed and static society based on the class position to which one is born, the SES model implies a far more open and fluid social structure in which individuals either rise on the basis of merit or fall for lack thereof.

On this latter point of **social mobility**—the upward or downward movement of individuals or groups from one position in the social stratification system to another position—both models are probably in error with regard to Canadian society. At least at the top end, and also at the very bottom, social mobility in Canada is relatively low, contrary to the implications of the SES model. At the same time, the opportunities for members of the working class and new middle class to rise higher in their individual lifetimes (intra-generational social mobility) are greater than envisioned by the Marxist model.

But is the age effect lessening for young people entering the labour market today? That is, will the current cohort of younger workers experience less social mobility over time than their parents have? Recent figures show that, between 1999 and 2012, the median net worth of those aged 35 to 44 increased by 46 percent; the net worth of those 45 to 54 increased by 55 percent; and the net worth of those 65 and older increased by 70.2 percent (Statistics Canada, 2014e). But the same data also show that, during this same period, the net worth of those younger than 35 rose only 8.6 percent, raising questions about whether the children of baby boom and Generation X parents will have the opportunity to rise higher than their parents (what is termed intergenerational social mobility).

Fourth, the SES model explicitly ignores wealth (the total amount of money and other financial assets owned by individuals or families) in favour of income (money earned through the sale of labour or through investments). By contrast, the Marxist model concerns all sources of wealth, particularly those that arise out of the ownership of the means of production, for this is also a source of major political power.

Social Stratification in Canada Today

What does Canada's social stratification system look like today? Table 4.1 (Chapter 4) provides a partial answer to this question, showing that in 2012 the median income of Canadian families was $74,540 (non-constant dollars). Table 8.3 provides additional information to address this question, by looking instead at the median net worth of families. The table divides the Canadian population into 5 groups of 20 percent each (quintiles), from the poorest 20 percent of families to the richest 20 percent of families. Note that the median net worth (in 2012 constant dollars) of families in the poorest quintile both declined from 1999 to 2012, and became increasingly negative (–$10,826 in 2012). The net worth of the second quintile also declined marginally over the period from 2005 to 2012, while that of the third and fourth quintiles rose slightly. Finally, the net worth of the fifth quintile group also declined slightly, but overall this group still captured 67.4 percent of Canada's net wealth in 2012, with a median net worth of $1,380,000.

Table 8.3: Distribution and Median Net Worth of Family Units, by Quintile, in Canada, 1999, 2005, 2012 (2012 Constant Dollars)

	1999			2005			2012			Median Net Worth	
	Net Worth by Quintile	Total Net Worth	Median Net Worth	Net Worth by Quintile	Total Net Worth	Median Net Worth	Net Worth by Quintile	Total Net Worth	Median Net Worth	Percentage change	
	%	Millions $	$	%	Millions $	$	%	Millions $	$	1999–2012	2005–2012
All family units	100	3,903,014	137,000	100	5,530,509	168,700	100	8,073,585	243,800	78	44.5
Lowest quintile	-0.1	-4,161	1,300	-0.1	-7,234	1,100	-0.1	-10,826	1,100	-15.4	0
Second quintile	2.6	102,036	39,600	2.3	124,739	42,400	2.2	180,292	56,100	41.7	32.3
Third quintile	8.8	343,419	137,000	8.4	465,147	168,700	9	728,655	245,000	78.8	45.2
Fourth quintile	20.1	785,529	313,400	20.2	1,118,333	410,900	21.5	1,735,014	575,500	83.6	40.1
Highest quintile	68.6	2,676,191	763,700	69.2	3,829,524	981,400	67.4	5,440,451	1,380,000	80.7	40.6

Source: Statistics Canada. 2014e. "Survey of Financial Security, 2012." The Daily (Table 3), February 25 (www.statcan.gc.ca/daily-quotidien/140225/t140225b003-eng.htm).

The median (for income, as used in Table 4.1, and net worth, as used in Table 8.3) can be a useful statistic, but it is only one of three **measures of central tendency**, the others being the mean (or average) and the mode. In various circumstances, one measure may be more appropriate than another. Additionally, note that every statistic both reveals and simultaneously conceals something about that which it measures. Consider, for example, data taken from Statistics Canada (2013e). The median income for individual men in 2011 was $36,600, while that for individual women was $24,300. (The overall median was $30,180.) But the average income for individual men was $48,100, while that of women was $32,100. While the ratio of women's to men's incomes was roughly the same using either measure (median 66.5, mean 66.7), each statistic tells a somewhat different story. Which story is more informative?

In contrast to the statistical evidence presented in Table 8.3, other evidence suggests that Canada's middle income groups are feeling increasingly squeezed. An internal report done for Employment and Social Development Canada in September 2013 states that "wealth is not distributed equally among the middle class" and "middle-income families are increasingly vulnerable to financial shocks" (ESDC, 2013:19–20).

Finally, consider also that the net wealth reported in Table 8.3 is not evenly distributed within the quintiles. This is particularly important in looking at the fifth quintile. The net worth of those at the very top—the one percent, or even smaller, identified by Occupy movement protesters after the financial collapse of 2007—are the primary holders of much of Canada's wealth.

In 2012, the wealthiest 86 individuals or families in Canada, many of whom are household names, had as much wealth ($178 billion) as the bottom 11.4 million Canadians (Macdonald, 2014:1). Within this select group is an even smaller group, those who are billionaires. Table 8.4 lists the names, as identified by *Forbes* (2014), of Canada's 31 billionaires in 2014—up from 20 in 2009—part of the 1,584 billionaires in the world, as noted earlier.

What is the source of this wealth? If asked, many average Canadians would respond that these billionaires are CEOs of major companies. Surprisingly, however, this is not the case. Canada's CEOs are generously reimbursed. Hugh Mackenzie (2009) shows that CEO compensation in Canada soared between 1995 and 2007, from 85 times the average salary of workers to 398 times. In 2007, the top 100 CEOs in Canada received an average compensation of $10,408,054, compared to an average salary of $40,237 for Canadian workers. But only 10 of Canada's CEOs are part of the 86 wealthy individuals and families noted above (Macdonald, 2014).

The very wealthy obtain most of their wealth through "creating or trading assets" (Macdonald, 2014:12) and lucrative tax breaks on capital gains that reward speculation; this is a phenomenon commensurate with neo-liberalism's veneration of finance capital that, in turn, has seen inequality skyrocket throughout the world in recent decades (see Piketty, 2014).

Unlike the very wealthy, most people rely heavily on paid income and not investments, a situation made worse by the recent recession. While the stock markets initially collapsed after 2007, they have since recovered entirely. This is not the case for wages, however, thus

Table 8.4: Primary Source of Wealth, Estimated Wealth (2009 and 2014), and 2014 World Ranking of Canada's 31 Billionaires

Name	Primary Source of Wealth	Estimated Wealth in Billions $ 2009	Estimated Wealth in Billions $ 2014	World Ranking
Thompson, David, and family	Inherited, media	13.0	24.0	25
Weston, Galen, Sr., and family	Retail	5.0	9.5	134
Pattison, Jim	Diversified	2.1	7.1	196
Tsai, Joseph	E-commerce	n/a	6.4	222
Irving, Arthur	Oil	n/a	6.3	225
Irving, James	Diversified	n/a	6.2	231
Saputo, Emanuele (Lino)	Cheese	1.3	5.2	291
Desmarais, Jacqueline and family	Financial services	2.6	4.7	328
Riddell, Clayton	Oil and gas	n/a	4.1	377
Sherman, Bernard (Barry)	Pharmaceuticals	2.5	4.0	390
Katz, Daryl	Pharmacies	1.5	3.5	473
Cheriton, David	Google	1.1	3.4	498
Coutu, Jean	Pharmacies	n/a	2.4	737
Miller, Robert	Electronics	2.1	2.4	749
Stroll, Lawrence	Retail	n/a	2.3	800
Edwards, N. Murray	Oil and gas	n/a	2.1	861
Bronfman, Charles	Liquor	1.8	2.1	880
Bouchard, Alain	Retail	n/a	2.1	889
Fidani, Carlo	Real estate	n/a	2.1	907
Wilson, Chip	Lululemon	n/a	2.0	941
Laliberté, Guy	Cirque du Soleil	2.5	1.9	958
Goldhar, Mitchell	Real estate	n/a	1.9	1000
Schwartz, Gerald	Finance	n/a	1.9	1001
Gilgan, Peter	Homebuilding	n/a	1.7	1064
Southern, Ronald	Structures, utilities	n/a	1.7	1069
Jarislowsky, Stephen	Money management	1.2	1.7	1096
Joyce, Ronald	Restaurants	n/a	1.3	1345
Stronach, Frank	Auto parts	n/a	1.3	1366
Adams, Marcel	Real estate	n/a	1.2	1433
Slaight, Allan	Broadcasting	n/a	1.2	1449
Sahi, K. Rai	Real estate	n/a	1.2	1465

Source: *Forbes*. 2014. "The World's Billionaires." New York: Forbes Media (www.forbes.com/billionaires/list/#tab:overall).

contributing to rising inequality in Canada and to the increased insecurity felt by the middle class. In fact, the average salary of most workers in Canada has steadily declined in relative terms (and remained largely static in real terms) since the 1980s. This is the case even in Alberta, where—despite the oil boom—the bottom 90 percent of people have seen a real increase in incomes of only $6,000 since 1986 (Macdonald, 2014:9).

The Labour Market's Periphery

For those outside of the labour market, the decline in living standards has been even greater. Compare, for example, the net wealth of the bottom quintile in 1999 and 2012 as shown in Table 8.3. As noted in Chapter 7, Canada's welfare state—like that in other Western countries—was created at the end of the Second World War in part as a counter-cyclical strategy to deal with the inevitable fluctuations that occur in a capitalist (market) economy. The strategy worked well until the mid-1970s, but globalization since has transferred economic clout to large corporations, especially the owners of finance capital (e.g., banks, investment houses). Unable or unwilling to challenge corporate power, many countries have reduced the role and capacity of welfare states in meeting the needs of the most vulnerable (Wahl, 2011).

This reduction has also occurred in Canada (see McBride and Whiteside, 2011; Rice and Prince, 2013:208–209). Shortly after the adoption of free trade in 1989, Canada began making changes and cuts to its social safety net. These changes have given greater power to "the market" and have had the effect of disciplining workers to accept a reduction in wages, other benefits, and protections. Individuals and families who rely upon non-market sources of income have been especially impacted by these changes. There has been a steady increase, for example, in the use of food banks throughout Canada. Reports show the number of people using food banks in Canada has risen steadily since the 1980s. In 2014, Canadian food banks assisted, on average, 850,000 people each month, more than 36 percent of whom were children and youth (Food Banks Canada, 2014). Tied partly to food bank usage, homelessness has also become a feature of Canadian urban life, even in very small towns. A report published in 2013 estimates that "at least 200,000 Canadians access homeless emergency services or sleep outside in a given year" and that "at least 30,000 are homeless on a given night" (Gaetz et al., 2013:5). It is important to note, however, that not all of those using food banks and shelters are entirely outside the labour market. Many users, often young people, do in fact have part-time or temporary—but also poorly paying—jobs. This phenomenon has led to recent depictions of a new social class, emerging throughout the developed nations: the **precariat** (Standing, 2011, 2014).

As a sociologist, you will have observed that, when it comes to great poverty, great wealth, and positions in between, not all people are treated equally (Grabb et al., 1999). Gender provides one example. Women, as noted above, earn roughly two-thirds of what men earn. Women's incomes closely approximate those of men in similar occupations—though there are still differences, even within (for example) the university professoriate. But women remain often concentrated in lower-paying job ghettos while men occupy the highest-paid professions (Krahn et al., 2015). Additionally, women do not often own or control large corporate enterprises, the major source of wealth (note the gender of Canada's billionaires in Table 8.4). Women, however, do disproportionately number among Canada's poor, especially those on some form of public assistance. Income and poverty rates are particularly high for single-parent female-headed families and single, widowed, or divorced female seniors (Curtis et al., 1999; Morissette and Zhang, 2001). The fact that women are disproportionately represented among the poor has led some policy-makers to speak of the **feminization of poverty**.

Besides age, gender, education, and occupation, other factors also impact Canada's system of social stratification. Region of residence is important. As earlier noted, employment is generally higher in the western provinces than in those further east, especially in the Maritime region. Ethnicity and race are also central among these other factors. The influence of ethnicity and race is not as stark as when John Porter published his seminal tome, *The Vertical Mosaic*, in 1965 (see Nakhaie, 1997; Lian and Matthews, 1998), but they still play a major role in defining life chances among both recent and established immigrants (Fleras, 2007), as well as in the case of Canada's Aboriginal peoples, whose place within the system is conditioned by a history of colonialism and attendant discrimination (Part 3).

Conclusion

The term *social engineering*, often voiced on talk radio, is usually employed to describe actions taken by governments in the form of rules given for preferential hiring or laws prohibiting discrimination against minorities. A good case can be made, however, that the market, aided and abetted by governments, has engaged in the most significant act of social engineering since the 1970s, transforming the relationships between states and citizens, individuals and communities, and the past and present—and future.

But we have also seen this before. Capitalist globalization, war, inequality, and social discord: these are not new phenomena, nor are threats to Canada's independence. Canadians have always faced the task of carving out an existence and an identity as a northern people on the margins of the world economy and under the aegis of empire.

Canada's fate lies not in the stars or in the inexorable workings of some imaginary manifest destiny imposed by others; rather, it lies in the will of its people to find or create new reasons to continue as a society, a country, and a different kind of nation. In this quest, they might look no further for answers than among Canada's Aboriginal peoples who, earlier than most, faced the onslaught of global imperial forces.

Note

1. In May 2011, Osama bin Laden—Al-Qaeda's leader and mastermind of the 9/11 attacks— was killed by a special operations unit of the U.S. Central Intelligence Agency.

Key Terms

double movement
externalities
feminization of poverty
measures of central tendency
military-industrial complex
neo-liberalism
precariat
social capital
social class
social cohesion
social mobility
socio-economic status

Critical Thinking Questions

1. Why did neo-liberalism become the dominant ideology of the late 20th century?
2. In what ways is the American Empire similar to or different from past empires?
3. Do values and beliefs either create or arise out of material conditions?
4. Which model of stratification described in the chapter fits Canada best?
5. Is a state's invasion of another country ever justified?

Recommended Readings

Clarkson, Stephen. 2008. *Does North America Exist?* Toronto: University of Toronto Press.
In this book, Clarkson examines the results of NAFTA, with specific focus on institutions of governance in the three signing countries.

Diamond, Jared. 2005. *Collapse: How Societies Choose to Fail or Succeed.* New York: Viking Press.
This very readable book presents a wealth of case studies on how human behaviour can result in ecological disasters that impact the survival of societies.

Grant, George. 2005. *Lament for a Nation: The Defeat of Canadian Nationalism.* 40th anniversary edition. Originally published in 1965. Montreal and Kingston: McGill-Queen's University Press.
Though often disputed, Grant's lament for Canada remains, nearly a half-century on, a keystone of philosophical discourse on Canada's relationship to the United States.

Klein, Naomi. 2014. *This Changes Everything: Capitalism vs. the Climate*. Toronto: Alfred A. Knopf Canada.
One of Canada's and the world's foremost critics, Klein argues that the earth is imperiled by the logic and practice of neo-liberal capitalism.

Smith, Graeme. 2013. *The Dogs Are Eating Them Now: Our War in Afghanistan*. Toronto: Alfred A. Knopf Canada.
Written by an acclaimed journalist, this book brings home to readers the horror and senselessness of war.

Related Websites

Canadian Council of Chief Executives
www.ceocouncil.ca
This organization is composed of the chief executive officers of roughly 150 major Canadian corporations. Founded in 1976 as the Business Council on National Issues, it was a chief proponent of free trade in 1988.

LittleSis
littlesis.org
Founded in 2009 and located in Buffalo, New York, LittleSis (i.e., not "Big Brother") is a non-profit, grassroots watchdog network that collects information on government and corporate connections, including lobbyists, think tanks, and board directorships.

World Social Forum
www.wsfprocess.net
This loose organization of non-governmental, non-partisan social movements from around the world meets every year in Brazil to discuss alternatives to neo-liberalism.

Canadian Society on Video

Tar Sands: The Selling of Alberta. 2008. Canadian Broadcasting Corporation, 60 minutes.
A critical look at the social and environmental costs associated with the development of the Alberta oil sands.

The Corporation. 2004. Big Picture Media Corporation, 160 minutes.
This documentary traces the development of the contemporary business corporation, from a legal entity that originated as a government-chartered institution to the rise of the modern commercial institution entitled to most of the legal rights of a person.

View from the Summit. 2001. National Film Board of Canada, 75 minutes, 15 seconds. Examines the events surrounding the April 2001 Quebec City meeting of world leaders to discuss an agreement for a free trade area of the Americas and the popular groups that assembled to oppose to such an agreement.

PART THREE

CANADA AND THE ABORIGINAL NATIONS

It may seem a bit unorthodox to discuss Canada's First Nations at the end of this volume rather than at the beginning. Our argument, however, is that Aboriginal peoples not only should not be historicized, but should be seen as constituting, if Canadians play fairly, the sector with the most promising future. Indeed, Aboriginal peoples are a young and thriving cultural, political, and economic force that holds a key to Canada's future as a whole.

In Part One, we examined Canada's French and English "solitudes." But Aboriginal and non-Aboriginal peoples in Canada constitute another pair of solitudes, separated by history, culture, class, and experience. This separation continues even though Aboriginals, especially in western Canada, are increasingly part of the urban landscape. Instead, state institutions such as the federal Department of Indian Affairs, children's service agencies, welfare agencies, and the courts often mediate this relationship, with the result that the knowledge that non-Aboriginals possess of Aboriginals is largely abstract or anecdotal, indeed stereotypical.

Part Three of this book explores relations between Aboriginal and non-Aboriginal peoples in Canada. As in the previous two sections, the first chapter of Part Three, Chapter 9, provides an historical overview. Chapter 10 then examines a part of Canada not yet discussed here in detail: the North, a place where Aboriginal peoples still predominate and yet one that is a prime source of Canadian identity. Chapter 11 examines the genesis of recent Aboriginal demands and growing militancy. Finally, Chapter 12 concludes with a portrait of Aboriginal peoples today in Canada, an examination of the major issues still to be resolved in this area, and a discussion of the profound impact that Aboriginals may have in shaping Canadian society in the future.

CHAPTER 9

WHEN CULTURAL
WORLDS COLLIDE

We had a cross made thirty feet high, which was put together in the presence of a number of the Indians on the point at the entrance to this harbour, under the cross-bar of which we fixed a shield with three *fleurs-de-lys* in relief, and above it a wooden board, engraved in large Gothic characters, where was written, LONG LIVE THE KING OF FRANCE. We erected this cross on the point in their presence and they watched it being put together and set up.

—Jacques Cartier, *Diary*, 1534

But the face of the red man is now no longer seen. All traces of his footsteps are fast being obliterated from his once favourite haunts, and those who would see the aborigines of this country in their original state, or seek to study their native manners and customs, must travel far through the pathless forest to find them.

—artist Paul Kane, 1859

All men were made by the same Great Spirit Chief. They are all brothers. The earth is the mother of all people, and all people should have equal rights upon it.

—Chief Joseph, Nez Perce Nation, 1877

Introduction

On June 11, 2008, Prime Minister Stephen Harper issued a formal apology to the First Nations of Canada for the government's treatment of Aboriginal children in residential schools. Among other things, Harper said, "The treatment of children in Indian residential schools is a sad chapter of our history. Some sought, as was infamously said, to 'kill the Indian in the child.' This policy was wrong, caused great harm, and has no place in our country."

Reactions to the prime minister's announcement varied greatly. Some Aboriginal leaders and interested observers demanded immediate concrete action—fearing more empty promises—to ameliorate social problems emanating from residential school experiences. Others were more positive, believing the apology was a good start toward creating better relations between Canada's Aboriginal peoples and other citizens.

Improving relations between Aboriginal and non-Aboriginal peoples is a huge task, however. The vast majority of non-Aboriginals have little knowledge of Aboriginal history or Aboriginal ways. As the late Aboriginal leader Harold Cardinal (1945–2005) put it, "We have been fighting for so long now that the original misunderstandings and differences [that] have created this conflict have been forgotten" (Cardinal, 1977:7). Moreover, unlike other minority groups, of whom Canada's dominant cultures also have little understanding, Canada's Aboriginals face a range of challenges, including economic underdevelopment, substandard education, often deplorable social conditions, and public misunderstanding, prejudice, and racism.

How did we—Aboriginal and non-Aboriginal peoples alike—get to where we are? And how will we get to the future? In order to understand, we have to retrace our steps.

This chapter examines the cultural world of Canada's Aboriginal peoples before and after the arrival of Europeans, including the political economy of the two peoples' early relations. The discussion examines how the dominant-subordinate relationship between the non-Aboriginal and Aboriginal peoples became institutionalized, with consequences for both parties and for Canadian society as a whole.

Pre-Contact Aboriginal Societies

Archaeologists inform us that the Aboriginal peoples of North America have been on this continent for 10,000 to 12,000 years, but the truth is that no one really knows when the first Aboriginal peoples arrived. Some evidence points to an arrival as long as 30,000 to 50,000 years ago (Dickason, 2002:6).

For decades, the prevailing theory was that they arrived in North America thousands of years ago via an ice bridge that temporarily linked Asia to this continent. The Bering Strait theory may explain some migrations, but this theory is now seriously questioned. Today, evidence suggests the first immigrants may have arrived by various routes, by boat or raft, across both major oceans.

Initial encounters between the Europeans and indigenous North Americans were limited to the south and central regions of the continent. Northern contact occurred much later. The first Europeans who arrived often failed to make distinctions among resident tribes, but in fact the people they encountered represented a variety of different civilizations and cultures.

In what is today Canada, six distinct cultural areas may be identified among the Aboriginal peoples. These include the Northwest Coast, the North, the Plateau, the Plains, the Mackenzie District, and the Eastern Woodlands. Authorities differ regarding the linguistic varieties, but today three language groups comprise most Aboriginal language families (Wilson and Urion, 1995:32). The first of the three major linguistic groups is Algonquian, which includes most Canadian Aboriginals and the vast majority in southern Canada east of the Rockies. Two Algonquian groups, Cree and Ojibway, are closely related, implying recent separation. The Blackfoot also appear to be distantly related.

The second major language family in Canada is Athapaskan, with the majority of speakers occupying much of northwestern Canada and Alaska. Because of the limited diversity among this language group, linguists believe this area was fairly recently occupied.

The third language family is Eskimo-Aleut, represented in Canada by Inupik (Inuktitut), is identified only in the northern regions from northern Alaska across to eastern Greenland. Apart from any archaeological evidence, this seems to imply that the region has only recently been occupied (see Chapter 10).

Addicted as we are to the magic of the technological age, it is sometimes hard to realize the dramatic cultural changes that have occurred these last several centuries in Canada. The impact on Aboriginal cultures has been considerable, and while many First Nations have successfully adjusted to elements of the technological revolution, others are still determining how they can best participate in this transition.

Cultures may differ materially and non-materially (through their particular languages, values, beliefs, norms, and behaviours) in ways passed on from one generation to the next. From a functionalist perspective, however, all cultures, Aboriginal or other, possess certain elements (Durkheim, 1912/1978; Wissler, 1923). These elements include (1) language; (2) artefacts (i.e., physical objects) that serve functional purposes; (3) social organization; (4) authority and decision-making arrangements; (5) underlying spiritual or religious beliefs and structures; (6) forms of welfare arrangements whereby the aged, the sick, and the young are taken care of; (7) arts and music; (8) forms of property ownership or usage; and (9) a means of educating the young to assure perpetuation of the system.

Pre-contact Aboriginal lifestyles represented a very present-oriented way of life. They enjoyed day-to-day living and took time for leisure activities. Unlike their 21st-century counterparts, Canada's First Nations were never in a hurry to get somewhere else; they were already where they needed to be. They did not have the luxury of placing things in a freezer to save for another day, though they had ways of preserving some foods. Nor did they make use of such future-oriented facilities as savings accounts, pension plans, or registered retirement savings plans; they relied instead on each other and the environment around them. Primary to all considerations was their relationship to nature, the elements—sun, earth, water, wind, fire—and the cycle of natural growth and change.

The Aboriginals' awe of nature did not hinder them from developing elaborate metaphysical belief systems or developing complex forms of food gathering, food preparation, art, and weaponry. Often these cultural elements were related. Food gathering and religion, for example, were highly related activities in nearly all pre-technological societies, but people were still able to live a satisfying way of life. The late Chief Walking Buffalo (Tatanga Mani) of the Stoney (Nakoda Sioux) Nation put it as follows:

> We were on pretty good terms with the Great Spirit and Ruler of all . . . . We saw the Great Spirit's work in almost everything: sun, moon, trees, wind and mountains. Sometimes we approached Him through these things. Was that so bad? Indians living close to nature and nature's Ruler are not living in darkness. (Friesen, 1998:30)

The primary unit of traditional social structure among Aboriginal peoples was the band, often considered a sub-unit of a tribe (now called a "First Nation"). The chiefs who headed the bands often possessed valuable talents, with varying gifts for leadership in hunting or war, or in other contexts. Chiefs were mentors or servants of the people rather than managers or rulers (Snow, 2005). Real authority within the bands or tribe, however, might reside with the elders, individuals perceived as having wisdom or medicinal knowledge gathered through years of living (Meili, 2012). This diffuse power structure confused the Europeans, who were used to rigid and hierarchical authority structures.

Bands were often formed on the basis of numbers; if a band got too large to set up or shut down camp easily, the people might divide into two sub-units. Hunting and gathering bands tended to be small. By contrast, bands engaging in horticulture could accommodate larger populations. Other factors—disagreements or the emergence of a charismatic leader with a following—could also lead to the division of a band. The nomadic bands of western Canada would sometimes meet during the summer months to renew acquaintances, socialize, or celebrate the sun dance.

The Aboriginal peoples of the West Coast and Eastern Woodlands developed elaborate clan systems of social organization. The clans were exogamous and bore animal names such as "Bear" or "Turtle." They were subdivided on a matrilineal basis, and clan mothers were guardians of clan traditions and sacred practices. Clan mothers alone had the right to select and depose chiefs and councils, and had primary authority in such matters as land allotment, supervision of field labour, care of the treasury, the ordering of feasts, and dispute settlement (Johnston, 1964). Chieftainships were not primarily hereditary along patrilineal lines, so a man might pass on his office to his sister's son, the latter not being a member of the chief's clan (Trigger, 1969).

First Contact

Beginning in the 15th century, a series of European visitors reached North America. They represented a host of states and nationalities, including Spain, Portugal, England, and France. They arrived unprepared to meet a people whose way of life featured an entirely different view of social organization and government, grounded in an allegiance to high spiritual powers centred in the universe. The Europeans ignored these differences. Armed with a strong sense of **ethnocentrism**, the tendency of people to see the world only from their own cultural perspective, they boldly went where no one had gone before.

Jacques Cartier and Samuel de Champlain were the most important of these Europeans in early Canadian history because of their role in fostering further explorations of the New World. In the mid-16th century, when Cartier returned to France with descriptions of the new land and its inhabitants, the whole of France attended him with extraordinary interest. As proof of his feats, Cartier even kidnapped two young Aboriginals, the sons of Iroquois Chief Donnacona, and brought them back to France with him. Later he returned and endured a most severe winter, but thanks in large part to assistance from the Iroquois, he and his crew managed to survive an onslaught of scurvy. This experience could have dampened the enthusiasm Cartier displayed in his first evaluation of the potential of the new country, but explorations continued. When Champlain arrived at the beginning of the 17th century, he, following Cartier's lead, made friends with the Iroquois and established colonies in Acadia and New France (Chapter 1).

In 1610, the English built their first colony in the New World, in Newfoundland. Further settlements followed along the eastern coast and along the St. Lawrence, heightening contact, competition, and conflict between the French and English and their Aboriginal allies.

In Newfoundland, the Europeans (mainly English, Portuguese, and French) encountered the Beothuk. The Beothuk's practice of colouring everything in red ochre—clothing, belongings, weapons, burial goods, and so on—resulted in the phrase "Red Indian" (Friesen, 1997:49). There was intense conflict between the two cultures and in the early 19th century, the last Beothuks disappeared, though there is disagreement about whether or not this resulted from intentional **genocide**, an organized attempt by one society to eradicate another society or subgroup, often, but not always, violently (see Dickason, 1984; Cook, 1995).

Yet not all contacts were negative. By contrast, for example, European contact with the Mi'kmaq (Micmac), a neighbouring tribe of the Beothuk, was by all accounts mutually beneficial. The invaders were quite impressed with the Mi'kmaq way of life, particularly their well-built wigwams, their methods of procuring food from both the land and the sea, and their socio-political structures.

Moreover, it was not immediately obvious that contacts between Aboriginal peoples and the Europeans, beginning in the late 15th century, would prove disastrous to the former (Cook, 1995:22). Aboriginal peoples were central to the fur trade (see below) and also instrumental politically and militarily during both the European wars for dominance of the fur trade in North America and post-revolutionary America's attempt to take over Canada. However, Cook (1995:22) remarks, "the long-term advantages . . . lay with the Europeans: a growing economy, an increasingly complex technology, an expanding population, and a centralized political system supported by military power." Aboriginal power, in relation to the Europeans, rose and fell with the fur trade.

The Fur Trade

Early 20th-century writings portrayed Aboriginal peoples as victims of the fur trade, but more recent writings provide a more complex view. Cook (1995:28) stresses three points concerning the fur trade. First, trade among Aboriginals in North America preceded the coming of the Europeans and was occasionally accompanied by conflict. The arrival of the Europeans only intensified the level of both. Second, insofar as eastern and coastal tribes had more immediate contact with Europeans than did the more western and inland tribes, the latter were able to preserve their cultures and base of power for a longer period. Third, Aboriginal peoples were not passive participants in the fur trade, but willing and motivated, and in the early period frequently did very well in bargaining. Not only did local Aboriginals quickly learn to demand better quality in the goods they were purchasing, but they became quite discriminating about the quantity of goods offered to them. Experience was a good teacher.

The beaver was central to the fur trade. Beaver pelts could be "felted" and used for making what became the treasured beaver pelt hat. The popularity of this unique item persisted in the 17th and 18th centuries, and became a badge of social status (Innis, 1962). Everyone in Europe with pretensions to "respectability" wanted a beaver hat, and when the hats began to age, they were refurbished and shipped to South America to grace less particular heads. As Lower (1977:99) puts it,

> So close was the relationship between the fur trade and the beaver hat that when early in the eighteenth century fashion in Europe decreed that brims should be a little narrower, a crisis ensued in the backwoods of Canada.

When the first Europeans settled along the eastern coast of North America, the First Nations brought them furs in exchange for European goods. Almost immediately, some Aboriginal peoples became intermediary traders between their counterparts further inland and the newcomers. Very soon, this established pattern had to be altered as the heavy European demand for furs resulted in a scarcity of pelts, which drove the fur traders further inland. As Innis (1962) later observed, the search for staples—in this case, furs—led to Canada's economic development.

The Europeans quickly learned the value of Aboriginal peoples and their culture in procuring the desired furs. Aboriginal peoples not only trapped and transported the pelts, but, more importantly, knew how to survive in the New World. They knew the habits of the sought-after animals, which plants were suitable as food and medicine, and the best routes to take (Cook, 1995:27–28). Aboriginal women, in particular, also proved adept as translators and trade negotiators, not to mention valued companions to the European traders (van Kirk, 1999; Saul, 2008). For these reasons, it was to the advantage of Europeans in Canada, unlike the Spanish invaders to the far south, to develop harmonious relations with the Aboriginal peoples (Conrad, Finkel, and Jaenen, 1993).

The fur trade gradually carried dangerous consequences for the Aboriginal peoples. Little did the First Nations realize that the enterprise was soon to heap devastating consequences on their traditional way of life through institutional restructuring, deadly diseases, revisionist philosophies, and severe changes to their economic circumstance.

Intensified conflict, both with Europeans and with each other, was one obvious consequence. The introduction of guns raised conflict to new levels and changed the balance of power between Aboriginal nations. No less lethal were the recurrent epidemics unleashed by the Europeans. In 1634, smallpox or measles killed large numbers of Montagnais and Algonquians. Similarly, between 1636 and 1639, a series of epidemics reduced the Huron population from 25,000 to around 10,000 (Dickinson and Young, 2008:20). In the main, the devastation experienced by Aboriginal peoples from epidemics was unintentional, with a single, notable exception: During the Seven Years War (1756–1763), General Jeffery Amherst (1717–1797) appears to have been the first person to utilize germ warfare when he ordered blankets contaminated by smallpox to be distributed among France's Aboriginal allies.

Liquor was another danger. Motivated by economic desires, the fur traders did whatever it took to obtain furs. Various items were traded or even given as gifts, but liquor was easily the most damaging. The English traded rum, while the French relied on brandy. Not familiar with either commodity, the Aboriginals did not differentiate between the liquids, which made the traders quite happy, particularly since the two were equally effective as trade items. The long-term effects of the dispersal of liquor led to the alcoholism that eventually destroyed the structure of tribal life.

As the fur trade flourished, European traders used the arrangement to enhance the status of tribal leaders in the eyes of their people and to reward them for their efforts on behalf of the trading companies (Ray, 1974). If a band later failed to obtain a sufficient quantity of furs or provisions to pay off its debts, the leader was denied the symbols of office. If, on the other hand, the crop was ample or abundant, Aboriginal leaders were paid in more generous terms.

In the latter years of the 16th century, France attempted to form a monopoly on trade. The attempt failed. Over the next two centuries, France and England repeatedly went to war, ending with the former's final defeated in 1763 (Chapter 1).

The Royal Proclamation

The end of war saw the British government pass the Royal Proclamation of 1763. Fully one-third of the Royal Proclamation was devoted to matters pertaining to First Nations (Johnston, 1989) and remains the founding document for all written negotiations between First Nations and the federal government of Canada. Some critics argue that the Royal Proclamation was intended to dispossess First Nations of both their sovereignty as well as their lands. According to Boldt (1993:3), the document was based on the "self-serving, villainous doctrine which held that, by right of 'first discovery' a Christian nation was Divinely mandated to exercise dominion over conquered 'non-Christian primitives.'"

The Royal Proclamation decreed that Aboriginals would be allowed to live unmolested on their traditional lands at the Crown's pleasure, the British government thus being established as protector of those lands that "have not been ceded or purchased by us." Boldt (1993:4) states that the Royal Proclamation set forth five important principles. First, the Crown legally held title to all Aboriginal lands. Second, the Crown allowed Aboriginal peoples **usufructuary rights** (that is, rights of possession) to their traditional lands. Third, possession of these lands could be surrendered only to the Crown; thus, incoming settlers could take over Aboriginal lands and use them for their own purposes only after these legal rights had been surrendered by formal agreements such as treaties with the Crown (and, by later extension, the federal government of Canada). Fourth, the Crown could extinguish Aboriginal rights of possession at its discretion, subject to reasonable compensation. And fifth, selected lands described as reserves would be set aside for Aboriginal domicile (on these points, see also Angus, 1991:67). None of these conditions included the entrenchment of Aboriginal rights as a principle of justice for First Nations, as we will later note.

Yet, before leaving the Royal Proclamation, it should be noted that Aboriginal peoples do not view the document as entirely negative. Some view the Royal Proclamation as also protecting their legal rights. A document prepared by the Union of Ontario Indians (UOI) in 1970 argues that while the British colonial legal system denied aboriginal sovereignty, it did not deny the existence of Aboriginal rights as grounded in the possession of tribal lands; and that, in fact, the Royal Proclamation of 1763 arose out of efforts to protect these territory rights that had led to conflict during the preceding seven years (Plain, 1988; see earlier discussions of the Seven Years War in Chapters 1 and 5).

In short, the UOI views the Royal Proclamation, the first constitutional document for British North America, as recognizing the existence of Aboriginal peoples' rights and establishing legal procedures for the surrender of land (Plain, 1988:31). Likewise, the Penner Commission, formed in 1983 to study Aboriginal self-government (see Chapter 11), argued that the subsequent writing of treaties was based on the principles of the Royal Proclamation of 1763 (Russell, 2000:7), but that the treaties in practice did everything the Royal Proclamation said not to do (Krotz, 1990:166).

The Royal Proclamation is legal; whether its interpretation and application have always been just is another question. As the UOI document notes further, many lands in Canada were never ceded or purchased by the colonial power. Today, as new treaties are being signed, will the procedures established by the Royal Proclamation be applied for the ceding of Aboriginal lands? In Chapter 12, we will examine the making of new treaties.

Decline, Response, and the Birth of the Métis

The end of war and France's defeat did not immediately change the contours of the fur trade, and so did not immediately impact the economic basis of Aboriginal existence. The French merchants were soon replaced in Montreal by a new organization of American and British merchants and French-Canadian voyageurs. The North West Company, as it was called, challenged the Hudson's Bay Company for supremacy in the fur trade, especially in the West.

Nonetheless, the fur trade was in trouble. By the early 19th century, overharvesting, changes in European fashion, and the impact of settlement upon habitat were taking their toll (Innis, 1962). After a long and sometimes bloody struggle (including the battle of Seven Oaks in 1816) to gain control of the fur trade, the Hudson's Bay Company and the North West Company merged in 1821. The merger ended the bitter rivalry between the two companies, but did not end the fur trade's decline. Thus, the company's new governor, George (later Sir George) Simpson (1792–1860) made several policy changes. To increase profits, he ordered that cheaper goods be traded for furs, reduced the use of alcohol as a trade item, and forbade the use of steel traps. He also tried to dissuade Aboriginals from trapping endangered species and taking furs out of season. This augured poorly with the Aboriginal trappers, whose way of life now revolved around the fur economy, and who reasonably insisted they had no choice but to keep on trapping in areas where food was in short supply.

Unaccustomed to long-range planning, the Cree and Ojibway's attitudes toward conservation, territoriality, and trespassing were particularly negative. Simpson fought back, requesting that the British government place the First Nations on permanent, well-defined territories as a means of better implementing his policies. In time, Simpson took even more extreme measures by closing redundant trading posts. By the middle of the 19th century the fur trade labour force was cut back by as much as two-thirds (Ray, 1974:205).

The Simpson incident is reminiscent of previous Aboriginal expressions of opposition to European actions. Aboriginal bitterness over land-grabbing had been growing since 1760, when Pontiac (1720–1769), an Ottawa chief, organized a pan-Aboriginal confederacy to oppose British policy ("Pontiac's Rebellion," as White historians named it) (Francis, Jones, and Smith, 1988:166). In 1811, Shawnee Chief Tecumseh led an Aboriginal confederacy of some 30 nations on a series of raids to challenge the cessions of territory, particularly those in Indiana. The raids helped pave the outbreak of the War of 1812 (Chapter 5).

In western Canada, Aboriginal resistance arose on another front. One of the unexpected results of the cultural clash between European fur traders and First Nations was the birth of the Métis people. Among the Europeans, the French proved the most inclined to merge culturally and biologically with the Aboriginals. Traditionally, intermarriage between French settlers and Aboriginal wives has been attributed to a shortage of women in New France and the value of securing interests in the fur trade. More recently, however, Saul (2008:3) has argued that "By marrying into the indigenous world, most of the newcomers were marrying up. They were improving their situations socially, politically, and economically." And though Dickason (1984:147) suggests that "Amerindians and French were still distinct entities at the end of the French Regime in 1760," Saul (2008:2) contends that "[a]nyone whose family arrived before the 1760s is probably part Aboriginal."

Children of these unions were commonly called "half-breeds" or Métis, meaning "mixed." Eventually, there were enough Métis people to be identified as a separate cultural group. Morton (1970:46) has described the Métis as hunters, trappers, fishermen, voyageurs, horsemen, and farmers, but, above all, soldiers. Between 1820 and 1869, the Métis settlement at Red River, in what became Manitoba, was one of the most populated settlements in the West (Sprague, 1988:ix). The Métis represented the chief labour force of the western fur trade and were hit particularly hard by that trade's demise.

The Métis resented previous British indifference to their fate and worried that Canada's politicians would do no better. To protect themselves, the charismatic Métis leader Louis Riel and his colleagues set up a provisional government and took control of the Red River region. Riel today remains a controversial figure. Was he a traitor or a hero? Was he insane or not (Flanagan, 1977; Braz, 2003)? Was he tried fairly, or was he railroaded (Thomas, 1977)?

In the end, this first act of Aboriginal resistance in western Canada ended more or less peacefully with Manitoba's entry into Confederation (1870), though Riel was forced to flee to the United States. The second act played out 15 years later at Batoche (near Prince Albert), with Riel and his followers—Métis and First Nations peoples together—defeated, and Riel tried and hanged.

Métis resistance has often been portrayed in derogatory terms such as *rebellion, insurrection*, or *defiance*, but a strong argument can be made that the Métis were simply defending their native lands. Moreover, the Métis have a unique place in Canadian history, being the only charter group in the country with a history of national political independence before joining Confederation. Under Riel's leadership, the Métis formulated the charter of the Province of Manitoba (Friesen and Friesen, 2004).

Despite these accomplishments, it was only in 1972 that the Canadian federal government acknowledged the Métis as a separate national entity. Since then, the Métis have worked hard to attain additional historical and cultural recognition through political action. This was partially achieved in 2003 when the Supreme Court of Canada announced that the Métis were to be regarded as an Aboriginal people. The implications of this status are yet to be determined.

Confederation and the Numbered Treaties

The conflict in Red River and Manitoba's entry into Confederation were only the beginning of Canadian expansion, an expansion that necessarily involved the signing of treaties in the western provinces. By 1870, treaty making in Canada was already well established, the First Nations of Canada having often engaged in friendship treaties and treaties concerning territorial and hunting rights with neighbouring bands prior to European contact, and even having engaged in treaties with Europeans on a nation-to-nation basis going back more than two centuries (Warry, 1998:19).

Still, the form and intent of these treaties had changed over time. The first treaties between Aboriginals and Europeans were conducted on the stated basis of "friendship and peace." After that, the treaties focused primarily on land (Dickason and Newbigging, 2010). The later pre-Confederation treaties carried out in the Maritimes generally dealt with military and political arrangements involving land transfers, annuities, or compensation for rights that were given up (Frideres and Gadacz, 2001:169). By contrast, the post-Confederation treaties, conducted in the West, dealt explicitly with the transfer of land from Aboriginal peoples to the Canadian government. (The BNA Act of 1867 makes reference to Aboriginal rights as follows: Section 91[24] gives the federal government exclusive jurisdiction to make laws in relation to Aboriginal tenure and rights in lands reserved for Aboriginals. No constitutional authority exists for provincial jurisdictions to make laws concerning lands reserved for Aboriginals.)

The opening up of the West for agricultural settlement meant the displacement of the Aboriginal peoples of the region. In counterpoise to the American experience, where a century of warfare and forced internment cleared the way for settlement, Canada (with the notable exception of 1885) resorted to signing what are known as the "numbered treaties."

Treaty no. 1, signed in 1871, involved the Ojibway (Saulteaux) people on the Peguis Reserve, a tribe of Swampy Cree, and others in southern Manitoba (see Box 9.1). Treaty no. 1 is called the Stone Fort Treaty because negotiations took place at Lower Fort Garry, which was built of stone. This began the process by which the government hoped to justify the formation of the Province of Manitoba as a place for incoming non-Aboriginal settlers to reside (Dickason and Newbigging, 2010).

Box 9.1: Provisions of Treaties no. 1 and no. 2, Signed with the Peguis (Ojibway) First Nation in 1871

1. The relinquishment of the Indian right and title to specified lands
2. Certain hunting privileges
3. Annual payments of $5 as compensation to every Indian person involved in these dealings (head chiefs and councillors each received $25 and $15 respectively, as well as a suit of clothes, a British flag, and silver medals)
4. Certain lands, allocated as "Indian reserves," amounting to 160 acres per family of five
5. Agricultural implements, oxen, and cattle to form the nuclei of herds were offered on a one-time basis to the tribes
6. Provision for the establishment of schools for the instruction of Indian children

Source: Aboriginal Affairs and Northern Development Canada. "Treaty Texts – Treaties No. 1 and No. 2" (www. aadnc-aandc.gc.ca/eng/1100100028664/1100100028665).

By 1877, six more treaties had been signed; by 1899, three more were signed; an 11th treaty was signed in the Northwest Territories in 1921. These numbered treaties were not like earlier ones, however. Whereas previous treaties implied an agreement between equals, the numbered treaties imposed the will of the new colonial government. Thus, Aboriginals were enjoined to divide themselves into bands and elect chiefs and councillors to govern themselves. Likewise, Status Indians who wanted to have a vote in Canada or even leave a reserve and go to a bar would have to disavow their "Indian-ness." It is not an exaggeration to suggest that these treaties determined virtually every aspect of Aboriginal peoples' everyday lives.

Two specific factors appear to have determined the approach of Canadian government officials to treaty making. First, the government wanted to set aside specific areas for European settlement; by contrast, as Chief John Snow (2005:62–63) points out, the land set aside for Indian reserves was very poor and unsuitable for farming. Second, establishing reserves constituted a convenient way for governments to manage Indian affairs, since the nomadic First Nations would be settled on relatively small pieces of land (Melling, 1967:37).

The terms offered in these numbered treaties were generally similar. These terms included surrender of Aboriginal rights and title to traditional lands, and the creation of reserves not to exceed one square mile (1.6 square kilometres) per family of five. The government also agreed to provide a measure of military protection, a small per capita annuity, instruction in the basics of farming, and some form of education (Buckley, 1993:34). The location of each reserve was determined, after consultation with First Nations, by someone sent by the chief superintendent of the Indian Affairs Branch (IAB) of the Department of Indian Affairs and Northern Development. Other terms included a ban on intoxicating beverages, a guarantee of hunting and fishing rights, the provision of a school, and the annual award of a few dollars per individual. In Treaty no. 6, for example, the amount was $12 per year. In addition, the government would make provisions of implements, twine, and farm animals so that the reserve residents could take up agriculture.

Some chiefs objected to the amounts of land prescribed for them and voiced their objections. The chiefs rejected the terms of Treaty no. 6 three times before signing it, and the negotiations ended with a fourfold increase in assigned lands, as well as a "medicine chest."

These treaties remain a point of conflict today. In part, this is because the meanings of words are unstable (as post-structuralists would observe). Many elders did not view signing a treaty as meaning the giving up of land, but rather an agreement to share land for the benefit of both sides. Evidence suggests also that some of the treaties were formulated by government agents and simply presented to Aboriginals who did not know what they were signing, and that in many cases hard-won oral promises gained by Aboriginals during treaty signing were never recognized or honoured by the government (Frideres and Gadacz, 2001:173). Finally, Aboriginal activist and Métis leader Howard Adams (1921–2001) further suggested the treaties are worthless because they primarily furthered the process of colonization (Adams, 1989).

It should also be noted that this view of the treaties is not universally held. Some academics argue that, far from being weak or passive victims of the process, the Aboriginal leaders made the best of an admittedly difficult situation. Friesen (1986), for example, points out that some Aboriginal leaders discussed the terms of the agreements handed to them and, when necessary, manoeuvred, stalled, appeased, and compared offers to get the best deal. Finally, as flawed in content and application as they might be, the treaties, in the eyes of some Aboriginal leaders, represent a binding contract. In the words of former president of the Indian Association of Alberta Harold Cardinal (1969), the treaties are an Aboriginal "Magna Carta" because they were entered into with faith and hope for a better life with honour. In a speech two months before the First Ministers' meeting held in Ottawa on March 15 and 16, 1983, Chief John Snow stated,

> The Indian treaties with the Crown are real, and we must see to it that the terms of those treaties and related documents are fully included with the new constitution. Without our treaties we would be in the same unfortunate situation as the non-Status and non-treaty Indians. I remind all treaty and registered Indians that the treaties are sacred covenants; they are binding documents and they must not be altered unilaterally by the Government of Canada. (Snow, 1988:42)

From Hunting and Gathering to Agriculture

As the conditions brought about by the treaties gradually became reality, the Aboriginal peoples were informed that they would soon become sedentary farmers instead of nomadic hunters. Father Albert Lacombe, missionary to the Blackfoot, urged Chief Crowfoot (1830–1890) to lead his people to a way of life that would eventually provide them with a new kind of prosperity. Chief Starblanket (1816–1896) of Saskatchewan optimistically stated, "we Indians can learn the ways of living that made the white man strong" (Buckley, 1993:34).

A decade after the first treaty signing, Aboriginal peoples on the Prairies were increasingly motivated to adopt an agriculture mode of economy with the demise of the "supermarket of the plains," as the buffalo has been called. Many Aboriginal leaders could not fathom what was happening to their way of life. Competition among First Nations for the remaining bison grew. Many former warriors resisted the idea of digging in the ground with a stick. Others grasped at spiritual straws, some believing their religious leaders when they spoke of the Great Spirit's anger with humankind for replacing hunting with ploughing, while some prophets also predicted the eventual return of the animal, perhaps in some other form. (A few years ago, a spokesman for the Smallboy band of Cree in Alberta declared that the buffalo were now coming back out of the ground in the form of oil and gas.)

These incidents aside, how enthusiastic were Aboriginal farmers in the West toward the idea of taking up an agrarian lifestyle? In 1936 historian G. F. G. Stanley (1936/1975) fostered the view, later promoted by Hanks and Hanks (1950) in their study of the Blackfoot Reserve in Alberta, that Aboriginal warriors and hunters looked upon farming with disdain. According to this view, most Aboriginal peoples shunned the concepts of steady work and acquisitiveness promoted by the dominant Euro-Canadian society, though some chiefs changed their minds about farming when they saw the rewards that could be theirs: axes, blankets, and beads.

Carter (1993:9–10) argues that the view promoted by Stanley and others is based on a dualism theory that recognizes two distinct and largely independent thinking patterns, modern and traditional. In this view, the modern perspective is characterized by high productivity and a market orientation, and is quite receptive to change. It pursues rational and maximizing aims. By contrast, the more traditional (Aboriginal) perspective is regarded as pre-capitalist, subsistence-oriented, primitive, and small-scale. It is depicted as resistant to change and affected by incentives quite different from the modern model. Instead of saving or building for the future, the traditional perspective emphasizes an orientation to the present.

Carter (1993) argues against such an essentialist view of European and Aboriginal perspectives. Europeans have consistently regarded First Nations as adherents to traditional ways of thinking and thus presumably opposed to taking up farming, but Carter notes that East Coast Aboriginals were long involved in horticulture and agriculture; for example, Woodland First Nations were already solidly entrenched in agriculture (growing corn, beans, and squash) when the first Europeans arrived. Similarly, the Iroquois received acceptable land grants on the Grand River in Upper Canada, and met with success in farming comparable to that of their Euro-Canadian neighbours.

Though intentionally hindered by government actions (Carter, 1993), Aboriginal farmers in western Canada also met with success. Carter cites studies by Tobias (1977) and Carlson (1981) as proof that many Plains First Nations in the West were actually quite anxious to take up farming. The Cree people, for example, adopted farming, and much of the political activity of their leaders was taken up with a concern about the lack of promised assistance rendered to them in that regard. Likewise, the Dakota of Manitoba initially showed great enthusiasm about farming until environmental setbacks and government restrictions brought about a period of stagnation (Laviolette, 1991).

The Dakota have continued to thrive as agriculturalists but, since they are relatively recent arrivals from the United States, some authorities have always considered them outsiders. Today the federal Conservative government is attempting to buy out Dakota treaty rights and terminate federal government provisions for Dakota health, education, and welfare. The government insists that technically, the Dakota are immigrants from the United States. While they are considered Status Indians, they do not have a treaty and are entitled to only half the reserve land that treaty nations get. Naturally, the Dakota are resisting the move (Couture, 2008).

Colonialism

With the collapse of the fur trade, its replacement by an agricultural and industrial economy, and the easing of tensions with the Americans, in 1830 the British government transferred management of Aboriginal affairs in Canada from military to civil authority. Canada's Aboriginal peoples, lacking an economic base for continued political control of their lives, experienced an abrupt change as civil authorities now sought to "take care of" (i.e., dominate) them.

Until Confederation, protection of First Nations and their lands was the paramount goal. The notion that Aboriginals needed to become civilized gained in importance, but assimilation was regarded as a gradual and long-term process. In 1869, the goals of civilization and assimilation were officially added to government objectives with the passing of the Act for the Gradual Enfranchisement of Indians (Tobias, 1983:43). Thereafter, Aboriginal peoples were denied any of the original or residual political power recognized in the Royal Proclamation's treaty process. Colonial interests simply dictated that plenary power would be centralized in the Constitution (Schouls, 2003:41). What is colonialism?

Colonialism is a complex national system of racial, cultural, and political domination that produces privileges beyond the surplus value generated by capitalism (Adams, 1999:7). As a process, colonialism shapes the culture and life of both the colonizer and the colonized, with the important difference, of course, that the former assumes a superior position and assigns the latter an inferior status. Frideres and Gadacz (2001:4–7) delineate the process of colonization in terms of seven characteristics.

The first characteristic is a colonizing group's invasion of a geographic territory occupied by an indigenous group. The second characteristic is a campaign of deliberate destruction of the indigenous group's social and cultural structures. In Canada, formal programs to carry out destructive policies were enacted between 1830 and 1875 (Surtees, 1969), particularly involving religious denominations and the provision of education designed to assimilate the Aboriginal peoples to European values and norms (see below).

The third and fourth characteristics of colonialism are the interrelated processes of exerting external control while encouraging economic dependency among the conquered people. Typically, the invading nation sends out governors to run things in the newly acquired territory, rather than assigning such responsibilities to leaders of the colonized peoples. In Canada the federally appointed "Indian agent" filled this role, often admirably, but frequently became a most despised foreign despot among the Aboriginals, whose lives he made miserable (Halliday, 1935). Nearly every activity on a reserve had to be approved by the Indian agent, including requesting seed, farm implements, or livestock, or even leaving the reserve on a temporary basis.

The fifth characteristic of colonialism is the provision of low-quality social services, including health, education, and welfare. This characteristic continues to be manifested in First Nations communities in a host of statistics showing reduced life expectancy, high mortality rates, poverty, inadequate education, high incidence of infectious diseases such as tuberculosis, poor housing, and heavy reliance on social assistance, not to mention alcohol and substance abuse, suicide, physical assaults, child abuse, and family breakup.

The last two characteristics of colonialism are the practice of racism (see Chapter 6) and the establishment of a "colour line." Analytically, racism may be defined as the perspective that tends to stress the real or alleged features of race and supports the use of them as grounds for group and intergroup action (Fairchild, 1967:246). In practice, this means that some people simply believe one racial category is innately superior or inferior to another. If the practice of **endogamy** (marriage within one's own group) is any indication, the enforcement of a colour line has certainly worked in Canada; Aboriginal peoples have the highest rate of marriage within their own ranks—almost 94 percent (Frideres and Gadacz, 2001:7).

Colonialism continues today, though it is more subtle—what some observers suggest is a form of **internal colonialism**, the process of continuing settler control and domination of Aboriginal peoples. Ponting (1986:86) points to several indicators of internal colonialism: (1) manipulation of information as a form of social control; (2) excessive secrecy or overburdening band members with information; (3) obstructionism versus facilitation in so far as getting information is concerned; (4) manipulation of discretionary funds; (5) withholding of funds; and (6) other means of socio-fiscal control.

Adams (1999) similarly insists that colonialism is alive and well, but argues it is often fostered by Aboriginal organizations themselves. He alleges that leaders in these organizations often manipulate government grants to benefit themselves and not band members. In turn, this arrangement works well for government: By using reactionary Aboriginal regimes, governments can hide their own colonial policies, while crushing Aboriginal efforts toward self-sufficiency by dispersing and disorganizing the population.

Echoing Adams's concerns, Boldt cautions Aboriginal peoples to carefully monitor their own leaders if they are to attain justice, arguing that their leaders "often manifest the same degree of paternalism, authoritarianism, self-interest and self-aggrandizement in their leadership as their non-Native counterparts" (Boldt, 1993:141). A corollary to this concern is the matter of accountability. Flanagan (2000:197) argues that Aboriginal leaders will never be held accountable by their people as long as the money they spend comes from the public treasury. Therefore, a new definition of Indian self-government is needed. Self-government, however, requires some degree of economic self-sufficiency, something that reserves, where many Aboriginals still reside, were not set up to provide.

The Reserve System

Indian reserves in Canada were first established following negotiation of the treaties in the late 19th century between representatives of Queen Victoria and the various Aboriginal chiefs. Wuttunee (1971:111) argues that reserves were designed to take Aboriginal peoples away from their natural habitat and segregate them on small parcels of land so that the surrounding areas would be safe for incoming settlers. Melling (1967:37f) supports this argument, noting, for example, that no reserves were created in areas where settlers did not migrate, such as the Yukon, Labrador, or the Northwest Territories. It also could be argued that reserves were at least partially designed for the administrative convenience of government. It was a lot easier to deal with Aboriginal "problems" if they were all located on a specific plot of land rather than trying to minister to the needs of a group of nomadic wanderers.

Whatever the underlying reasons, it is clear that much of the land reserved for Aboriginals was unsuitable for farming, the new mode of Prairie economy. Thus, the period after the treaty signings saw Canada prosper under the National Policy (see Chapter 6), while Aboriginal peoples languished. The reserve inhabitants suffered from malnutrition and disease in primeval silence, often far from the hurly-burly of mainstream Canadian life and thus unseen, in semi-permanent havens from the modern world.

Until the 1960s, there was practically no economic development on Aboriginal reserves. Were it not for government transfer payments such as relief family allowance, youth allowances, blind and disabled people's allowances, and old age assistance, few Aboriginal peoples would have survived, though it can be cogently argued that the money provided was insufficient to launch them out of dependency. In 1959, the average income of Aboriginals in Saskatchewan was $200 per year. That same year, the average Saskatchewan citizen was making $1,245. In monetary terms, Aboriginal peoples were making only one-sixth the income of their non-Aboriginal counterparts.

There were exceptions. There are regional differences in the circumstances of Aboriginal peoples. In contrast to their western counterparts, the Algonqian and Iroquois nations did quite well. In farming, as already noted, Aboriginals in eastern Canada, when given the opportunity, did quite well. The same was the case in other areas of economic life. For example, Aboriginal males who had previously been successful voyageurs became river pilots and guided boats and barges loaded with supplies through the rapids to the port in Montreal. When the Grand Trunk Railway began building the Victoria Bridge, some of the same river men learned the skills of the high-beam steel workers, a prestigious occupation that many Iroquois continued to practise today. In short, eastern Aboriginals had built up over time a repertoire of skills usable in the changing economy.

By contrast, when the railway cut through the western plains, Aboriginals were not approached with prospective employment. Likewise, their efforts at becoming successful farmers were actively opposed by the Department of Indian Affairs, which viewed them as unable to adapt (Carter, 1993). The reserve system, so heavily concentrated in the West, promoted the public's view that Aboriginals constituted at best an alien and dying society, at worst an obstacle to progress (Buckley, 1993:60).

Aboriginal Education

Colonialism is not merely an economic or political phenomenon. It is also cultural. Where colonial systems have been most successful, they have entered into the psychology of the colonized. The truly colonized individual "apes" the language, beliefs, and behaviours of the colonizer, while denigrating his or her own cultural heritage (Fanon, 1968). Educational institutions have always played a key role in this process.

The campaign to colonize Aboriginal culture via schooling has a long history in Canada. Mission schools were tried in early New France, but soon proved unsuccessful due to low attendance. An alternative plan saw young Aboriginal boys and girls sent directly to France, where they could be "properly educated" and later returned as teachers for their own people, but again, the results were not favourable; more often than not the young Aboriginals returned as marginalized individuals, unable to function in either society. A few died. By 1639, scarcely a dozen had returned to the colony to assist the missionaries. As a result, the practice was ended (Cornish, 1881; Hawthorn, 1966/1967; Jaenen, 1986).

The Hudson's Bay Company operated Canada's first schools designed to educate Aboriginal children. The company built and operated them primarily for the children of their employees, but a few Aboriginal children were enrolled. Later, religious orders became the main administrators of schools for Aboriginal students. In 1658, Sister Marguerite Bourgeoys (1620–1700), who later founded the Ursulines, opened a school for French girls in a converted stable, where eventually Aboriginal children were also enrolled (Chalmers, 1974). Around this same period, the Jesuits developed day schools in permanent settlements in New France and tried to lure Aboriginal students, with a view to teaching them the Catholic faith and French culture.

The Catholic Oblates, founded in the 1840s, dominated the early stages of missionary schools in Canada. The Grey Nuns (Sisters of Charity), responsible for the education of Aboriginal girls, established their first school, St. Joseph's Academy, in St. Boniface in 1845. Further west, a host of well-known individuals, Catholic and non-Catholic alike, laboured for the same cause. These included James Evans, Robert Rundle, Father Albert Lacombe, Henry Steinhauer (an Aboriginal missionary), and others. Typical of the educational philosophy of the time, Methodist missionaries George McDougall and his son John strove to "Christianize, educate and civilize" the Aboriginals, in their case the Woodland Crees and the Stoneys (McDougall, 1903:71).

A dramatic shift in policy occurred in 1830 with a scheme to assimilate the Aboriginal peoples. The plan was to establish the First Nations in permanent settlements and commence instruction so that an agricultural form of lifestyle would be possible. Missionaries and schoolmasters were brought in to instruct the children and to teach them to pray, read the Scriptures, and pursue "moral lives" (Friesen, 1991:14). In 1857, legislation to design education for Aboriginals was passed, entitled An Act for the Gradual Civilization of the Indian. The Civilization and Enfranchisement Act followed in 1858.

This same period saw the start of Canada's experiment in residential schooling for Aboriginal children. Between 1833, when missionary Peter Jones petitioned the Methodist Church to build a residential school among the Ojibway people of Ontario, and 1996, when the last residential school in Canada closed (the Gordon Residential School in Punnicky, Saskatchewan), 80 such schools were in operation.

Among the first of these were industrial schools, begun shortly after 1830 when the civil branch of government took over Aboriginal matters from the military (Titley, 1992). The industrial school experiment in Aboriginal education was short-lived, however.

Late enrollment for many students, short periods of attendance, and lack of funds to support the students in jobs after graduation were some of the problems. More tellingly, Aboriginal parents (with justification) disliked the removal of their children, often to places that were very far away; the industrial schools' deliberate attempts to convert and "civilize" their children at the cost of their heritage; the restrictions on the use of Aboriginal languages; the teaching of "women's chores" to young men (rather than teaching them to read and write); and the work component of the industrial schools, arguing that their children had been sent to school to learn literary skills, not to become unpaid apprentices with full-time jobs (Miller, 1987:3f)—complaints that echoed through the other types of residential schools that followed.

Confederation in 1867 saw responsibility for educating Aboriginal youth fall to the federal government. The treaties signed shortly thereafter specified that Her Majesty (Queen Victoria) agreed to maintain schools for instruction in such reserves (Brookes, 1991:168), but the quality and mode were not specifically spelled out. Given governmental assumptions about the demise of Aboriginal culture, why bother providing them with a first-class education? Besides, since the missionaries were already involved in the enterprise, why not continue to finance the residential schools for a few more years until they were no longer required?

Despite Aboriginal protests, the push to have residential schools continued, and by the end of the 19th century every region of the nation had boarding schools for Aboriginal children. Promoted by Egerton Ryerson (1803–1882), who in 1844 became the first superintendent of schools in English-speaking Canada, the federal government financed these schools, while churches provided spiritual guidance and management. Ryerson suggested that Aboriginals could not accomplish civilization without a "religious feeling," and thus "the animating and controlling spirit of each residential school should be a religious one" (Brookes, 1991:20). The Province of Canada endorsed Ryerson's plan, acknowledging "the superiority of the European culture and the need to raise them [the Aboriginals] to the level of the whites" (Haig-Brown, 1993:29).

A shift in policy was signalled in 1947 in a paper entitled (with admirable honesty), *A Plan to Liquidate Canada's Indian Problem in Twenty-five Years* (Pauls, 1984:33). The scheme outlined a plan to transfer the authority for the operation of Aboriginal schools from federal to provincial governments, a stance later reiterated in the White Paper of 1969 (see Chapter 11). Integration, rather than assimilation, was to be the basis of the new policy, though given that "integration" was still to be one way, it seemed a distinction without a difference. Aboriginal students would interact with their non-Aboriginal peers, thereby slowly absorbing the values of the dominant European culture (Allison, 1983:119).

In 1949 the federal government took steps to place administration of residential schools directly into the hands of government bureaucrats instead of religious leaders. That same year, a Special Joint Committee of the Senate and the House of Commons recommended that, wherever possible, Aboriginal children should be educated in association with other children (Friesen, 1983:48). Despite considerable input from Aboriginal leaders, however, education according to the traditional European format was still perceived as a vehicle for assimilating First Nations (Hawthorn, 1966/1967). Likewise, despite mounting criticism, the residential schools continued to operate.

Life in a Residential School

Indian residential schools conformed to what the Canadian sociologist Erving Goffman (1961:xiii) terms a **total institution**, defined as a place of residence and work where a large number of like-situated individuals, cut off from the wider society for an appreciable period of time, together lead an enclosed, formally administered round of life.

Although only 30 to 35 percent of Aboriginal children attended residential schools (Steckley and Cummins, 2008:191), many of them remember with deep pain the experiences they suffered in those institutions (Friesen, 1999:251f). Life in residential schools meant participating in an entirely different cultural milieu, replete with such alien features as corporal punishment, strict discipline, hard work, loneliness, and, worst of all, confinement.

A common feature of total institutions is **identity stripping** (Goffman, 1961), essentially the removing of articles, personal identification, and other elements that tell individuals who they are. Children arriving at residential schools were often given Christian names to replace their own (though students in a few schools were referred to only by assigned numbers), stiff uniforms in place of their Aboriginal clothing, and a haircut, the latter a sufficient form of insult to a culture that revered long hair. The children also quickly learned that use of their native language was forbidden, and that using it would result in severe punishment, including beatings. The intent of stripping was to make Aboriginal children ashamed of their culture and heritage.

Students quickly found themselves coping with a highly structured hierarchical institution. Church-employed staff constituted the power structure and the ideological ethos of the school. Many of them were from lower socio-economic backgrounds, were minimally educated, and were often only recent immigrants to Canada, with little understanding of Canada's history or value system, and knew even less about the Aboriginal way of life (King, 1967:58). They were armed with a strong sense of mission that, when frustrated, found vent in aggression toward the children. Since their identity was derived theologically, they held more authority than parents or students, surpassed in status only by school administrators.

Daily activities in a residential school were quite crude and very public. Initially the huge brick buildings, built on the factory model, had sealed windows. Often, the heavily occupied buildings produced a foul smell and a rank odour, contributing no doubt toward the spread of diseases, notably tuberculosis, which took a fearful toll on Aboriginal youth. At other times, the residences were cold and drafty (Grant, 1996:123). Bathing was a group activity, with the younger students bathing first. The water was often too hot when they started the ritual, but by the time the older students got their turn, the water was cold and dirty.

The quality of residential food was poor, the quantity scanty, and today former residents frequently recall long periods of hunger. Students sometimes would wolf down their food as fast as possible in hopes of getting an additional helping. Students sometimes stole bread from the kitchen, though punishment was severe if caught; thus, stealing food became a complex operation involving a number of participants in a particular institutional subcultural practice (Haig-Brown, 1993:99). Once eaten, food was seldom allowed to digest naturally, so the condition of the children's bowels was a major staff concern for which a daily routine was the administration of a laxative to the children, whether they needed it or not.

Even more than in non-Aboriginal schools of the period, the curriculum of the residential schools was primarily based on the three R's—readin', 'ritin', and 'rithmetic—plus a fourth staple, large doses of religion, the latter indubitably the most important of the four components (Perley, 1993:123). As in the old industrial schools, there was also gender-specific training in some areas: farming and trades for boys, and housekeeping, mending, and knitting for girls. As noted, however, the use of Aboriginal languages was forbidden; likewise, the history or cultures of First Nations was completely ignored. Music and songs reflected only the themes of the new dominant society.

Learning was by rote and academic achievement low. This was partially because teachers had low expectations of their Aboriginal students, but Barman and colleagues (1986) and Grant (1996:89) argue that the residential school education was never intended in any case to fully educate Aboriginal youngsters. Had they been properly educated, Aboriginal children may have become so well prepared that they might successfully enter the socio-economic order and become a threat to dominant society. The real purpose of residential schooling was to "kill the Indian in the child"; the real lessons to be learned every day were discipline and obedience. When students later transferred to provincial schools for high school training, they were often ashamed of their poor records; small wonder that less than three percent of those children attending residential schools ever graduated from high school.

Residential schools did provide some training in communication arts imported from Europe, and today many Aboriginal leaders can trace their literary beginnings to the years they spent in residential schools. This in no way justifies the existence of that form of teaching and learning, but it offers some measure of consolation. In addition to mastering the basic forms of communication required to negotiate effectively with governments, many students formed lasting friendships with their peers that have endured to this day. (It is interesting, though not necessarily reassuring, to note that the majority of Aboriginal leaders today are products of residential schools.) In some ways these bonds may have partially alleviated painful memories of the cruelties and hardships endured in residential schools.

Perhaps surprisingly, a few residential school survivors have quite positive memories of the experience and today even speak highly of the education they received. For example, interviews conducted with 80 elders from the Kainai (Blood) reserve in southern Alberta, authorized by the Kainai administration in 1995 and 2003, convey several instances of pride and gratitude felt by some former residents (Sikotan and Mikai'sto, 1995; Sikotan, Mikai'sto, and Omahksipootaa, 2003).

These few positive memories aside, the more general long-term impacts of residential schools were negative. According to Grant (1996), these impacts include an inability to express feelings, apathy and unwillingness to work, values confusion and culture shock, anti-religious attitudes, and a long-term negative impact on succeeding generations. Many former residential school dwellers have had to work very hard to overcome the psychological, spiritual, and sexual abuses they suffered. Wax and colleagues (1964:46) observed that the overwhelming majority of complaints by Aboriginal children were directed against other Aboriginal children rather than against teachers or school conditions. In turn, those abused in residential schools often became abusers themselves (O'Hara, 2000:18). The cycle continued with many former inmates' transmitting the abuses they witnessed and experienced at the hands of the staff and teachers on to their own children.

Why did Aboriginal parents enroll their children in such dreadful environments? The answer has many sides. First, residential school conditions were not well known. But, second, parents had no real choice. In many situations members of the Royal Canadian Mounted Police took their children away. Some parents who were having a difficult time supporting their families grudgingly released their children with hopes they would have a better chance in life attending the school and developing their skills (Furniss, 1995). Others followed the recommendation of the local Indian agent, partly in the belief that doing so might gain the agent's approval.

Sadly, when the residential system ended, it was not because the system failed. That should have been the reason, but instead its end came about because of increased government intervention motivated by citizen concern (King, 1967:87). As a first step toward liquidation, schools run by missionaries were taken over by government bureaucrats in the 1950s, but this stage was brief. Aboriginal parents, some of them educated in residential schools themselves, grew increasingly involved in the education of their children. In 1970, the residential school in St. Paul, Alberta, was turned over to local control after nearly 300 Aboriginals conducted a sit-in at the school (Persson, 1986). Fifteen years later, two-thirds of reserve schools in the nation were either partly or completely managed by Aboriginal school boards.

Over the years, many closed residential schools were simply torn down. Some, however, were converted to other purposes. First Nations bands managed a few; in 1995, for example, Aboriginal management operated six residential schools in Saskatchewan. Several former residential schools became cultural centres, adult learning centres, or private schools. When administration of these schools was transferred to Aboriginal control, the influence of Aboriginal input was quickly evident. It is more than symbolic that, when the final closing exercises of several residential schools transpired in the 1980s and 1990s (for instance, at Qu'Appelle Indian Residential School in Saskatchewan), Aboriginal dancing and social events often took precedence over denominational activities (Gresko, 1986:89). Aboriginal culture began its slow rebirth.

Conclusion

Contact between Aboriginals and non-Aboriginals in North America occurred in several stages. During the first stage, Aboriginal peoples had a degree of control over the relationship. The outsiders wanted a valuable commodity: furs. They also relied on local know-how in learning how to live in inclement climates. The Aboriginals were pleased to supply furs and expertise in return for various imported products, but the fur trade also carried hidden dangers such as disease and war, including conflict among Aboriginal tribes. In the long term, the fur trade also eroded Aboriginal culture.

By the time the fur trade collapsed in the early 19th century, the relationship between Aboriginals and non-Aboriginals was no longer that of equals. The Aboriginal peoples were excluded from the agricultural and industrial economies that followed, while Canadian expansion westward exacerbated the decline of Aboriginal culture. Viewed by successive governments as a dying people, Aboriginal peoples gradually vanished from the Canadian landscape into places of physical and psychological retreat and subjugation. For a time, modernity passed them by.

Like the trains that brought western settlement, Canada's economic development proceeded, seemingly unstoppable. On the West Coast in 1896, eyes turned suddenly northward in search of gold. Southern Canada was about to discover its North.

Key Terms

colonialism
endogamy
ethnocentrism
genocide
identity stripping
internal colonialism
total institution
usufructuary rights

Critical Thinking Questions

1. In what ways does the existence of Aboriginal peoples complicate our conventional notions of the nation-state?
2. In what ways does the dominant mode of economic production shape the organizational structure of a society?
3. What lessons does the fur trade hold for Canadian economic development as a whole?
4. What are the similarities and differences between residential schools and other types of total institutions?
5. In what ways are Aboriginal peoples in Canada still subject to colonial rule?

Recommended Readings

Braz, Alberta. 2003. *The False Traitor: Louis Riel in Canadian Culture.* Toronto: University of Toronto Press.
Not everyone in Canada perceived Louis Riel as a national villain, certainly not his Métis followers. Braz explores both sides of the question and concludes that Riel's contributions to nationhood have been overlooked.

Cardinal, Harold. 1977. *The Rebirth of Canada's Indians.* Edmonton: Hurtig Publishers. Considered somewhat of a classic over time, this book by a young Aboriginal leader reached back into history to reveal the many shortcomings of both Canadians and their government in negotiating with Canada's Aboriginal peoples.

Friesen, John W., and Virginia Lyons Friesen. 2005. *First Nations in the Twenty-first Century: Contemporary Educational Frontiers.* Calgary: Detselig.
The authors explore six educational challenges facing Canada's First Nations today: (1) spirituality, (2) leadership, (3) language maintenance, (4) Aboriginal self-identity, (5) school curriculum, and (6) preparation of teachers.

Henlin, Calvin. 2006. *Dances with Dependency: Indigenous Success through Self-Reliance.* Vancouver: Orca Spirit Publications and Communications.
This book is touted as somewhat of a bible for Aboriginal economic success, and Chief Henlin, the author, is a strong proponent of Aboriginal-originated and operated business and economic development.

Steckley, John I., and Bryan Cummins. 2008. *Full Circle: Canada's First Nations.* 2nd ed. Toronto: Pearson Education Canada.
Written in everyday language, this text is a good primer for those not acquainted with Aboriginal affairs in Canada. Topics include prehistory and traditions, culture areas, legal definitions, effects of colonialism, and contemporary issues.

Related Websites

Historical Society of St. Boniface
www.shsb.mb.ca/en
This is the oldest francophone historical society in western Canada. Among its online offerings is information on Louis Riel.

McGill University's Digital Library
digital.library.mcgill.ca/nwc
This library contains a large number of documents and maps dealing with the fur trade in Canada.

Métis National Council
www.metisnation.ca
Recognition of the Métis people as one of Canada's three distinct Aboriginal peoples in the Constitution Act, 1982, paved the way for the creation in 1983 of the Métis National Council. Today, the MNC represents the Métis nation nationally and internationally.

Canadian Society on Video

Maïna. 2012. Telefilm Canada, 100 minutes.
A movie set in pre-European times, it follows the story of the daughter of an Innu chief as she tries to rescue a boy stolen by Inuit from her community. The film is in English, Inuktitut, and Inupiaq with English subtitles.

The Learning Path. 1993. National Film Board of Canada, 56 minutes, 50 seconds.
A moving film that describes the devastating effects of residential/boarding schools on Canadian Aboriginals and the widespread sexual and physical abuse to which they were subjected. One of five videos in the *As Long as the Rivers Flow* series produced by the NFB.

Women in the Shadows. 1991. National Film Board of Canada, 55 minutes, 55 seconds.
The story of one Métis woman's reconciliation with her past and her people.

CHAPTER 10

KEEPERS OF
THE NORTH

What happens in the North will ... tell us what kind of a country Canada is; it will tell us what kind of people we are.

—Justice Thomas Berger, 1977

Canadians have never strayed far either physically or spiritually from the Canada-U.S. boundary. We are [a] northern nation in fantasy and imagery only.

—Ken Coates, P. Whitney Lackenbauer, William R. Morrison, and Greg Poelzer,

in *Arctic Front: Defending Canada in the Far North*, 2008

What would a north where we actually respected Aboriginal and treaty rights look like? It will take an enormous popular struggle to answer a question that no one in the highest reaches of power today wants to hear.

—Peter Kulchyski, activist and author, 2013

Introduction

The vast majority of Canadians live within about 240 kilometres of the American border. Few have ever travelled to any of the territories, yet the North holds a special place in most Canadian hearts. It is a source of national identity.

Unlike elsewhere in Canada, Aboriginal peoples predominate throughout much of the North. They represent a majority in the Northwest Territories and Nunavut. While making up only 3.8 percent of the Canadian population as a whole, Aboriginal peoples constitute roughly 24 percent of the resident population of the Arctic and Subarctic regions (Harrison, 2012). Canadians at large see the North as part of Canada, but as overwhelmingly Aboriginal land, with Canadians as its guardians.

The North is also a major source of Canada's present and future, a rich treasure trove of minerals, and oil and gas reserves. But it is threatened, first by global warming, and second by international challenges to Canada's jurisdiction from other polar countries. For all of these reasons, the North is very much in the news today.

This chapter briefly explores the peoples and history of the North, and the changing relationship of the region with the rest of Canada. Special attention is given to the state's role in the North's gradual integration into Canada and the North's social, economic, political, and environmental challenges.

A Portrait of the North

Outsiders to the Far North are amazed that anyone could enjoy life in an environment almost entirely void of trees, and surrounded by great amounts of snow and ice. For about eight months of the year, most of the Arctic is covered with snow and extensive portions of its seas are frozen. The Subarctic seems only slightly more hospitable, a place of pesky blackflies in summer and cold winter twilight. To those raised in the North, however, life in the crowded, fast-paced urban centres of the South seems equally strange and even tantamount to suicide. Besides, the long periods of daylight in Inuit country balance the long, bleak winter.

Canada's North consists of Arctic and Subarctic regions and stretches north from 60 degrees latitude to the North Pole. The Arctic comprises 3 million square kilometres of ice, water, and tundra, while the Subarctic includes more than 4.5 million square kilometres of land. Combined, these regions amount to nearly 80 percent of the land and water mass of Canada, an area populated by nearly 1.5 million people. While these areas together make up the largest geographic region in Canada, they have by far the smallest economy and population.

The Arctic's unique physical environment is primarily a result of the sun's relative absence. The tilt of the earth on its axis keeps the northern area facing away from the sun throughout the winter months and facing toward the sun throughout the summer months. For as long as four consecutive months, from mid-October to mid-February, the Arctic is plunged into darkness. During the summer, it becomes the land of the midnight sun, experiencing constant daylight for a few short months.

During the very short Arctic summers, snow melts, plants grow, and the midnight sun shines over most of the land area. Spring and fall are virtually non-existent in the area. Most Arctic regions experience January temperatures as cold as –40°C or –45°C with a mean temperature of only 12°C during the warmest months, though this is rapidly changing (see below). The 200 varieties of vegetation in the Arctic (shrubs, scrub trees, herbs, and lichen) are well suited. They are low to the ground, grow away from the wind, and thrive on a brief and intense growing period.

The Arctic Ocean and surrounding lakes and rivers begin to freeze over in October and remain frozen until May in most areas. The frozen ocean extends the Arctic coastline by hundreds of kilometres, but the ice is not always safe to travel on, and in recent years has been growing thinner. Strong winds often drive vast floating fields of ice across the waterways. Often these islands of ice crash into one another, creating upheavals. A sudden spring breakup can create ice floes that may carry off unsuspecting hunting parties or migrating families (Osborn, 1990:27–28).

Traditionally, the peoples of the Arctic relied on a variety of game and birds for food. This included the Arctic hare, the Arctic fox, the muskox, and a variety of birds such as rock ptarmigans, sandpipers, plovers, elder ducks, red-throated loons, and ruddy turnstones. Little-appreciated life forms included a variety of obnoxious insects such as small flies, mosquitoes, and bumblebees. Today, many Arctic species, such as the polar bear, are threatened by **climate change** (see below).

An obvious treeline separates the Subarctic from the Arctic and consists of four distinct zones: (1) the wooded tundra, (2) the lichen woodland, (3) the closed boreal forest, and (4) the forest parkland. The wooded tundra forms the transition zone. This wooded area contains sporadic patches of spruce and larch trees, and the lichen woodland has a few stands of spruce and pine. The closed boreal forest offers a denser stand of fir, spruce, and pine, while the forest parkland combines elements of forest and grass milieu (Bone, 1992:21). Subarctic wildlife is more plentiful and includes some 50 species of birds and 600 species of plants.

Bone (1992:27) points out that the North's fragile physical environment poses unique challenges for modern times. Its cold climate and slow rate of natural growth means it takes longer to recover from modern industrial accidents such as oil spills. Unfortunately, considerations of the environment and the people have not always influenced the North's development.

The North's Aboriginal Peoples

The North's Aboriginal peoples are made up of three primary groups: (1) the Inuit of the Arctic, (2) the Algonquian-speaking people of the eastern Subarctic (the Cree, the Naskapi, and the Montagnais, with those located in Labrador referred to as Innu), and (3) the Athapaskan-speaking people (the Dene), located in the western Subarctic (Brody, 1987:29). The latter two groups also span the northern portions of several provinces, including Quebec and Labrador, as well as the western provinces.

The Inuit

Most historians and archaeologists today believe the Inuit are descendants of the Thule Inuit, who spread from the northern coast of Alaska to the Mackenzie Delta in the 11th century, replacing the Dorset people (Crowe, 1974; Wilson, 1976; Purich, 1992). Linguistically, the Inuit language is unique, with no discernible relationship with any New World Aboriginal people. The Inuit language probably descended from Aleut, from which it diverged about 6,000 years ago, and thereafter evolved into two distinct subfamily units, Yupik and Inupik. This includes all dialects between western Alaska and Greenland (Jennings, 1978).

The land of the Inuit is divided into a western portion, which includes the Aleut on the Aleutian Islands as well as the Inuit of Alaska, and a central and eastern region, which embraces all the Inuit from the Mackenzie River Delta east to Greenland. At the time of first contact with Europeans, some 22,000 Inuit lived in the North. The groups broadly identified as Inuit include Mackenzie, Copper, Netsilik, Sadliq, Caribou, Iglulik, South Baffin Island, Ungava, and Labrador (Crowe, 1974; Brody, 1987). There is evidence of a fairly widespread exchange of various minerals, including soapstone, iron, and copper, and products made from raw materials like ivory, among the tribes before the arrival of Europeans (Crowe, 1974).

Essentially an ocean-oriented culture, the Inuit obtained most of their food supply from the sea. Seals and other sea mammals were a chief source of food, though in the summer months fishing and caribou hunting supplemented the Inuit diet. Taylor (1974) describes a typical annual cycle utilized by the Netsilik around the turn of the 20th century. The sea began to freeze around October, the caribou herds departed for the South, and the building of snow houses commenced. Char continued to be taken from the sea until the middle of November, and the women were busy making winter clothes. During December and January the people remained at home, relying on provisions laid up during the previous summer and fall. The breathing-hole seal hunting began in February when the snow on the ice was deep; other hunting techniques were employed when April and May arrived. These included sneaking up on the seal or catching new pups at the breathing holes. A few stray caribou showed up, and in June when the snow houses caved in from the hot sun, the people moved into tents. Kayaks were prepared for caribou hunting, which continued until the herd disappeared south again.

In many ways, the Inuit had a sophisticated culture, fitted to the materials and circumstances of their climate and geography. The Alaskan Inuit and Aleuts, for example, developed the two-holed kayak and, in place of the toggling harpoons that other Inuit used for large sea mammals, also developed a multi-barbed harpoon dart head (Dumond, 1977). Housing construction—from portable summer tents made of seal or caribou skin to winter homes of the classic igloo type (Baldwin, 1967) to (in the south) rectangular, semi-subterranean, turf-covered houses of logs—reflected a firm grasp of such things as ventilation and insulation.

The Inuit were probably unique among Canada's Aboriginals in functioning with a simple social system, unencumbered by elaborate hierarchical forms of governing individuals or bodies. They had no chiefs among them. Contrary to the Western dichotomy of individualism versus collectivism, the Inuit way of life involved a form of **individual egalitarianism**. When food was scarce, supplies were stretched out as far as possible and a spirit of goodwill prevailed. Friendliness was expected; anger was viewed as a form of madness (Coates et al., 2008:31). Age and gender determined one's status, though the sexes were more equal than in European countries of the day. In hunting, for example, women assisted their husbands in driving animals into an ambush. Still, women had the chief role in raising children and preparing food (Giffen, 1930). Long before it became popular in the mainstream, Inuit clothing was unisex, with both sexes wearing loose-fitting fur trousers and shirts, usually made of caribou hide, but sometimes of polar bear or other animal fur (Josephy, 1968).

Polygyny, the marriage of one man to more than one woman, was not uncommon. Since the Inuit sometimes practised female infanticide, however, there was often a scarcity of women. This being the case, on occasion, and subject to strict clan-related rules, a man might lend the use of his wife to a friend on a short-term basis, a practice that elicited both sensationalist intrigue and condemnation among European outsiders (Mowat, 1952; Balikci, 1970; McMillan, 1995).

Storytelling, along with everyday modelling, were means of transmitting valued Inuit cultural beliefs and values to the young. In some tribes storytellers were designated, while in others both men and women of respect could relate stories. Among the Labrador Inuit, each village had a designated storyteller, while in Alaska certain old men monopolized this art (Giffen, 1930).

The Dene

The Dene (sometimes spelled Dinneh) speak a dialect of the Athapaskan language (Chapter 9). They share this language family with the Apache and the Navajo of the

American Southwest. Abel (1993) suggests these northern people traditionally used the word *Dinneh* to identify the larger population and distinguished a wide range of separate groups by adding the name of a river or lake associated with their particular hunting grounds. Irwin's (1994) comprehensive list of Dene tribes includes the Chipewyan, of the Canadian interior (not to be confused with the Chippewa-Ojibway of Lake Superior); the Dogrib, between Great Slave lake and Great Bear Lake; the Beaver, along the lower Peace River in northern Alberta; the Slavey, along the southern shore of Great Slave Lake; the Hare, northwest of Great Bear Lake; the Klaska or Nahani, west of the headwaters of the Mackenzie River; the Sekani, in central British Columbia; the Carrier (named for their widows' custom of carrying the charred bones of their dead husbands on their backs); the Chilcotin, south of Carrier lands; the Tahlan, on the upper Stikine River in northwestern British Columbia; and the Tuchone in southern Yukon Territory (see also Crowe, 1974; Ryan, 1995; Massey and Shields, 1995).

Like the Inuit, the traditional Dene people were primarily hunters and trappers. Huge herds of caribou and moose were vital components of the Dene diet and culture, supplemented by the fish of lakes and rivers. Predictability of supply was important. The Chipewyan people, for example, followed the migration patterns of the caribou, and if there was even a slight shift in their migration paths, the band's food supply was affected. In fall these animals were slaughtered by waiting hunters as they passed a certain point, and the meat was cut into strips, dried in the sun, and pounded into pemmican for the winter food supply (McMillan, 1995).

It was customary for the Dene to function as groups of friendly neighbours. Each tribe adapted to its immediate terrain. For example, the Hare, so named for their use of rabbit skins for clothing and shelter, lived in small extended families that divided relatives into two opposing groups. Cross-relatives were in-laws, while parallel relatives were akin to parents, siblings, or one's own children (Ives, 1990). A similar situation prevailed in Slavey country, where the people identified two kinds of relatives—kinsmen and in-laws.

The Dene had quite explicit social rules (Ryan, 1995). These rules covered three specific areas: (1) natural resources, (2) families, and (3) governance or decision making. In turn, these rules were intertwined with the Dene's holistic view of the universe. Rule-breakers were punished in various ways. For minor offences, an elder might deal verbally with the guilty party. Individuals committing more serious offences were often made the subject of a gathering in which they were required to admit guilt and make restitution, followed by a process of reconciliation. If this failed, shunning, and even the death penalty, though rarely used, was possible.

A 19th century visitor to Dene country, Father Petitot, noted that Dene beliefs were reflected in daily practices, but not formalized (Savoie, 1970). A series of celestial beings were worshipped as deities: the midnight sun, for example, was a real national and tutelary god, supremely recognized and worshipped. Father Petitot described the Dene as having a primordial knowledge of a Good Being who was placed above all other beings and possessed a multitude of names, the most common one being Bettsen-nu-unli ("He by whom the earth exists"). Frequently, spirit beings would personify themselves in the form of birds, such as the eagle; the male spirit brought the day and the female spirit brought the night (Savoie, 1970). As in the South, the trickster was recognized, in the form of a raven, as a creator, culture hero, and miracle worker (Merkur, 1991:215).

Roman Catholic priests who later arrived in Dene territory introduced concepts that blended well with traditional Dene beliefs: love your spouse, be kind to your neighbours, take good care of your children and raise them well, and stay together forever (Ryan, 1995). In many instances, priests were perceived as emissaries from God possessing spiritual power and authority, and served as wisdom elders, providing advice and direction, resolving disputes, and meting out disapproval for acts of violation.

There is little doubt that conflict with European society caused some First Nations cultural and spiritual traditions to be altered or even lost (Brody, 1987:205). Many sacred practices that the priests frowned upon continued in secret; sometimes, as well, Christianity merged with Aboriginal beliefs—in a process known as **syncretism**—in ways the missionaries did not recognize. In short, Christianity had important effects on Indigenous cultures, but Aboriginal peoples also took what they wanted from the new religion, while retaining many of their old beliefs and values, the shoots of which are seen today in a strong cultural and spiritual renaissance in most Aboriginal communities (Lincoln, 1985; McGaa, 1990).

The Coming of the Europeans

Initial contacts between the northern people and Europeans in the 10th century were not friendly. Erik the Red, a Norwegian who explored Greenland, and whose son, Leif, later returned to establish a colony in Newfoundland, viewed the locals as quite primitive "little people" who had no iron and used missiles made of walrus tusks and sharp stones for knives (Osborn, 1990:77). It was a pattern of contact repeated several centuries later with the arrival of a new band of explorers.

Among these early explorers were John Cabot (in 1497 and 1498), Martin Frobisher (in 1576, 1577, and 1598), John Knight (in 1606), and Henry Hudson (in 1609 and 1610). Why did they come? In part, they were searching for precious metals, especially copper and gold, but they also had a larger quest: finding a northwest passage to the Orient.

European exploration, beginning in the 15th century with Cabot, was inextricably linked to mercantilism (Chapter 1). In the modern context, we can see this period as an early expression of globalization, with its search for new products and markets, and the expansion of trade. While considerable trade occurred overland between Europe and Asia, it also occurred by sea. But a ship sailing to the Orient from Europe, either eastward around Africa or westward around South America, might journey more than a year. By contrast, a passage more directly westward would save time and money, hence the search for what Berton (1988) termed "the Arctic Grail."

Ultimately, the Northwest Passage was found. It was not mastered, however, until the Norwegian Roald Amundsen sailed his sloop, the *Gjoa*, through the ice in 1905 (see Berton, 1988). By then, the North had claimed a host of explorers and their ships. Among these was Hudson, who steered a course into a strait that later bore his name and became icebound, whereupon his crew mutinied and set him and a few loyal crew-men adrift in a small boat, never to be seen again. Hudson's lurid fate and that of other disastrous expeditions that followed—from Jens Munk in 1619 to Sir John Franklin in 1845 to 1849 (see Beattie and Geiger, 1987)—did not dissuade outsiders, however. Far from it; the North became transformed into a place both mystical and mythical. (Note that Mary Shelley's monster in *Frankenstein*, published in 1819, dies on an Arctic ice floe.) And where mystery's allure failed to attract, Europeans came in search of profit.

And profit there was. In 1665, two disgruntled fur traders from New France, Pierre-Esprit Radisson and Médard Chouart, sieur des Groseilliers, having been turned down by the French government, went to London to meet King Charles II and local merchants to seek their support. The English were more responsive to Radisson and des Groseilliers, and shortly thereafter, in 1670, Charles II issued the Hudson's Bay Company charter, granting the company rights to all lands whose waters drained into Hudson Bay. The Hudson's Bay Company (HBC) thus became "the vastest empire any private company ever controlled" (Morton, 1997:75; also Newman, 1998:54–61).

The HBC did not immediately thrive. Over the next decades, the French captured company forts and burned them to the ground several times, only to see them rebuilt. Gradually, however, the Hudson's Bay Company grew. Defeat of the French in 1763 and amalgamation with the rival North West Company in 1821 left the company unas-sailable in the North. For roughly the next 50 years, the HBC represented a kind of quasi-government, making rules and regulations, enforcing order, and even providing social services, such as education.

With the advent of the fur trade, the lifestyle and political economy of the northern Aboriginal peoples changed dramatically. Some initially did quite well with the arrange-ment. For a hunting people, rifles and ammunition were a real advantage. Likewise, certain tribes also initially did well, notably the Cree, who quickly became middlemen and spread westward across Canada. But, as we have noted (Chapter 9), the fur trade also brought negative consequences. In the words of Brody (1987:199), the "fur trade was built upon the economics of dependency." Trade with the forts became habitual. Hunters became trappers and changed their lifestyles accordingly. The role of women also changed, as they now had to clean and tan additional furs for market.

Not all northern peoples were brought into the world economy all at once. Beginning in the 17th and 18th centuries, some tribes in the Subarctic had initial contact with fur traders pushing north from the St. Lawrence and whalers arriving from the North Atlantic. Others, however, experienced their first contact only in the 19th century. At that time, European ships began regular trips to the Arctic to garner whale oil, baleen (whalebone, used in making corsets), and walrus ivory. In the 1850s, the ships began to winter over, and contact between Europeans and Inuit intensified. The establishment of whaling stations upset the seasonal economic cycle of the settlements, which became handout stations, soon known as places where "weekly biscuits were handed out" (Wilson, 1976:85).

This increased contact brought other material and cultural changes. By the time com-mercial whaling came to an end (around 1912), "hunters were using rifles, telescopes, sheath knives, jack-knives, hatchets, saws, drills, awls, steels and files. Women cooked in metal pots and kettles, and used steel needles, cotton thread and metal scissors in sewing" (Brody, 1987:193). Clothing materials and styles also changed, as did music and dancing.

Some changes were decidedly negative, although the Aboriginal people further west were less affected (Finnie, 1948:40). Overhunting depleted the whale pods and led to starvation in some instances. Alcoholism, suicide, and disease also took their toll. As early as 1887, Father Emile Petitot quoted a chief of the Chiglit Eskimos on the terrible living conditions among the Inuit: "We are all dying . . . . [W]e are getting snuffed out day by day and nobody cares about us. No one looks after our sick or pities our misfortunes" (Petitot, 1999:15). In 1912, Captain Henry Toke Munn described the Inuit of Baffin Island as a "passing race" destined for extinction because of the coming blight of complex European civilization, without whose influence he felt they would be better off. Brody (1987:193) notes that around this same period, the Inuvialuit of the Mackenzie Delta were reduced from a community of 2,000 to about 30.

> [T]hey were the healthiest and finest looking Indians I have ever seen in the northern country. Most of the men were fine specimens, and also the women, who bore children abundantly and reared them in health and vigour. They were absolutely honest and lived a primitive Indian life. (Finnie, 1948:40)

The life of northern peoples was about to experience further change, however. As so often in the history of the Americas (see Wright, 1993), the catalyst for change was gold.

The Yukon Gold Rush

The California gold rush of 1849 begat the British Columbia gold rush of 1858, followed in 1896 by the discovery of gold on a tributary of the Klondike River by George Washington Carmack and his two Aboriginal brothers-in-law, Skookum Jim and Tagish Charley. Even earlier, Robert Campbell, a trader with the Hudson's Bay Company, found gold in the gravel near his trading post at the junction of the Yukon and Pelly rivers in the early 1850s. An Anglican missionary, Robert McDonald, reported traces of gold in Birth Creek near the Yukon-Alaska border in the 1870s (Cruikshank, 1998:434). This time, however, gold fever became a pandemic.

By the summer of 1897, however, hordes of men (women were scarce) were swarming over the Yukon region, some arriving by water, many taking the arduous journey over the White Pass and Chilcoot Pass, then down the Yukon River by a colourful assortment of handmade boats and rafts. By 1898, a total of 30,000 people lived in the Klondike region, of whom about 16,000 resided in Dawson City, which became Yukon's capital. Most of the newcomers knew only three things about the Yukon: it was cold, it was remote, and gold nuggets were available for the picking.

While many of the fortune seekers sought female companionship among the locals, few of these relationships lasted very long. Most of the men soon drifted back to the

South, often leaving children behind them. Those who stayed and struck it rich were few. Like other booms, it was the traders, hoteliers, or other providers of goods and services, not to mention the con artists, who made money (Cruikshank, 1998:451; Berton, 1958). Most of those who remained ended up working for wages, their stay occasioned by either a love of the North or dreams still nursed of becoming wealthy (Fried, 1969).

The 1896 gold rush ended quickly. The boom-and-bust pattern of Canadian development, so familiar to the South, was replicated in the North. Dawson City's fortunes and population experienced a steep decline. Between 1902 and 1903 alone, $12 million left the northern territories, but—for all the wealth generated—little remained to be invested locally. Residents blamed both an uninterested government and lack of local control for this loss of revenue.

First, the gold rush augured the North's full integration into the world capitalist economy. It was a slow process. The fur economy remained strong throughout the 1920s, bringing considerable wealth to Yukon and the Northwest Territories. Fur towns like Aklavik sprang up, and a few local families got rich, but prosperity was again short-lived. For many people tied only tangentially to the labour market, however, the downturn was not critical. Meanwhile, companies were increasingly entering the region, searching for exploitable resources. Gold remained in high demand, leading to the foundation of towns at Noranda, Quebec; Kirkland Lake, Ontario; and Flin Flon, Manitoba. Other minerals such as radium and uranium were mined in places like Great Bear Lake, high in the Northwest Territories (Careless, 1970:353).

It had long been known that the North possessed rich pockets of oil. Writing in his diary in the 18th century, the explorer Peter Pond wrote about the thick pitch oozing from the Athabasca River's banks in what is today northern Alberta. In 1907, Alfred von Hammerstein, known as "the Count," acquired surface and mineral rights to about 48,600 hectares of freehold land downstream of where Fort McMurray now stands, and set about drilling wells. He was unsuccessful. In 1920, however, the Imperial Oil Company announced the discovery of large amounts of oil at Norman Wells. The announcement temporarily spurred the Canadian government to seek a treaty with the local Dene to pave the way for development. The small amount of oil produced soon discouraged the government from further development in the area.

Second, while the North's economy as a whole was being transformed, local Aboriginal peoples were frequently left on the margins of these changes. The pattern began with the gold rush, and was repeated in the 1920s and 1930s, which saw an influx of white southerners seeking their fortunes at a time when jobs "back home" were growing scarce (Brody, 1987). Locals now found themselves hard pressed to find employment, while incoming outsiders claimed jobs in the new economy: mining, oil, and government bureaucracies.

Third, the gold rush signalled the growing involvement of the Canadian government in the lives of northerners. Canada had gained jurisdiction over the West, Rupert's Land, and the North-West Territories in 1870. In 1880, the British government ceded responsibility over the Arctic Islands to Canada, in large part to thwart American and other efforts to claim Baffin Island (Purich, 1992:31). Canada's failure to enforce jurisdiction, however, subsequently resulted in claims pressed by other countries. Thus, the late 19th century saw a host of countries—particularly Britain, the United States, and Norway— sending polar expeditions, ostensibly in the name of exploration, but also to "plant their flags" (see Coates et al., 2008).

The Canadian government responded to these threats in various ways. In 1897, the Canadian government sent a reconnaissance mission to Hudson Bay and Baffin Island, where Captain William Wakeham declared Canada's sovereignty over that and surrounding islands. Similar missions followed, leading up the First World War. Between 1913 and 1918, the Canadian government also funded the research of Vilhjalmur Stefansson (1921; 1938), whose work quickly popularized for Canadians "their" northern heritage. The government also expanded the number of North-West Mounted Police (NWMP) posts in the Arctic, the first having been established two years before the Yukon gold rush (Coates et al., 2008:20), increasing to three by 1903, and several more by the 1920s.

In 1922, the Canadian government instituted a yearly patrol of the eastern Arctic to enforce its claims to sovereignty over the North (Purich, 1992:32–33; also Brody, 1987). The NWMP, now expanded, and renamed the Royal Canadian Mounted Police in 1920, played an important role in this enforcement, while performing a multitude of other functions and roles, including the North's administrators, social workers, and, perhaps most importantly, explorers. From 1940 to 1942, the RCMP vessel the *St. Roch*, a kind of floating detachment, travelled the Northwest Passage from west to east, then from east to west in 1944, becoming the first ship to navigate the passage in both directions, while also engaging in unofficial wartime reconnaissance.

In less than 50 years, Canada's North had been transformed from a peripheral and even exotic appendage to a politically, economically, culturally, and administratively integrated colony of the South. In 1939, the North also began to be militarily integrated into the modern world.

The Second World War and the Post-War South

The Second World War and the subsequent Cold War brought renewed but brief interest in the North, this time not only for its resources, but more immediately for strategic reasons. A major supply route for oil and other military supplies for Alaska moved down the Mackenzie River and along a new highway. Local centres like Fort Smith and Whitehorse suddenly burgeoned with population, and Frobisher Bay became a vast military complex. A former ghost town, Churchill, Manitoba, became a military base with a satellite town of skilled and unskilled workers and a large number of unemployed Aboriginal "squatters."

The Second World War saw a number of large-scale construction projects launched in the North. These included the construction of a series of landing fields, a military base at Goose Bay, the expansion of oil production at Norman Wells, the building of a pipeline from Norman Wells to Whitehorse, and the construction of the Alaska Highway. Both Goose Bay and Gander became strategic links in the North American chain of defence and, between them, supplied more than 900 warplanes to the United Kingdom (Bone, 1988, 1992).

The Alaska Highway was a particularly monumental task for its time. Originally proposed in the 1930s, construction began finally in the 1940s, partially motivated by the Japanese bombing of Pearl Harbor in December 1941. The road was built both to supply Russians with needed materials to fight the Nazi invasion of their country and as a safeguard against a Japanese invasion of North America. The road was over 2,500 kilometres in length, built over muskeg and unstable fields of tundra, and required 11,000 men, including U.S. Army engineers and civilians, to complete the job. Although 80 percent of the highway was built on Canadian soil, the United States government paid the entire cost of $133 million, while Canada absorbed the costs of upkeep. The road had two long-term impacts outlasting the war. First, it stimulated oil and gas exploration in the North. Second, the road's construction had the effect of reinforcing American influence in western Canada, especially Alberta (see Chapter 7).

As important as the military intrusion into the North was, the role of the Canadian government was more crucial in bringing about change (Vallee, 1971). This presence increased markedly after 1945, with the federal government taking over direct responsibility for economic and social affairs as the Hudson's Bay Company no longer felt obligated to buffer Aboriginals from economic swings in the marketplace.

Soon government facilities existed for services that touched on every aspect of Aboriginal life. To some extent, this intervention improved the local way of life. Housing standards were raised, and famine became virtually a thing of the past. Instead of hunting and trapping, new sources of income were generated, including wages, the sale of handicrafts, family allowances, various pensions, and social assistance.

Education was a key area of increased government involvement. As in the South, missionary schools had long existed in the North. Mission schools were opened as early as 1867 at Fort Providence on Great Slave Lake, and in 1874 at Fort Chipewyan on Lake Athabasca (Fisher, 1981). Others followed, with a spate of residential schools set up by missionaries for Arctic and Subarctic children in the 1940s and 1950s (Brody, 1987:143). The purpose of the "new education" was acculturation and assimilation (see also Chapter 9). Thus, local language training was downplayed, and religious practices related to Aboriginal culture and spirituality were discouraged. Boys no longer hunted or trapped with their fathers, and girls were removed from situations where they could take up traditional domestic responsibilities (Cline, 1975:173). Health and educational facilities were virtually non-existent in northern regions (Rea, 1968:184), although a federally sponsored program to train young women as nurses in mission hospitals was initiated in the Northwest Territories in 1939 (Drees, 2013:148). After the 1950s, however, government intervention increased in the form of social and educational assistance as a means of integrating Aboriginal peoples into the body of national life. During the 1930s and 1940s, for example, the fur economy was still a mainstay of northern families. After 1947, however, the price of furs collapsed and remained low until the 1960s. Many Canadian officials viewed trapping as a dying way of life and were determined to drag the North and its residents into the "modern world." Education and economic development were seen as key elements of this process.

Increasingly, the Dene and Inuit found themselves backed into a corner by the realities of a shrinking resource base, their own geography, and the forces of international markets (Abel, 1993:268). In the 1950s, settlements based on the fur industry declined. Farther north, some were able to live off the land, living in fishing camps in the summer and organizing hunting parties in the winter (Massey and Shields, 1995), part of what Stabler (1989) has identified as a **dual economy**, a livelihood earned by both traditional and modern means. (In 1989, two-thirds of family breadwinners in the Northwest Territories still hunted and trapped.) In the southern Subarctic, however, planned resource towns like Thompson, Manitoba, became major producers of minerals, attracted sizable populations, and sometimes employed local Aboriginals (Bone, 1992:69).

Northern Visions

In the late 1950s, English-speaking Canada was beginning to discover or, rather, create itself. Having broken with Britain over the period of the two world wars, Canada was also in the early stages of trying to separate itself from the United States. In part, these efforts were economic. Thus, in the elections of 1957 and 1958, Conservative leader John Diefenbaker spoke out regarding Canada's need to diversify trade, seek out new markets in Asia, and revive those in Britain. But Diefenbaker also lit a fire in many Canadians' imaginations with visions of opening up the North in much the same way that Sir John A. Macdonald had opened up the West in the 19th century. The Diefenbaker government was particularly concerned about growing dependence on social assistance in the North, and so addressed increasing demands for forest products, minerals, and energy. The plan was to transform the fur-trading economy of the North into a resource-based, urban-like economy.

Under Diefenbaker's leadership, Canadian Aboriginals garnered unconditional federal voting rights. Before 1960, they had had to surrender their Indian Status, a process known as **enfranchisement**, if they wanted to vote as Canadian citizens. During the Diefenbaker years, assimilation as an official government policy toward First Nations was also downplayed. For these and other liberating manoeuvres, some observers have jokingly referred to Diefenbaker as "the Lincoln of the North" (McMillan, 1995:314).

By the late 1950s, Diefenbaker's "northern vision" had growing cultural support. Years before, Vilhjalmur Stefansson's book *The Friendly Arctic* (1921) and his subsequent speeches, and Robert Flaherty's silent film *Nanook of the North* (1922), the world's first full-length documentary, had popularized the North among Canadians and non-Canadians alike (Brody, 1987; Srebrnik, 1998). (*Nanook* began touring Canada again in 2014, with a new soundtrack featuring the sounds of Tanya Tagaq, an Inuk throat singer.) The harrowing tales of bush pilots in the years after, followed by the popular writings of people like Farley Mowat and Pierre Berton in the 1950s, added further lustre to the North's reputation and its role in Canadian identity.

From the beginning, however, development of the North has faced economic challenges unlike those of any other area of the country. First, the terrain (largely muskeg or rock) is unwieldy. Second, the North's summer season, when outside work is most feasible, is very short. Third, a lack of skilled labour means that bringing in people from the outside is required. Fourth, the North is far from markets and supplies, resulting in high transportation costs in both directions. Fifth, economic development in the North requires a lot of capital investment, supplied in the past by the state, either directly or through loans, or by private, often foreign, investors who frequently demand generous terms or conditions that ignore the environment and local job creation and training.

Beyond these purely economic factors, there are also significant political, social, and environmental considerations that came to the fore after the 1970s. On the one hand, Aboriginal peoples increasingly developed the political organizations and skills to press their demands for a greater role in economic development and the use of their lands (see Chapter 11). On the other hand, the period from 1965 to 1975 also witnessed a renewed interest in the North on the part of many provincial governments, driven by a belief in activist government and a spirit of province building (Chapter 7). Megaprojects, featuring employment in modern industries, became a feature of the northern part of nearly every province: forestry in British Columbia, the oil sands in Alberta, potash and uranium in Saskatchewan, hydroelectricity and mining in Manitoba and Quebec, and mining in Ontario.

In the early 1960s, the Quebec government began searching for a northern supply of power (see Chapter 2). These ideas were finally realized in 1971 with Premier Robert Bourassa's announcement of a land agreement between the Cree First Nation at James Bay and the Quebec government that would allow construction of a dam (see Chapter 11). A key part of the agreement was Aboriginal employment in the project. Later, however, there were criticisms that the project involved massive unforeseen social and environmental costs borne largely by the Cree people (Clerici, 1999; see also Frideres and Gadacz, 2001).

Similar stories arise from other projects, such as the Nelson River Hydroelectric Project at Pike Lake, Manitoba; the Dryden Chemicals plant at Kenora, Ontario; and the oil sands developments in Fort McMurray. When the Pike Lake project began, local Aboriginal peoples were told that tremendous benefits would accrue from the project. The end result, however, was that little job training took place and instead outside labour was brought in. At Dryden, the plant flushed its waste of chlorine and other chemicals directly into the Wabigoon River, creating a relatively high level of mercury. Eventually, the mercury worked its way up the local food chain, severely damaging the mental and physical health of people in the local Aboriginal communities who ate the contaminated fish (Bone, 1992:167). The Aboriginal peoples of Fort Chipewyan in northern Alberta, meanwhile, have been experiencing high rates of unusual cancers that many attribute to contaminated water runoff from the Fort McMurray oil sands seeping into the Athabasca River (see Marsden, 2007; Nikiforuk, 2010).

In the 1970s, however, the people of the North reacted to the devastating results of modernization. The oil crises of that decade suddenly made financially feasible the pos-sibility of shipping northern oil and gas to southern markets via an overland pipeline crossing Yukon and the Northwest Territories. Large companies were eager to exploit the moment. Federal government approval was required, however, and though technically able to make decisions for the northern territories, which lack the status of provinces, the federal government suddenly became sensitive to northern residents' concerns. The government struck a commission of inquiry.

The Mackenzie Valley Pipeline Inquiry (better known as the Berger Inquiry, after its chair, Justice Thomas Berger) went on for three years (1974–1977) and may properly be described as the first significant public study of the environmental and social effects of economic development ever conducted in Canada. Altogether, 1,000 people, including 300 experts in 35 communities, testified at the hearings, which resulted in 204 volumes of relevant data. Berger's final recommendation was blunt. He outright rejected the pipeline proposal, based on the threat of damage to the local ecosystem, and recommended an alternative route through the Mackenzie Valley after a delay of 10 years. Subsequently, however, a number of complaints about development not ceded by treaty have been resolved including Inuvialuit, Nunavut, Nunatsiavut, and Nunavik in Yukon as well as certain areas in the Northwest Territories (Frideres, 2011:185).

Today, the North—if not the people inhabiting the region—is nearly fully integrated into the rest of Canada and the world economy. Many traditional jobs have been replaced by work in the new economy: the hydrocarbon industries (including diamonds), government bureaucracies, tourism, and the manufacture of cultural products (such as narwhal carvings and beadwork). Unemployment remains stubbornly high: The official unemployment rate for the three northern territories in 2011 was over 9 percent, and over 15 percent in Nunavut (Canadian Northern Economic Development Agency, 2013), but hope for improvement lingers on the horizon (Cooke and Long, 2011:305).

To an extent, cultural integration is also happening. Most northern peoples today live in permanent settlements. The pickup truck and the snowmobile have long replaced the dog team, and the same assortment of large stores, schools, churches, hospitals, sports arenas, and other institutions found in many small Canadian towns in the South can be seen in the North (Condon, 1987).

Moreover, Aboriginal languages (see Chapter 12) and cultures are no longer being explicitly attacked; though still facing enormous pressures, they are instead encouraged (Brody, 1987:163). The training of Aboriginal teachers has been undertaken and curricula have been amended to reflect local themes.

But old problems remain, to which new ones—especially acute in Nunavut—have been added: poor housing, food insecurity, poor health—as evidenced by new diseases, such as diabetes and, since the 1990s, AIDS, as well as the return of an old nemesis, tuberculosis—school absenteeism and dropout, and (as noted above) unemployment. These social problems in turn provide a backdrop to alarmingly high rates of sexual violations against children, homicide, violence against women, and suicide (Hicks, 2013:14–15). Regarding the latter, in 2013 alone, there were 45 suicides in Nunavut, nearly all among the Inuit—a rate of 166 per 1,000 (Alexander, 2014).

Amid these changes and challenges, and in the context of renewed fears about world energy shortages, the idea of a northern pipeline is being revisited. The proposed $18.2 billion Mackenzie Gas Project has the potential to deliver 30 trillion cubic feet of natural gas from the Mackenzie Delta and areas further south to meet the needs of the southern (especially American) market. As in 1977, a joint review panel has been holding public meetings to consider social, economic, and environmental implications of such a development (Gregoire, 2007:58). This time around, however, the project has garnered support from northern people, including Aboriginals; former justice Berger has even come out in support of a pipeline, saying the North is now ready to handle the associated difficulties while taking advantage of the opportunity.

Ironically, just as the North seems prepared to embrace the pipeline, it may lose out to a competing bid, the construction of a gas pipeline from Alaska to Alberta. Nonetheless, the original Berger Inquiry stands as a landmark in Canada's relations with the North and its peoples. The inquiry was the first time the wishes of local northerners themselves became central to decision making. The North gained a voice, but the inquiry also had the effect of informing many Canadians elsewhere about the North and about environmental issues generally. In this sense, the North has played a role in shaping Canadians' growing concern over environmental matters; a concern, one might add, that has slowly worked its way into sociology (see Box 10.1).

Global Warming and the North

There is near consensus around the world in favour of the **global warming thesis** that, first, worldwide temperatures are increasing and, second, human activity is a major contributor to this temperature rise. Since 1988, when it was founded, the United Nations Intergovernmental Panel on Climate Change (IPCC) has compiled the scientific evidence dealing with global warming. The IPCC's Fifth Report, a product of hundreds of scientists from as many as 70 countries, makes several summary statements about the world's climate, rating the confidence level in each statement:

- Each of the last three decades has been successively warmer at the Earth's surface than any preceding decade since 1850.... In the Northern Hemisphere, 1983–2012 was *likely* the warmest 30-year period of the last 1400 years (*medium confidence*).[1]
- Ocean warming dominates the increase in energy stored in the climate system, accounting for more than 90% of the energy accumulated between 1971 and 2010 (*high confidence*). It is *virtually certain* that the upper ocean (0–700 m) warmed from 1971 to 2010 ... and it *likely* warmed between the 1870s and 1971.
- Over the last two decades, the Greenland and Antarctic ice sheets have been losing mass, glaciers have continued to shrink almost worldwide, and Arctic sea ice and Northern Hemisphere spring snow cover have continued to decrease in extent (*high confidence*).
- The rate of sea level rise since the mid-19th century has been larger than the mean rate during the previous two millennia (*high confidence*). Over the period 1901 to 2010, global mean sea level rose by 0.19 [0.17 to 0.21] m.
- The atmospheric concentrations of carbon dioxide, methane, and nitrous oxide have increased to levels unprecedented in at least the last 800,000 years. Carbon dioxide

Box 10.1: The Ecological Challenge to Sociology

Catton and Dunlap (1980) argue that traditional sociology is premised on a set of assumptions that human society is exempt from ecological considerations, a broader rubric they term the Human Exemptionalist Paradigm, which comprises four central beliefs:

1. Humans have a cultural heritage in addition to (and distinct from) their genetic inheritance, and thus are quite unlike all other animal species.
2. Social and cultural factors, including technology, are the major determinants of human affairs.
3. Social and cultural environments are the crucial contexts for human affairs, and the biophysical environment is largely irrelevant.
4. Culture is cumulative, thus technological and social progress can continue indefinitely, making all social problems ultimately soluble.

By contrast, they argue for a New Ecological Paradigm, based on four very different assumptions:

1. While humans have exceptional characteristics (e.g., culture, technology), they remain one among species that are interdependently involved in the global ecosystem.
2. Human affairs are influenced not only by social and cultural factors, but also by intricate connections of cause, effect, and feedback in a web of nature; thus, purposive human actions have many unintended consequences.
3. Humans live in and are dependent upon a finite biophysical environment that imposes physical and biological restraints on human affairs.
4. Although the inventiveness of humans, and the powers derived from this inventiveness, may seem for a while to extend carrying capacity limits, ecological laws cannot be repealed.

Source: Catton, William R., and Riley E. Dunlap. 1980. "A New Ecological Paradigm for Post-Exuberant Sociology." *American Behavioral Scientist* 24(1):34.

concentrations have increased by 40% since pre-industrial times, primarily from fossil fuel emissions and secondarily from net land use change emissions. The ocean has absorbed about 30% of the emitted anthropogenic carbon dioxide, causing ocean acidification. (United Nations, 2014a)

What are the causes of climate change? The report is clear: (1) "The largest contribution to total radiative forcing is caused by the increase in the atmospheric concentration of CO since 1750" and (2) "It is extremely likely that human influence has been the dominant cause of the observed warming since the mid-20th century" (United Nations, 2014a).

According to some, global warming (at the extreme) will result in a massive loss of human and animal life as rising sea levels inundate much of the planet, while many other areas would be rendered uninhabitable due to heat and drought. In turn, these temperature changes will have massive economic, social, and political impacts, including dramatic population shifts and intensified competition for scarce resources, leading, some predict, to war (Dyer, 2008). A briefing note prepared by researchers for the Centre for Climate and Security (a recently created branch of the U.S. Central Intelligence Agency) noted that climate change is both directly and indirectly a "national security threat." The Centre's researchers, Femia and Werrell (2014:4), conclude the following:

> There is a high enough degree of certainty that climate change is, and has the capacity to be, a multiplier of direct and indirect threats to the United States. That's why U.S. national security planners put time, personnel and resources into mitigating and adapting to its effects. Climate change as a security threat is not just a narrative, or a political talking point. It's a reality. The U.S. military and the U.S. intelligence community get it. Our policy-makers should too.

Policy-makers in Canada should also be concerned about global warming. Lemmen and Warren (2004:23–24) argue that global warming, accompanied by changes in precipitation, will impact all of Canada, but its northern regions and the south-central Prairies the most.

Many of these impacts involve geopolitical arguments over jurisdiction and Canadian sovereignty. Chief among these are (1) the opening up of the Northwest Passage for year-round shipping, which poses both environmental risks from oil leaks and other forms of contamination and risks to Canadian jurisdiction; and (2) disputes over subsurface rights in the Arctic, which geological surveys suggest may hold as much as 25 percent of the world's undiscovered oil and gas, as well as valuable minerals, such as diamonds. But it is the United States, and not other northern states (i.e., Russia, Norway, and Denmark), that is Canada's main challenger, with its Alaskan territory giving the U.S. its foothold (legal and otherwise) to make claims.

In response to threats to Canada's jurisdiction, Prime Minister Stephen Harper announced in 2007 plans to "build military ice-breakers, upgrade underwater and aerial surveillance capabilities, build a deep-water port, and expand Canada's military presence in the area" (Coates et al., 2008:172; also see Griffiths, Huebert, and Lackenbauer, 2011). This was followed in 2009 with a document outlining Canada's "Northern Strategy," which continues to be revised (Government of Canada, 2014). To date, however, few of the promises embedded in these policy statements have been implemented; the North remains a prime backdrop for political photo-ops and symbolic speeches, but little real or meaningful action (see Byers, 2014).

Indeed, in the case of environmental challenges facing Canada's North, some view Canada's political leadership and the actions it has taken as not only woefully indifferent but even, at times, hostile. A recent report by the Commissioner of the Environment and Sustainable Development (CESD) (2014) stated the following:

Despite some initiatives and progress in certain areas, there remain many unanswered questions. In many key areas that we looked at, it is not clear how the government intends to address the significant environmental challenges that future growth and development will likely bring about.

The government does not know what Environment Canada's role will be in oil sands monitoring beyond March 2015. It has not made clear the rationale for what projects will be subject to environmental assessments, and I am concerned that some significant projects may not be assessed. It has also not determined what level of service it will provide in the Arctic to support increased navigation and minimize environment and safety risks. And it has not defined a national plan, with the provinces and territories, to achieve Canada's international greenhouse gas emission reduction target.

The failure to implement meaningful environmental policies and initiatives to deal with global warming is not specific to any single governing party. Critics argue that neither the previous Liberal governments of Jean Chrétien (1934–) and Paul Martin nor the current Conservative government of Stephen Harper has seriously tackled the issue, though many view the latter as expecially hostile to scientific evidence. Indeed, one author has referred to a "war on science" (Turner, 2013) that has seen restrictions on what government scientists can publically say, the termination of hundreds of Environment Canada positions in 2011, the destruction of several scientific library collections, and the defunding of several environment-related departments, including the closure of the Polar Environment Atmosphere Research Laboratory (PEARL) in Nunavut, whose research had informed the discovery of a large hole in the Arctic's ozone layer (see Linnitt, 2013). Upset with what has happened, in July 2012 a number of scientists organized a mock funeral for the "death of evidence," the protest since resulting in the creation of a small organization of the same name dedicated to defending and restoring the role of scientific evidence in decision making.

As a country, Canada is lagging behind earlier commitments to reduce greenhouse gas emissions (GHG), the chief cause of global warming. Canada's current level of GHG emissions is marginally below that of 2005, largely due to a drop in electricity generation in Ontario. It is far off, however, the targets set when Canada signed the 2009 Copenhagen Accord through the United Nations Framework Convention on Climate Change—targets that will be further from Canada's reach if and when the plethora of pipelines carrying oil from the oil sands get approved (see again the CESD report above).

The causes of the government failure to protect the ecological commons are complex and not based solely on opposition to scientific evidence. Of greater weight are political and economic considerations concerning the value of the petroleum industry to Canadian governments, corporations, and individuals. Prime Minister Harper stated in June 2014, for example, that his government viewed the environment and economic growth as largely incompatible issues: "No country is going to undertake actions on climate change, no matter what they say … that is going to deliberately destroy jobs and growth" (*Maclean's*, 2014). Others question, however, whether one can speak of an economy separate from a healthy and sustainable climate and environment.

What does global warming mean for the people of the Far North? Put simply, it could prove particularly disastrous. As Grossmen and Parker (2013:13–14) suggest, "Climate change is already here … climate change is a potential culture killer"—a harsh verdict, if correct, for Northern peoples.

According to Ford and Wandel (2013:114), Nunavut is particularly vulnerable to global warming due to changes, such as "the erosion of traditional Inuit knowledge, weakening of social networks, and reduced harvesting flexibility," that have lessened the people's adaptive capacity. In response to the looming crisis, the government of Nunavut began consultations in the summer of 2014, working with "communities, Inuit organizations and university researchers" to start mapping areas vulnerable to climate change (Government of Nunavut, 2014). More broadly, Aboriginal communities in the North have increasingly begun mounting legal challenges against the actions—and inactions—of Canadian governments that have failed to deal with climate change (Sniderman and Shedletzky, 2014).

At the same time, the issues surrounding climate change have rekindled debate regarding **Aboriginal ecology** and whether First Peoples have ever lived up to Western-imposed ecological stereotypes (Porter, 2012:xiii).

Aboriginal Ecology

Some scholars insist that Indigenous approaches to the environment were founded on a superior philosophical basis to that imported from Europe. Against this view, anthropologist Shepard Krech III's book *The Ecological Indian* garnered considerable criticism in 1999 for questioning the notion that American Indians were evologists whose cultural practices took into account the complexities of natural systems, waste, or future sustainability. Krech was accused of being anti-environmental and anti-Indian, but he defended himself by stating that his intent in the book was to encourage discussion on the matter.

Harvey Feit of McMaster University has since criticized Krech for neglecting to take fur trade history into account to consider what the policy choices or questions should be today. He suggests that Krech's book not only

> fails to present credible analyses of both nineteenth century Euro-American fur traders and Native Americans, and of the politics of Indigenous rights today, but that it also disappoints and misleads readers about present circumstances and possibilities for North Americans and Native Americans. (Feit, 2007:85–86)

Krech (2007) later defended his research by asking whether it is better to promote biodiversity or to relieve poverty; but his response invites the question "Why not both?" while also ignoring simple calls for justice or political accountability.

Amid these debates, Hull University historian Joy Porter (2012:xv) states, regarding Aboriginal perspectives on the environment, that "It is not argued here that native thinking about American land is always necessarily better that Euro-American thinking, rather it is suggested that a close examination of each is fruitful and important if we are to think anew of the most pressing issues of the future." However, Porter's approach may be seen as less than even-handed, given her defence of a whale hunt undertaken by the West Coast Makah First Nation that was opposed by 350 groups from 27 countries (Porter, 2012:33). Porter justified the hunt by suggesting that the whale hunt was environmentally sound on several levels. It invigorated the Makah community and almost every part of the whale was used. Moreover, the hunt offered symbolic and intercultural power, and highlighted a people's right to determine its way of life.

Against efforts to bridge the gap, Christine Elsey (2013:13) of the University of the Fraser Valley emphasizes the polarity that exists between traditional Aboriginal and Western thought, arguing that the former perspective applies to more than land and climate as connected spiritual gifts from the Creator, and has never been fully explored. This difference is echoed in the work of a retired anthropologist, Julie Cruikshank, who has worked extensively with the Athapaskan and Tlinget elders who have cautioned newcomers to the region to respect the glaciers that tradition suggests are living, sentient beings. The glaciers, Cruikshank observes, "were seen as animate as any animals.... They responded to people. They took offence easily. You had to be very circumspect in the way you behaved around them, or you would be served catastrophic consequences" (Montgomery, 2007:76). Kathleen Absolon (2011:31) concurs, pointing out that the contemporary age is not particularly attuned to appreciate a holistic and relational viewpoint; issues of the environment, as seen by many Aboriginal people in the North, are not merely technical, and certainly not purely economic; they are inherently spiritual—issues that we will return to in Chapter 12.

Conclusion

For most Canadians, Canada's North remains a place of fantasy and imagery only, a land rich in symbolism and myth, but largely unknown, yet it is important to all of Canada in ways that Canadians have not yet recognized.

Since the 1980s, Canada has started to forge a new relationship with the North and its peoples, but progress has been slow and uneven, and today poses new perils as well as possibilities. The creation of Nunavut in 1999 was an important step; some land claim issues there have been settled, though many remain. Among the most important issues remaining are calls for self-government. This is a call heard elsewhere in Canada by Aboriginal peoples—one that, unheeded, has often led to conflict in recent decades, the subject of the chapter to follow.

Note

1. The United States National Oceanic and Atmospheric Administration reported in late 2014 that September had been the warmest month on record (going back to 1880) and that combined land and sea average surface temperatures for the year were 0.68°C above the 20th century average of 14.1°C, tying with 1998 as the hottest year on record (Goldenberg, 2014).

Key Terms

Aboriginal ecology
climate change
dual economy
enfranchisement
global warming thesis
individual egalitarianism
polygyny
syncretism

Critical Thinking Questions

1. Why do places such as the North gain such a hold on the human imagination?
2. What examples of syncretism can you identify from other cultures?
3. In what ways are the kinds of megaprojects in the Canadian North similar to those underway in many underdeveloped countries?
4. How might Catton and Dunlap's "New Ecological Paradigm," if adopted, alter the way sociologists look at issues?
5. Is climate change only an issue for northern Indigenous communities or should it be an important issue to Canadians as a whole?

Recommended Readings

Bone, Robert. 1992. *The Geography of the Canadian North: Issues and Challenges*. Toronto: Oxford University Press.
Considered a watershed work on Canada's North, this book expertly details the topography of the region and outlines the challenges faced by people living there.

Coates, Ken S., P. Whitney Lackenbauer, William R. Morrison, and Greg Poelzer. 2008. *Arctic Front: Defending Canada in the Far North*. Toronto: Thomas Allen.
This book provides an environmental, historical, political, and economic overview of the issues facing the Canadian North today.

Grossman, Zoltán, and Alan Parker, eds. 2013. *Asserting Native Resilience: Pacific Indigenous Nations Face the Climate Crisis*. Corvallis, OR: Oregon State University Press.
This book offers a series of perspectives on Indigenous responses to climate change.

Harkin, Michael E., and David Rich Lewis, eds. 2007. *Native Americans and the Environment: Perspectives on the Ecological Indian*. Lincoln, NE: University of Nebraska Press.

The focus of this book is to elaborate the environmental perspectives of a group of inter-disciplinary scholars.

Porter, Joy. 2012. *Native American Environmentalism: Land, Spirit, and the Idea of Wilderness*. Lincoln, NE: University of Nebraska Press.
This book explores the conflict between traditional Indigenous attitudes toward nature and that of Christian environmentalists.

Related Websites

Death of Evidence Organization
www.deathofevidence.ca/media
A protest of scientists on Parliament Hill in July 2012 led to the formation of a permanent Internet-based organization dedicated to the defence of empirical evidence in decision making.

Government of Nunavut
www.gov.nu.ca
The official website for the government of Nunavut.

Intergovernmental Panel on Climate Change
www.ipcc.ch
The United Nations Environment Programme and the World Meteorological Organization established the Intergovernmental Panel on Climate Change (IPCC) in 1988 to provide scientific information on the current state of climate change and its potential environmental and socio-economic consequences.

Canadian Society on Video

People of the Ice. 2003. National Film Board of Canada, 52 minutes.
Examines the Inuit way of life and how it is threatened by global warming today.

The Necessities of Life. 2008. 102 minutes.
The film traces the removal by boat of an Inuit hunter (played by Natar Ungalaaq) from Baffin Island to a Quebec City sanatorium in 1952.

Vanishing Point. 2012. 82 minutes, 23 seconds.
The film examines the unprecedented changes facing all Arctic peoples. A stunning scene features a dog team pulling an Inughuit family across the vast sea ice of Greenland. As the team forges ahead, the terrain melts beneath them, and the dogs break through the surface, plunging into frigid polar waters.

CHAPTER 11

THE FIGHT
FOR JUSTICE

The day will come when Indians will not be concerned with struggling for their basic rights only, but for the basic rights of all.

—Cree lawyer William Wuttunee, 1971

However noble and necessary justice is to our struggles, its gaze will always be backward. By itself, the concept of justice is not capable of encompassing the broader transformations needed to ensure coexistence. Justice is one element of a good relationship; it is concerned with fairness and right and calculating moral balances, but it cannot be the end goal of a struggle.

—author and professor Taiaiake Alfred, 2005

It is those who are being healed within their deepest wounds who will be the strongest healers. They will be the most generous for it is they who, blessed as they are, respond so completely in it. They will be the new Persons, the New Indians, so long awaited.

—Joseph E. Couture, 2013

Introduction

Well into the 20th century, Aboriginal peoples remained hidden from mainstream Canadian society. Occasionally, some—like Tom Longboat—became quite famous athletes, or found employment in towns and cities, and thus left the reserves. The two world wars of the 20th century provided yet another opportunity to leave. During the Second World War, some 4,000 Status Indians and an unknown number of Métis and other Native peoples enlisted, with several of them being decorated for valour (see Winegard, 2012). In general, however, the colonial reserve system fulfilled its function of segregating Aboriginal peoples from Canadian society. But, gradually, Aboriginal peoples did begin reclaiming their voices. This chapter examines this process of reclamation and the search for justice, a process that continues today, sometimes in conflict, sometimes in co-operation. The chapter begins with a discussion of the emergence of Aboriginal organizations capable of fighting for positive change.

Aboriginal Capacity and the Hawthorn Report

Under the Indian Act, enacted in 1876, members of Indian organizations were prevented from meeting by a pass system that forbade individuals from leaving their reserves without permission of the Indian agent. Under Section 141 of the same act, introduced in 1927, it was an offence to raise money for the purpose of advancing Aboriginal claims (Purich, 1986:185).

Despite these impediments, a few Aboriginal organizations *did* emerge in Canada during the 1930s and 1940s. These included the Native Brotherhood of British Columbia, the Indian Association of Alberta, and, with the encouragement of Saskatchewan's

CCF government, the Union of Saskatchewan Indians. In the 1960s the federal government's decision to fund Aboriginal organizations meant the further growth of additional organizations. The National Indian Brotherhood (NIB) was formed in 1968 when the National Indian Council split into two factions, the NIB and the Canadian Métis Society. These and other, newer Aboriginal organizations experienced some success through lobbying, organizing, and protesting. Together, these organizations drew attention to a wider range of concerns that went beyond individual First Nations (Frideres and Gadacz, 2001), and finally convinced governments to also take a hard look at a community within Canada that had been too long ignored. The result was the Hawthorn Report.

In 1963, the federal government asked University of British Columbia anthropologist Harry Hawthorn to study the living conditions of Canada's Aboriginal peoples. This was at a time when Canada was rapidly becoming urbanized, but Aboriginals, rural and confined to reserves, still made little impression upon most Canadians. Hawthorn's subsequent study (1966–1967) stunned everyone, however, including government leaders. Few knew or had taken the time to find out about the devastating conditions under which most Canadian Aboriginals were living. The Hawthorn Report catalogued the plight of Aboriginals, from high rates of unemployment and poverty to health problems, including malnutrition, and a resultant life expectancy that was dismally below that of other Canadians. It made clear that Aboriginal housing was substandard and education was inadequate. Finally, the report made an important plea that Aboriginal peoples should be extended the same rights as other citizens *and* be assured that their legal rights as Status Indians also be honoured, a plea captured in the term **citizens plus**.

The Hawthorn Report was delivered in the context of a great deal of discussion of human rights and fundamental freedoms. The American civil rights movement spilled over into Canada and forced the government to focus attention on neglected minorities. The Red Power movement and Vietnam War demonstrations in the U.S. threatened many Canadians who feared that similar protests might occur in their country, fears amplified by the armed occupation of Anicinabe Park in Kenora, Ontario, and a near-riot on Parliament Hill (Purich, 1986:188).

Fear alone does not explain the majority reaction, however. The 1960s in Canada, as elsewhere, reflected a sincere, if paternalistic, belief in providing opportunities for neglected communities to "join" the rest of society. Unfortunately, these efforts implied that all responsibility for accommodation lay within the minority camp. These efforts further assumed that education and good teaching were the chief vehicles for equalizing opportunity and minimizing differences (Friesen, 1993:7).

In 1967, Canada celebrated 100 years as a nation. It was also a time of civil unrest, and there were many questions about relationships between people and institutions, including provincial and federal governments. Similarly, the role of the United States in the Vietnam War was under scrutiny, city parks were full of "hippies," universities were sites of sit-ins, and anti-establishment marches protesting all sorts of things were frequent. Against this background, while clutching the Hawthorn Report, in 1969 Pierre Trudeau's Liberal government made public its new Aboriginal policy in a White Paper.

White Paper, Red Paper

The Trudeau administration was modernist to a fault; that is, it believed firmly in the role of the state in society and, at the same time, the values of liberal individualism and economic progress. In this vein, the Liberal government decided to adopt a new Aboriginal policy, the intent of which was to resolve Aboriginal land claims and to eliminate distinctions between Aboriginal peoples and other Canadians. Aboriginal peoples were to be made individually self-reliant. Indian Status was to disappear as a meaningful term in law (Boldt, 1993:18).

The White Paper (Government of Canada, 1969) was the instrument designed to lay out the new policy. It proposed the following government actions:

1. Abolish the Department of Indian Affairs and Northern Development.
2. Repeal the Indian Act.
3. Transfer all responsibility for Indian programs to provincial administration. Provide economic assistance to those reserves that are furthest behind.
4. Formulate a policy to end treaties.
5. Appoint an Indian claims commissioner.
6. Recognize the contributions that Indian people have made to Canadian society.

Many Aboriginal leaders immediately and vigorously denounced the government's White Paper and were joined in their repudiation by a number of non-Aboriginal social and political organizations. In his book *The Unjust Society*, a prominent young Aboriginal leader, Harold Cardinal, contrasted the White Paper with Pierre Trudeau's vision of a "just society," calling the White Paper "a programme which offers nothing better than cultural genocide" (Cardinal, 1969:1).

The first official reaction to the White Paper came from the Indian Chiefs of Alberta (1970), who claimed that it was a document of despair, not hope, whose proposals (if implemented) would see Aboriginal peoples within a generation or two left with no land and threatened by complete assimilation. The Indian Chiefs' "Red Paper," as it was called, itself drew strong criticism, however, notably from Cree lawyer William Wuttunee (1928–) in his book *Ruffled Feathers* (1971), which accused the Alberta Chiefs of fostering a treaty mentality and supporting a buckskin-and-feather culture.

A second major paper (the "Brown Paper") critical of the White Paper emanated from the Union of British Columbia Indian Chiefs. The Brown Paper argued that the special relationship between Aboriginals and the federal government, developed through the years, should not be negated; indeed, that this relationship carried immense moral and legal force and should constitute the foundation for future co-operative policy making. The Brown Paper also made reference to the principle of self-determination and suggested that bands should take over aspects of reserve administration at local levels. In this, the authors of the Brown Paper joined with other Aboriginal organizations in asking the Indian Affairs Branch to provide the necessary financial resources to develop their plans, programs, and budgets toward that end.

Officials of the Government of Canada were surprised and dismayed by the response of Aboriginals to the White Paper. Their surprise was due not solely to the forcefulness of the response, but to the articulate and organized manner of its expression. Faced with such opposition, in 1970 the federal government decided not to proceed with implementing the White Paper (Purich, 1986:187).

Nonetheless, the White Paper and the ensuing controversy had three important impacts. First, the White Paper resulted in the renewed growth of Aboriginal organizations on the Canadian scene. Second, it led to an immediate change in government land claims policy, with the appointment of an Indian claims commissioner in 1969. (The appointment was one of the few recommendations in the White Paper acceptable to most Aboriginals.)

This second impact subsequently led (in August 1973) to the federal government announcing a comprehensive land claims policy recognizing two broad categories of claims: comprehensive claims based on Aboriginal rights, and specific claims based on specific legal commitments. Funding to pursue these claims was made possible through a newly established Office of Native Claims. In 1975, the Dene of the Northwest Territories became one of the first Aboriginal groups to claim First Nation Status. The following year, the Inuit Tapirisat proposed a land claim settlement that eventually gave birth to the territory of Nunavut on April 1, 1999 (Geddes, 2000) (see Chapter 12).

The White Paper's third impact is harder to measure, but is no less important. The debate surrounding the White Paper and Aboriginal response to it educated many in the non-Aboriginal community about the issues facing Aboriginal peoples. It was knowledge reinforced on many occasions over the next 45 years through commission reports, constitutional meetings, and conflict.

Aboriginal Peoples and the 1982 Constitution

In February 1980, Prime Minister Pierre Trudeau declared his intention to bring home Canada's Constitution (Chapter 3). Immediately, a number of Aboriginal organizations began lobbying both the federal government and the British Parliament to include Aboriginal rights in the process of patriation. The lobbying worked, for in January 1981 then–Minister of Justice Jean Chrétien introduced an amendment to the proposed Constitution that would "recognize and affirm" the Aboriginal and treaty rights of Canada's Aboriginal peoples. The amendment included in its recognition the existence of Indian, Inuit, and Métis peoples. Chrétien also proposed that a conference to define Aboriginal rights be held within two years of the date when the patriation process was complete.

Almost immediately, however, these amendments ran into problems. On November 5, 1981, all provinces except Quebec agreed to repatriation, but this incomplete consensus was achieved by dropping Aboriginal rights from the Constitution. The first ministers then reversed their position, agreeing to the inclusion of these rights, on condition that the word *existing* be added. In effect, Aboriginals could expect no new rights;

the Constitution endorsed only those rights already possessed. Many feared that this condition would hinder the development of **Aboriginal self-government**—fears that have since proved well justified (see below).

On April 17, 1982, Canadians could finally say that they had their own Constitution. For Aboriginal peoples, while the new Constitution remained incomplete, it nonetheless represented an important step. It affirmed existing Aboriginal rights in broad terms and thus opened the door for making land claims. For the first time, the Métis, along with the Inuit, garnered specific mention in Canada's Constitution. Furthermore, the document set out a process of ongoing constitutional conferences aimed at defining Aboriginal rights and giving Aboriginal peoples the opportunity to present their views. Finally, the Canadian Charter of Rights and Freedoms not only recognized and affirmed Aboriginal and treaty rights, it also put a spotlight on what some observers saw as the Indian Act's discriminatory provisions.

Who Is an Indian?

Since the establishment of the Indian Act in 1876, legislation governing Aboriginals had defined who was an Aboriginal in a way that discriminated against women. To begin with, on "the day that the government counted the Indians," all who "stood in line" became Status Indians by law. This afforded them the privilege of having matters pertaining to health, education, and welfare delivered directly through federal auspices. Children born to Status Indians were added to the Indian Register.

But what happened if a Status Indian woman married a non-Status male (either Aboriginal or non-Aboriginal)? In these cases, she lost her Status rights. Likewise, any children born to her were also deprived of Status. This was not true for males, however. In fact, if a Status Indian man married a non-Status woman (either Aboriginal or non-Aboriginal), that woman became a Status Indian. Such gender discrimination bothered many people, particularly since the 1973 case of *A. G. (Can) v. Lavell*, which upheld this discriminatory provision of the Indian Act. The terms of the Charter of Rights and Freedoms may have been influenced by the 1975 case of Sandra Lovelace, who took her complaint of gender discrimination to the Human Rights Committee of the United Nations. In 1981 this committee decided that her case was one of "an unjustifiable denial of her rights under the United Nations' Covenant on Civil and Political Rights" (Miller, 2000:357–358).

The issue of how Aboriginals traditionally viewed women's rights was complex. Aboriginal women were not unanimous in endorsing Bill C-31, the equal rights amendment that would end Status women's loss of their rights through marriage to non-Status males. Of eight national First Nations organizations, only four endorsed the bill. One group of Aboriginal women launched a demonstration in Ottawa protesting the bill. Some argued that women who married "outside" knew very well what they were doing. Insofar as Aboriginals believe tribal spirituality is mainly transferred through women, who alone have the power to give life, marrying outside was viewed by some Aboriginals, male and female alike, as disregarding the spiritual welfare of the band. Hence, some believed that women doing so deserved to lose their Status and should not be permitted to opt back in. There were also bands that refused to return band membership to women who were able to regain Status through the auspices of Bill C-31. The result has been a new division in First Nations communities. This is illustrated by a remark made by an Aboriginal to one of the authors when a neighbour regained Status: "Oh, so now she is a Bill C-31 Indian!"

The arguments put forward by those who objected to Bill C-31 were decidedly out of step with Canadian society and with many in the Aboriginal community. In 1985, Bill C-31 was passed, eliminating sexual discrimination, abolishing the concept of enfranchisement, and providing for those who had lost their Aboriginal Status to gain partial reinstatement. The bill had the almost immediate effect of greatly enlarging Canada's Aboriginal population. By 2001, more than 105,000 people had regained Indian Status under Bill C-31, fuelling the growth of the Aboriginal identity population (Frideres and Gadacz, 2001:35) (see Chapter 12).

The first conference specified in the Constitution was held on March 15 and 16, 1983, and was followed by three additional conferences. From the beginning, at least one practical problem beset these conferences: that of representation. Through tradition and the Indian Act, Status Indians had a recognized seat at the gatherings. This was not the case, however, for Métis people and non-Status Indians. In the past, the Native Council of Canada (NCC) had spoken for Métis people, but the Métis disagreed with the NCC's definition of Métis (anyone of mixed blood) and wanted a more explicit definition, including the origins and domicile of the Métis in the Red River area. Similarly, non-Status Indians demanded equal rights with Status Indians. By contrast, the Métis were not requesting Status rights; they simply wanted to be recognized as a distinct Aboriginal group.

In the end, Prime Minister Trudeau asked the NCC to represent Métis interests, a move that caused a further split in the Aboriginal community. A new organization, the Métis National Council, was then formed by a group of dissidents who launched a court case to demand that their interests also be represented at constitutional conferences. When the first conference was over, it was agreed that no constitutional changes affecting Aboriginal rights would be made without a constitutional conference for that explicit purpose, to which Aboriginal representatives would be invited (Schwartz, 1986:127). It was further agreed that future land claims would include a definition of "existing rights" and that sexual equality would be guaranteed, hence the later passing of Bill C-31.

From Meech Lake to Oka and Beyond

The failure of the Meech Lake Accord in 1990 had important consequences for Quebec-Canada relations (Chapter 3). But the Meech Lake Accord likewise had important consequences for Aboriginal peoples and Canada.

From the beginning, groups of First Nations opposed the Meech Lake Accord. They feared that the accord's provisions recognizing Quebec's specificity would lead to a similar delegation of powers to the other provinces, including jurisdiction over Aboriginal affairs. Symbolically, the phrase respecting Quebec as a "distinct society" also rankled with many Aboriginals who believed that the accord completely overlooked their historical traditions; indeed, it identified Quebec as the "foremost distinct society" in Canada, implicitly building on the notion of "two founding races" (French and English) while ignoring the pre-existence of Aboriginal peoples on the continent. Aboriginals were further upset that Canada's first ministers had long rejected the entrenchment of Aboriginal rights on the grounds that the concept was too vague and undefined, yet suddenly they were quite willing to grant similar rights to the province of Quebec (York, 1989:266).

Technically, the Meech Lake Accord died on the East Coast when the Newfoundland legislature failed to vote on it. In fact, as earlier recounted (Chapter 3), the accord's final defeat came at the hands of Elijah Harper, an Aboriginal NDP member of the Opposition in the Manitoba legislature. By the spring of 1990, the House of Commons and most provinces had given the accord approval. Newfoundland and Manitoba had not, however, and time was running out. The agreed-upon procedure required that for the Manitoba legislature to vote on the accord, and thus make the deadline, there had to be unanimous approval by the members. When the proposal to cut debate short was put forward, however, Harper stood alone in refusing approval. Without this approval, the accord could not be passed in time. Newfoundland's government already knew of this outcome on the day that it also refused to vote on the accord.

The accord's failure had profound consequences for Aboriginal/non-Aboriginal relations, not only in Quebec but elsewhere in Canada. The first consequence of this failure was a series of actual confrontations between Aboriginal peoples and Canadian governments that escalated, in several instances, to armed conflict.

The most immediate and famously publicized of these conflicts occurred in Oka, Quebec. Cross and Sévigny (1994:80) describe the events:

> Everything began on a nice day in March 1990, when the Municipal Council of the Village of Oka [outside Montreal] adopted the proposal to expand the area's golf course. In one stroke, Oka's Pines and Mohawk cemetery at Kanehsatake were threatened. To protect their land and the graves of their ancestors, the Mohawks erected a barricade to make the Whites understand that they intended to protect their land against all invaders.

As with any conflict, however, the roots of the Oka Crisis (as it quickly became known) were much older. In fact, the conflict dated back to 1717, when King Louis XV of France granted the land in question to the Seminary of St. Sulpice to set up a mission for the resident Aboriginals, mainly Huron, Algonquin, and Iroquois. By French law (which never recognized **Aboriginal land title**), later confirmed by British and Canadian governments, the lands of Kanehsatake (Oka) did not legally belong to the Aboriginal inhabitants; to Aboriginal peoples, however, this was their land (Dickason, 2002:343–346). Indeed, for many Mohawks and their supporters, such legal decisions merely reinforced the notion that law and justice are often strangers, and that the Canadian legal system is simply another tool for state oppression—an idea with which many conflict theorists would sympathize.

The crisis escalated into violence when the Quebec police decided to attack and take down the barricades, resulting in the death of a police officer, although the exact circumstances of the incident are uncertain to this day. The Canadian government quickly sent in 2,500 soldiers to surround the reserve now guarded by khaki-clad Mohawk "warriors" bearing automatic rifles. Sympathy barricades arose on other Mohawk reserves nearby. The crisis lasted 11 weeks, during which many Canadians, Aboriginal and non-Aboriginal alike, feared a horrible bloodbath (Alfred, 1995:100); fortunately, this did not occur. On September 26, 1990, the crisis ended with the Mohawk warriors putting down their weapons and walking out from behind the barricade. Only a few dozen Mohawk warriors were tried in court; a few were convicted on minor offences and sentenced to short periods in jail.

Today, there remains a great deal of mistrust between Mohawks and the Quebec and federal governments, and between Mohawks and the surrounding non-Aboriginal community. But there are also fractures within the Mohawk community between moderate and hard-line Mohawk nationalists, worsened since 1990 by the emergence of criminal gangs thriving on gambling and smuggling (primarily of cigarettes, but also guns). As for the disputed land, in June 2000 the Kanehsatake Mohawk band signed a deal with Ottawa, gaining control (but not legal title) of their affairs, while the Mohawk band council has gained the right to establish bylaws, zoning regulations, and a process for resolving disputes on those lands, a situation akin to self-government (see below).

The Oka Crisis must be viewed in a larger context of Aboriginal resistance dating back centuries (Chapter 9). Aboriginal peoples have never given up—nor can they give up—the fight (whether militantly or politically expressed) for self-governance. Long before Oka, there were similar confrontations. In 1969, for example, Mohawk Indians from the St. Regis Reserve blocked the international bridge between Canada and the United States near Cornwall, Ontario. In September 1989, the Barriere Lake Algonquin of Quebec blockaded six logging roads in an effort to save their traditional hunting grounds and way of life.

After Oka, the number of confrontations increased and were no longer confined to Quebec. Among them were conflicts at Ipperwash in Ontario (where an Aboriginal protester, Dudley George, was killed by the Ontario Provincial Police), the Old Man Dam in Alberta, and Gustafson Lake in British Columbia. Today, such confrontations still occur (see Box 11.1).

Why have Aboriginal protests increased in recent decades? Clearly, the protests reflect a great deal of frustration on the part of Aboriginals. Anger and discontent do not alone lead to political action, however. Examining the increase in Aboriginal protests in recent years, the sociologist Howard Ramos (2006) has concluded that the increase in Aboriginal-launched protests is positively related to the number of Aboriginal organizations; that is, while a pan-Indigenous ideology (or consciousness) or the availability of

Box 11.1: The Caledonia Story

Karl Marx once remarked that history repeats itself, the first time as tragedy, the second time as farce. Canada's longest Aboriginal occupation began on February 28, 2006. The dispute, which involves the Six Nations of Grand River, Ontario, centres on a 40 hectare parcel of land at Caledonia, Ontario, near Hamilton. Like Oka, the origins of the dispute go back a long way, in this case to 1784 when the British government awarded the Six Nations 385,000 hectares of land in exchange for their allegiance during the American War of Independence. According to the federal government, the land was bought back in 1841; according to the Six Nations, however, the land was only leased to the government at that time. The dispute simmered in later years, with the government selling the land (first in 1848), an action that the Six Nations insist they never agreed to nor for which have they received adequate compensation.

Despite litigation, a developer bought the land in 1992 and in 2005 registered plans to build a housing development. This action sparked protests that began in early 2006, causing work at the site to cease immediately. In April 2006, the Ontario government obtained a court injunction to have the protesters removed, leading the Ontario Provincial Police to raid the site and arrest more than a dozen people. However, as word of the arrests spread, hundreds of Aboriginal peoples quickly descended on the site and set up barricades that remained up for several months. Meanwhile, relations between the Six Nations and the residents of Caledonia deteriorated, with several incidents of violence reported and accusations that the police have played a less-than-neutral role.

In 2007, the federal government made an undisclosed offer to the developer and pledged $1 million in compensation to Caledonia's businesspeople. The Six Nations leaders refused the federal offer of $26 million and in 2008 erected new barricades. The saga of protests, violence, and land claims continues. The dispute is over for the developer: the Ontario government has compensated it to the tune of $16.5 million.

Source: Lawson, James C. B. 2006. "The Caledonia Occupation." *Relay* 30:12–14. www.socialistproject.ca/relay/r12_caledonia.pdf; and Humphreys, Adrian. 2014. "Caledonia Developers Vindicated as Government Ordered to Pay Legal Costs for Tax Battle over Standoff Settlement." *National Post On-Line*, September 30 (news.nationalpost.com/2014/09/30/caledonia-developers-dont-have-to-pay-legal-costs-for-tax-battle-over-16m-standoff-settlement-court).

resources may be necessary, they are insufficient factors in explaining Aboriginal political action; the necessary factor is organization.

Oka and these other confrontations alarmed many Canadians, Aboriginals and non-Aboriginals alike. (Regrettably, in some quarters, racism and prejudice also reared their heads.) The sight of Canadian soldiers and police squaring off against Aboriginal protesters revealed the stark divide between Canada's other "two solitudes" and the possible dangers if that gulf was not addressed. For 20 years, Canada-Quebec issues had dominated the political agenda. In the context of the failures of the Meech Lake and Charlottetown accords, and in the aftermath of Oka, Aboriginal/non-Aboriginal issues came to be seen as parallel to Canada-Quebec issues. They became better known to the general public and gained support, albeit sometimes grudgingly. Within government circles, a heightened sense of urgency over treaties and the Aboriginal right to self-government also emerged (Mercredi and Turpel, 1993:209–210). The creation of the Royal Commission on Aboriginal Peoples was a tangible result of this changed mood.

The Royal Commission on Aboriginal Peoples

In the wake of the failure of the Meech Lake Accord and the Oka Crisis, in 1991 the federal government established the Royal Commission on Aboriginal Peoples (RCAP) (Indian and Northern Affairs Canada, 1996). Chaired by former Assembly of First Nations (AFN) Chief George Erasmus and Quebec Judge René Dussault, the commission included seven members, four of them Aboriginal and three of them non-Aboriginal. A number of public meetings were held, transcripts were analyzed, and a great deal of research was undertaken, though it is clear both from the structure of the report and from the public hearings that the commissioners regarded their task as an exercise in public education as well as a government investigation (Miller, 2000:385).

Altogether, the Royal Commission cost $50 million. Its final report in 1996 consisted of five volumes, more than 3,500 pages, and 400 recommendations. The report's main findings were contained in five sections.

In essence, the report recommended a major reconstruction of Canadian society so that justice and equality would be better assured for Aboriginal Canadians. Two specific and urgent concerns of the report had to do with the high suicide rates in Aboriginal communities and the high incidence of incarceration for Aboriginals, especially in the western provinces, which raised issues regarding the fairness of Canada's criminal justice system. The report recommended swift action in these areas, starting with a meeting of the various bars, law societies, and lawyers' associations. It also urged increased government expenditures on preventive programs.

More broadly, the RCAP also recommended rewriting the principles of the Royal Proclamation to reflect the new nation-to-nation concept of negotiation, as well as a new constitutional foundation by which to perceive the past treaty-making process. In the words of University of Calgary sociologist Rick Ponting (1997a:470), the report recommended at its core "the re-balancing of political and economic power between Aboriginal nations and Canadian governments." Among its many recommendations was the formation of an Aboriginal parliament with an advisory but no law-making authority. This was seen as a first step toward creating a House of First Peoples as the third chamber of the Parliament of Canada. The commission also recommended the abolition of the Department of Indian Affairs and Northern Development and its replacement by two departments: the Department of Aboriginal Relations and the Department of Indian and Inuit Services.

The RCAP also recommended creating a number of new organizational structures, including an Aboriginal Peoples' international university along with Aboriginal student unions and Aboriginal residential colleges, and an Aboriginal languages foundation, which would parallel the work of the international university and supplement its efforts to maintain Aboriginal languages and culture.

The Liberal government's response to the report was to set up, in 1998, a special healing fund in the amount of $350 million to be used over a four-year period as a token of the government's apology for the treatment of Aboriginals in residential schools, and to approve an increase of $250 million in their next year's budget as a means of supporting the Aboriginal cause. However, the response of others was often critical.

While Phil Fontaine (1944–), then grand chief of the AFN, generally approved of the recommendations, suggesting that they were the best that one could hope for at the time, most Métis, Inuit, and non-Status Indians were critical of it, and subsequent government actions, as favouring Status Indians. Others noted the report's lack of emphasis on the situation of urban Aboriginals, privileging reserve life and cultural persistence over solving socio-economic problems across the board (Alan Cairns cited in Miller, 2000:385), a particularly important consideration, since more than one-half of Canada's First Nations now live in urban centres (see Chapter 12).

Likewise, the report also met with strong criticism in the non-Aboriginal community. University of Calgary political scientist Thomas Flanagan (2000) is one of the report's harshest critics. Flanagan disagrees with the assumption that first habitation gives Aboriginals any particular rights over later arrivals; he argues that because Aboriginal peoples never continuously settled the land, but were nearly always in motion, they have no legitimate territorial claims. Flanagan contends that Aboriginal peoples are not nations, but rather subordinate communities within the nation of Canada, and hence lack a legitimate basis for claims to self-government.

While Flanagan acknowledges the current plight of Aboriginal peoples and their communities, he argues the solution does not lie in collective, racially based claims for political Status and Aboriginal community property rights. Instead, Flanagan argues for a "realistic" interpretation of the ongoing relationship between Aboriginals and non-Aboriginals, including a full integration of Indian peoples into the modern economy, implying a willingness to leave the reserves, if necessary, and relocate to where there are jobs and investment opportunities (Flanagan, 2000:7).

What can we make of Flanagan's criticisms? Setting aside counters to his particular arguments, the interesting foundations of his position are the "modernist" values upon which they are based. Seen this way, Flanagan's arguments point to the wide cultural gap remaining between Aboriginal and non-Aboriginal understandings of such things as social relationships, individualism, private property, capitalism, and notions of state and nation.

Today, few of the Royal Commission's recommendations (see Indian and Northern Affairs Canada, 1996) have been implemented. Nonetheless, its report set Canadian society on a new path in handling several Aboriginal issues. These issues include dealing with residential claims, revising or eliminating the Indian Act, settling existing land claims, signing modern treaties, and defining and implementing self-government, to which we now turn.

Residential School Claims

We have seen the role that residential schools played in the colonization of Aboriginal peoples (Chapter 9). Not all Aboriginals are products of Canada's residential schools, the last of which was closed in 1996. In fact, only about 30 to 35 percent of Aboriginal children ever attended residential schools. While some residents enjoyed life in these schools and report no unfortunate experiences, many more experienced years of physical, sexual, and psychological abuse, the effects of which were often visited upon later generations. The evidence for these claims is not seriously challenged. The ramifications, however, have been enormous.

Seeking legal redress for the abuses they had suffered, former residents of the schools were encouraged to bring forward their demands for justice. In response, the Canadian government established a fund worth $1.9 million in 2005 to address these claims. In 2007, the Indian Residential Schools Settlement Agreement, the largest class action settlement in Canadian history, was negotiated and approved, covering 9 jurisdictions and 139 schools, including 64 Roman Catholic, 35 Anglican, and 14 United Church–run schools. The settlement agreement was meant to reach reconciliation with an estimated 80,000 former students still living (Edmond, 2014) and contains the following elements:

- a common experience payment to be paid to all eligible former students who resided at a recognized Indian residential school;
- an independent assessment process for claims of sexual or serious physical abuse;
- the introduction of the Truth and Reconciliation Commission;
- commemoration activities; and
- measures to support healing, such as the Indian Residential Schools Resolution Health Support Program and an endowment to the Aboriginal Healing Foundation.

By the 2012 deadline, Canada had received "over 105,000 applications for Common Experience Payments, of which over 79,000 were found eligible and paid, the average amount being $19,412" (Edmond, 2014). Sadly, in too many cases, the plaintiffs received little of the money won through litigation; lawyers were often the big winners.

The Truth and Reconciliation Commission (TRC) was established in June 2008 as a separate part of the settlement agreement. Based on the court-like restorative justice body assembled in South Africa after the abolition of Apartheid in that country, the TRC was given a budget of $60 million over 5 years to investigate claims of mistreatment and abuse with regard to government-run residential schools dating back to the 1870s. Since its inception, the Commission has travelled across Canada, receiving submissions from former residential school students. A final report is expected in 2015.

The Indian Act

The Indian Act has not been substantially changed since its enactment in 1876. The federal government has on several occasions suggested either revising or even abandoning the act, most notably in the White Paper of 1969 and again in 1999. Aboriginal responses to the idea of changing the Indian Act have been mixed, with most First Nations and their organizations rebuffing these suggestions, a response that will likely surprise non-Aboriginal readers. Why is this the case? Why are many Aboriginals reluctant to eliminate an act at the heart of colonial oppression?

While some Aboriginal leaders clearly view the Indian Act as hindering efforts to get ahead, others view it as actually protecting certain of their rights, while still others support changing the Indian Act, but dislike the federal government's process for making changes, especially efforts at speaking over the head of the AFN leadership to the Aboriginal grassroots directly. They want the government to work through the AFN, which represents about half of Canada's Aboriginal peoples.

Disagreements aside, most Aboriginals nonetheless view three key issues in the Indian Act as needing redress. First, the Indian Act does not make clear the powers of chief and council or the legal standing and capacity for Aboriginal bands and band councils to sue, to contract, to borrow, and so on. Second, the act does not outline a clear and consistent system of determining band leadership selection and voting rights. Some bands follow procedures outlined in the Indian Act for the election of chiefs and councils, while others continue to follow a hereditary system of appointment, with which the government has no power under the Indian Act to interfere. Additionally, while the Indian Act allows off-reserve Aboriginals to vote in band elections, they cannot run for the office of councillor, but can apply for the office of chief; in fact, one does not have to live on a reserve or even be a band member to run for that office. Third, the Indian Act has few rules ensuring that First Nations communities will be run in a fair and equitable manner. While many First Nations bands have in place their own system of accountability, these vary in structure and function, with many Aboriginal band members feeling that they have no control or say in bylaws, annual reports, accounting, and band budgeting. Many Aboriginals likely agree that changes to the Indian Act are required in these three areas.

The push for changes to the Indian Act has gained momentum from recent court rulings in such areas as reserve elections and matrimonial and property rights for Aboriginal women. Today, legislation to replace the Indian Act continues winding its way through Parliament. A few years ago the government set aside a budget of $13 million for the project, though the recent economic downturn has hindered attempts at making progress.

Existing Land Claims and Modern Treaties

We have previously examined the historical development of treaties in Canada (Chapter 9). Two types of claims under the treaty process need differentiation. Aboriginal peoples' claims under negotiation with the federal government involving promises not fulfilled or interpretations of what was promised by either the treaties or scrip are referred to as

specific claims. Aboriginal peoples' claims involving lands that they have never legally surrendered are referred to as **comprehensive claims**. The latter include large areas of British Columbia and the North.

The need to deal with both specific and comprehensive claims has intensified in recent decades for two reasons. First, as Canadian economic development has shifted northward, governments and companies have wanted to ensure jurisdiction. For example, failure to make agreements in the Northwest Territories and Yukon, where Aboriginal land claims have been based on the customary principle of Aboriginal rights (see Wittington, 1985), is currently holding up the transfer of Crown lands and the consequent construction of pipelines.

Second, Aboriginal peoples themselves have become more politically aware and adept in pressing their claims. An example of this is a pact signed in 2000 between the Blood, Peigan, and Siksika of Alberta and the Blackfeet of Montana nations, all members of the once mighty Blackfoot Confederacy that, before Treaty No. 7 was signed in 1877, controlled the southern third of Alberta, stretching into Saskatchewan and Montana. The pact was meant to draw the government's attention to their concerns, including honouring Aboriginal rights, renewing tribal customs, and restoring lands that they insist were wrongfully appropriated from the Confederacy (*Edmonton Journal*, 2000).

In some instances, Aboriginal claims have received sympathetic treatment from non-Aboriginals. An example is the decades-long claim of the Lubicon band of northern Alberta for about 10,000 square kilometres of land where oil production is underway and where the Peace River Pulp Mill has been operating. A significant amount of development has been undertaken in the area in the form of new roads and drilling sites, which have had a detrimental effect on wildlife, but the Lubicons have not benefited from the arrangement (Goddard, 1991). In 2008, NOVA Gas Transmissions, a Trans-Canada Corporation subsidiary, applied to the Alberta Utilities Commission to construct a major gas pipeline through Lubicon land. Unlike previous projects, the Lubicon band was consulted, but did not give approval, and was denied formal intervener status on hearings into the project. As of today, the project appears to be going ahead.

In some instances, Aboriginal claims have faced strong opposition, sometimes resulting in violence between Aboriginals and non-Aboriginals. In the summer of 2000, for example, riots over lobster fishing broke out in Burnt Church, New Brunswick. A Department of Fisheries and Oceans boat had rammed an Aboriginal boat broadside, demolishing it and overturning several occupants into the water. The dispute was resolved later that fall when the Burnt Church band agreed to stop fishing three weeks earlier than they had planned. By then, the lobsters had already started their seasonal migration to colder waters, making them harder to catch.

It is the settlement of comprehensive claims that has caused the most concern, however. As noted in Chapter 10, the first comprehensive agreements were signed in the late 1970s by the Quebec government with the James Bay Cree of northern Quebec. The Inuvialuit agreement, dealing with lands in Canada's Far North, followed in 1984, extinguishing Aboriginal title to the western Arctic in return for ownership of 96,000 square kilometres of territory and $55 million (combined) in benefits and money for economic development (Dickason, 2002:405). After 14 years of negotiation, a similar agreement, regarding the Dene/Métis Western Arctic Land Claim, was cancelled by the federal government, which refused to renegotiate the extinguishing of Aboriginal title (Dickason, 2002:406; see also Geddes, 2000). This was quickly followed, however, by a series of other, smaller agreements signed with bands in Yukon and the Northwest Territories.

Finally, in 1999, the territory of Nunavut was created. Nunavut (meaning "our land") began as a proposal submitted in 1976 by the Inuit Tapirisat of Canada organization. After years of exhaustive negotiations, boundary disputes, and meetings with Dene and Métis representatives who had their own agendas, the residents of the Northwest Territories passed their own plebiscite on the issue in 1992 (Momatiuk and Eastcott, 1995). The federal government eventually accepted the proposal, and in 1999 Nunavut became the permanent home of the Inuit. About 85 percent the territory's population is of Inuit heritage, and the area they occupy comprises more than 2.2 million square kilometres, more than one-fifth of Canada's land surface. The area represents the largest land claim in Canada's history (Dickason and Newbigging, 2010). The territory's capital is the town of Iqaluit, formerly known as Frobisher Bay.

As many of these agreements have dealt with sparsely populated northern lands inhabited mostly by Aboriginal peoples, non-Aboriginal Canadians have raised few questions. Not so, however, in the case of treaty claims and land settlements further south, especially in British Columbia.

The situation of treaty negotiations in British Columbia is unique. Aside from 14 minor treaties, signed with Governor James Douglas in the middle of the 19th century, and the overlapping of Treaty no. 8 into their territory, British Columbia had never, until recently, negotiated treaties with First Nations. For years, the Province of British Columbia denied having any legal obligations to Aboriginal peoples. In 1992, however, a newly elected New Democratic government opened discussions pertaining to 47 land claims, promising to resolve them (Dickason and Newbigging, 2010).

The total area of British Columbia is 932,000 square kilometres. By October 1999, negotiations were in process for claims amounting to 703,832 square kilometres of the province (Frideres and Gadacz, 2001:223). The Nisga'a people of northern British Columbia, whose claim was settled in 1999, provide a kind of case study of contemporary land claims.

The Nisga'a were never militarily defeated, nor did they ever sign a treaty with the Government of Canada ceding lands. They first pressed their claims in 1887 when a group of Nisga'a chiefs travelled to Victoria. The government ignored them and took no action until 1976. Even then, it was a token acknowledgement. Twenty years later, in March 1996, the government and the Nisga'a leadership signed an agreement in principle. The agreement gave the Nisga'a a cash payment of $190 million (later increased to $500 million) and established a Nisga'a central government with administrative, municipal-like responsibilities for 2,000 square kilometres of land in the Nass River Valley. Additionally, Nisga'a ownership of surface and subsurface resources was safeguarded, as well as rights to salmon stocks and wildlife harvests. In 1999, the 5,000 members of the Nisga'a First Nation ratified the treaty and in April of the same year, the British Columbia government and the federal Parliament passed the agreement into law. The Senate passed the bill on April 13, 2000, completing the treaty process (Steckley and Cummins, 2008:143).

In a bold subsequent move, in November 2013 the Nisga'a became the first Aboriginal nation in British Columbia to privatize land (Lynch, 2013). Some observers believe that, when individuals are able to take loans against home equity in order to establish a business, more opportunities will be provided for the Nisga'a to move out of poverty. Critics contend, however, that private ownership means that citizens can transfer, sell, or will their property to anyone, including non-Nisga'a—an issue of obvious importance to Aboriginal culture, community, and identity.

As a model for other agreements, the Nisga'a treaty has encountered criticism, not least from some Aboriginals who dislike the fact that, under the agreement, federal and provincial income tax laws, the Charter of Rights and Freedoms, and the Criminal Code now apply to Nisga'a government. (A group of dissidents have launched a court challenge to the agreement.)

By far the strongest criticisms of the Nisga'a and similar treaties have come, however, from the non-Aboriginal community (Frideres and Gadacz, 2001:184, 227). Many non-Aboriginal concerns over comprehensive claims are unfounded. There is no likelihood, for example, that Aboriginals will confiscate the lands on which Vancouver sits and have non-Aboriginals evicted, as is sometimes argued. But more legitimate concerns about the process and outcomes of land claims negotiations have been expressed.

Smith's (1995) argument that there is no legal basis for comprehensive land claims is today unsupported by the Supreme Court. His other four concerns, however, bear consideration: (1) that such land claims agreements are actually constitutional agreements that are binding upon subsequent generations and therefore do not provide for sufficient flexibility; (2) that such agreements open the way for endless negotiations, ever-escalating demands, the creation of more bureaucracy, and mounting costs; (3) that the land claims agreements (and concomitant rights and benefits provided to Aboriginal peoples) are race-based and will actually hinder the chances of ordinary Aboriginals from entering fully into Canadian society; and (4) that land claims raise jurisdictional concerns, including whether Aboriginals under the agreements will be subject to Canadian law, including the Constitution's Charter of Rights and Freedoms. Ultimately, many of these concerns speak to a larger issue addressed by the Royal Commission: the issue of self-government.

In a landmark June 2014 decision bearing on future land claims, the Supreme Court of Canada, by a unanimous vote, granted the Tsilhqot'in First Nation of British Columbia title to their historic lands, which were traditionally used for hunting, fishing, and other cultural activities. The decision is expected to have repercussions across the nation (Stueck, 2014). Among these, a problem of historical overlapping land use often occurs when such land claims are granted (Pemberton, 2014). (Historically, for example, First Nations shared hunting grounds with other bands, but individual First Nations may now have to attempt to determine title to those lands.)

But even larger repercussions may result from the ruling. The immediate reaction of the Tsilhqot'in community to the Supreme Court decision was to threaten the building of the northern Gateway Pipeline (see Chapter 8) and to put a stop to other non-Aboriginal developments. However, Mulgrew (2014) contends that the decision is not without its complexities. First, members of the band must establish "they are the same people who have been living on and using the land forever, and then their rights will be decided by governments through talks or, in the end, by its appointed judges." Second, and more importantly, the decision appears to end talk of Aboriginal sovereignty. No more government-to-government, or nation-to-nation discussions. If Mulgrew is correct, the decision will go a long way in determining the meaning and extent of Aboriginal self-government in Canada.

Self-Government and Self-Determination

Long before the arrival of the Europeans, Aboriginal peoples in Canada successfully governed themselves. Historical examples of self-government in Aboriginal communities include the Iroquois Confederacy, circa 1570 (from which some elements of the American Constitution were drawn) and the eastern Maritime Mi'kmaq First Nation, which existed prior to European contact and operated a seven-state democratic system presided over by seven chiefs and a grand chief who lived on Cape Breton Island. Subsequent colonialism destroyed many of these organizational structures, but First Nations peoples have never ceased their fight to regain control over their lives.

Aboriginal claims for self-government rest on three planks (Schouls, 2003:115–116). First, as originally sovereign nations, Aboriginal nations have an inherent right to create and maintain their own identities, cultures, languages, values, and practices, and therefore they should have the right to choose their own form of governance. Second, even though Canada's Aboriginal peoples live under the Crown's protection, this in no way reduces or diminishes their historical right to self-government. The original agreements between government and First Nations (treaties) were signed as equal partners—nation to nation. Therefore, any model of self-government must constitute more than mere self-administration. Third, because the original treaty-making process was initiated on a principle of reciprocity and consent, there is no valid reason to ignore or even seek to improve this arrangement; the original agreements should simply be adhered to. Ultimately, the desire for self-government may also be justified as a means of redressing the harm done by a "foreign" government—that of Canada—and ensuring it does not happen again (Buckley, 1993).

Aboriginal peoples have been demanding the right of self-government within Canada for quite some time, but these demands either have been ignored or have faltered amid efforts to arrive at a workable application of the meaning of self-government. In language reminiscent of Jean Lesage's Liberals in Quebec in the early 1960s (see Chapter 2), the Union of British Columbia Indian Chiefs, for example, defined its position on self-government in this way:

> We must be masters in our own house, in order to survive as Indian people. There is
> no basis in the laws of Canada to restrict the recovery of Aboriginal rights because
> we have never given up our rights to control our own lives and means to live. (Wall,
> 2000:144)

Paternalism, an offshoot of colonialism, has continued to infuse government-Aboriginal relations. During the constitutional discussions in the early 1980s, however, real efforts were begun in earnest to define self-government.

In 1983, the federal government released a report prepared by the Special Committee on Indian Self-Government in Canada (also known as the Penner Report). The Penner Report dismissed the terms and intent of the Indian Act as being out of date and ineffective for contemporary negotiations and made several recommendations calling for the government to establish a new kind of relationship with Aboriginal peoples based on the notion of Aboriginal self-government. Among specific recommendations, the report recommended that Aboriginal governments be made accountable to their own people; that bilateral federal-Aboriginal agreements govern respective jurisdictions, with the federal government ceding all areas of competence required for First Nations to govern themselves effectively and ensuring that provincial laws would not apply to Aboriginal land except with Aboriginal consent; and that complete control be given to First Nations over their lands and resources, with financial backing through federal grants and the settlement of land claims. Finally, the report also originated the concept of a third order of government with respect to Aboriginal self-government (Tennant, 1988:329).

The federal government's response to the Penner Report was to try to entrench Aboriginal self-government for Status Indians at a first ministers' meeting in 1984. At that meeting, Prime Minister Pierre Trudeau pursued the report's initiatives, but found little agreement among the premiers. Brian Mulroney's government made similar proposals in 1985 and 1987, but again consensus was lacking. The governments of Alberta, British Columbia, Newfoundland, and Saskatchewan in particular were reluctant to support federal proposals for Aboriginal self-government without a full definition of costs and terms (Miller, 1988:304).

Additionally, some Aboriginal organizations have found the self-government proposals inadequate while, for its part, the federal government appears to only tacitly recognize the "inherent right" of Aboriginal peoples to negotiate for self-government (Asch, 2002:67), a recognition that carries no fundamental meaning. (Ottawa has left the door open for the negotiation of self-government in the Dene-Métis and Yukon claims, but only on the condition that this kind of right does not receive the same constitutional protection accorded the rest of the settlements, meaning that any constitutional recognition of the Aboriginal right to self-government gained by the Dene-Métis constituency cannot be used as a precedent in any other sector of the Aboriginal community.)

Several specifically contentious issues lie at the heart of the problems of defining and implementing self-government.

Timing

There is little doubt that Canada's First Nations communities—weary of being regarded as wards of the government—desire self-government (Kulchyski, 2005:15–17). Thus far, however, the Department of Indian Affairs and Northern Development has continued to exercise control and to decide which bands are at a sufficiently advanced stage to be ready for self-government (Angus 1991:33), raising questions about the government's sincerity in pursuing the matter.

Territoriality

The intent of recent land claims settlements has been to define the idea of Aboriginal self-government. It is less clear how one might implement self-government in urban areas where a significant and growing number of Aboriginal peoples live, some on urban reserves (Barron and Garcea, 1999) (see Chapter 12). Implementing self-government is difficult enough when confined to a single, uncontested geographical space. It is even more problematic when different institutions and rules govern different groups of people within the same space.

Level and Form of Government

The Canadian government has tended to view "self-government" as approximating the level of Canadian municipalities, often transferring certain responsibilities to local Aboriginal bands and councils, which, in turn, act as financial administrators (Asch, 2000:67). By contrast, Aboriginal organizations want assurances that the Constitution will protect their actual institutions—unlike municipal governments, which are not protected—and that such self-governing institutions would be on more or less the level of provincial counterparts. Kulchyski (2005:15–17) argues, moreover, that for many Aboriginal leaders, achieving a measure of self-government is not simply a matter of transferring powers from government to local bands, but of clarifying and determining the kind of governance that will be initiated.

Governance Structure

Whatever form it takes, if Aboriginal self-government is ever realized, there will have to be a recognized structure for exercising that authority (Angus, 1991:32). Kulchyski (2005:15–17) notes, however, that federal negotiators have attempted to fit Aboriginal self-government into the existing operations of the Canadian state, and thus failed to recognize that existing governmental structures are not necessarily appropriate or functional in Aboriginal communities.

Jurisdiction

Angus (1991:32) states that in order for Aboriginal self-government to succeed, the Canadian government must recognize Aboriginal authority in specific areas of jurisdiction. Fleras (2007:192) suggest that Aboriginal jurisdiction will likely include control over (1) the delivery of social services such as policing, education, and health and welfare; (2) resources and use of land for economic development; (3) the means to protect and promote distinct cultural values and language systems; (4) band membership and entitlements; and (5) local expenditures according to Aboriginal priorities rather than those of government or bureaucracy, with some variation at play with regard to the different Indian bands. On this latter point, Kulchyski (2005:15–17) similarly argues that Aboriginal self-government must be tailored to meet local needs if it is to succeed. Unfortunately, such a degree of flexibility is often lacking in Canada's national programs.

Citizenship

Is the notion of Aboriginal citizenship, and all the rights and privileges that entails, commensurate with that of Canadian citizenship? Flanagan (2000) argues that Aboriginal militants tend to define self-government in racial terms, and cautions that the idea of Aboriginal self-government, embedded in broader notions of Aboriginal self-determination, contributes to cultural exclusiveness and divisions that others contend may have unanticipated and negative consequences. Cairns (2000) opines, for example, that the notion "we are not you" (Denis, 1997), if carried too far, may give non-Aboriginals a convenient excuse for withdrawing responsibility, financial or otherwise, for the condition of Aboriginal peoples.

Others view such fears as unwarranted, however. Frideres and Gadacz (2001:251; Frideres, 2011:162) suggest that First Nations will never gain the rights of self-determination and status of self-government envisioned by their more radical members. Governments will see to it that any arrangement for Aboriginal self-government will harmonize with existing Canadian laws, including the Charter of Rights and Freedoms. To date, this appears to be the case.

Economic Self-Sufficiency

Many of Canada's reserves do not have a strong economic base and cannot support the people who live there. In consequence, large numbers of Aboriginals have moved or are moving to Canadian cities in search of jobs and other opportunities, while many of those remaining on the reserves are supported by government social assistance and welfare. But how can a people be termed self-governing if they are dependent upon financial support from "external" governments? Boldt (1993:261) argues that

> Any proposal that Indian political autonomy and culture should be financed by another government makes a mockery of Indian nationhood. It is a manifestation of the "culture of dependence" in the political sphere. Such an arrangement is a design for continued subordination and paternalism.

It has often been said that Canada does not work in theory, but does in practice. This holds particularly true for current efforts at Aboriginal self-government. Despite seemingly interminable debates about how it will work, at the concrete level things are progressing. In 1986, for example, the Sechelt band of British Columbia gained a form of self-government that has since served as a model for other bands. The Sechelt band assumed powers to legislate matters that range from zoning and land use to education on their reserve. Today, both federal and provincial governments respect the application of these rights so long as they are consistent with federal and provincial laws. Moreover, the Sechelt agreement has paved the way for similar recognition of rights for all Indian bands in Canada that previously had to negotiate with the federal government even over peripheral matters (Russell, 2000:163; Asch, 2000:67; Bird, Land, and McAdam, 2000).

In the meantime, efforts toward the very tedious and complex process of reaching agreement on self-government continue (Ponting and Henderson, 2005). Few observers are optimistic about fast results. Henderson (2000:167) accuses legal bureaucrats of unreflectively asserting colonial privileges and power when dealing with the issue of self-government, but others are a bit more optimistic. Hylton observes that some progress toward Aboriginal self-government has been made in terms of both federal attitude and experiences reported by some Aboriginal bands. He notes the following;

> Aboriginal people in Canada are increasingly engaged in the practice of self-government . . . .
> [A] number of Aboriginal nations have already negotiated far-reaching self-government
> agreements . . . . [T]he federal government appears more ready than previous administra-
> tions to enter into new arrangements with Aboriginal people. (Hylton, 1999:432)

Finally, others suggest that the debate over self-government actually obscures the more important notion of self-determination. In the words of McDonnell and Depew (1999:353), "The processes associated with self-government are so powerfully unilateral in their focus that they have all but displaced considerations relating to self-determination." Boldt (1993) similarly argues that beyond self-government, the survival of Aboriginal cultures requires Aboriginal peoples to develop a clear vision and consensus about their future. They must assess the damage that colonialism has inflicted on them in the past and continues to do today, and invent ways to stop the processes of assimilation and acculturation. They must further critically evaluate what must be done and mobilize their people in an effort to make that identity a reality. "Such a process of cultural revitalization will necessitate a purge of corrupting colonial institutions, and of traits derived from the culture of dependence and from Euro-Western acculturation" (Boldt, 1993:219). Self-government alone will not do these things.

Conclusion

In December 2012, four Native women organized a grassroots movement known as Idle No More. The purpose of the organization, which operated without a budget, was to show Canadians that Aboriginal peoples across the land would no longer sit back and be run over by inappropriate legislation. Their strongest protest was against the Conservative government's passing of the omnibus Bill C-45, which—among other things—gave the federal government the right to encroach on Native lands with a minimum of consultation. The movement quickly galvanized Aboriginal youth, many of whom took to marching in protest.

Idle No More suggests the continuing emergence of Aboriginal peoples from Canada's backstage to the front stage of Canadian life. The path has not always been peaceful. Like Oka, the actions of the Idle No More activists have sometimes engendered conflict and criticism, especially from government officials angered by a series of protests and blockades. But, as conflict theorists would argue, such conflict has also paved the way for dealing with a host of problems previously ignored. The result, in this early part of the 21st century, has been a renewal within Aboriginal society and recognition within non-Aboriginal society of Canada's Aboriginal roots. These developments will affect every sector of contemporary Aboriginal—and non-Aboriginal—life in Canada for decades to come. The following chapter examines Aboriginal society today and what its transformation might hold for Canada.

Key Terms

Aboriginal land title
Aboriginal self-government
citizens plus
comprehensive claims
specific claims

Critical Thinking Questions

1. Why did so many studies such as the Hawthorn Report arise in Canadian society during the 1960s?
2. What lessons does the Oka Crisis provide for governments in conflict with minority groups?
3. Why have so few of the Royal Commission's recommendations been enacted?
4. What problems do notions of Aboriginal self-government pose for mainstream ideas of state and nation?
5. What problems and opportunities might arise from the introduction of individual property ownership on Nisga'a territory?

Recommended Readings

Bird, John, Lorraine Land, and Murray McAdam, eds. 2000. *Self-Government in the New Millennium: Nation to Nation: Aboriginal Sovereignty and the Future of Canada*. Toronto: Irwin Publishing.
This is one of the first books to address the question of Aboriginal self-government, and does so from the perspective of informed authorities.

Dickason, Olive Patricia, and William Newbigging. 2010. *A Concise History of Canada's First Nations*. Don Mills, ON: Oxford University Press.
Written from an Aboriginal perspective, this book delivers what its title professes.

Fleras, Augie, and Jean Leonard Elliott. 2007. *Unequal Relations: An Introduction to Race, Ethnic, and Aboriginal Dynamics in Canada*. 5th ed. Toronto: Pearson Canada.
The authors expertly juxtapose the various socio-economic and cultural challenges faced by both Aboriginal peoples and immigrant communities in Canada.

Snow, Chief John. 2005. *These Mountains Are Our Sacred Places: The Story of the Stoney People*. Calgary: Fifth House.
Although primarily an in-depth case study of the Stoney First Nation in Alberta, the narrative outlines much broader implications for other First Nations as well.

Warry, Wayne. 2007. *Ending Denial: Understanding Aboriginal Issues*. Peterborough, ON: Broadview Press.
This is an in-depth, objective appraisal of a variety of legal and socio-economic frontiers faced by Canada's First Nations.

Related Websites

Canadiana
www.canadiana.ca/citm/index_e.html
This is a national body made up of distinguished scholars and representatives of major research libraries from across Canada. The organization hosts a digital archive, Canada in the Making, containing a collection of narrative text, primary documents, maps, and photos.

Royal Commission on Aboriginal Peoples
www.aadnc-aandc.gc.ca/eng/1307458586498/1307458751962
In the wake of the Oka Crisis, the Canadian government established the Royal Commission on Aboriginal Peoples. The commission's final report can be found at this site.

The Truth and Reconciliation Commission
www.trc.ca/websites/trcinstitution/index.php?p=26
This is the website of the historic commission whose final report is scheduled for 2015.

Canadian Society on Video

Oka: Behind the Barricades. 1998. National Film Board of Canada, 311 minutes, 29 seconds.
This collection of four videos examines the events of summer 1990, when the Mohawk community faced off against the governments of Quebec and Canada. The four videos are *Acts of Defiance* (104 minutes, 34 seconds); *Kanehsatake: 270 Years of Resistance* (119 minutes, 15 seconds); *Spudwrench-Kahnawake Man* (57 minutes, 50 seconds); and *My Name is Kahentiiosta* (29 minutes, 50 seconds).

The Invisible Nation. 2012. National Film Board of Canada, 93 minutes, 20 seconds.
The lifestyle of Canada's Algonquin was changed forever when the Europeans arrived. Today, barely 9,000 Algonquin are left. They live in about 10 communities, and are suffering the threat to their very existence in silence. Richard Desjardins and Robert Monderie have decided to sound the alarm before it's too late.

The Journey of Nishiyuu. 2013. The Grand Council of the Crees, 14 minutes, 18 seconds.
Nishiyuu means "human beings" or "modern people" in the Cree language. Between January and March of 2013, a group of Cree youth walked from Northern Quebec to Ottawa, a distance of more than 1,600 kilometres, in support of the Idle No More movement.

CHAPTER 12

NEW
LEARNING
PATHS

Our people have come into their own—there's no doubt about it—but now we have to build an audience. We have to do what we can to ensure that the beautiful power of our voices is heard.... Our stories are full of both sorrow and joy and it is important that we share them.

—actor Gary Farmer, 2005

We are a Métis civilization.

—author John Ralston Saul, 2008

It is only a matter of time for this growing cultural self-confidence to express itself, and be listened to, in other arenas as well. A key area is education, and the First Nations have demonstrated their effectiveness in taking control of the schooling of their children.

— Olive Patricia Dickason and William Newbigging in
A Concise History of Canada's First Nations, 2010

Introduction

There is much unfinished business surrounding Aboriginal and non-Aboriginal relations: land claims, new treaties, the abolishment in time of the Indian Act, and the implementation of genuine self-government, not to mention real economic and social equality. Above all, there is the need for healing. But that is to be expected. Every society has unfinished business, although matters pertaining to Aboriginal peoples have specific urgency. In this regard, Drees (2013:121) emphasizes that Aboriginals should be encouraged to heal in accordance with traditional Indigenous "medicines" that—although not always visible—are very much available. As noted in the Introduction, societies are not a static thing; they are a process, and in this instance, the process of healing may mean listening more closely to Aboriginal voices.

This concluding chapter of Part 3 examines Aboriginal society in all its complexity today, including some of the current experiments going on in Aboriginal communities and the new group of Aboriginal leaders. Along the way, the chapter also examines how Aboriginal values embedded within a traditional world view might fit into a modern Canada. Finally, the chapter looks at how Canadian society could benefit—if it chooses—from rediscovering its Aboriginal roots.

Population Dynamics

When Christopher Columbus first arrived from Europe, the total population of North and South America was about 57 million people, 4.5 million of whom lived north of Mexico (Cook, 1995:33). Of these, about 500,000 lived in what is today Canada. Shortly after Confederation, however, Canada's Aboriginal population sank to 102,000 (Ponting, 1997b:68) and did not rise again until the 1940s. Since then, however, the population of Status Indians in Canada has steadily risen. Today, the number of Status Indians in Canada totals 851,560 while 1.4 million people report Aboriginal ancestry. Overall, the proportion of Aboriginals in Canada has also increased, today making up 4.3 percent of the Canadian population, up from 3.8 percent in the 2006 census (Statistics Canada, 2013f). While the Status Indian population remains the largest segment, it should be noted that the largest increase in recent years has occurred among the Métis population (see Table 12.1 for a breakdown of related groups).

Table 12.1: Aboriginal Identity Population, Canada, 2011[1]

Aboriginal Identity Population	Number	Percentage
Total Aboriginal identity population	1,400,690	100.0
First Nations single identity	851,560	60.8
- First Nations single identity (Registered or Treaty Aboriginal)	637,660	45.5
- First Nations single identity (not a Registered or Treaty Aboriginal)	213,900	15.3
Métis single identity	451,795	32.3
Inuit single identity	59,445	4.2
Multiple Aboriginal identities	11,415	0.8
Aboriginal identities not included elsewhere	26,475	1.9

Note: 1. The response rate for the 2011 National Household Survey was much lower than the response rate on previous censuses and raises questions of accuracy or comparability with earlier data. See Chapter 1 regarding this change.

Source: Statistics Canada. 2011f. "Aboriginal Peoples in Canada: First Nations People, Métis and Inuit, Table 1: Aboriginal Identity Population, Canada, 2011." *National Household Survey*, 2011. Cat. no. 99-011-X2011001 (www12.statcan.gc.ca/nhs-enm/2011/as-sa/99-011-x/99-011-x2011001-eng.pdf).

Why has Canada's Aboriginal population increased so rapidly in recent years? The increase is particularly impressive given both the high infant mortality rate that stalks many First Nations communities and the much lower life expectancy generally for Aboriginal peoples. (The **infant mortality rate** is calculated as the number of infants who die during their first year after birth for every thousand live births within a certain population.) Smylie and colleagues (2010:147) note, for example, that the infant mortality rate for First Nations peoples (on and off reserve) and Inuit ranges "from 1.7 to over 4 times the overall Canadian and/or non-Aboriginal rates." While the life expectancy of Aboriginal peoples is projected to rise in coming years, that of Métis and other Aboriginal peoples (both male and female) in 2017 will still be five years less than their counterparts in the Canadian population as a whole. Life expectancy rates for Inuit are projected to fall short by 15 years for men and 10 years for women (Statistics Canada, 2010b).

So, again, what are the causes of the increase in Canada's Aboriginal population? First, the passage of Bill C-31 in 1985 (see Chapter 11) allowed many Aboriginal women to regain their status. A little more than a decade after Bill C-31 was passed, some 105,000 individuals had regained their status (Frideres and Gadacz, 2001:35). A second possibility is that a growing sense of pride in Aboriginal ancestry has led to an increase in voluntary identification among Aboriginal peoples. Most researchers, however, attribute the primary cause of the population increase to birth rates that remain higher than the Canadian average within the Aboriginal community. A further consequence of high birth rates is that Canada's Aboriginal population, again compared with the general population, is also very young—and fertile. As shown in Table 12.2, while the median age of the non-Aboriginal population is 41 years, the median age of the total Aboriginal population is 28 years, ranging from the Métis median, at 31 years, to the Inuit, at 23 years.

Looking ahead, demographers with Statistics Canada (2011h) have mapped out four possible scenarios regarding Canada's Aboriginal identity population in 2031. Employing such variables as fertility and mortality rates and intergenerational migration and ethnic mobility (factors that might impact self-identification), demographers project Canada's Aboriginal population to be between 1,682,000 and 2,220,000 in 2031. In the latter scenario, Aboriginal people would constitute 5.6 percent of the total Canadian population. As noted earlier, the importance of Aboriginal peoples in shaping Canadian society now and in the future is not solely related to numbers per se, but rather to the population's geographic location. We have seen previously that a population shift is occurring throughout Canada (Chapter 7) as people migrate to the economically vibrant and relatively young West. A similar shift is occurring within Canada's Aboriginal population, though it is birth rates, rather than interprovincial migration, that are the primary factor. As Table 12.3 shows, while Ontario has the largest Aboriginal population (201,100), the Aboriginal populations of the western provinces are not far behind; indeed, more than half of Canada's Aboriginal population today resides in western Canada, where birth rates are also among the highest in Canada.

Administratively, governments describe First Nations communities as tribes with subdivisions known as bands, of which there are more than 600 in Canada. The term **band** referred originally to small cultural and linguistic groups living together, or coming together at various seasons and times, as part of a larger Aboriginal society, such as the Cree, Blackfoot, or Inuit. Today, however, the term describes a local unit of administration, operating under the Indian Act (see Chapter 11). Most bands consist of about 500 members, though some, such as the Six Nations band in Ontario, with 25,660 members, and the Kainai Reserve in southern Alberta, with 12,000 members, are quite large.

While many Aboriginal peoples in the northern parts of Canada's provinces and in the territories continue to live in rural areas, Table 12.3 also shows that, increasingly, many Aboriginals, both Status and non-Status, are moving to Canada's cities and towns; indeed, slightly more than half of Status Indians (50.7 percent) today live off reserve, mainly in urban centres. The urbanization of Canada's Aboriginal peoples has received considerable attention from sociologists over the last three decades. Much of this

Table 12.2: Age Distribution and Median Age for Selected Aboriginal Identity and Non-Aboriginal Populations, Canada, 2011

Age Groups and Median Age	Total Aboriginal Identity Population		First Nations Single Identity		Métis Single Identity		Inuit Single Identity		Non-Aboriginal Identity Population	
	Number[1]	%	Number	%	Number	%	Number	%	Number	%
Total age groups	1,400,690	100.0	851,565	100.0	451,790	100.0	59,440	100.0	31,451,640	100.0
0–14 years	392,105	28.0	258,795	30.4	104,415	23.1	20,160	33.9	5,200,695	16.5
15–24 years	254,515	18.2	156,865	18.4	80,035	17.7	11,950	20.1	4,069,550	12.9
25–64 years	671,380	47.9	389,215	45.7	237,705	52.6	24,905	41.9	17,712,545	56.3
65 years and over	82,690	5.9	46,690	5.5	29,635	6.6	2,425	4.1	4,468,850	14.2
Median age in years	28	—	26	—	31	—	23	—	41	…

Note: 1. The estimates for the three Aboriginal groups do not add to the total Aboriginal identity population because only selected Aboriginal identity categories are shown.

Source: Statistics Canada. 2011g. "Aboriginal Peoples in Canada: First Nations People, Métis and Inuit, Table 4: Age Distribution and Median Age for Selected Aboriginal Identity Categories, Canada, 2011." *National Household Survey, 2011.* Cat. no. 99-011-X2011001 (www12.statcan. gc.ca/nhs-enm/2011/as-sa/99-011-x/2011001/tbl/tbl04-eng.cfm). Modified April 24, 2014.

Table 12.3: Distribution of First Nations People by Status, Canada, Provinces, and Territories, 2011[1]

	First Nations People		First Nations People with Registered Aboriginal Status			
	Number	Distribution Percentage	Number	Distribution Percentage	On Reserve Percentage	Off Reserve Percentage
Canada	**851,555**	**100**	**637,655**	**100**	**49.3**	**50.7**
Newfoundland and Labrador	19,315	2.3	8,015	1.3	35.1	64.9
Prince Edward Island	1,515	0.2	765	0.1	56.2	43.8
Nova Scotia	21,895	2.6	12,910	2.0	68.0	32.0
New Brunswick	16,120	1.9	10,275	1.6	68.8	31.3
Quebec	82,425	9.7	52,645	8.3	72.0	28.1
Ontario	201,100	23.6	125,560	19.7	37.0	63.0
Manitoba	114,225	13.4	105,815	16.6	57.9	42.1
Saskatchewan	103,210	12.1	94,160	14.8	57.3	42.7
Alberta	116,670	13.7	96,730	15.2	47.3	52.7
British Columbia	155,020	18.2	112,400	17.6	44.2	55.8
Yukon[2]	6,585	0.8	5,715	0.9	—	—
Northwest Territories[3]	13,350	1.6	12,575	2.0	2.1	97.9
Nunavut[4]	125	0.01	90	0.01	—	—

Notes: 1. This table shows data for First Nations people with registered Aboriginal status living on and off reserve. The 2006 Census release on Aboriginal people, entitled "Aboriginal Peoples in Canada in 2006: Inuit, Métis and First Nations, 2006 Census" (Cat. no. 970558-XIE), showed data for the total First Nations populations living on and off reserve without a breakdown by registered Indian status. 2. Yukon has no Indian reserve or Indian settlements included in the "on reserve" definition. 3. There are only two Aboriginal reserves in the Northwest Territories. 4. There are no Aboriginal reserves or Aboriginal settlements in Nunavut.

Source: Statistics Canada. 2011i. "Aboriginal Peoples in Canada: First Nations People, Métis and Inuit, Table 3: Distribution of First Nations People with and without Registered Indian Status, and First Nations People with Registered Indian Status Living on or off Reserve, Canada, Provinces and Territories, 2011." *National Household Survey, 2011.* Cat. no. 99-011-X2011001 (www12.statcan.gc.ca/nhs-enm/2011/as-sa/99-011-x/99-011-x2011001-eng.pdf).

attention has centred on negative statistics emanating from the great difficulties that many Aboriginals have in adjusting to urban life. Despite these difficulties, exacerbated by discrimination, prejudice, and racism, Aboriginals continue to migrate to Canada's cities, drawn by educational and employment opportunities in particular, though other factors may also be important (Cooke and Bélanger, 2006; Frideres, 2011:169), a significant consequence of which has been the emergence of **urban reserves**.

Urban Reserves

Saskatchewan is the birthplace of urban reserves. In 1976, the Saskatchewan and federal governments and Aboriginal leaders signed an agreement, the Saskatchewan Formula, through which land equity would be worked out. A change of provincial government (from NDP to Conservative) saw the deal temporarily abandoned, but the NDP's later return to power assured the signing of the Saskatchewan Treaty Land Entitlement Framework Agreement in 1992. The agreement set aside $446 million to purchase land on which to develop urban reserves (Barron and Garcea, 1999:15). That same year, 28 of Saskatchewan's 70 Indian bands signed on, and 28 urban reserves were created, 9 of them in larger centres (Steckley and Cummins, 2008:141). Today there are 120 Aboriginal urban reserves operating throughout Canada.

Barron and Garcea (1999:24) state three reasons for the creation of urban reserves. The first reason is that they are directly related to treaties and treaty land entitlement. When treaties 4, 6, and 7 were drawn up (see Chapter 9), the conditions were that every family of five would be awarded a full section of land, but the federal government often failed to live up to this arrangement and simply shortchanged the Aboriginals. A century after the first 10 numbered treaties were signed, Aboriginal peoples made up a full 3 percent of Canada's population, but possessed only 0.02 percent of available land. (In Saskatchewan alone, almost 30 bands were shortchanged when land entitlements for reserves were negotiated.) In effect, the 1992 agreement settled an outstanding claim by offering bands compensatory funds with which to buy private real estate holdings.

A second reason is that urban reserves are closely associated with First Nations' desires to develop and diversify economic opportunities. Federal land was found for economic development in Saskatoon, for example, and transferred, after negotiations, to Aboriginal ownership.

A third reason is that for many Aboriginal peoples, urban reserves are a territorial expression of the inherent right of self-government. They want to be full players in the dominant society, not as assimilated members of that society, but as people with their own distinct cultural identity. Urban reserves function as an extension of a band's national land patrimony and authority to make decisions over their own lives.

On this latter point, urban reserves clearly tie into demands for self-government (see Chapter 11). The concept of a bonded community offers not only strong encouragement for economic development but also the opportunity necessary for participants to formulate some kind of self-government to determine rules for living, show respect for others, and set community goals.

Aboriginal peoples on urban reserves continue to face stiff opposition, particularly from local non-Aboriginal politicians, though politicians at other levels have also expressed concern. This opposition often stems from concerns that any form of reserve government could establish rules and laws that might contradict those passed by city council; that the establishment of a different kind of neighbourhood might affect federal and provincial grants to cities and towns; and that urban reserves might turn into ethnic ghettos. Without doubt, some of these objections are grounded in prejudice and discrimination. But urban reserves do raise some legitimate jurisdictional questions, reflecting the complexity and newness of such ventures (Frideres, 2011:222).

By law, the federal government has responsibilities to Aboriginal peoples. In the case of urban reserves, however, it appears to have abdicated these responsibilities, instead turning governance matters over to the provinces, which, in turn, have handed over control of Aboriginal programs and service funds to Aboriginal peoples. Bobiwash (1997:91) notes that in Saskatchewan, for example, the provincial government identified up to $550 million a year in the areas of health, education, justice, and social services that could eventually be transferred to band administration. Such a move may have commendable features, but it too easily allows the federal government to shirk its responsibilities toward First Nations communities. Moreover, the legality of whether provinces have authority to negotiate agreements with Aboriginal governments is in question. As Bobiwash (1997:91) notes,

> Among the arguments used by the federal government in regards to provision of social services for off-reserve Native people has been that if provinces are the main beneficiaries for lands and resources under Lands and Resources Transfer Agreements and Acts (by which the provinces also became parties to later treaties such as the Williams Treaty of 1923), then some of those benefits ought to go to off-reserve Native People.

At the same time, one may observe that new arrangements sometimes have a way of bringing various parties together, and often the exchange of ideas fosters goodwill. As Makela (1999:89) suggests, "The development of urban reserves presents great opportunities for both Aboriginal and non-Aboriginal people ... with the issues at stake reaching beyond matters of tax-loss compensation or bylaw compatibility." Above all, urban reserves express the hope of sharing wealth and power in the pursuit of providing equal opportunity for education, employment, adequate housing, and other social benefits.

Health and Social Conditions

As earlier noted, First Nations infant mortality rates are higher than rates in the general Canadian population, and life expectancy among both First Nations and Inuit peoples, for both men and women, is lower than among their non-Aboriginal Canadian counterparts. These results are largely attributable to the Third World conditions of poverty found on many First Nations reserves or in the North. On-reserve housing, for example, is generally substandard and often poorly ventilated. The homes are too hot in summer and too cold in winter. Running water is frequently a luxury. (For example, in November 2007, 31 people on the Peigan reserve in southern Alberta were evacuated from five homes that were condemned in part due to serious mould problems.) Many First Nations' reserves have limited capacity when natural disasters strike, as occurred in the spring of 2013 in southern Alberta, when a massive rain-fed flood forced 1,000 people from the Siksika (Blackfoot) reserve to evacuate their homes, and 510 homes on the Stoney Nakoda Reserve west of Calgary were similarly flooded, contributing to hazardous health conditions for some families that remained.

Poor housing is a significant cause of Aboriginal health problems. Tuberculosis is somewhat less of a threat than in the recent past, but other scourges, such as diabetes, AIDS, and drug and alcohol abuse, have taken its place. Keep in mind also that, while on-reserve conditions are generally poor, the situation of Aboriginals migrating to urban areas is often not much better. Though cities may provide some families with increased opportunities and more accessible services, many Aboriginals also find they have to contend with a myriad of other challenges not experienced on the reserve, such as cultural alienation and racism (Buckley, 1993; Fox and Long, 2000).

Unfortunate social facts are not disconnected from other factors and consequences. Thus, in general, poor health and poor social outcomes tend to correlate highly with low socio-economic status (SES), especially related to an individual's family of origin. Though the situation is improving, many Aboriginals continue to live below the poverty line, and many are also on some form of social assistance (Frideres and Gadacz, 2001:120; Kerr and Beaujot, 2011:173–174). A report by Citizens for Public Justice (2012:14) notes that, in the aftermath of the financial crisis that began in 2008, the poverty rate for Aboriginals rose markedly, reaching 15.2 percent for those living off reserve in 2010, compared with 9 percent for all Canadians.

Poverty and a host of allied conditions contribute to the fact that, for a substantial number of Aboriginals on and off the reserves, life is fraught with danger and hopelessness. Suicide rates, especially among young Aboriginals (15 to 34 years), eclipse the Canadian average; as noted in Chapter 10, suicide rates in Nunavut are especially high. Interpersonal violence within Aboriginal communities also plays a part in early mortality.

In western Canada particularly (Sinha and Kozlowski, 2013), each year a disproportionate number of Aboriginal children are taken into care by provincial welfare agencies, many simply because their parents are too poor to take care of them. Statistics Canada (2014f) reports that in 2011, of the roughly 30,000 children aged 14 years and younger in foster care in Canada, nearly half (48.1 percent) were Aboriginal children; in fact, 3.6 percent of all Aboriginal children in Canada in 2011 were foster children, compared with 0.3 percent of non-Aboriginal children.

Not surprisingly perhaps, Aboriginals who were wards of the state as children also make up a disproportionate number of inmates within adult correctional institutions. Dauvergne (2012) reports that, in 2010 and 2011, Aboriginal people made up 27 percent of the adult population in provincial and territorial custody, and 20 percent in federal custody—meaning that the proportion of Aboriginals in custody is about seven to eight times that of adult Aboriginals in Canada as a whole.

Labour Force Participation and Income

Sociologists note that an individual's place in the labour market influences much regarding their social circumstances. The economic and social conditions of Canada's First Nations have gradually improved in recent decades, with Aboriginals making up a growing percentage of Canada's labour force. At the same time, the economic circumstances of the various Aboriginal communities in Canada are not uniform. As in the non-Aboriginal community, one's life chances are influenced by such factors as place of residence, gender, and class. Aboriginal peoples in the Atlantic region and Quebec tend to have lower employment and participation rates compared with their counterparts in the West, notably in the oil sands region of Alberta; Aboriginal women tend to earn less than Aboriginal men; and, within Aboriginal bands, there are sometimes also class and status differences.

One obvious factor influencing successful employment is whether Aboriginals remain on reserve or not. On-reserve Aboriginals are less likely than their off-reserve counterparts to enter the labour force for a very good reason: There are fewer jobs to be had. The situation of off-reserve Aboriginals seeking employment is often not much better, however.

Frideres (2011:214) notes that the overall unemployment rate for First Nations people in Canada is three times that of the general population, a point given further emphasis by data looking at the impact of the recent economic downturn (discussed in Chapter 8) on the Aboriginal labour force. Table 12.4 shows that, between 2008 and 2010, Aboriginal workers experienced a decrease in labour force participation and employment, and an increase in unemployment exceeding that of their non-Aboriginal counterparts.

Nonetheless, Aboriginal peoples are participating in the labour market more today than in the past, a fact raising an important point for Canada's future. One of Canada's fast-emerging challenges is its aging population, with consequences, among other things, for the country's labour force needs. Might Aboriginals be the solution? Might the Aboriginal birth rate rescue Canada from demographic decline? Politicians and corporate leaders (for example, the Canadian Chamber of Commerce, 2013) have noted this possibility and, in some instances, made well-publicized efforts to open up opportunities for Aboriginal people in the work force. How is the increased participation of Aboriginals in the labour market reflected in their economic circumstances? Answering this question is difficult because Statistics Canada no longer collects the data necessary to adequately address the question. The most recent comparative data, drawn from the 2006 census, showed that the median income for Aboriginal people was $18,962 compared with $27,097 for non-Aboriginals, a difference of 30 percent; while the average income for Aboriginal people was $23,935 compared with $35,872 for non-Aboriginals, a difference of 33 percent (see Chapter 8 for a discussion of the pros and cons of medians and averages). The same data showed, however, that Aboriginal incomes are also stratified, with Métis workers having generally higher incomes, Inuit workers lower incomes, and First Nations people falling in between (and varying between on- and off-reserve residents) (Statistics Canada, 2006b; see also Parriag and Chaulk, 2013). Usalcas (2011:21) reports that, in 2010, Aboriginal workers earned $22.15 per hour on

Table 12.4: Employment, Unemployment, and Participation Rates among Aboriginal and Non-Aboriginal Peoples, by Age, 2008 and 2010

	Aboriginal Population			Non-Aboriginal Population		
	2008	2010	Percentage Change 2008–2010	2008	2010	Percentage Change 2008–2010
Employment Rate by Age						
15–24 years	52.5	45.0	−7.5	60.0	55.3	−4.7
25–54 years	70.8	65.8	−5.0	82.6	80.9	−1.7
55 years and older	33.7	30.3	−3.4	32.6	33.7	1.1
Unemployment Rate by Age						
15–24 years	15.3	21.1	5.8	11.5	14.6	3.1
25–54 years	9.3	12.3	3.0	5.0	6.8	1.8
55 years and older	n/a	n/a	n/a	n/a	n/a	n/a
Participation Rate by Age						
15–24 years	62.0	57.0	−5.0	67.7	64.8	−2.9
25–54 years	78.0	75.0	−3.0	86.9	86.7	−0.2
55 years and older	36.0	34.6	−1.4	34.3	36.0	1.7

Source: Adapted from Tables 3, 6, 7, and 8 in Usalcas, Jeannine. 2011. "Aboriginal People and the Labour Market: Estimates from the Labour Force Survey, 2008–2010." Labour Statistics Division, Statistics Canada. Cat. no. 71-588-X, no. 3 (www.statcan.gc.ca/pub/71-588-x/71-588-x2011003-eng.pdf).

average, compared to $24.46 per hour for their non-Aboriginal counterparts, or roughly 91 percent of non-Aboriginal wages. But information on per hour wages provides no relevant information about yearly income unless the number of hours worked per year is reported.

While credit for much of the progress that has been made can be attributed to several First Nations bands, led by a new generation of young, entrepreneurial leaders who are changing the culture of First Nations reserves, the path of continued hope for Canada's Aboriginal peoples lies in education and economic development.

Box 12.1: Profiles in Aboriginal Leadership

The Osoyoos Indian band of south-central British Columbia is a storied economic success. Led by Chief Clarence Louie (1961–), one of the new generation of Aboriginal leaders emerging today, the Osoyoos band boasts nearly a dozen successful local businesses, including a golf course/hotel/residential complex, a vineyard, a campground, a recreational vehicle park, a construction company, a ready-mix concrete company, a gas bar, and a convenience store. Together, these business ventures bring in revenues of more than $15 million annually—seven times the revenue the band receives from the federal government.

Similar success stories can be found throughout Canada:

- The Fort McKay First Nation in northern Alberta and Suncor recently launched a joint partnership to establish a business "incubator" to encourage, support, and promote entrepreneurial activities and start-up businesses in the community.
- The Membertou First Nation of Sydney, Nova Scotia, has partnered with the Cape Breton YMCA to deliver entrepreneurial courses to its members. The deal will offer free training in business ventures to 1,100 Mi'kmaq who may be interested in turning their ideas into business ventures.
- In July 2008, the Stoney Nation of Morley, Alberta, opened a $65 million casino complex.

Education

Education is a known influence on occupational attainment and economic opportunity. Historically, Aboriginal educational levels have lagged behind those of other Canadians. Today, however, educational achievement among Aboriginal youth is at an all-time high.

The 1981 Canadian census revealed that only 2 percent of Aboriginal youth held university degrees, compared with 8.1 percent of the non-Aboriginal population. The 1996 Report of the Royal Commission on Aboriginal People (RCAP) indicated that 4.2 percent of Aboriginal individuals held university degrees, and that 21 percent of Aboriginal peoples had completed college certificates. Data from the recent National

Household Survey conducted in 2011, while subject to caution due to sampling error, suggests that the level of educational attainment among Aboriginal peoples continues to increase, especially for Aboriginal women. As Table 12.5 shows, in 2011, nearly 10 percent of Aboriginals between the ages of 25 and 64 hold university degrees, more than 20 percent have college diplomas, and more than 14 percent are educated in the trades. The latter is perhaps no surprise, given the number of jobs involved in the northern resource extraction industries.

At the same time, Aboriginal educational attainment continues to trail that of Canadians overall, whose post-secondary levels have also continued to rise since 1991. Moreover, a large proportion of Aboriginal people, nearly 29 percent, do not have high school equivalency, compared with only 12.7 percent of the Canadian population as a whole. This is especially the case among Aboriginal men. At the same time, the educational gains made by Aboriginal women, who now make up nearly two-thirds of university degree-holders within the Aboriginal community, are also worth noting.

The increasing educational success of Aboriginals reflects in part the growing responsiveness of universities to Aboriginal needs. For example, as of fall 2008, York University has sanctioned graduate research in Aboriginal languages, with graduate students now able to defend their research in any of 50 Aboriginal languages. Elsewhere, special pre-medicine courses for Aboriginal students are available, and medical faculties are beginning to accept mature students with community-based experiences in place of university degrees (Warry, 2007). These victories have begun showing positive results.

The seeds of later educational success are sewn early on. Even greater efforts at innovation and experimentation have been undertaken at the K–12 level. Some schools in British Columbia, for example, are inviting local elders to share their knowledge and celebrate ceremonies with students and teachers. The Qualicum School District even has an Elder-in-Residence program in which an elder will spend one day a week in local schools, demonstrating traditional cultural activities and teaching life lessons.

More recently, in April 2014, the Government of Canada introduced Bill C-33, intended to provide First Nations students with higher standards of education, supports, and opportunities, which most Canadians take for granted. The bill would have required First Nations schools to teach a core curriculum that would ensure students being able to transfer their credits between schools on- and off-reserve; to ensure that students meet minimum attendance requirements; to hire properly certified teachers; and to award widely recognized diplomas or certificates. The Assembly of First Nations (AFN) rejected the bill, much to the surprise of the Conservative government, leading to the resignation of AFN Grand Chief Shawn Atleo. The bill is now on hold.

Why was the bill rejected? The reasons are complex, but one reason touches on the meaning of education and its broader relation to culture and identity. Education in modern, non-Aboriginal society is often viewed as merely a means to occupational attainment, and, true enough, education is positively correlated with high occupational and economic attainment. Within Aboriginal communities, however, there have been growing demands for the right to educate youth in the ways of their traditional knowledge and heritage (Battiste and Henderson, 2000:87).

Table 12.5: Population Aged 25–64, by Level of Educational Attainment and Sex, Canadian Population as a Whole and Individuals Reporting Aboriginal Identity, Canada, 2011

	All Canadians						Aboriginal Identifiers					
	Both Sexes	%	Men	%	Women	%	Both Sexes	%	Men	%	Women	%
< High school	2,330,575	12.7	1,238,845	13.8	1,091,735	11.6	193,785	28.9	100,075	31.8	93,705	26.3
High school or equivalent	4,270,660	23.2	2,049,355	22.8	2,221,305	23.6	152,840	22.8	70,550	22.4	82,295	23.1
Trades	2,218,800	12.1	1,435,395	16.0	783,410	8.3	96,460	14.4	62,810	20.0	33,645	9.4
College	3,913,710	21.3	1,674,815	18.6	2,238,895	23.8	138,600	20.6	50,000	15.9	88,595	24.8
University certificate below Bachelor's level	894,750	4.9	385,980	4.3	508,770	5.4	23,605	3.5	8,255	2.6	15,350	4.3
University	4,755,420	25.9	2,199,995	24.5	2,555,420	27.2	66,095	9.8	22,875	7.3	43,215	12.1
Total	18,383,915	100.1	8,984,385	100.0	9,399,535	99.9	671,385	100.0	314,565	100.0	356,805	100.0

Source: Adapted from Statistics Canada. 2014g. "The Educational Attainment of Aboriginal Peoples in Canada." *National Household Surveys 2011.* Cat. no. 99-0012-X (www12.statcan. gc.ca/nhs-enm/2011/as-sa/99-012-x/99-012-x2011003_3-eng.cfm). Modified January 14, 2014; Statistics Canada. 2014h. "Education and Labour." *National Household Surveys 2011.* Cat. no. 9-0012-X2011037 (www12.statcan.gc.ca/nhs-enm/2011/dp-pd/dt-td/Lp-eng.cfm?). Modified March 4, 2014.

Language is an important element of a people's cultural heritage, as we saw in Part 1, dealing with French culture in Canada. Similarly, many view the revival of Aboriginal languages as key to the transmission and survival of Aboriginal knowledge and culture (Kirkness, 1998a). Many also believe that the Canadian government must play a greater role in ensuring the vitality of Aboriginal languages. Fettes and Norton (2000), for example, argue that the federal government should establish a program for Aboriginal languages within the Department of Canadian Heritage (see also Battiste, 2000:199). While there is a diversity of Aboriginal languages in Canada, spoken by 213,490 people, the fact is that only three particular languages dominate: Cree, 83,475 (39.1 percent); Inuktitut, 34,110 (16 percent); and Ojibway, 19,275 (9 percent) (Statistics Canada, 2011j). These three languages will likely persist into the 22nd century. Research shows that for these languages to prevail, however, they must first become a priority within Indigenous communities themselves (Friesen and Friesen, 2005:150).

Aboriginal concerns related to linguistic concerns involve a broader understanding that includes self-esteem, cultural pride, and indeed the very survival of the community (Antone, 2000). Effective cultural renewal goes beyond the mere adding of Aboriginal components, even language, to the content of non-Aboriginal curricula in schools. It is important to emphasize that Aboriginal teachings must have a broad cultural foundation (Witt, 1998:270; see also Marker, 2000). As Verna Kirkness (1998b:12–13), a Cree professor emeritus at the University of British Columbia, argues, the survival of Aboriginal culture must move beyond mere rhetoric to the actual practice of culture in everyday life beyond the school.

Things are gradually improving. Young Aboriginals are increasingly aware of their history, assisted by elders who pass on cultural lessons, often in traditional ways—through storytelling, modelling, and on-the-job training—and by Aboriginal teachers who have been trained to work in their own communities. Likewise, there have been improvements in educational facilities, local control of schooling, counselling services and support groups, and school curricula have been revised to include culturally relevant content. From kindergarten to grade 12 and beyond, Aboriginal peoples are slowly gaining control of their own schools, their own education, and their own lives. In doing so, Aboriginals are also preserving a way of being in the world that challenges modern non-Aboriginal values.

Contrasting World Views

Classical sociologists, such as Émile Durkheim (see the Introduction), often contrasted the fundamental values and beliefs of traditional society with those of the modern industrial society that was emerging; that is, they contrasted the overarching **world view** by which each society defined reality.

It is simplistic—and sometimes dangerous—to dichotomize world views, yet if we employ them as Weberian "ideal types" and do not reify them, such descriptions can serve a heuristic purpose.

At the macro-level of cultural analysis, one can identify several differences between the world views held by traditional and modern societies, differences that often continue to manifest in day-to-day misunderstandings between Aboriginals and non-Aboriginals in Canada.

The Sacred and the Profane

Durkheim (1912/1978) described two exclusive philosophical worlds existing side by side. The first is the **profane world**: the world of the everyday, the expected, the mundane, and the explainable. The second is the **sacred world**: the world of mystery, uncertainty, and even danger. The latter existed before time, and will continue to live after; it is perpetual. According to Durkheim, the sacred cannot and should not be approached with the idea of exploitation or domination, nor should one tamper with the elements or workings of the universe. The sacred is to be treated with awe, even reverence. This contrast between the sacred and the profane well describes a fundamental difference between traditional and modern societies, between the traditional Aboriginal and dominant Canadian societies. However, it yields nothing to the notion of flexibility or transition, a fact that is readily visible in contemporary Aboriginal communities.

The early European invaders underestimated the extent to which spirituality was valued by Aboriginal peoples in their daily lives (Friesen, 1995; Witt, 1998; Hanohano, 1999). This emphasis on spirituality remains underestimated and misunderstood by non-Aboriginals today who have long ago abandoned the spiritual roots of their society. For many Aboriginal leaders, their spirituality serves as a foundation for education, land claims, and language revitalization programs. Current negotiations between non-Aboriginal industries and Indian bands have altered this stance in the interests of coping with and even expanding economic development in Aboriginal communities.

Many other differences between traditional Aboriginal and non-Aboriginal culture follow from the former's greater acceptance of this spiritual or sacred realm.

Spiritual Holism versus Scientific Empiricism

In contrast to modern cultures, traditional cultures experience no uneasiness at the thought of multiple realities, spiritual or phenomenological, simultaneously operating in the universe. Likewise, the world is seen as a single, if complex, phenomenon; its elements cannot be studied and tested in isolation. Dreams, visions, and other spiritual experiences are considered to be as valid sources of knowledge as scientifically and empirically derived truths. Today's successful Aboriginal entrepreneurs often add to their traditional repertoire of knowledge such things as university research, innovation, and strategic economic planning.

Cyclical versus Linear Notions of Time

For traditional (pre-industrial) peoples around the world, time is cyclical, tied to hunting and growing seasons. The Industrial Revolution and the advent of capitalism resulted in a changed conception of time ("wasting time," "lost time," "time is money") that sees time as linear, a direct offshoot of this being the notion of "progress," the notion that "Every day, in every way, things must get better and better." Conflicts over the meaning of time remain a constant and frequent element in relations between Aboriginals and non-Aboriginals, but also within Aboriginal communities that are attempting to take control of their own economies.

Competing Notions of Cause and Effect

Both traditional and modern world views recognize the notion of cause and effect. The modern world view, however, subscribes to the belief that such effects can be controlled; indeed, that by designing the right tools and approaches, people can even improve upon nature and perhaps tailor effects to their own advantage. By contrast, people in traditional societies view themselves as part of a great chain of existence in which all elements of creation are interrelated and interdependent (Ross, 1992). Moreover, as with time, this chain is not linear, but rather a continuous series. If any single element is subjected to pressures or is otherwise tampered with, there are sure to be repercussions in the grand scheme of things. The implications of this belief are profound, and bear similarity to what sociologists refer to as **unintended or unanticipated consequences** (Merton, 1968). Aboriginal culture includes an inherent warning not to attempt to dominate or exploit the mysterious workings of nature, but to work in harmony with them (Suzuki, 1992). It is a warning against hubris. Given escalating concerns over the environment, Aboriginal peoples may be correct in suspecting both the idea of progress and the further assumption that damages caused by technology can always be rectified by still another scientific discovery or adjustment.

The Collective versus the Individual

As previously noted (Chapter 4), modernity's greatest invention, and perhaps also its greatest illusion, is that of "individualism," often contrasted with the "collectivism." Non-Aboriginals tend to view Aboriginal culture as collective and conformist, in contrast to modern non-Aboriginal society's extolling of individualism. This view is simplistic, to say the least. Family loyalty *does* have a high priority in traditional Aboriginal thinking, and the individual is expected to submit to group and community demands (Dion, 1979; Surtees, 1969). And, in turn, this *does* put limits on one's individuality and may hinder achievements in the contemporary socio-economic culture of the nation. (Plant managers are rarely sympathetic to individuals who take time off to tend to personal family matters, though perhaps they should. Might this change as Aboriginals become industrial managers?)

There is a paradox, however. Beyond these restraints, the community also guarantees the individual emotional security, support, and a particular identity. This identity is assigned and sometimes amended, and, if need be, taken away from the individual. Generally, the process also fosters a subtle kind of non-interference, though this too has limitations in a post-modern society. The community, for example, will soon "put in line" individuals who "show off" too much. In extreme cases, individuals who step beyond community limits may find themselves shunned as punishment.

Egalitarianism versus Hierarchy

Modern Western societies frequently parade their democratic political cultures. The foundational element of democracy is equality, however, and on this measure traditional societies, including those of Canada's First Nations societies, were exceedingly democratic. Age and sex were the only certain markers of status; otherwise, authority rules tended to be complex and shifting. This confused the Europeans, whose own traditions were akin to a caste system; Aboriginal decision-making processes still confuse many Euro-Canadians today.

Few followers of *Robert's Rules of Order* (a widely used guide to Parliamentary procedure), for example, could endure a traditional Aboriginal meeting. Aboriginal rules are different from those of non-Aboriginals. Elders, chiefs, and respected spokespeople prescribe the procedures for a meeting simply by their behaviour, and no one takes issue with this. In the most traditional format, every challenge faced by a tribe must be resolved communally. Industrial and government negotiators frequently become quite impatient with such processes, especially when elders decide that a lengthy sweet-grass ceremony should precede the deliberations. If negotiations toward industrial development are to continue, it will require a significant "rewriting of rules and attitudes" (Fleras, 2007:347).

Seeking a Third Way

We have previously noted (Chapter 9) that the intent of the original non-Aboriginal educational establishment—both residential schools as well as day schools—was to silence expressions of Aboriginal culture. Over time, the process of educational imperialism had a crushing effect on Aboriginal communities. Several generations lost their languages and transformed their cultures, sometimes resulting in psychological and social upheaval for community members. In recent years, a crescendo of Aboriginal voices has emphasized the importance of reviving traditional knowledge and spirituality (Meili, 2012; Cajete, 1994; Couture, 1991; McGaa, 1995; Johnston, 1995; Bear Heart, 1998; Weaver, 1998; Battiste, 2000; Battiste and Henderson, 2000). But there have also been repeated calls from some, in both Aboriginal (Henlin, 2006) and non-Aboriginal communities (see Flanagan, 2000), for Aboriginals to adopt modern ways, or to "get with the program." Is it possible to combine traditional Aboriginal world views and values with those of modernity, to adapt them to the dominant socio-economic environment? Is there a third way between traditional and modern values? This is a major challenge facing not only Aboriginal peoples, but Canadians as a whole. Yazzie (2000) argues that if First Nations want to retain elements of their traditional belief systems, they must first throw off the yoke of epistemological colonialism and commence the truth-finding process within themselves. Political self-determination begins with internal sovereignty, which means taking control of one's personal, family, clan, and community life. Essentially this will require the valuing of tradition while mingling aspects of contemporary Euro-Canadian value systems. This task will not be easy. As Findley (2000) notes, despite increasing challenges from Euro-Canadian and Aboriginal scholars alike, modernity's orthodoxies remain dominant and are even expanding their domain.

Maintaining or even retrieving traditional Aboriginal culture is made problematic by the fact that many First Nations today are significantly "modernized," while others are marginalized between their traditional and Western cultures. Those who attempt to remain oriented to traditional ways ironically find themselves joined by some elements within the dominant non-Aboriginal community who have themselves rejected modern Western values (materialism, individualism, secularism) and seek in Aboriginal culture a solution to modernity's perceived ills.

How have Aboriginal peoples adapted to the challenges of modern Western and capitalist society? Friesen and Friesen (2005:156–158) and Schultz and Kroeger (1996) describe five types of responses by groups within the Aboriginal community.

Traditionalists make up the first group, and respond to the challenge by clinging tenaciously to "the old ways" and ignoring or denying any form of change. Traditionalists have strong ties to the past, culturally as well as spiritually, and are therefore able to ignore modern developments while continuing to live with both eyes on the past.

The second group is made up of lost-identity individuals who feel powerless in the current of socio-economic change and often fall prey to social and cultural breakdown. They often develop confused identities and exhibit characteristics of deprivation, grief, and dependency, and often drift into poverty.

The third group are new traditionalists or "born-again" Aboriginals with little knowledge of the old ways, but who like to dress in traditional garb by wearing braids, sporting ribbon shirts, and displaying items of beadwork. Unaware of the impracticality and difficulty of such an existence today, they nonetheless often extol the virtues of hunting, gathering, and fishing societies. Often youthful, articulate, and college-educated, members of this group seek a cultural renaissance of sorts.

The fourth group are those assimilated completely into the modern world, albeit often unconsciously. This requires adopting new norms and forming new social alliances. For this group and its proponents, maintaining an Aboriginal cultural identity is secondary to economic development (Henlin, 2006).

The fifth group comprises those who might be called internationally minded persons of First Nations background. (There are increasing contacts among Aboriginal peoples in Australia, New Zealand, South America, Scandinavia, the United States, and Canada.) These individuals seek to balance and appreciate the contributions of both Aboriginal and non-Aboriginal cultures, placing a great deal of value on their own heritage without belittling that of others. They are often quite open to alternative ways of thinking, such as finding ways to protect the environment while also supporting technological and industrial advancement.

Mainstream Canadian society need not romanticize traditional Aboriginal culture or its values; nor, however, can these things be ignored. The fact is that there is still a large gap between the values and beliefs embedded in First Nations' culture and those of modern society. The latter has little understanding, and even less appreciation for a lifestyle focused on living in harmony with nature, respecting the earth, believing in the interconnectedness of all living phenomena, and honouring the Creator in one's daily life (Friesen, 1995; Brascoupé, 2000). In the words of well-known Métis architect Douglas Cardinal, Aboriginal culture amounts to a "different way of being human" (Buckley, 1993:174). The question for non-Aboriginal Canadians at the start of the 21st century is whether they are open enough to accommodate, learn from, and perhaps even embrace such a divergent world view.

We Are You: Canada as an Aboriginal Society

In Chapter 8, we looked at how various political philosophers have described the nature of Canadian society. For Lipset (1990), you will recall, Canada is a British Tory country; for Grant (2005), Canada was a Tory country, but is now a modern Liberal (and liberal and, hence, American) country; while for Resnick (2005), Canada is a European country; and on and on.

More recently, John Ralston Saul (2008) proffered a very different, even radical, thesis: that Canada is a Métis civilization, an Aboriginal country. Saul points out the many practical contributions that Aboriginal peoples have made to Canada, from various kinds of foods to canoes. But Saul's argument goes beyond a historical homage to a lost culture; rather, he argues that Aboriginal ways of thinking and behaving, of solving problems, continue in the kind of society that Canada has become. He argues that several strategic elements linked to Canada's Aboriginal nature shape how Canadians see themselves:

> Our obsession with egalitarianism. Our desire to maintain a balance between individuals and groups. The delight we take in playing with our non-monolithic idea of society—a delight in complexity. Our tendency to try to run society as an ongoing negotiation, which must be related to our distaste for resolving complexities. Our preference, behind a relatively violent language of public debate, for consensus—again an expression of society as a balance of complexity, a sort of equilibrium. Our intuition that behind the formal written and technical face of our society lies something more important, which we try to get at through the oral and through complex relationships. Our sense that the clear resolution of differences will lead to injustice and even violence. And related to that our preference for something that the law now calls minimal impairment, which means the obligation of those with authority to do as little damage as possible to people and to rights when exercising that authority. (Saul, 2008:54–55)

Ultimately, Saul's call is for Canadians to escape colonially imposed ways of thinking, to thereby see—to imagine—ourselves based on the truth of how Canada has been built; if we are unable to do this, Canadian society may continue to stumble and fail.

In issuing his call, however, Saul also reverses a centuries-old practice of Euro-Canadian ethnocentrism. There are many observers, sympathetic or otherwise, who claim that Aboriginal traditions and practices have no relevance in a modern, competitive society (see Flanagan, 2000). Indeed, they argue that Aboriginals have "much to learn" from modern Euro-Canadian society; that the way forward lies in becoming more like the dominant culture. Saul's critique (2008), and that of Davis (2009), take us in a more interesting and challenging direction, enjoining us to ask such questions as What have we lost? What, if anything, can traditional cultures teach us?

What lessons might non-Aboriginals learn from Aboriginals, their values, and their heritage? We provide one example, dealing with crime and justice.

Despite a general decrease in incidence of crime, many Canadians remain fearful, and because they are afraid, Canadians are often persuaded that more police officers, stiffer sentences, and bigger jails are the solution. Most criminologists view such policies as ineffective except in dealing with a few select types of crime; the United States is a shining testament to the failure of "getting tough on crime," leading even many conservative voices in that country to rethink such policies. Severe punishment seems ineffective in dissuading criminal behaviour, while victims themselves often feel unsatisfied—sometimes even revictimized—by a legal system that often seems remote and uncaring.

Consider the example of traditional Aboriginal justice. In pre-contact days, Aboriginal peoples employed storytelling, ridicule, and shaming as methods of keeping people in line. In more serious cases, they would put an offender in a circle of elders, who would offer advice and mete out punishment to the offender (Warry, 2007:173–174). This gathering of elders would demand change in the offender's behaviour and determine an appropriate punishment for the misdeed. Sometimes called a **sentencing circle**, this approach has been revived in many Aboriginal communities, although it has been altered slightly. Today, such circles include offenders, victims, community members, and justice professionals who meet and discuss face to face the offences and determine ways to ensure that justice is administered (Chiste, 2005:224–225). Re-established in the Yukon in the 1990s, where some 300 sentencing circles soon emerged, the practice has since spread to Saskatchewan, British Columbia, Manitoba, and Quebec (Steckley and Cummins, 2008:241). The central purpose of sentencing circles is to encourage the offender to deal directly with the victim and the community at large. Wrongdoing involves a tearing of the social fabric; the intent of the sentencing circle is to repair the harm done. Might such an approach also work better than conventional approaches to crime in non-Aboriginal communities?

Conclusion

Our world continues to change at an accelerating speed. Ironically, however, many of the biggest changes in Canada today and in the foreseeable future involve Aboriginal peoples—those who were there at the forefront of changes 400 years ago, then forgotten, are now once more prominent.

But this is not a situation peculiar to Canada. Throughout many parts of the world long ago colonized, Aboriginal peoples have begun reasserting their political rights and cultural identities. This has particularly been the case in the former British colonies— Canada, the United States, Australia, and New Zealand (see Fleras and Elliott, 1992). But there has also been a growing resurgence of Indigenous peoples in many parts of Latin America since the 1990s (e.g., Mexico's Zapatista movement) and Asia (e.g., the Ainu of Japan).

We began our search for Canadian society with a discussion of the notions of country, nation, and state. We noted the problematic nature of these terms, and the uniqueness of Canada in trying to fit them into the Canadian experiment. The case of Aboriginal peoples in Canada provides perhaps the most striking example. Canada remains a country. It also constitutes, we would argue, a unique society. Part of Canada's uniqueness, however, resides in the complex manner in which states and markets have been involved in its creation, and the creative manner in which more than one nation has been accommodated into that grand design.

One thing is particularly clear: Canada's Aboriginal nations will play a major and growing role in shaping the kind of society Canada will become in the remaining years of the 21st century. As Phil Fontaine, former grand chief of the Assembly of First Nations, has observed, "The future of First Nations and Canada's future are intricately linked."

Key Terms

band
infant mortality rate
profane world
sacred world
sentencing circle
unintended or unanticipated consequences
urban reserves
world view

Critical Thinking Questions

1. As Aboriginal communities in Canada change and adapt, what kinds of conflicts might we expect to arise within the communities?
2. What factors might explain the differences in educational attainment between men and women in both Aboriginal and non-Aboriginal communities?
3. Are the inequalities between Aboriginals and non-Aboriginals in Canada more similar to a class system or a caste system?
4. Is a "third way" between traditional and modern world views possible? What might it look like?

5. What lessons might non-Aboriginal societies learn from Aboriginal societies in meeting the challenges of the 21st century?

Recommended Readings

Davis, Wade. 2009. *The Wayfinders: Why Ancient Wisdom Matters in the Modern World*. Toronto: House of Anansi.
Destined to be a classic, Davis's book, the 2009 Massey Lecture, examines traditional cultures around the world and "why ancient wisdom matters."

Drees, Laurie Meijer. 2013. *Healing Histories: Stories from Canada's Indian Hospitals*. Edmonton: University of Alberta Press.
This book essentially traces the formation, development, and operation of Canada's Indian hospitals, while at the same time carefully mingling traditional Aboriginal healing philosophies and techniques.

Frideres, James S. (2011). *First Nations in the Twenty-First Century*. Don Mills, ON: Oxford University Press.
This book offers a comprehensive view of First Nations' legal and historical identity as well as an analytic treatment of contemporary issues affecting Aboriginal communities.

Friesen, John W., and Virginia Lyons Friesen. 2008. *Western Canadian Native Destiny: Complex Questions on the Cultural Maze*. Calgary: Detselig.
The authors document a series of contemporary Aboriginal issues, including urban adjustment, health, justice, education, cultural identity, land claims, economic development, and self-government.

Warry, Wayne. 2007. *Ending Denial: Understanding Aboriginal Issues*. Peterborough, ON: Broadview Press.
Warry examines the problems and obstacles that confront Canada's First Nations in their quest to wrest control of their institutions away from the federal government.

Related Websites

Aboriginal Affairs and Northern Development Canada
www.aadnc-aandc.gc.ca/eng
The Canadian government's primary department for managing Aboriginal issues.

Assembly of First Nations
www.afn.ca
The Assembly of First Nations is the national representative organization of the First Nations in Canada.

Turtle Island Native Network
www.turtleisland.org/news/news-justice.htm
This is Canada's Aboriginal news and information network.

Canadian Society on Video

Circles. 1997. National Film Board of Canada, 57 minutes, 45 seconds.
Circles examines justice and community healing, hope, and transformation, bringing together the traditional Aboriginal justice circle and the Canadian justice system.

Mohawk Girls. 2005. National Film Board of Canada, 62 minutes, 45 seconds.
This film examines the lives of three teenage Mohawk girls on the Kahnawake reserve and the hope, despair, heartache, and promise of growing up Aboriginal at the beginning of the 21st century.

No Turning Back: The Royal Commission on Aboriginal Peoples. 1997. The National Film Board of Canada, 47 minutes, 20 seconds.
The video begins with footage of the Oka standoff and other First Nations' protests of the 1990s, then interviews the commissioners of this inquiry and highlights some of the presentations.

CONCLUSION

CANADA
IN THE WORLD
AND IN THE FUTURE

Much will have to change in Canada if the country is to stay the same.

—Abraham Rotstein, 1964

The Global Village is nothing more than Canadian culture writ large.

—author John Gray, 1994

The world needs more Canada.

—U2 lead singer Bono, 2003

Introduction

In the introductory chapter, we defined *society* as

> the product of relatively continuous and enduring interactions, within a political terri-
> tory, between people more or less identifying themselves as members of the society, these
> interactions being maintained by an ensemble of political, economic, cultural, and other
> institutions, the sum of such interactions being in excess of interactions occurring with
> similarly defined societies external to the given territory.

We have taken as a given throughout this text the notion that something termed
"Canadian society" exists as a sociological construct amenable to study.

The approach taken in this text has emphasized four themes. First, that the study of
any social phenomenon, including society, cannot be adequately conducted without
consideration of its historical context. Equally, time—and timing—must be viewed as a
variable. That is, when and if something occurs is of central importance to the creation
and maintenance of society's elements, including its underlying structures of power (see
the Introduction).

Second, the study of society, specifically, cannot be hived off from its relation to the
state and the market. Indeed, the authors argue for a critical sociology that puts back
together in its analyses the triumvirate of state-market-society that has too often been
separated over the past century of scholarship. Only in this way can students (especially)
begin to understand the complex world that is the 21st century.

The text's third theme, if subtly expressed throughout the text, is that sociological
theory must not be employed in a decorative or didactic fashion (e.g., "Look here: an
example of conflict theory!"), but used rather as a genuine lens for examining and understanding events and issues. Students and instructors who, at times in reading this text,
wondered "Where is the theory?" are encouraged to go back into the text with an eye
to answering their own question. How might, for example, the theories described in the
Introduction be used regarding the socio-historical events and meanings surrounding
Louis Riel (Chapters 2 and 9)?

Fourth, this text should be viewed as enjoining sociologists to commit to using its
insights to study real-world issues and problems. This need is especially important in

the wake of the Great Recession that bludgeoned much of the world between 2007 and 2009 (and still continues in some quarters); the attendant conflicts, both large and small, that dominate our daily news; and a host of other critical issues, notably environmental damage and global warming, which are transforming the world at a rapid pace.

Being critical and engaged means actively examining the choices people make and do not make. In this, comparisons to other countries are useful, indeed imperative, in terms of the choices that Canadians will face in the future.

Comparing Canada: Methodology

In the recent age of globalization, comparisons among various countries have been commonplace. International organizations, such as the United Nations and World Bank, regularly put out lists of data for every country on the planet.

Comparisons must be meaningful, however. Imagine, for example, comparing the slapshot of Steven Stamkos, a professional hockey player, to that of an eight-year-old player or, worse, to that of either of this text's authors. The point is that there must be a legitimate basis for comparison. Usually this means that, at least on some factors, the groups compared are the same. The presence of constants on some variables makes any differences meaningful. Which countries might provide a sound basis for comparisons with Canada?

Several countries are often grouped together on different bases. For example, the Anglo democracies (Australia, Canada, New Zealand, the United Kingdom, and the United States) share cultural similarities, including legal and political systems. Slightly overlapping the Anglo-democracy group is another group termed the "white" dominions (Argentina, Australia, Canada, New Zealand, and Uruguay), countries in the New World largely settled by Europeans (Laxer, 1989). A third grouping can be derived from Olsen's (2002) typology of different types of welfare states (Chapter 7), and his own specific study of Canada, the United States, and Sweden—Canada's system being a kind of hybrid. Finally, we might construct a group for specific comparison with Canada comprising its former imperial rulers, Britain and France.

Putting together all of these groups, we arrive at the following countries for comparison with Canada: Argentina, Australia, France, New Zealand, Sweden, the United Kingdom, the United States, and Uruguay.

Canada and Its Comparates: The Human Development Index Report

There are a number of organizations, including the International Labour Organization and the U.S. Central Intelligence Agency, that provide reliable national and international data on a host of subjects. The United Nations' Human Development Report Office (HDRO) (United Nations, 2014b) is another of these. It publishes an annual report assessing country achievements in different areas of human development based on an index. The countries classified in the **Human Development Index** are compared according to four criteria: (1) life expectancy at birth; (2) mean years of expected schooling; (3) mean years of actual schooling; and (4) gross national income (GNI).[1] The aggregate of these scores provides an overall index score. In 2014, 187 countries were examined. Based on their index scores, the human development of each of these countries was defined as either very high, high, medium, or low. Of the nine countries examined here, only Uruguay was not defined as having very high human development (high only), though Argentina only marginally made it into the very high category.

Table 13.1 shows the overall index scores for the nine countries examined. Canada's rank among all countries in 2013 was number eight.[2] Among the nine countries shown in Table 13.1, Canada's index score (0.902) falls somewhere in between the highest (Australia, 0.933) and the lowest (Uruguay, 0.790). But likewise, Canada is nearly at the mid-point between its two "mother countries" (France and the United Kingdom) and its current suitor (the United States). Canada's closest comparate is Sweden (0.898), another northern country with a small population, established welfare-state traditions—and reindeer!

Why the differences between these respective countries? Some of the factors underlying these differences are suggested in Table 13.2.

Table 13.1: Human Development Index Trends for Select Countries, 1980–2013

Country	1980	1990	2000	2010	2011	2012	2013	Rank 2013
Argentina	0.665	0.694	0.753	0.799	0.804	0.806	0.808	49
Australia	0.841	0.866	0.898	0.926	0.928	0.931	0.933	2
Canada	**0.809**	**0.848**	**0.867**	**0.896**	**0.900**	**0.901**	**0.902**	**8**
France	0.722	0.779	0.848	0.879	0.882	0.884	0.884	20
New Zealand	0.793	0.821	0.873	0.903	0.904	0.908	0.910	7
Sweden	0.776	0.807	0.889	0.895	0.896	0.897	0.898	12
United Kingdom	0.735	0.768	0.863	0.895	0.891	0.890	0.892	14
United States	0.825	0.858	0.883	0.908	0.911	0.912	0.914	5
Uruguay	0.658	0.691	0.740	0.779	0.783	0.787	0.790	50

Source: United Nations. 2014b. *Human Development Reports*. New York: United Nations Development Programme (hdr. undp.org/en/content/table-2-human-development-index-trends-1980-2013).

Table 13.2: Gender-Related Development Index (GDI[1]) for Select Countries, 2013

Country	Life Expectancy at Birth, Men	Life Expectancy at Birth, Women	Mean Years of School, Men	Mean Years of School, Women	GNI per Capita (2011 PPP (US$)), 2013, Men	GNI per Capita (2011 PPP (US$)), 2013, Women	Percentage (Women to Men) GNI per Capita, 2013	Overall GDI Rank, 2013
Argentina	72.6	79.9	9.6	10.0	22,849	11,975	52.4	74
Australia	80.3	84.8	13.1	12.5	47,553	35,551	74.8	19
Canada	79.3	83.6	12.2	12.3	49,272	34,612	70.2	23
France	78.3	85.2	11.4	10.9	44,139	29,580	67.0	12
New Zealand	79.2	83.0	12.6	12.5	38,656	26,695	69.1	34
Sweden	79.7	83.9	11.4	11.8	48,365	38,071	78.7	4
United Kingdom	78.6	82.5	11.8	12.8	42,632	27,589	64.7	35
United States	76.5	81.3	12.9	13.0	63,163	41,792	66.2	47
Uruguay	73.7	80.6	8.2	8.7	22,730	13,789	60.7	70

Note: 1. The GDI is a compilation of Human Development Indices that focuses on issues related to women.

Source: United Nations. 2014b. *Human Development Reports*. New York: United Nations Development Programme (hdr.undp.org/en/content/table-5-gender-related-development-index-gdi). Percentages calculated by authors.

Life expectancy is generally a good proxy measure for such things as income, education, social equality, and welfare supports. Note, for example, that the life expectancy (at birth) in Canada is high for both men and women; indeed, with the exceptions of Australia and Sweden, Canada ranks above the others. Note, too, that Canada's mean years of schooling for both men and women is quite high, though challenged by several other countries, especially the United States and (again) Australia.

The United States scores particularly high on income. In 2013, the gross national income per capita for American men was $63,163 and for women $41,792 (US dollars). The gross national income per capita for Canadian men that year was $49,272 and for women $34,612. Women in Canada in 2013 earned roughly 70 percent of what their male counterparts earned, compared with women in the United States, whose earnings were 66 percent that of men in the U.S. Looked at another way, Canadian men earned 78 percent of what their U.S. male counterparts earned, while Canadian women earned 83 percent of what their U.S. counterparts made.

Globally, Canada stands third on the list in terms of gender parity, behind Australia and Sweden. These gender differences in income are not explainable by education. Note, for example, the mean years of schooling for women versus men in the United States and, even more strikingly, in the lowest-ranking countries, Uruguay and Argentina. A more likely explanation is the perseverance of patriarchy (see the Introduction) and its impact on gender roles at home and in the workplace. In turn, social and economic inequalities translate into the political realm: Sweden, for example, regularly scores high on indexes of gender equality in government and in broader issues of democratic participation. These issues, in turn, bear on questions of distributional justice and social cohesion, elements of the welfare state discussed in Chapters 7 and 10.

Redefining the Welfare State

Wherever people live, they require many of the same services. The difference lies in whether these services are publicly provided, requiring larger tax revenues, or paid for by individuals out of their own pocket, in which case state taxes may be reduced. To the extent that services are paid for out of the public purse, they are de-commodified (Chapter 7); to the extent they are paid for privately, they are made into commodities, or **marketized**—becoming something purchased in the marketplace.

As the recent recession began in 2007, Canada spent 16.9 percent of its GDP on social expenditures (i.e., pensions, income support to people of working age, health, and social services), compared to the United States' 16.2 percent. But also compare Canada's total with Germany (25.2 percent), France (28.4 percent), Sweden (27.3 percent), and Norway (20.8 percent). By 2012, Canada's expenditures had risen to an estimated 19.3 percent, but were actually surpassed by the U.S. (19.5 percent) (all figures in Adema et al., 2011:21, Table 1.2).

Since the 1980s, Canada has faced increased pressure from business lobbyists and their political and media supporters to lower corporate and personal taxes and to accept the minimalist welfare state model of its American counterpart (Li, 1996) in the name of competitiveness. Table 13.3 shows the 2014 individual, corporate, and indirect tax rates for the countries examined here. Despite popular perceptions, often given heft by media and politicians, it will perhaps come as a shock that Canada, in fact, has the lowest individual tax rate (29 percent), one of the lowest corporate tax rates (26.5 percent)—both considerably below that of the United States—and an indirect tax rate (i.e., the Goods and Services Tax [GST], at 5 percent) that is second-lowest among the nine countries examined.

Table 13.3: Comparative Tax Rates for Select Countries, 2014

Country	Individual Tax Rate (%)	Corporate Tax Rate (%)	Indirect Tax Rate (%)
Argentina	35	35	21
Australia	45	30	10
Canada	**29**	**26.5**	**5**
France[1]	45	33.3	20
New Zealand	33	28	15
Sweden	57	22	25
United Kingdom	45	21	20
United States	39.6	40	0
Uruguay	30	25	22

Note: 1. Individual tax rate for 2013 only.
Source: KPMG International. 2014. "Tax Tools and Resources." KPMG (www.kpmg.com).

Note, of course, that high taxes do not necessarily mean high social expenditures. The money taken through taxes could go into state bureaucracies, the military, or infrastructure. These are choices that people, through their governments, make.

Ultimately, as the saying goes, "there is no free lunch." To quote another common expression, "taxes are the price of civilization"—of a functioning society. But what is society? And how large is it? We began with these questions, and briefly return to them now.

A Global Society?

The world today is clearly more interconnected—through trade, telecommunications, and travel—than ever before. To manage and assist these connections, world governments, corporations, and civil society groups have formed a number of organizations (e.g., the United Nations, the World Bank, the International Labour Organization,

Amnesty International, the Aga Khan Development Network). But, far from creating a harmonious **global village**, globalization has revealed and even fomented "hot spots" of tension, conflict, and war. What is the way forward? The answer to this question is not clear.

The noted sociologist Daniel Bell (quoted in Swedberg, 1990:222) once remarked that "people can only identify with society if the society feels a responsibility to them." At the global level, this would have to mean more than loans (often given at usurious rates of interest) or handouts. It would mean an entire rethinking of social and economic relationships (and interests) beyond the nation and state. It would, in fact, require the enactment at a deep psychological level of an "imagined community" (Anderson, 1983; see the Introduction) to which all people would see themselves belonging. This seems, at the present time, unlikely.

In the absence of broad-based levels of social justice and equality, it is understandable that conflicts will arise, some large, many small. For some, the fact of conflict raises issues of governance and power; or simply law and order. Centuries ago, Thomas Hobbes (Hobbes, 1651/2014) argued that human beings were incapable of governing themselves, that only through a strong, authoritarian figure could human beings be saved from an endless war of "all against all." The modern version of Hobbesian thinking is found in arguments that the United States and the American Empire are the lynchpin of economic, political, and military order in the world and must remain that way, otherwise chaos.

Others argue, however, that the problems currently facing the world are the result of too much power being centralized in the hands of a few states and economic actors (see Harvey, 2010) whose power is preventing the planet from dealing with issues such as warming, and thus impacting global society (Klein, 2014). To address the growing power imbalance, some have called for measures that will enhance economic and social justice. Piketty (2014), for example, has called for tax changes to deal with the increasing accumulation of wealth at the very top; as noted in Chapter 8, the richest 85 people in the world today own 50 percent of the world's wealth. Standing (2014) has called for a global extension of human rights that would protect the growing number of individual workers who find themselves in precarious employment. But others suggest that the way forward is in fact to break up the world's largest corporations and to return power to people through "de-globalizing" the economy (Bello, 2002)—an idea that harkens back to ideas of subsidiarity in Chapter 4 regarding the level at which decisions should be made for reasons of both efficiency and democracy.

Conclusion

For several hundred years, the people inhabiting the political territory of Canada have interacted, sometimes in hostility, sometimes in amity, often in tolerance, and perhaps even more often in unconsciousness. The creation of a Canadian society has meant the intensification of these interactions and knowledge (or at least imagined knowledge) of a large assortment of others, from Cape Spear to Vancouver Island to the Arctic Circle. No society remains static, however, and even less so in the 21st century.

Canada still faces many challenges, such as ensuring that all citizens are included socially, politically, and economically—note the continuing discrepancy between men's and women's incomes (shown in Table 13.2)—and ensuring the enactment of **deep democracy** as the lived experience in the daily lives of all Canadians, no matter their class, race, gender, or religion, whether in their workplaces, their homes, or their communities.

Canada is one of the world's wonders. Against many odds, Canadians through the centuries have constructed a society that, for the most part, is prosperous and tolerant, progressive and civil. The torch is thus passed to future generations to continue the Canadian experiment into the 21st century.

Notes

1. The HDRO defines GNI per capita as aggregate income of an economy generated by its production and its ownership of factors of production, less the incomes paid for the use of factors of production owned by the rest of the world, converted to international dollars using purchasing power parity (PPP) rates, divided by mid-year population (United Nations, 2014b).
2. For several years in the early 2000s, Canada held first place on the human development index. As recently as 2006, Canada ranked number three in the world, just behind Iceland and Norway. In 2014, Norway ranked number one. Canada's slip to eighth place is partly due to other countries' improving their scores on the components making up the index.

Key Terms

deep democracy
global village
Human Development Index
marketized

Critical Thinking Questions

1. Do you think the countries chosen here are good comparates with Canada?
2. What is meant by "development"?
3. Is a global society possible?
4. Is democracy compatible with economic inequality?
5. What do you think Canada will be like in 2050?

Recommended Readings

Bell, Daniel. 1996. *The Cultural Contradictions of Capitalism*. 20th anniversary ed. New York: Basic Books.
Bell's book remains a classic in sociology, arguing that capitalism brings about cultural changes that, in turn, destroy capitalism's underpinnings.

Galbraith, John Kenneth. 1997. *The Great Crash 1929*. Boston: Mariner.
Written by Canada's greatest contributor to the economics profession, Galbraith's account of the 1929 crash is humorous, concise, and remarkably current in explaining some of the reasons for market instability.

Harvey, David. 2010. *The Enigma of Capital and the Crises of Capitalism*. New York: Oxford University Press.
This book explains in clear terms the concept of finance capital and how it has contributed to the ongoing economic and political crises of our time.

Pickett, Kate, and Richard Wilkinson. 2011. *The Spirit Level: Why Greater Equality Makes Societies Stronger*. London: Bloomsbury Press.
Pickett and Wilkinson present a strong case that individuals, both rich and poor, are healthier and happier the greater the degree of equality in the society around them.

Piketty, Thomas. 2014. *Capital in the Twenty-First Century*. Translated by A. Goldhammer. Cambridge, MA: Belknap.
Piketty's book is already approaching the status of a classic. He uses an array of data sets covering 20 countries, going back to the 19th century, to examine and explain current inequalities of wealth and how this can be addressed.

Related Websites

Central Intelligence Agency (CIA)
www.cia.gov/library/publications/the-world-factbook/index.html
This agency was established in 1947 as a civilian intelligence agency of the United States government. As such, it gathers a huge amount of information, much of which can be found on its site.

International Labour Organization (ILO)
www.ilo.org/global/lang--en/index.htm
This is a United Nations organization that deals with labour issues.

United Nations' Human Development Reports
hdr.undp.org/en
This United Nations office is housed in New York.

APPENDIX 1

CANADIAN FEDERAL ELECTION RESULTS SINCE CONFEDERATION

Year	Conservatives	Liberals					Other	Total
1867	101	80						181
1872	103	97						200
1874	73	133						206
1878	137	69						206
1882	139	71						210
1887	123	92						215
1891	123	92						215
1896	89	117					7	213
1900	78	128					8	214
1904	75	139						214
1908	85	133					3	221
1911	133	86					2	221
			Unionists					
1917		82	153					235
			Liberal Conservatives	**Progressives**				
1921		116	50	65			4	235
1925	116	101		24			4	245
			Liberal Progressives		**United Farmers**			
1926	91	116	9	13	11		5	245
1930	137	88	3	2	10		5	245
			CCF	**Social Credit**				
1935	39	171	7	17			11	245
1940	39	178	8	10			10	245

Year	Conservatives	Liberals				Other	Total
	Progressive Conservatives						
1945	67	125	28	13		12	245
1949	41	190	13	10		8	262
1953	51	170	23	15		6	265
1957	112	105	25	19		4	265
1958	208	48	8			1	265
			NDP				
1962	116	99	19	30		1	265
1963	95	129	17	24			265
					Créditistes		
1965	97	131	21	5	9	2	265
1968	72	155	22		14	1	264
1972	107	109	31		15	2	264
1974	97	136	17		9	5	264
1979	136	114	26		6		282
1980	103	147	32				282
1984	211	40	30			1	282
1988	169	83	43				295
				Reform	Bloc Québécois		
1993	2	177	9	52	54	1	295
1997	20	155	21	60	44	1	301
				Alliance			
2000	12	172	13	66	38		301
	Conservatives						
2004	99	135	19		54	1	308
2006	124	103	29		51	1	308
2008	143	77	37		49	2	308
2011	166	34	103		4	1	308

Source: Elections Canada On-Line, "Past Elections" (www.elections.ca/content.aspx?section=ele&document=index&dir=pas/41ge&lang=e). Modified February 10, 2014.

APPENDIX 2

CANADIAN PRIME MINISTERS, GOVERNMENTS, AND MAJOR POLICIES SINCE CONFEDERATION

Prime Minister	Party	Dates of Administration	Major Policies/Events
Sir John A. Macdonald	C	July 1867–Nov. 1873	Confederation; Red River Rebellion; Manitoba, British Columbia, and Prince Edward Island join Canada
Alexander Mackenzie	L	Nov. 1873–Oct. 1878	Supreme Court of Canada established; Intercontinental Railway completed; first Indian Act passed
Sir John A. Macdonald	C	Oct. 1878–June 1891	National Policy; the North-West Rebellion; Louis Riel hanged
Sir John J. C. Abbott	C	June 1891–Nov. 1892	
Sir John S. Thompson	C	Dec. 1892–Dec. 1894	
Sir Mackenzie Bowell	C	Dec. 1894–Apr. 1896	
Sir Charles Tupper	C	Apr. 1896–July 1896	
Sir Wilfrid Laurier	L	July 1896–Oct. 1911	Manitoba Schools Act; Klondike Gold Rush; Boer War; free trade election (lost)
Sir Robert Borden	C	Oct. 1911–Oct. 1917	First World War; Conscription Crisis; income tax introduced
Sir Robert Borden	U	Oct. 1917–July 1920	War ends; White women gain federal vote; Winnipeg general strike
Arthur Meighen	U	July 1920–Dec. 1921	
W. L. Mackenzie King	L	Dec. 1921–June 1926	King-Byng Constitutional Affair

Prime Minister	Party	Dates of Administration	Major Policies/Events
Arthur Meighen	C	June 1926–Sept. 1926	
W. L. Mackenzie King	L	Sept. 1926–Aug. 1930	Great Depression begins; Cairine Wilson appointed Canada's first female senator
R. B. Bennett	C	Aug. 1930–Oct. 1935	Statute of Westminster; Co-operative Commonwealth Federation (CCF) founded; Regina riot; Social Credit elected in Alberta
W. L. Mackenzie King	L	Oct. 1935–Nov. 1948	Second World War; beginning of welfare state; second Conscription Crisis; CCF elected in Saskatchewan
Louis St. Laurent	L	Nov. 1948–June 1957	Korean War
John Diefenbaker	PC	June 1957–Apr. 1963	Avro Arrow cancelled; Canadian Bill of Rights; Status Indians gain vote
Lester B. Pearson	L	Apr. 1963–Apr. 1968	Maple Leaf flag; medicare
Pierre Trudeau	L	Apr. 1968–June 1979	Bilingualism; multiculturalism; the FLQ Crisis; capital punishment abolished; PQ elected in Quebec
Joe Clarke	PC	June 1979–March 1980	
Pierre Trudeau	L	March 1980–June 1984	Quebec Referendum; National Energy Program; the Constitution Act, 1982
John Turner	L	June 1984–Sept. 1984	
Brian Mulroney	PC	Sept. 1984–June 1993	Free Trade Agreement; Meech Lake Accord; Charlottetown Accord and Referendum; Goods and Services Tax (GST); Oka Crisis
Kim Campbell	PC	June 1993–Oct. 1993	First female prime minister
Jean Chrétien	L	Oct. 1993–Nov. 2003	North American Free Trade Agreement; Quebec Referendum; Clarity Act; 9/11 attacks; Canadian military involvement in Afghanistan War
Paul Martin	L	Nov. 2003–Feb. 2006	Gomery Inquiry; same-sex marriage becomes law

Prime Minister	Party	Dates of Administration	Major Policies/Events
Stephen Harper	C	Feb. 2006–	GST cuts; end of Afghan War; recognition of Quebec "nation"; political scandals (robo-calls, expenditures, the Senate, the Duffy Affair); residential schools apology; increased use of omnibus bills and prorogation; petroleum policies

Legend: C = Conservative; L = Liberal; U = Unionist; PC = Progressive Conservative

Source: Matheson, W. A. 2009. "Prime Minister." *Canadian Encyclopedia On-Line* (www.thecanadianencyclopedia.com/index.cfm?PgNm=TCE&Params=A1ARTA0006474). Modified May 5, 2014.

REFERENCES

Abel, Kerry. 1993. *Drum Songs: Glimpses of Dene History*. Montreal and Kingston: McGill-Queen's University Press.

Abella, Irving, and Harold Troper. 1982. *None Is Too Many: Canada and the Jews in Europe, 1933–1948*. Toronto: Lester and Orpen Dennys.

Aboriginal Affairs and Northern Development Canada. "Treaty Texts – Treaties No. 1 and No. 2" (www.aadnc-aandc.gc.ca/eng/1100100028664/1100100028665).

Abrams, Philip. 1988. "Notes on the Difficulty of Studying the State." *Journal of Historical Sociology* 1(1):58–89.

Absolon, Kathleen E. (Minogiizhigokwe). 2011. *Kaandossiwin: How We Come to Know*. Halifax, NS: Fernwood.

Adams, Howard. 1989. *Prison of Grass: Canada from a Native Point of View*. 2nd ed. Saskatoon: Fifth House Publishers.

Adams, Howard. 1999. *Tortured People: The Politics of Colonization*. Revised ed. Penticton, BC: Theytus Books.

Adams, Michael. 1998. *Sex in the Snow: Canadian Social Values at the End of the Millennium*. Toronto: Penguin.

Adams, Michael. 2003. *Fire and Ice: The United States, Canada, and the Myth of Converging Values*. Toronto: Penguin.

Adams, Michael. 2007. *Unlikely Utopia: The Surprising Triumph of Canadian Pluralism*. Toronto: Viking Press.

Adema, Willem, Pauline Fron, and Maxine Ladaique. 2011. "Is the European Welfare State Really More Expensive?" *OECD Social, Employment, and Migration Working Papers* No. 124. Paris, France: OECD.

Aitken, Hugh G. J. 1959. "The Changing Structure of the Canadian Economy." Pp. 3–35 in *The American Economic Impact on Canada*, edited by H. G. J. Aitken. Durham, NC: Duke University Press.

Albrow, Martin. 1997. *The Global Age: State and Society beyond Modernity*. Stanford, CA: Stanford University Press.

Alexander, Colin. 2014. "In Canada's North, a Suicide Epidemic." *National Post On-Line*, September 10.

Alford, B. W. E. 1996. *Britain in the World Economy since 1880*. London: Longman.

Alfred, Gerald R. 1995. *Heeding the Voices of Our Ancestors: Kahnawake Mohawk Politics and the Rise of Native Nationalism*. Toronto: Oxford University Press.

Alfred, Taiaiake. 2005. *Wasâse: Indigenous Pathways to Action and Freedom*. Peterborough, ON: Broadview Press.

Allain, Kristi A. 2012. "'Real Fast and Tough': The Construction of Canadian Hockey Masculinity." Pp. 359–372 in *Rethinking Sociology in the 21st Century*, edited by M. Webber and K. Bezanson. 3rd ed. Toronto: Canadian Scholars' Press.

Allison, Derek. 1983. "Fourth World Education in Canada and the Faltering Promise of Native Teacher Education." *Journal of Canadian Studies* 18(3):102–119.

Anderson, Benedict. 1983. *Imagined Communities*. London: Verso.

Angus, Murray. 1991. *And the Last Shall Be First: Native Policy in an Era of Cutbacks*. Toronto: NC Press.

Antone, Eileen M. 2000. "Empowering Aboriginal Views in Aboriginal Education." *Canadian Journal of Native Education* 24(2):92–101.

Asch, Michael. 2000. "Self-Government in the New Millennium." Pp. 65–73 in *Nation to Nation: Aboriginal Sovereignty and the Future of Canada*, edited by J. Bird, L. Land, and M. McAdam. Toronto: Irwin.

Baer, D., E. Grabb, and W. Johnston. 1993. "National Character, Regional Culture, and the Values of Canadians and Americans." *Canadian Review of Sociology and Anthropology* 30(1):13–36.

Baker, Maureen. 1996. "Social Assistance and the Employability of Mothers: Two Models from Cross-National Research." *The Canadian Journal of Sociology* 21(4):483–504.

Baldwin, Gordon C. 1967. *How Indians Really Lived*. New York: G. P. Putnam's Sons.

Baldwin, John R., and Guy Gallatly. 2005. *Global Links: Long-Term Trends in Foreign Investment and Foreign Control in Canada, 1960 to 2000*. Statistics Canada, Cat. no. 11-622-MIE, no. 08. Ottawa: Statistics Canada.

Baldwin, John R., and Walong Gu. 2004. *Trade Liberalization: Export Market Participation, Productivity Growth, and Innovation*. Statistics Canada Cat. no. 11-F0027-MIE. Ottawa: Statistics Canada.

Balikci, Asen. 1970. *The Netsilik Eskimo*. Garden City, NY: The American Museum of Natural History.

Balthazar, Louis. 1993. "The Faces of Quebec Nationalism." Pp. 92–107 in *A Passion for Identity: An Introduction to Canadian Studies*, edited by D. Taras, B. Rasporich, and E. Mandel. Scarborough, ON: Nelson Canada.

Balthazar, Louis. 1997. "Quebec and the Ideal of Federalism." Pp. 45–60 in *Quebec Society: Critical Issues*, edited by M. Fournier, M. Rosenberg, and D. White. Scarborough, ON: Prentice-Hall Canada.

Barber, Benjamin. 1996. *Jihad vs. McWorld*. New York: Ballantine.

Barman, Jean, Yvonne Hébert, and Don McCaskill. 1986. "The Legacy of the Past: An Overview." Pp. 1–22 in *Indian Education in Canada*, vol. I: *The Legacy*, edited by J. Barman, Y. Hébert, and D. McCaskill. Vancouver: UBC Press.

Barron, F. Laurie, and Joseph Garcea. 1999. "The Genesis of Urban Reserves and the Role of Governmental Self-Interest." Pp. 22–52 in *Urban Indian Reserves: Forging New Relationships in Saskatchewan*, edited by F. L. Barron and J. Garcea. Saskatoon: Purich.

Battiste, Marie. 2000. *Reclaiming Indigenous Voice and Vision*. Vancouver: UBC Press.

Battiste, Marie, and James (Sa'ke'j) Youngblood Henderson. 2000. *Protecting Indigenous Knowledge and Heritage*. Saskatoon: Purich.

Bauch, Hubert. 2006. "Quebec 'Nation' Debate Divides French, English: Poll." *Montreal Gazette*, November 11 (www.canada.com/story.html?id=23ba4837-5854-458d-b513-0c2d2d0b5ea3).

Bear Heart. 1998. *The Wind Is My Mother: The Life and Teachings of a Native American Shaman*. New York: Berkley Books.

Beattie, Owen, and John Geiger. 1987. *Frozen in Time: Unlocking the Secrets of the Franklin Expedition*. Saskatoon: Western Producer Prairie Books.

Behiels, Michael D., and Matthew Hayday. 2011. *Contemporary Quebec: Selected Readings and Commentaries*. Montreal and Kingston: McGill-Queen's University Press.

Bell, Daniel. 1993. "The Third Technological Revolution and Its Possible Socioeconomic Consequences." Pp. 351–365 in *Sources: Notable Selections in Sociology*, edited by K. Finsterbusch and J. Schwartz. Guilford, CT: Dushkin.

Bell, Daniel. 1996. *The Cultural Contradictions of Capitalism*. 20th anniversary ed. New York: Basic Books.

Bell, Edward, 1993. *Social Classes and Social Credit*. Montreal and Kingston: McGill-Queen's University Press.

Bellamy, Donald, and Allan Irving. 1981. "Pioneers." Pp. 27–46 in *Canadian Social Welfare*, edited by J. Turner and F. Turner. Don Mills, ON: Collier Macmillan Canada.

Bello, Walden. 2002. *Deglobalization: Ideas for a New Economy*. London: Zed Books.

Bercuson, David, and Barry Cooper. 1991. *Deconfederation: Canada without Quebec*. Toronto: Key Porter Books.

Berdahl, Loleen, and Roger Gibbins. 2014. *Looking West: Regional Transformation and the Future of Canada*. Toronto: University of Toronto Press.

Berger, Carl. 1976. *The Sense of Power: Studies in the Ideas of Canadian Imperialism 1867–1914*. Toronto: University of Toronto Press.

Bernard, Paul. 1996. "Canada as a Social Experiment." *The Canadian Journal of Sociology* 21(2):245–258.

Berton, Pierre. 1958. *The Klondike Fever: The Life and Death of the Last Great Gold Rush*. New York: Knopf.

Berton, Pierre. 1980. *The Invasion of Canada, 1812–1813*. Toronto: McClelland & Stewart.

Berton, Pierre. 1988. *The Arctic Grail*. Markham: Penguin.

Berton, Pierre. 1991. *The Great Depression, 1929–1939*. Toronto: Penguin.

Bird, John, Lorraine Land, and Murray McAdam, eds. 2000. *Self-Government in the New Millennium: Nation to Nation: Aboriginal Sovereignty and the Future of Canada*. Toronto: Irwin Publishing.

Bissoondath, Neil. 1994. *Selling Illusions: The Cult of Multiculturalism in Canada*. Toronto: Penguin.

Black, Conrad. 1977. *Duplessis*. Toronto: McClelland & Stewart.

Bobiwash, A. Rodney. 1997. "Native Urban Self-Government and the Politics of Self-Determination." Pp. 84–94 in *The Meeting Place: Aboriginal Life in Toronto*, edited by F. Sanderson and H. Howard-Bobiwash. Toronto: Native Canadian Centre.

Boldt, Menno. 1993. *Surviving as Indians: The Challenge of Self-Government*. Toronto: University of Toronto Press.

Bone, Robert M. 1988. "Cultural Persistence and Country Food: The Case of the Norman Wells Project." *The Western Canadian Anthropologist* 5:61–79.

Bone, Robert M. 1992. *The Geography of the Canadian North: Issues and Challenges*. Toronto: Oxford University Press.

Bourgault, Pierre. 1991. *Now or Never: Manifesto for an Independent Quebec*. Toronto: Key Porter Books.

Bowler, Arthur. 1993. "Introduction." Pp. 291–309 in *Reappraisals in Canadian History: Pre-Confederation*, edited by A. D. Gilbert, G. M. Wallace, and R. M. Bray. Scarborough: Prentice-Hall Canada.

Boyer, Robert, and Daniel Drache (eds). 1996. *States against Markets*. London: Routledge.

Bradley, Paul G., and G. Campbell Watkins. 2003. "Canada and the U.S.: A Seamless Energy Border?" *The Border Papers*, no. 178, April. Toronto: C. D. Howe Institute.

Brascoupé, Simon. 2000. "Aboriginal Peoples' Vision of the Future: Interweaving Traditional Knowledges and New Technologies of the Heart." Pp. 411–432 in *Canadian Aboriginal Issues*, edited by D. Long and O. P. Dickason. Toronto: Harcourt Canada.

Braz, Albert. 2003. *The False Traitor: Louis Riel in Canadian Culture*. Toronto: University of Toronto Press.

Brimelow, Peter. 1986. *The Patriot Game*. Toronto: Key Porter Books.

Brodie, Janine. 1990. *The Political Economy of Canadian Regionalism*. Toronto: Harcourt Brace Jovanovich Canada.

Brody, Hugh. 1987. *Living Arctic: Hunters of the Canadian North*. Vancouver: Douglas & McIntyre.

Brookes, Sonia. 1991. "The Persistence of Native Educational Policy in Canada." Pp. 163–180 in *The Cultural Maze: Complex Questions on Native Destiny in Western* Canada, edited by J. W. Friesen. Calgary: Detselig.

Brown, Wallace. 1993. "Victorious in Defeat: The American Loyalists in Canada." Pp. 241–250 in *Reappraisals in Canadian History: Pre-Confederation*, edited by A. D. Gilbert, G. M. Wallace, and R. M. Bray. Scarborough, ON: Prentice-Hall Canada.

Brunelle, Dorval. 1999. "Free Trade Illusions in Quebec." *Le Monde Diplomatique* (April), 15.

Brunet, M. 1993. "The British Conquest and the Decline of the French-Canadian Bourgeoisie." Pp. 198–215 in *Reappraisals in Canadian History: Pre-Confederation*, edited by A. D. Gilbert, G. M. Wallace, and R. M. Bray. Scarborough, ON: Prentice-Hall Canada.

Brym, Robert J. 2014. "Politics and Social Movements." Pp. 438–461 in *New Society*, edited by R. J. Brym. 7th ed. Toronto: Nelson Canada.

Brym, Robert J., and R. James Sacouman, eds. 1979. *Underdevelopment and Social Movements in Atlantic Canada*. Toronto: New Hogtown Press.

Buckley, Helen. 1993. *From Wooden Ploughs to Welfare: Why Indian Policy Failed in the Prairie Provinces*. Montreal and Kingston: McGill-Queen's University Press.

Burbach, Roger, Orlando Nunez, and Boris Kagarlitsky. 1997. *Globalization and Its Discontents*. London: Pluto Press.

Byers, Michael. 2014. "The North Pole Is a Distraction." *The Globe and Mail*, August 20, p. A11.

Cairns, Alan C. 2000. *Citizens Plus: Aboriginal Peoples and the Canadian State*. Vancouver: UBC Press.

Cajete, Gregory. 1994. *Look to the Mountain: An Ecology of Indigenous Education*. Durango, CO: Kivaki Press.

Campbell, Bruce, and Ed Finn. 2006. *Living with Uncle*. Toronto: James Lorimer.

Canadian Association of Petroleum Producers (CAPP). 2014. "Basic Statistics." Canadian Association of Petroleum Producers. Retrieved October 1, 2014 (www.capp.ca/library/statistics/basic/Pages/default.aspx).

Canadian Chamber of Commerce. 2013. *Opportunity Found: Improving the Participation of Aboriginal Peoples in Canada's Workforce*. Ottawa: Canadian Chamber of Commerce. (www2.viu.ca/aboriginal/docs/Opportunity-Found-131217.pdf).

The Canadian Encyclopedia. 2014. "Quebec Values Charter."

Canadian Northern Economic Development Agency. 2013. "Northern Economic Index, 2011–12." Ottawa: Canadian Northern Economic Development Agency (www.cannor.gc.ca/eng/1387900596709/1387900617810).

Cardinal, Harold. 1969. *The Unjust Society: The Tragedy of Canada's Indians*. Edmonton: Hurtig.

Cardinal, Harold. 1977. *The Rebirth of Canada's Indians*. Edmonton: Hurtig.

Careless, J. M. S. 1970. *Canada: A Story of Challenge*. Toronto: Macmillan and Company.

Carlson, Leonard. 1981. *Indians, Bureaucrats, and the Land: The Dawes Act and the Decline of Indian Farming*. Westport, CT: Greenwood Press.

Carr, Edward H. 1990. *What Is History?* Markham: Penguin Books.

Carroll, William K. 2010. *The Making of a Transnational Capitalist Class: Corporate Power in the 21st Century*. London: Zed Books.

Carter, Sarah. 1993. *Lost Harvests: Prairie Indian Reserve Farmers and Government Policy*. Montreal and Kingston: McGill-Queen's University Press.

Catton, William R., and Riley E. Dunlap. 1980. "A New Ecological Paradigm for Post-Exuberant Sociology." *American Behavioral Scientist* 24(1):15–47.

Chalmers, J. W. 1974. "Marguerite Bourgeoys, Preceptress of New France." Pp. 4–20 in *Profiles of Canadian Educators*, edited by R. S. Patterson, J. W. Chalmers, and J. W. Friesen. Toronto: D. C. Heath.

Chiste, Katherine Beaty. 2005. "Getting Tough on Crime the Aboriginal Way: Alternative Justice Initiatives in Canada." Pp. 218–232 in *Hidden in Plain Sight: Contributions of Aboriginal Peoples to Canadian Identity and Culture*, edited by D. Newhouse, C. Voyageur, and D. Beavon. Toronto: University of Toronto Press.

Chodos, Robert, and Eric Hamovitch. 1991. *Quebec and the American Dream*. Toronto: Between the Lines.

Chomsky, Noam. 2001. *9–11*. New York: Seven Stories Press.

Chorney, Harold. 1989. *The Deficit and Debt Management: An Alternative to Monetarism*. Ottawa: Canadian Centre for Policy Alternatives.

Citizens for Public Justice. 2012. "Poverty Trends Scorecard 2012." Ottawa: Citizens for Public Justice (www.cpj.ca/poverty-trends-scorecard-canada-2012).

Citizenship and Immigration Canada. 1996. "Citizenship and Immigration Statistics 1996." Cat. no. MP22-/1996. Ottawa: Citizenship and Immigration Canada.

City of Toronto. 2014. "Labour Force Survey Data—Educational Attainment." Toronto: Data Centre. Retrieved July 28, 2014 (www1.toronto.ca/wps/portal/contentonly?vgnextoid=0bb e3c6d9c8ba310VgnVCM10000071d60f89RCRD&vgnextchannel=e71032d0b6d1e310V gnVCM10000071d60f89RCRD&vgnextfmt=default).

Clark, Samuel D., J. Paul Grayson, and Linda M. Grayson. 1975. *Prophecy and Protest: Social Movements in Twentieth-Century Canada.* Toronto: Gage.

Clarkson, Stephen. 1985. *Canada and the Reagan Challenge.* Toronto: Lorimer.

Clarkson, Stephen. 2002a. *Uncle Sam and Us: Globalization, Neoconservatism, and the Canadian State.* Toronto: University of Toronto Press.

Clarkson, Stephen. 2002b. "What Uncle Sam Wants...." *The Globe and Mail,* December 2, p. A13.

Clarkson, Stephen. 2008. *Does North America Exist?* Toronto: University of Toronto Press.

Clarkson, Stephen, and Christina McCall. 1990. *Trudeau and Our Times,* vol. 1: *The Magnificent Obsession.* Toronto: McClelland & Stewart.

Clement, Wallace. 1975. *The Canadian Corporate Elite.* Toronto: McClelland & Stewart.

Clement, Wallace, ed. 1997. *Understanding Canada: Building on the New Canadian Political Economy.* Montreal and Kingston: McGill-Queen's University Press.

Clement, Wallace, and Glen Williams. 1989. *The New Canadian Political Economy.* Montreal and Kingston: McGill-Queen's University Press.

Clerici, Naila. 1999. "The Cree of James Bay and the Construction of their Identity for the Media." Pp. 143–165 in *Futures and Identities,* edited by M. Behiels. Montreal: Association for Canadian Studies.

Cline, Michael S. 1975. *Tannik School: The Impact of Education on the Eskimos of Anaktuvuk Pass.* Anchorage: Alaska Methodist University Press.

Coates, Ken S., P. Whitney Lackenbauer, William R. Morrison, and Greg Poelzer. 2008. *Arctic Front: Defending Canada in the Far North.* Toronto: Thomas Allen.

Cohen, Andrew. 1990. *A Deal Undone: The Making and Breaking of the Meech Lake Accord.* Vancouver: Douglas & McIntyre.

Collins, Randall. 1982. *Sociological Insight: An Introduction to Non-Obvious Sociology.* Oxford: Oxford University Press.

Colombo, John Robert. 1994. *Colombo's All-Time Great Canadian Quotations.* Toronto: Stoddart.

Commissioner of the Environment and Sustainable Development. 2014. *Commissioner of the Environment and Sustainable Development Releases Fall 2014 Report.* October 7. Ottawa: Office of the Auditor General of Canada.

Condon, Richard G. 1987. *Inuit Youth: Growth and Change in the Canadian Arctic.* Newark, NJ: Rutgers University Press.

Conrad, Margaret, Alvin Finkel, and Cornelius Jaenen. 1993. *History of Canadian Peoples: Beginnings to 1867.* Toronto: Copp Clark Pitman.

Conway, John. 2004. *Debts to Pay: The Future of Federalism in Quebec.* 3rd ed. Toronto: James Lorimer and Company.

Conway, John. 2014. *The Rise of the New West: The History of a Region in Confederation.* 4th ed. Toronto: James Lorimer and Company.

Cook, Ramsay. 1995. *Canada, Quebec, and the Uses of Nationalism.* 2nd ed. Toronto: McClelland & Stewart.

Cooke, Martin, and Daniéle Bélanger. 2006. "Migration Theories and First Nations Mobility: Towards a Systems Perspective." *Canadian Review of Sociology and Anthropology* 43(2):141–165.

Cooke, Martin, and David Long. 2011. "Moving Beyond the Politics of Aboriginal Well-being, Health, and Healing." Pp. 292–327 in *Visions of the Heart: Canadian Aboriginal Issues*, edited by D. Long & O.P. Dickason. 3rd ed. Don Mills, ON: Oxford University Press.

Cormier, Ryan. 2014. "Alberta Court of Appeal Rules Provincial Laws Don't Have to Be Bilingual." *Edmonton Journal*, February 21.

Cornellier, Manon. 1995. *The Bloc*. Toronto: James Lorimer and Company.

Cornish, George H. 1881. *Encyclopedia of Methodism in Canada*. Toronto: Methodist Book and Publishing Company.

Costs of War. 2014a. "US and Allies Killed." Watson Institute (costsofwar.org/article/us-killed-0).

Costs of War. 2014b. "Afghanistan: At Least 21,000 Civilians Killed." Watson Institute (costsofwar.org/article/afghan-civilians).

Coulombe, Pierre A. 1998. "Quebec in the Federation." Pp. 187–197 in *Challenges to Canadian Federalism*, edited by M. Westmacott and H. Mellon. Scarborough, ON: Prentice-Hall Canada.

Courchene, Thomas. 1997. *The Nation State in a Global/Information Era: Policy Challenges*. Kingston: John Deutsch Institute for the Study of Economic Policy, Queen's University.

Courchene, Thomas. 1998. *From Heartland to North American Region State: The Social, Fiscal, and Federal Evolution of Ontario*. Toronto: University of Toronto Press.

Couture, Claude. 1998. *Paddling with the Current: Pierre Elliott Trudeau, Etienne Parent, Liberalism, and Nationalism in Canada*. Edmonton: University of Alberta Press.

Couture, Joseph E. 1991. "The Role of Native Elders: Emergent Issues." Pp. 201–218 in *The Cultural Maze: Complex Questions on Native Destiny in Western Canada*, edited by J. W. Friesen. Calgary: Detselig.

Couture, Joseph E. 2008. "First Nations Say No but Gov't Continues to Persist with Offer." *Saskatoon SAGE* (August 8):1.

Creighton, Donald. 1970. *Canada's First Century, 1867–1967*. Toronto: Macmillan of Canada.

Cross, Ronald, and Héléne Sévigny. 1994. *Lasagna: The Man behind the Mask*. Vancouver: Talonbooks.

Crowe, Keith J. 1974. *A History of the Original Peoples of Northern Canada*. Kingston: Queen's University Press.

Cruikshank, Julie. 1998. "Discovery of Gold on the Klondike: Perspectives from Oral Tradition." Pp. 435–458 in *Reading beyond Words: Contexts for Native History*, edited by J. S. H. Brown and E. Vibert. Peterborough: Broadview Press.

CTV. 2014. "Timeline: Canada's Involvement in Afghanistan." CTV (www.ctvnews.ca/canada/timeline-canada-s-involvement-in-afghanistan-1.1814698).

Curtis, James, Edward Grabb, and Neil Guppy. 1999. *Social Inequality in Canada: Patterns, Problems, and Policies*. Scarborough, ON: Prentice-Hall Canada.

Dauvergne, Mia. 2012. "Adult Correctional Statistics in Canada, 2010/2011." *Juristat*. Ottawa: Statistics Canada (www.statcan.gc.ca/pub/85-002-x/2012001/article/11715-eng.htm#r11).

Davis, Wade. 2009. *The Wayfinders: Why Ancient Wisdom Matters in the Modern World*. Toronto: House of Anansi Press.

Denis, Claude. 1989. "The Genesis of American Capitalism: An Historical Inquiry into State Theory." *Journal of Historical Sociology* 2(4):328–356.

Denis, Claude. 1993. "Quebec-as-Distinct-Society as Conventional Wisdom: The Constitutional Silence of Anglo-Canadian Sociologists." *Canadian Journal of Sociology* 18(3):251–270.

Denis, Claude. 1997. *We Are Not You: First Nations and Canadian Modernity*. Peterborough, ON: Broadview Press.

Denton, Frank. 1983. "The Labour Force." *Historical Statistics of Canada*. 2nd ed. Ottawa: Statistics Canada.

Deutsch, Karl W., ed. 1980. *Politics and Government: How People Decide Their Fate*. Boston: Houghton Mifflin.

Diamond, Jared. 2005. *Collapse: How Societies Choose to Fail or Succeed*. New York: Viking Press.

Dickason, Olive Patricia. 1984. *The Myth of the Savage and the Beginnings of French Colonialism in the Americas*. Edmonton: University of Alberta Press.

Dickason, Olive Patricia. 2002. *Canada's First Nations: A History of Founding Peoples from Earliest Times*. Toronto: McClelland & Stewart.

Dickason, Olive Patricia, and William Newbigging. 2010. *A Concise History of Canada's First Nations*. Don Mills, ON: Oxford University Press.

Dickinson, John, and Brian Young. 2008. *A Short History of Quebec*. 4th ed. Montreal and Kingston: McGill-Queen's University Press.

Dilthey, Wilhelm. 1961. *Pattern and Meaning in History*. London: Harper and Row.

Di Matteo, Livio. 2014. "Quebec and the Economics of Diminishment." *Troy Media*, March 18 (www.troymedia.com/2014/03/18/quebec-and-the-economics-of-diminishment).

Dion, Joseph F. 1979. *My Tribe: The Crees*. Calgary: Glenbow Museum.

Dobbin, Murray. 2008. "Afghanistan Transforms Canada: To Play Junior Partner to Empire, We've Militarized Our Identity." *The Tyee*, August 11 (thetyee.ca/Views/2008/08/11/AfghanCan).

Doern, B., and B. W. Tomlin. 1991. *Faith and Fear: The Free Trade Story*. Toronto: Stoddart.

Drache, Daniel. 1995. "Introduction: Celebrating Innis: The Man, the Legacy." Pp. xiii–lix in *Staples, Markets, and Cultural Change. Selected Essays*, edited by D. Drache. Montreal and Kingston: McGill-Queen's University Press.

Drees, Laurie Meijer. 2013. *Teaching Histories: Stories from Canada's Indian Hospitals*. Edmonton: University of Alberta Press.

Driedger, Leo. 1991. *The Urban Factor: Sociology of Canadian Cities*. Oxford: Oxford University Press.

Dubuc, Alain. 2001. "The Lafontaine-Baldwin Lecture: Canadian Nationalism." In *Dialogue on Democracy: The LaFontaine-Baldwin Lectures 2000–2005*, edited by R. Griffiths. Toronto: Penguin Canada.

Dufour, Christian. 1990. *A Canadian Challenge: Le defi quebecois*. Halifax, NS: Oolichan Books and the Institute for Research on Public Policy.

Dumond, Don E. 1977. *The Eskimos and Aleuts*. London: Thames and Hudson.

Duncan, Sarah J. 1971. *The Imperialist*. Originally published in 1904. Toronto: McClelland & Stewart.

Dunn, Christopher. 1995. *Canadian Political Debates*. Toronto: McClelland & Stewart.

Dunning, John. 1983. "Changes in the Level and Structure of International Production: The Last One Hundred Years." Pp. 84–139 in *The Growth of International Business*, edited by M. Casson. London: George Allen and Unwin.

Durkheim, Émile. 1964. *The Division of Labor in Society*. Originally published in 1893. New York: The Free Press.

Durkheim, Émile. 1978. *Elementary Forms of Religious Life*. Originally published in 1912. London: George Allen and Unwin.

Dyck, Rand. 1998. *Canadian Politics*. Concise ed. Toronto: Nelson Canada.

Dyer, Gwynne. 2008. *Climate Wars*. Toronto: Random House Canada.

Dymond, Bill, and Michael Hart. 2003. "Canada and the Global Challenge: Finding a Place to Stand." *The Border Papers* 180 (March). Toronto: C. D. Howe Institute.

Easterbrook, W. T., and Hugh G. J. Aitken. 1988. *Canadian Economic History*. Toronto: University of Toronto Press.

Eccles, W. J. 1993a. "The French Forces in North America during the Seven Years War." Pp. 162–174 in *Reappraisals in Canadian History: Pre-Confederation*, edited by A. D. Gilbert, G. M. Wallace, and R. M. Bray. Scarborough, ON: Prentice-Hall Canada.

Eccles, W. J. 1993b. "The Society of New France, 1680's–1760." Pp. 40–48 in *Reappraisals in Canadian History: Pre-Confederation*, edited by A. D. Gilbert, G. M. Wallace, and R. M. Bray. Scarborough, ON: Prentice-Hall Canada.

Edmond, John. 2014. "Indian Residential Schools: A Chronology." *Law Now*, July 7 (www.lawnow.org/indian-residential-schools-chronology).

Edmonton Journal. 2000. "New Confederacy Aims to Restore Blackfoot Nation," August 13, p. A8.

Edmonton Journal. 2008. "Separatism Dormant but Not Forgotten: Survey," June 2, p. A5.

Elsey, Christine J. 2013. *The Poetics of Land & Identity among British Columbia Indigenous Peoples*. Black Point, NS: Fernwood.

Employment and Social Development Canada (ESDC). 2013. *What We Know About the Middle Class in Canada*. Annex A, September 27.

Epps, Kenneth. 2011. "Canada's Largest Military Contractors: Military Contracting Is a Multi-Billion-Dollar Industry that Extends from Coast to Coast in Canada, Data Shows." *The Ploughshares Monitor* 32(4) (ploughshares.ca/pl_publications/canadas-largest-military-contractors-military-contracting-is-a-multi-billion-dollar-industry-that-extends-from-coast-to-coast-in-canada-data-shows).

Esping-Andersen, Gösta. 1990. *The Three Worlds of Welfare Capitalism*. Princeton, NJ: Princeton University Press.

Fairchild, Henry Pratt, ed. 1967. *Dictionary of Sociology and Related Sciences*. Totowa, NJ: Littlefield, Adams, and Company.

Fairclough, Norman. 1989. *Language and Power: Language in Social Life*. London: Longman.

Fanon, Frantz. 1968. *The Wretched of the Earth*. New York: Grove Press.

Feit, Harvey A. 2007. "Myths of the Ecological Whitemen: Histories, Science, and Rights North American—Native American Relations." Pp. 95–122 in *Native Americans and the Environment: Perspectives on the Ecological Indian*, edited by M. E. Harkin, M. E. and D. R. Lewis. Lincoln, NE: University of Nebraska Press.

Femia, Francesco, and Caitlin E. Werrell. 2014. "UPDATE: Climate and Security 101: Why the U.S. National Security Establishment Takes Climate Change Seriously." *Briefer* 23:1–4.

Ferguson, Niall, ed. 2003. *Virtual History: Alternatives and Counterfactuals*. London: Pan Books.

Ferguson, Niall. 2004. *Colossus: The Price of America's Empire*. New York: Penguin.

Fettes, Mark, and Ruth Norton. 2000. "Voices of Winter: Aboriginal Languages and Public Policy in Canada." Pp. 29–54 in *Aboriginal Education: Fulfilling the Promise*, edited by M. B. Castellano, L. Davis, and L. Lahache. Vancouver: UBC Press.

Fidler, Richard. 2006. "A 'Québécois Nation'? Harper Fuels an Important Debate." *Global Research*, December 22 (www.globalresearch.ca/index.php?context=va&aid=4244).

Findley, L. M. 2000. "Foreword." Pp. ix–xiii in *Reclaiming Indigenous Voice and Vision*, edited by M. Battiste. Vancouver: UBC Press.

Finkel, Alvin. 1989. *The Social Credit Phenomenon in Alberta*. Toronto: University of Toronto Press.

Finkel, Alvin. 2012. *Our Lives: Canada after 1945*. 2nd ed. Toronto: James Lorimer and Company.

Finnie, Richard. 1948. *Canada Moves North*. Toronto: Macmillan Company of Canada.

Fisher, A. D. 1981. "A Colonial Education System: Historical Changes and Schooling in Fort Chipewyan." *Canadian Journal of Anthropology* 2(1):37–44.

Flanagan, Thomas. 1977. "Louis Riel: Insanity and Prophecy." Pp. 15–36 in *The Settlement of the West*, edited by H. Palmer. Calgary: Comprint.

Flanagan, Thomas. 2000. *First Nations? Second Thoughts*. Montreal and Kingston: McGill-Queen's University Press.

Fleras, Augie. 2007. *Unequal Relations: An Introduction to Race, Ethnic, and Aboriginal Dynamics in Canada*. 5th ed. Toronto: Pearson Canada.

Fleras, Augie, and Jean Leonard Elliott. 1992. *The Nations within: Aboriginal-State Relations in Canada, the United States, and New Zealand*. Toronto: Oxford University Press.

Food Banks Canada. 2014. "About Hunger in Canada." Mississauga, ON: Food Banks Canada (www.foodbankscanada.ca/Learn-About-Hunger/About-Hunger-in-Canada.aspx).

Forbes. 2014. "The World's Billionaires." New York: Forbes Media (www.forbes.com/billionaires/list/#tab:overall).

Ford, James, and Johanna Wandel. 2013. "Responding to Climate Change in Nunavut: Policy Recommendations." Pp. 103–115 in *Moving Forward, Making a Difference*, vol. 3: Aboriginal Policy Research Series. Toronto: Thompson Educational.

Foreign Affairs, Trade and Development Canada. 2013. "The Economic Impact of the Canada-Chile Free Trade Agreement." Ottawa: Foreign Affairs, Trade and Development Canada (www.international.gc.ca/economist-economiste/analysis-analyse/studies-etudes/canada_chile-canada_chili/econo_impact_toc-tdm.aspx?lang=eng).

Fossum, Jon-Erik. 1997. *Oil, the State, and Federalism: The Rise and Demise of Petro-Canada as a Statist Impulse*. Toronto: University of Toronto Press.

Foucault, Michel. 1973. *Madness and Civilization: A History of Insanity in the Age of Reason*. New York: Vintage Books.

Foucault, Michel. 1977. *Power/Knowledge: Selected Interviews and Other Writings 1972–1977*, edited by C. Gordon. New York: Pantheon.

Foucault, Michel. 1980. *The History of Sexuality*, vol. 1: *An Introduction*. New York: Vintage Books.

Fournier, Marcel. 2001. "Quebec Sociology and Quebec Society: The Construction of a Collective Identity." *Canadian Journal of Sociology* 26(3):333–347.

Fournier, Marcel, Michael Rosenberg, and Deena White, eds. 1997. *Quebec Society: Critical Issues*. Scarborough, ON: Prentice-Hall Canada.

Fox, John, Robert Andersen, and Joseph Dubonnet. 1999. "The Polls and the 1995 Quebec Referendum." *The Canadian Journal of Sociology* 24(3):411–424.

Fox, Terry, and David Long. 2000. "Struggles within the Circle: Violence, Healing, and Health on a First Nations Reserve." Pp. 271–301 in *Visions of the Heart: Canadian Aboriginal Issues*, edited by D. Long and O. P. Dickason. 2nd ed. Toronto: Harcourt Canada.

Francis, Daniel. 1997. *National Dreams: Myth, Memory, and Canadian History*. Vancouver: Arsenal Pulp Press.

Francis, Diane. 2013. *Merger of the Century*. Scarborough, ON: HarperCollins.

Francis, R. Douglas, Richard Jones, and Donald B. Smith. 1988. *Origins: Canadian History to Confederation*. Toronto: Holt, Rinehart, & Winston of Canada.

Frank, Andre Gunder. 1975. *On Capitalist Underdevelopment*. Bombay, India: Oxford University Press.

Fraser, Blair. 1967. *The Search for Identity: Canada: Postwar to Present*. Toronto: Doubleday Canada.

Frideres, James S. 2011. *First Nations in the Twenty-First Century*. Don Mills, ON: Oxford University Press.

Frideres, James S., and Rene R. Gadacz. 2001. *Aboriginal Peoples in Canada: Contemporary Conflicts*. 6th ed. Scarborough, ON: Prentice-Hall Canada.

Fried, Jacob. 1969. "Boom Towns . . . Must They Bust?" Pp. 38–42 in *People of the Light and Dark*, edited by M. van Steensel. Ottawa: Department of Indian Affairs and Northern Development.

Friesen, Jean. 1986. Pp. 41–51 in *Magnificent Gifts: The Treaties of Canada with the Indians of the Northwest, 1869–70*. Series 5, vol. 1. Ottawa: Transactions of the Royal Society of Canada.

Friesen, Joe, and Ingrid Peritz. 2012. "New Bilingualism Taking Hold in Canada." *The Globe and Mail*, October 24 (www.theglobeandmail.com/news/national/new-bilingualism-taking-hold-in-canada/article4650408).

Friesen, John W. 1983. *Schools with a Purpose*. Calgary: Detselig.

Friesen, John W. 1991. "Introduction: Highlights of Western Canadian Native History." Pp. 1–22 in *The Cultural Maze: Complex Questions on Native Destiny in Western Canada*, edited by J. W. Friesen. Calgary: Detselig.

Friesen, John W. 1993. *When Cultures Clash: Case Studies in Multiculturalism*. 2nd ed. Calgary: Detselig.

Friesen, John W. 1995. *You Can't Get There from Here: The Mystique of Plains Indians' Culture & Philosophy*. Dubuque: Kendall/Hunt.

Friesen, John W. 1997. *Rediscovering the First Nations of Canada*. Calgary: Detselig.

Friesen, John W. 1998. *Sayings of the Elders*. Calgary: Detselig.

Friesen, John W. 1999. *First Nations of the Plains: Creative, Adaptable, and Enduring*. Calgary: Detselig.

Friesen, John W. 2008. *Western Canadian Native Destiny: Complex Questions on the Cultural Maze*. Calgary: Detselig.

Friesen, John W., and Virginia Lyons Friesen. 2004. *We Are Included: The Métis People of Canada Realize Riel's Vision*. Calgary: Detselig.

Friesen, John W., and Virginia Lyons Friesen. 2005. *First Nations in the Twenty-First Century: Contemporary Educational Frontiers*. Calgary: Detselig.

Frisby, David, and Derek Sayer. 1986. *Society*. London: Ellis Horwood/Tavistock.

Fuentes-Nieva, Ricardo, and Nicholas Galasso. 2014. *Working for the Few*. Oxfam briefing paper #178. Oxford: Oxfam International (www.oxfam.org/sites/www.oxfam.org/files/file_attachments/bp-working-for-few-political-capture-economic-inequality-200114-en_3.pdf).

Fukuyama, Francis. 1992. *The End of History and the Last Man*. New York: The Free Press.

Furniss, Elizabeth. 1995. *Victims of Benevolence: The Dark Legacy of the Williams Lake Residential School*. Vancouver: Arsenal Pulp Press.

Gaetz, Stephen, Jesse Donaldson, Tim Richter, and Tanya Gulliver. 2013. *The State of Homelessness in Canada 2013*. Homeless Hub Paper 4. Toronto: Canadian Homelessness Research Network Press.

Gagnon, Lysiane. 2000. "The October Crisis: Singular Anomaly." *The Beaver* 80(5):6–7.

Galbraith, John Kenneth. 1997. *The Great Crash 1929*. Boston: Mariner.

Gardner, Dan. 2002. "The First Casualty of Hollywood . . . Is Truth." *Edmonton Journal*, February 9, p. A16.

Gasher, Mike. 2014. "Media Convergence." Revised by A. McIntosh. *The Canadian Encyclopedia* (www.thecanadianencyclopedia.ca/en/article/media-convergence).

Gauvreau, Michael. 2005. *The Catholic Origins of Quebec's Quiet Revolution, 1931–1970*. Montreal and Kingston: McGill-Queen's University Press.

Geddes, John. 2000. "Northern Son." *Maclean's* 114(17):16–21.

Gervais, Stéphan, Christopher Kirkey, and Jarrett Rudy. 2011. *Quebec Questions: Quebec Studies for the Twenty-First Century*. Don Mills, ON: Oxford University Press.

Gibbins, Roger. 1979. *Prairie Politics and Society: Regionalism in Decline*. Toronto: Butterworths.

Gibson, Gordon. 1994. *Plan B: The Future of the Rest of Canada*. Vancouver: The Fraser Institute.

Giddens, Anthony. 1984. *The Constitution of Society: Outline of the Theory of Structuration*. Cambridge: Polity Press.

Giddens, Anthony. 1987. "Structuralism, Post-Structuralism, and the Production of Culture." Pp. 195–223 in *Social Theory Today*, edited by A. Giddens and J. Turner. Stanford, CA: Stanford University Press.

Giffen, Naomi Musmaker. 1930. *The Roles of Men and Women in Eskimo Culture*. Chicago: University of Chicago Press.

Gilbert, Martin. 1991. *The Second World War*. New York: Holt.

Gingras, Yves, and Jean-Philippe Warren. 2006. "A British Connection? A Quantitative Analysis of the Changing Relations between American, British, and Canadian Sociologists." *The Canadian Journal of Sociology* 31(4):509–522.

Giroux, Henry A. 2014. "Neoliberalism and the Machinery of Disposability." Truth-Out.Org, October 7 (www.truth-out.org/opinion/item/22958-neoliberalism-and-the-machinery-of-disposability).

The Globe and Mail. 2014. "Canada Threatens Retaliatory Tariffs." October 21, p. B1.

Goddard, John. 1991. *Last Stand of the Lubicon*. Vancouver: Douglas & McIntyre.

Goffman, Erving. 1961. *Asylums*. Garden City, NY: Anchor Books.

Goldenberg, Suzanne. 2014. "2014 on Track to Be Hottest Year on Record, Says US Science Agency." *The Guardian*, October 20 (www.theguardian.com/environment/2014/oct/20/2014-on-track-to-be-hottest-year-on-record-says-us-science-agency).

Gonzalez, Roberto J. 2001. "Lynne Cheney-Joe Lieberman Group Puts out a Blacklist." *San Jose Mercury News*, December 13.

Gordon, Walter. 1966. *A Choice for Canada: Independence or Colonial Status?* Toronto: McClelland & Stewart.

Government of Canada. 1963. *A Preliminary Report of the Royal Commission on Bilingualism and Biculturalism*. Ottawa: Queen's Printer.

Government of Canada. 1969. *The White Paper*. Statement of the Government of Canada on Indian Policy. Published under the Authority of the Honourable Jean Chrétien, Minister of Indian Affairs and Northern Development. Ottawa: Indian Affairs Branch.

Government of Canada. 1982. *The Canadian Constitution*. Ottawa: Public Works.

Government of Canada. 2013. *Facts and Figures 2012—Immigration Overview: Permanent and Temporary Residents*. Ottawa: Government of Canada (www.cic.gc.ca/english/resources/statistics/facts2012/permanent/01.asp). Modified August 7, 2013.

Government of Canada. 2014. "Canada's Northern Strategy." Ottawa: Government of Canada (www.northernstrategy.gc.ca/index-eng.asp).

Government of Nunavut. 2014. "Climate Change Community Consulations." Government of Nunavut News Release, August 26 (www.gov.nu.ca/eia/news/climate-change-community-consultations).

Government of Quebec. 2008. "Building the Future: Abridged Report of the Bouchard-Taylor Commission." Quebec: Government of Quebec (communiques.gouv.qc.ca/gouvqc/communiques/ME/Mai2008/22/c3134.html).

Government of the United States. 2002. *The National Security Strategy of the United States of America*. Washington, DC: Government of the United States.

Goyder, John. 1993. "The Canadian Syndrome of Regional Polarities: An Obituary." *Canadian Review of Sociology and Anthropology* 30(1):1–12.

Grabb, Edward. 2000. "Defining Moments and Recurring Myths: Comparing Canadians and Americans after the American Revolution." *Canadian Review of Sociology and Anthropology* 37(4):373–420.

Grabb, Edward, Douglas Baer, and James Curtis. 1999. "The Origins of American Individualism: Reconsidering the Historical Evidence." *The Canadian Journal of Sociology* 24(4):511–534.

Grabb, Edward, and James Curtis. 2005. *Regions Apart: The Four Societies of Canada and the United States*. Toronto: Oxford University Press.

Granatstein, Jack. 1996. *Yankee Go Home? Canadians and Anti-Americanism*. Toronto: HarperCollins.

Grant, Agnes. 1996. *No End of Grief: Indian Residential Schools in Canada*. Winnipeg: Pemmican Publications.

Grant, George. 2005. *Lament for a Nation: The Defeat of Canadian Nationalism*. 40th anniversary ed. Montreal and Kingston: McGill-Queen's University Press.

Gray, John. 1994. *Lost in North America: The Imaginary Canadian in the American Dream*. Vancouver: Talonbooks.

Gregg, Allan. 2005. "Quebec's Final Victory." *The Walrus* (February):50–61.

Gregoire, Lisa. 2007. "People of the Delta." *Canadian National Geographic* 127(3):42–58.

GRES. 1997. "Immigration and Ethnic Relations in Quebec: Pluralism in the Making." Pp. 95–122 in *Quebec Society: Critical Issues*, edited by M. Fournier, M. Rosenberg, and D. White. Scarborough, ON: Prentice-Hall Canada.

Gresko, Jacqueline. 1986. "Creating Little Dominions within the Dominion: Early Catholic Indian Schools in Saskatchewan and British Columbia." Pp. 88–109 in *Indian Education in Canada*, vol. 1: *The Legacy*, edited by J. Barman, Y. Hébert, and D. McCaskill. Vancouver: UBC Press.

Griffiths, Franklin, Rob Huebert, and P. Whitney Lackenbauer. 2011. *Canada and the Changing Arctic: Sovereignty, Security, and Stewardship*. Waterloo, ON: Wilfrid Laurier University Press.

Griffiths, Rudyard. 2008. *We're Prying French and English Canada Apart*. Ottawa: The Dominion Institute.

Grossman, Zoltán, and Alan Parker, eds. 2013. *Asserting Native Resilience: Pacific Indigenous Nations Face the Climate Crisis*. Corvallis, OR: Oregon State University Press.

Grunwald, Michael. 2002. "Security Fears Have U.S. and Canada Rethinking Life on the Border." *Guardian Weekly* (January 10–16):29.

Guevara, Che. 2003. *Che Guevara Reader: Writings on Politics & Revolution*, edited by D. Deutschmann. Melbourne, Australia: Ocean Press.

Gwyn, Richard. 1996. *Nationalism without Walls: The Unbearable Lightness of Being Canadian*. Toronto: McClelland & Stewart.

Haig-Brown, Celia. 1993. *Resistance and Renewal: Surviving the Indian Residential School*. Vancouver: Tillacum Library.

Hall, D. J. 1977. "Clifford Sifton: Immigration and Settlement Policy, 1896–1905." Pp. 60–85 in *Settlement of the West*, edited by H. Palmer. Calgary: Comprint.

Halliday, W. M. 1935. *Potlatch and Totem and the Recollections of an Indian Agent*. London: J. M. Dent and Sons.

Hamelin, J. 1993. "What Middle Class?" Pp. 215–223 in *Reappraisals in Canadian History: Pre-Confederation*, edited by A. D. Gilbert, G. M. Wallace, and R. M. Bray. Scarborough, ON: Prentice-Hall Canada.

Hamilton, Graeme. 2014. "A Dying Dream: Most Quebec Voters Want Nothing to Do with Sovereignty." *National Post*, April 5 (fullcomment.nationalpost.com/2014/04/05/graeme-hamilton-a-dying-dream-most-quebec-voters-want-nothing-to-do-with-sovereignty).

Hanks, Lucien M., Jr., and Jane Richardson Hanks. 1950. *A Study of the Blackfoot Reserve of Alberta*. Toronto: University of Toronto Press.

Hanohano, Peter. 1999. "The Spiritual Imperative of Native Epistemology: Restoring Harmony and Balance to Education." *Canadian Journal of Native Education* 23(2):206–219.

Harkin, Michael E., and David Rich Lewis, eds. 2007. *Native Americans and the Environment: Perspectives on the Ecological Indian*. Lincoln, NE: University of Nebraska Press.

Harrison, Trevor. 1995. *Of Passionate Intensity: Right-Wing Populism and the Reform Party of Canada*. Toronto: University of Toronto Press.

Harrison, Trevor. 1996. "Class, Citizenship, and Global Migration: The Case of the Canadian Business Immigration Program." *Canadian Public Policy* 22(1):7–23.

Harrison, Trevor. 1999. "Globalization and the Trade in Human Body Parts." *Canadian Review of Sociology and Anthropology* 36(1):21–36.

Harrison, Trevor. 2000. "The Changing Face of Prairie Politics: Populism in Alberta." *Prairie Forum* 25(1):107–122.

Harrison, Trevor. 2002. *Requiem for a Lightweight: Stockwell Day and Image Politics.* Montreal: Black Rose.

Harrison, Trevor. 2005. "Introduction." Pp. 1–20 in *The Return of the Trojan Horse and the New World (Dis)Order,* edited by T. Harrison. Montreal: Black Rose.

Harrison, Trevor. 2007. "Anti-Canadianism: Explaining the Deep Roots of a Shallow Phenomenon." *International Journal of Canadian Studies* 35:217–240.

Harrison, Trevor. 2012. "Resources and the Northern Colonies." Presentation to the 16th Annual Parkland Institute Conference, Edmonton, Alberta, November 24.

Harvey, David. 2010. *The Enigma of Capital and the Crises of Capitalism.* New York: Oxford University Press.

Hawthorn, Harry B. 1966/1967. *A Survey of the Contemporary Indians of Canada,* Part I and II. Ottawa: Indian Affairs.

Healing, Dan. 2014. "Oil and Gas Salaries Average $130,000: Survey." *Calgary Herald,* April 9 (www.calgaryherald.com/business/salaries+average+Survey/9719742/story.html).

Heath, Joseph. 2013. "In Defence of Sociology." *Ottawa Citizen,* April 30 (www2.canada.com/ottawacitizen/news/archives/story.html?id=24e9ec33-5809-4437-9a19-530c01e6c262).

Hedges, Christopher. 2009. *Empire of Illusion: The End of Literacy and the Triumph of Spectacle.* Toronto: Vintage Books.

Hedges, Christopher. 2010. *Death of the Liberal Class.* Toronto: Vintage Books.

Heilbroner, Eric. 1992. *Twenty-First Century Capitalism.* Concord, ON: Anansi.

Hemberger, Suzette. 1993. "Constitution." Pp. 189–190 in *The Oxford Companion to Politics of the World,* edited by J. Krieger. Oxford: Oxford University Press.

Hemispheric Social Alliance. 2003. *Lessons from NAFTA: The High Cost of "Free Trade."* Ottawa: Canadian Centre for Policy Alternatives.

Henderson, James (Sákéj) Youngblood. 2000. "Postcolonial Ledger Drawing: Legal Reform." Pp. 57–76 in *Reclaiming Indigenous Voice and Vision,* edited by M. Battiste. Vancouver: UBC Press.

Henderson, Robert, ed. n.d. *A Soldier's Account of the Campaign on Quebec, 1759.* Taken from *A Journal of the Expedition up the River St. Lawrence.* Originally published in 1759. Manotick, ON: The Discriminating General.

Henlin, Calvin. 2006. *Dances with Dependency: Indigenous Success through Self-Reliance.* Vancouver: Orca Spirit Publications and Communications.

Heron, Craig, and Robert Storey. 1986. "On the Job in Canada." Pp. 3–46 in *On the Job,* edited by C. Heron and R. Storey. Montreal and Kingston: McGill-Queen's University Press.

Hicks, Jack. 2013. "The Dissociative State of Nunavut." *Canadian Dimension* 47(31):14–15.

Hiller, Harry. 1987. "The Foundation and Politics of Separation: Canada in Comparative Perspective." *Research in Political Sociology* 3:39–60.

Hobbes, Thomas. 2014. *Leviathan*, edited by N. Malcolm. Originally published in 1651. Toronto: Oxford University Press.

Hobsbawm, Eric. 1992. *Nations and Nationalism since 1780*. 2nd ed. Cambridge: Cambridge University Press.

Hobsbawm, Eric. 1995. *Age of Extremes. The Short Twentieth Century 1914–1991*. London: Abacus.

Hofstadter, Richard, ed. 1958. *Great Issues in American History*, vol. I: *1765–1865*. New York: Vintage Books.

Hofstadter, Richard, William Miller, and Daniel Aaron. 1957. *The United States: The History of a Republic*. Englewood Cliffs, NJ: Prentice-Hall.

Honan, William. 1998. "Historians Warming to Games of 'What if?'" *New York Times*, January 7, p. B7.

Hood, Duncan. 2008. "How Canada Stole the American Dream." *Maclean's*, July 7, pp. 51–54.

Horowitz, Gad. 1966. "Conservatism, Liberalism, and Socialism in Canada: An Interpretation." *Canadian Journal of Economic and Political Science* 32:143–171.

Horsman, Reginald. 1993. "On to Canada: Manifest Destiny and United States Strategy in the War of 1812." Pp. 272–291 in *Reappraisals in Canadian History: Pre-Confederation*, edited by A. D. Gilbert, G. M. Wallace, and R. M. Bray. Scarborough, ON: Prentice-Hall Canada.

House, John D. 1978. *The Last of the Free Enterprisers*. Toronto: MacMillan of Canada.

Howard, V. 1999. "Unemployment Relief Camps." *The Canadian Encyclopedia*. Year 2000 ed. Toronto: McClelland & Stewart.

Hufbauer, Gary C., and Jeffrey J. Schott. 2004. "The Prospects for Deeper North American Integration." *The Border Papers* 195 (January). Toronto: C. D. Howe Institute.

Hum, Derek. 1983. *Federalism and the Poor: A Review of the Canada Assistance Plan*. Toronto: Ontario Economic Council.

Humphreys, Adrian. 2014. "Caledonia Developers Vindicated as Government Ordered to Pay Legal Costs for Tax Battle over Standoff Settlement." *National Post On-Line*, September 30 (news.nationalpost.com/2014/09/30/caledonia-developers-dont-have-to-pay-legal-costs-for-tax-battle-over-16m-standoff-settlement-court).

Hylton, John H. 1999. "Future Prospects for Aboriginal Self-Government in Canada." Pp. 432–455 in *Aboriginal Self-Government in Canada*, edited by J. H. Hylton. Saskatoon: Purich.

Ibbitson, John. 2001. *Loyal No More: Ontario's Struggle for a Separate Destiny*. Toronto: HarperCollins.

Ibbitson, John. 2009. *Open and Shut: Why America Has Barack Obama, and Canada Has Stephen Harper*. Toronto: McClelland & Stewart.

Igartua, Jose E. 2006. *The Other Quiet Revolution: National Identities in English Canada, 1945–1971*. Vancouver: UBC Press.

Ignatieff, Michael. 1993. *Blood and Belonging: Journeys into the New Nationalism*. Toronto: Penguin.

Ignatieff, Michael. 2009. *True Patriot Love: Four Generations in Search of Canada*. Toronto: Viking Press.

Indian and Northern Affairs Canada. 1996. "Highlights from the Report of the Royal Commission on Aboriginal Peoples: A Word from Commissioners." Ottawa: Indian and Northern Affairs Canada (www.ainc-inac.gc.ca/ap/pubs/rpt/rpt-eng.asp).

Indian Chiefs of Alberta. 1970. *Citizens Plus: A Presentation by the Indian Chiefs of Alberta to the Right Honourable P.E. Trudeau, Prime Minister and the Government of Canada*, a.k.a. "The Red Paper." Edmonton: Indian Association of Alberta.

Industry Canada. 2014. "Canadian Industry Statistics." Ottawa: Industry Canada (www.ic.gc.ca/app/scr/sbms/sbb/cis/definition.html?code=51&lang=eng). Modified July 15.

Innis, Harold. 1956. "Great Britain, the United States, and Canada." Pp. 394–412 in *Essays in Canadian Economic History*, edited by M. Q. Innis. Toronto: University of Toronto Press.

Innis, Harold. 1962. *The Fur Trade in Canada*. Toronto: University of Toronto Press.

Innis, Harold. 1995. "Recent Trends in Canadian-American Relations." Pp. 262–270 in *Staples, Markets, and Cultural Change: Selected Essays*, edited by D. Drache. Montreal and Kingston: McGill-Queen's University Press.

Irwin, R. Stephen. 1994. *The Indian Hunters*. Blaine, WA: Hancock House.

Ives, John W. 1990. *A Theory of Northern Athapaskan Prehistory*. Boulder, CO: Westview Press.

Jackson, Andrew. 1999. "From Leaps of Faith to Lapses of Logic." *Policy Options* (June):12–18.

Jaenen, Cornelius. 1986. "Education for Francization: The Case of New France in the Seventeenth Century." Pp. 45–63 in *Indian Education in Canada*, vol. I: *The Legacy*, edited by J. Barman, Y. Hébert, and D. McCaskill. Vancouver: UBC Press.

James, Lawrence. 1997. *The Rise and Fall of the British Empire*. London: Abacus.

Jaszi, Oszkar. 1961. *The Dissolution of the Habsburg Monarchy*. Originally published in 1929. Chicago: University of Chicago Press.

Jennings, Jesse D. 1978. *Ancient Native Americans*. San Francisco: W. H. Freeman and Company.

Jensen, Joan. M. 1988. *Passage from India: Asian Indian Immigrants in North America*. New Haven, CT: Yale University Press.

Jessop, Bob. 1993. "Towards a Schumpeterian Workface State? Preliminary Remarks on Post-Fordist Political Economy." *Studies in Political Economy* 40:7–39.

Johnson, Chalmers. 2006. *Nemesis: The Last Days of the American Republic*. New York: Holt.

Johnston, Basil. 1995. *The Manitous: The Spiritual World of the Ojibway*. Toronto: Key Porter Books.

Johnston, Charles M., ed. 1964. *The Valley of the Six Nations: A Collection of Documents on the Indian Lands of the Grand River*. Toronto: University of Toronto Press.

Johnston, Darlene. 1989. *The Taking of Indian Lands in Canada: Consent or Coercion?* Saskatoon: University of Saskatchewan Native Law Centre.

Josephy, Alvin M., Jr. 1968. *The Indian Heritage of America*. New York: Alfred A. Knopf.

Kaye, Julie, and Daniel Béland. 2014. "Stephen Harper's Dangerous Refusal to 'Commit Sociology'." *Toronto Star*, August 22 (www.thestar.com/opinion/commentary/2014/08/22/stephen_harpers_dangerous_refusal_to_commit_sociology.html).

Keegan, John. 1990. *The Second World War*. New York: Penguin.

Kelly, W. E. 1997. "Canada's Black Defenders." *The Beaver* 77(2):31–34.

Kendall, Diana, Jane L. Murray, and Rick Linden. 2007. *Sociology in Our Times*. 4th Canadian ed. Toronto: Nelson Canada.

Keohane, Robert O. 2002. "The Globalization of Informal Violence: Theories of World Politics, and the 'Liberalism of Fear'." *Dialogue IO* (Spring):29–43.

Kerr, Don, and Roderic Beaujot. 2011. "Aboriginal Demography." Pp. 149–188 in *Visions of the Heart: Canadian Aboriginal Issues*, edited by D. Long and O. P. Dickason. Don Mills, ON: Oxford University Press.

Kilpatrick, Sean. 2014. "Suicide Claims More Soldiers than Those Killed by Afghan Combat." *Toronto Star*, September 17 (www.thestar.com/news/canada/2014/09/16/suicide_claims_more_soldiers_than_those_killed_by_afghan_combat.html).

King, A. Richard. 1967. *The School at Mopass: A Problem of Identity*. New York: Holt, Rinehart, and Winston.

Kirkness, Verna J. 1998a. "Our Peoples' Education: Cut the Shackles; Cut the Crap; Cut the Mustard." *Canadian Journal of Native Education* 22(1):10–15.

Kirkness, Verna J. 1998b. "The Critical State of Aboriginal Languages in Canada." *Canadian Journal of Native Education* 22(1):93–107.

Klein, Naomi. 2014. *This Changes Everything*. Toronto: Alfred A. Knopf Canada.

Knuttila, Murray. 2002. *Introducing Sociology: A Critical Perspective*. Toronto: Oxford University Press.

Knuttila, Murray, and Wendee Kubik. 2000. *State Theories: Classical, Global, and Feminist Perspectives*. Halifax, NS: Fernwood.

Korten, David. 2001. *When Corporations Rule the World*. 2nd ed. San Francisco: Berrett-Koehler.

KPMG International. 2014. "Tax Tools and Resources." KPMG (www.kpmg.com/global/en/services/tax/tax-tools-and-resources/pages/default.aspx).

Krahn, Harvey, Trevor Harrison, Michael Haan, and William Johnston. 2009. "Social Capital and Democratic Political Engagement." *International Journal of Contemporary Sociology* 46(1):51–76.

Krahn, Harvey, Graham Lowe, and Karen Hughes. 2015. *Work, Industry, and Canadian Society*. 7th ed. Toronto: Nelson Canada.

Krech, Shephard, III. 1999. *The Ecological Indian: Myth and History*. New York: Norton.

Krech, Shephard, III. 2007. "Beyond the Ecological Indian." Pp. 3–31 in *Native Americans and the Environment: Perspectives on the Ecological Indian*, edited by M. E. Harkin and D. R. Lewis. Lincoln, NE: University of Nebraska Press.

Krotz, Larry. 1990. *Indian Country: Inside Another Canada*. Toronto: McClelland & Stewart.

Kulchyski, Peter. 2005. *Like the Sound of a Drum: Aboriginal Cultural Politics in Denendeh and Nunavut*. Winnipeg: University of Manitoba Press.

Kulchyski, Peter. 2013. "Focus: The North." *Canadian Dimension* 47(31):13.

Kurth, James. 1993. "Military-Industrial Complex." Pp. 587–588 in *The Oxford Companion to Politics of the World*, edited by J. Krieger. Oxford: Oxford University Press.

La Haye, Laura. 1993. "Mercantilism." Pp. 534–538 in *The Fortune Encyclopedia of Economics*, edited by D. R. Henderson. New York: Warner Books.

Lairson, T. D., and D. Skidmore. 1997. *International Political Economy: The Struggle for Power and Wealth*. Toronto: Harcourt Brace.

Lane, Jan-Erik, and Svante O. Ersson. 1994. *Politics and Society in Western Europe*. London: Sage.

Langer, W. L. 1948. *An Encyclopedia of World History*. Boston: Houghton Mifflin.

Laurendeau, André. 1985. "The Conditions for the Existence of a National Culture." Pp. 255–269 in *Canadian Political Thought*, edited by H. D. Forbes. Toronto: Oxford University Press.

Laviolette, Gontran. 1991. *The Dakota Sioux in Canada.* Winnipeg: DLM Publications.

Lawson, James C. B. 2006. "The Caledonia Occupation." *Relay* 30:12–14 (www.socialistproject. ca/relay/r12_caledonia.pdf).

Laxer, Gordon. 1989. *Open for Business: The Roots of Foreign Ownership in Canada.* Toronto: Oxford University Press.

Laxer, Gordon, ed. 1991. *Perspectives on Canadian Economic Development.* Toronto: Oxford University Press.

Laxer, Gordon. 1992. "Distinct Status for Quebec: A Benefit to English Canada." *Constitutional Forum* 3(3):57–61.

Laxer, Gordon. 1995. "Social Solidarity, Democracy, and Global Capitalism." *Canadian Review of Sociology and Anthropology* 32(3):287–314.

Laxer, Gordon. 2000. "Surviving the Americanizing Right." *Canadian Review of Sociology and Anthropology* 37(1):55–76.

Laxer, Gordon. 2002. "Alternatives to Secession." *Review of Constitutional Studies* 7(1/2):272–293.

Laxer, Gordon. 2010. "Superpower, Middle Power, or Satellite? Canadian Energy and Environmental Policy." Pp. 138–161 in *Canada's Foreign and Security Policy: Soft and Hard Strategies of a Middle Power*, edited by N. Hynek and D. Bosold. Toronto: Oxford University Press Canada.

Laxer, Gordon, and John Dillon. 2008. *Over a Barrel: Exiting from NAFTA's Proportionality Clause.* Edmonton: Parkland Institute.

Laxer, Gordon, and Trevor Harrrison, eds. 1995. *The Trojan Horse: Alberta and the Future of Canada.* Montreal: Black Rose.

Laxer, James. 2004. *The Border.* Toronto: Anchor.

Lee, Marc. 2012. "Northern Gateway Pipeline Jobs Far from the Number Promised." *CCPA Monitor* 19(1):12–13.

Leger Marketing. 2008. "Referendum Voting Intentions in Quebec." Montreal: Leger Marketing (www.leger360.com/admin/voting_int/Referendum_Voting_Intentions_in_Quebec2012.pdf).

Lemmen, Don, and Fiona Warren. 2004. *Climate Change Impacts and Adaptation: A Canadian Perspective.* Ottawa: Government of Canada.

Lepage, Jean-François, and Jean-Pierre Corbeil. 2013. "The Evolution of English-French Bilingualism in Canada from 1961 to 2011." Ottawa: Statistics Canada. Cat. no. 75-006-X.

Levant, Ezra. 2011. *Ethical Oil: The Case for Canada's Oil Sands.* Toronto: McClelland & Stewart.

Levitt, Kari. 1970. *Silent Surrender: The Multinational Corporation in Canada.* Toronto: Macmillan of Canada.

Li, Peter. 1996. *The Making of Post-War Canada.* Toronto: Oxford University Press.

Lian, Jason Z., and David Ralph Matthews. 1998. "Does the Vertical Mosaic Still Exist? Ethnicity and Income in Canada, 1991." *The Canadian Review of Sociology and Anthropology* 35(4):461–482.

Lincoln, Kenneth. 1985. *Native American Renaissance.* Berkeley, CA: University of California Press.

Linnitt, Carol. 2013. "Harper's Attack on Science: No Science, No Evidence, No Truth, No Democracy." *Academic Matters: The Journal of Higher Education* (May) (www.

academicmatters.ca/2013/05/harpers-attack-on-science-no-science-no-evidence-no-truth-no-democracy).

Lipset, Seymour M. 1968a. *Agrarian Socialism: The Co-operative Commonwealth Federation in Saskatchewan.* Garden City, NY: Doubleday.

Lipset, Seymour M. 1968b. *Revolution and Counter-Revolution.* New York: Basic Books.

Lipset, Seymour M. 1986. "Historical Conditions and National Characteristics." *Canadian Journal of Sociology* 11(2):113–155.

Lipset, Seymour M. 1990. *Continental Divide.* New York: Routledge.

Lipset, Seymour M. 1996. *American Exceptionalism: A Double-Edged Sword.* New York: Norton.

Lipsey, Richard. 2000. "The Canada–US FTA: Real Results versus Unreal Expectations." *World Economic Affairs* (Autumn):29–32.

Lowe, Graham S. 1987. *Women in the Administrative Revolution.* Toronto: University of Toronto Press.

Lower, Arthur R. M. 1977. *Colony to Nation: A History of Canada.* Toronto: McClelland & Stewart.

Lower, J. Arthur. 1983. *Western Canada: An Outline History.* Vancouver: Douglas & McIntyre.

Lynch, Laura. 2013. "B.C.'s Nisga'a Becomes Only First Nation to Privatize Land." *CBC News,* November 4 (www.cbc.ca/news/canada/british-columbia/b-c-s-nisga-a-becomes-only-first-nation-to-privatize-land-1.2355794)

Lyon, John Tylor. 1998. "'A Picturesque Lot': The Gypsies of Peterborough." *The Beaver* 78(5):25–30.

Macdonald, David. 2014. *Outrageous Fortune: Documenting Canada's Wealth Gap.* Ottawa: Canadian Centre for Policy Alternatives.

Mackenzie, Hugh. 2009. *Banner Year for Canada CEOs: Record High Pay Increase.* Ottawa: Canadian Centre for Policy Alternatives.

Maclean's. 2000. "Trudeau: His Life and Legacy." Special commemorative ed.

Maclean's. 2014. "Economy Trumps Climate Change Actions, PM Says." *Maclean's,* June 9 (www.macleans.ca/news/canada/economy-trumps-climate-change-actions-pm-says).

MacLennan, Hugh. 1959. *The Watch That Ends the Night.* Toronto: Macmillan.

MacLennan, Hugh. 1974. *The Rivers of Canada.* Toronto: Macmillan of Canada.

MacLennan, Hugh. 1998. *Two Solitudes.* Toronto: Stoddart.

Maclure, Jocelyn. 2011. "Quebec's Culture War: Two Conceptions of Quebec Identity." Pp. 137–148 in *Quebec Questions: Quebec Studies for the Twenty-First Century,* edited by S. Gervais, C. Kirkey, and J. Rudy. Don Mills, ON: Oxford University Press.

MacMillan, Margaret. 2008. *The Uses and Abuses of History.* Toronto: Viking Press.

Macrory, Patrick. 2002. "NAFTA Chapter 19: A Successful Experiment in International Trade Dispute Resolution." *The Border Papers* 168 (September). Toronto: C. D. Howe Institute.

Makela, Kathleen, 1999. "Legal and Jurisdictional Issues of Urban Reserves." Pp. 78–95 in *Urban Indian Reserves: Forging New Relationships in Saskatchewan,* edited by L. F. Barron and J. Garcea. Saskatoon: Purich.

Manchester, William. 1992. *A World Lit Only by Fire: The Medieval Mind and the Renaissance.* Boston: Little, Brown.

Mann, Michael. 2008. "American Empires: Past and Present." *Canadian Review of Sociology* 45(1):7–50.

Marchak, M. Patricia. 1988. *Ideological Perspectives on Canada*. Toronto: McGraw-Hill Ryerson.

Marchildon, Gregory. 1995. "From Pax Britannica to Pax Americana and Beyond." Pp. 151–169 in *Being and Becoming Canada: The Annals of the American Academy of Political and Social Science* 538, edited by C. Doran and E. Babby.

Margolis, Eric. 2008. "Time to Face Facts in Afghanistan." *Toronto Star*, October 6.

Marker, Michael. 2000. "Economics and Local Self-Determination: Describing the Clash Zone in First Nations Education." *Canadian Journal of Native Education* 24(1):30–44.

Marquis, Greg. 2000. *In Armageddon's Shadow: The Civil War and Canada's Maritime Provinces*. Kingston and Montreal: McGill-Queen's University Press.

Marsden, William. 2007. *Stupid to the Last Drop: How Alberta Is Bringing Environmental Armageddon to Canada (and Doesn't Seem to Care)*. Toronto: Alfred A. Knopf.

Martin, Ged. 1993a. "The Influence of the Durham Report." Pp. 437–448 in *Reappraisals in Canadian History: Pre-Confederation*, edited by A. D. Gilbert, G. M. Wallace, and R. M. Bray. Scarborough, ON: Prentice-Hall Canada.

Martin, Ged. 1993b. "History as Science or Literature: Explaining Canadian Confederation." Pp. 543–570 in *Reappraisals in Canadian History: Pre-Confederation*, edited by A. D. Gilbert, G. M. Wallace, and R. M. Bray. Scarborough, ON: Prentice-Hall Canada.

Martin, Lawrence. 1982. *The Presidents and Prime Ministers*. Markham: Paper Jacks.

Martin, Lawrence. 1993. *Pledge of Allegiance: The Americanization of Canada during the Mulroney Years*. Toronto: McClelland & Stewart.

Martin, Lawrence. 1999. "Canada Was on the Brink of Civil Strife Four Years Ago." *Edmonton Journal*, P. A19.

Marx, Karl. 1977a. "The Communist Manifesto." In *Karl Marx: Selected Writings*, edited by D. McLellan. Oxford: Oxford University Press.

Marx, Karl. 1977b. "Theses on Feuerbach." Pp. 156–158 in *Karl Marx: Selected Writings*, edited by D. McLellan. Oxford: Oxford University Press.

Mason, Gary. 2014. "What Happens When Fossil Fuels Run Out?" *The Globe and Mail*, January 31 (www.theglobeandmail.com/globe-debate/what-happens-when-fossil-fuels-run-out/article16625142).

Massey, Don, and Patricia N. Shields. 1995. *Canada: Its Land and People*. 2nd ed. Edmonton: Reidmore Books.

Mayes, Hubert G. 1999. "Resurrection: Tolstoy and Canada's Doukhobors." *The Beaver* 79(5): 39–44.

McBride, Stephen, and Heather Whiteside. 2011. *Private Affluence, Public Austerity: Economic Crisis and Democratic Malaise in Canada*. Halifax, NS: Fernwood.

McCall-Newman, Christina. 1982. *Grits: An Intimate Portrait of the Liberal Party*. Toronto: Macmillan of Canada.

McCallum, John. 1991. "Agriculture and Economic Development in Quebec and Ontario until 1870." Pp. 10–20 in *Perspectives on Canadian Economic Development*, edited by G. Laxer. Toronto: Oxford University Press.

McCue, William Westaway. 1999. "Crossing the Line." *The Beaver* 79(1):16–21.

McDaniel, Susan, and Heidi MacDonald. 2012. "To Know Ourselves—Not." *Canadian Journal of Sociology* 37(3):253–272.

McDonald, Kevin. 1994. "Globalisation, Multiculturalism and Rethinking the Social." *Australian-New Zealand Journal of Sociology* 30(3):239–247.

McDonnell, R. F., and R. C. Depew. 1999. "Self-Government and Self-Determination in Canada: A Critical Commentary." Pp. 352–376 in *Aboriginal Self-Government in Canada*, edited by J. H. Hylton. Saskatoon: Purich.

McDougall, John. 1903. *In the Days of the Red River Rebellion*. Toronto: William Briggs.

McGaa, Eagle Man, ed. 1990. *Mother Earth Spirituality: Native American Paths to Healing Ourselves and Our World*. New York: HarperCollins.

McGaa, Eagle Man, ed. 1995. *Native Wisdom: Perceptions of the Natural Way*. Minneapolis: Four Directions Publishing.

McKay, Ian, and Jamie Swift. 2012. *Warrior Nation: Rebranding Canada in an Age of Anxiety*. Halifax, NS: Between the Lines.

McKie, Craig. 1994. "A History of Emigration from Canada." *Canadian Social Trends* 35:26–29.

McMillan, Alan, D. 1995. *Native Peoples and Cultures of Canada*. 2nd ed. Vancouver: Douglas & McIntyre.

McNally, David. 2010. *Global Slump: The Economics and Politics of Crisis and Resistance*. Oakland, CA: PM Press.

McPherson, James. 1998. "Quebec Whistles Dixie." *Saturday Night* (March):13–14, 18, 20, 22–23, 72.

Meekison, J. Peter. 1993. "Canada's Quest for Constitutional Perfection." *Constitutional Forum* 4(2):55–59.

Meili, Dianne. 2012. *Those Who Know: Profiles of Alberta's Aboriginal Elders*. Edmonton: NeWest Press.

Melling, John. 1967. *Right to a Future: The Native Peoples of Canada*. Toronto: T. H. Best Printing Co.

Mercredi, Ovide, and Mary Ellen Turpel. 1993. *In the Rapids: Navigating the Future of First Nations*. Toronto: Viking Press.

Merkur, Daniel. 1991. *Powers Which We Do Not Know: The Gods and Spirits of the Inuit*. Moscow, ID: University of Idaho Press.

Merriam-Webster. 2003. *Merriam-Webster's Collegiate Dictionary*. 10th ed. Springfield, MA: Merriam-Webster.

Merton, Robert. 1968. *Social Theory and Social Structure*. New York: The Free Press.

Miliband, Ralph. 1969. *The State in Capitalist Society*. New York: Basic Books.

Miller, Alan D. 1988. *Native Peoples and Cultures of Canada*. Vancouver: Douglas & McIntyre.

Miller, Carman. 1999. "Canada's First War." *The Beaver* 79(5):6–7.

Miller, J. R. 1987. "The Irony of Residential Schooling." *Canadian Journal of Native Education* 14(2):3–14.

Miller, J. R. 2000. *Skyscrapers Hide the Heavens: A History of Indian-White Relations in Canada*. 3rd ed. Toronto: University of Toronto Press.

Mills, C. Wright. 1956. *The Power Elite*. Oxford: Oxford University Press.

Mills, C. Wright. 1961. *The Sociological Imagination*. New York: Grove Press.

Mills, Sean. 2005. "Modern, Postmodern, and Post-Postmodern." *The Beaver* (April/May):11–12.

Milne, Seumas. 2008. "Civilian Dead Are a Trade-Off in NATO's War of Barbarity." *Guardian Weekly*, October 16.

Milot, Micheline. 2011. "That Priest-Ridden Province? Politics and Religion in Quebec." Pp. 123–136 in *Quebec Questions: Quebec Studies for the Twenty-First Century*, edited by S. Gervais, C. Kirkey, and J. Rudy. Don Mills, ON: Oxford University Press.

Mittelman, J. H. 1996. "The Dynamics of Globalization." Pp. 1–19 in *Globalization: Critical Reflections*, edited by J. H. Mittelman. International Political Economy Yearbook, vol. 9. Boulder, CO: Lynne Rienner Publishers.

Moffett, Samuel E. 1972. *The Americanization of Canada*. Originally published in 1908. Toronto: University of Toronto Press.

Momatiuk, Yva, and John Eastcott. 1995. "'Nunavut' Means 'Our Land.'" *Native Peoples* 9(1):42–48.

Monahan, Patrick. 1995. *Cooler Heads Shall Prevail: Assessing the Costs and Consequences of Quebec Separation*. Toronto: C. D. Howe Institute.

Montgomery, Charles. 2007. "When Mountains Crumble." *Canadian National Geographic* 127(3):68–78.

Moore, Christopher. 1997. *1867: How the Fathers Made a Deal*. Toronto: McClelland & Stewart.

Moore, Christopher. 2012. "Colonization and Conflict: New France and Its Rivals (1600–1760)." Pp. 95–180 in *The Illustrated History of Canada*, edited by C. Brown. Toronto: Key Porter Books.

Morissette, Rene, and Xuelin Zhang. 2001. "Experiencing Low Income for Several Years." *Perspectives* (Summer):25–35. Cat. no. 75-001-XPE. Ottawa: Statistics Canada.

Morrow, Ray. 1994. "History of Sociological Theory." Pp. 1–22 in *An Introduction to Sociology*, edited by W. Meloff and D. Pierce. Scarborough, ON: Nelson Canada.

Morton, Desmond. 1997. *A Short History of Canada*. Edmonton: Hurtig Publishers.

Morton, Desmond. 2000. "1900: A New Century Begins." *The Beaver* 79(6):23–29.

Morton, William Lewis. 1970. "The Battle at Grand Coteau, July 13 and 14, 1851." Pp. 45–59 in *Historical Essays on the Prairie Provinces*, edited by D. Swainson. Toronto: McClelland & Stewart.

Mowat, Farley. 1952. *People of the Deer*. Toronto: McClelland & Stewart.

Mulgrew, Ian. 2014. "First Nations Mistaken in Their Celebration of Supreme Court Ruling." *Vancouver Sun*, June 29 (www.vancouversun.com/life/Mulgrew+First+Nations+mistaken+their+celebration+Supreme+Court/9986954/story.html).

Nakhaie, M. Reza. 1997. "Vertical Mosaic among the Elites: The New Imagery Revisited." *The Canadian Review of Sociology and Anthropology* 34(1):1–24.

Nanos. 2014. "Canadians and Americans Drifting Apart Says 10 Year Nanos Study. Appetite for Cooperation on the Border, Security Issues, Fighting Terror Down." *Nanos-UB North American Monitor* (August) (www.nanosresearch.com/library/polls/POLNAT-S14-T619.pdf).

Naylor, R. T. 1975. *The History of Canadian Business 1867–1914*. 2 vols. Toronto: Lorimer.

Nemni, Max, and Monique Nemni. 2006. *Young Trudeau: 1919–1944: Son of Quebec, Father of Canada*. Toronto: Douglas Gibson.

Nevitte, Neil. 1996. *The Decline of Deference*. Peterborough, ON: Broadview Press.

Newman, Peter C. 1998. *Empire of the Bay: The Company of Adventurers That Seized a Continent*. Toronto: Penguin.

Nikiforuk, Andrew. 2010. *Tar Sands: Dirty Oil and the Future of a Continent*. Vancouver: Greystone.

Nikiforuk, Andrew. 2012. *The Energy of Slaves: Oil and the New Servitude*. Vancouver: Greystone.

Norrie, Ken, and Douglas Owram. 1996. *The History of the Canadian Economy*. 2nd ed. Toronto: Harcourt Brace and Company, Canada.

O'Hara, Jane. 2000. "Abuse of Trust." *Maclean's* 113(26):16–21.

Ohmae, Ken'ichi. 1990. *The Borderless World: Power and Strategy in the Interlinked Economy*. New York: Harper Business.

Ohmae, Ken'ichi. 1995. *The End of the Nation State: The Rise of Regional Economies*. New York: The Free Press.

Olsen, Gregg. 2002. *The Politics of the Welfare State: Canada, Sweden, and the United States*. Oxford: Oxford University Press.

Orchard, David. 1998. *The Fight for Canada*. 2nd ed. Westmount, QC: Robert Davies Multimedia Publishing.

Orum, Anthony M., and John G. Dale. 2009. *Political Sociology: Power and Participation in the Modern World*. 5th ed. Oxford: Oxford University Press.

Orwell, George. 2008. *1984*. Toronto: Penguin.

Osberg, Lars, ed. 2003. *The Economic Implications of Social Cohesion*. Toronto: University of Toronto Press.

Osborn, Kevin. 1990. *The Peoples of the Arctic*. New York: Chelsea House.

Ouellet, Fernand. 1993. "The 1837/38 Rebellions in Lower Canada as a Social Phenomenon." Pp. 356–379 in *Reappraisals in Canadian History: Pre-Confederation*, edited by A. D. Gilbert, G. M. Wallace, and R. M. Bray. Scarborough, ON: Prentice-Hall Canada.

Palmer, Howard. 1982. *Patterns of Prejudice: A History of Nativism in Alberta*. Toronto: McClelland & Stewart.

Palmer, R. R., with Joel Colton. 1957. *A History of the Modern World*. New York: Alfred A. Knopf.

Panitch, Leo. 1977. *The Canadian State: Political Economy and Political Power*. Toronto: University of Toronto Press.

Panitch, Leo. 1981. "Dependency and Class in Canadian Political Economy." *Studies in Political Economy* 6:7–33.

Panitch, Leo, and Sam Gindin. 2012. *The Making of Global Capitalism: The Political Economy of American Empire*. London: Verso.

Panitch, Leo, and Donald Swartz. 1988. *The Assault on Trade Union Freedoms: From Consent to Coercion Revisited*. Toronto: Garamond.

Paquet, Gilles. 1997. "States, Communities, and Markets: The Distributed Governance Scenario." Pp. 25–46 in *The Nation State in a Global/Information Era: Policy Challenges*, edited by T. J. Courchene. Kingston: Queen's University Press.

Parliamentary Budget Officer. 2008. "The Fiscal Impact of the Canadian Mission in Afghanistan." Office of the Parliamentary Budget Officer, October 9 (www.parl.gc.ca/PBO-DPB/documents/2008-10-09%20Statement%20-%20Afghanistan.pdf).

Parriag, Anada, and Paul Chaulk. 2013. "The Urban Aboriginal Middle-Income Group in Canada: A Demographic Profile." *Aboriginal Policy Studies* 2(2):34–63.

Parsons, Talcott. 1951. *The Social System.* Glencoe, IL: The Free Press.

Parti Québécois. 1994. *Quebec in a New World: The PQ's Plan for Sovereignty.* Translated by R. Chodos. Toronto: James Lorimer and Company.

Pauls, Syd. 1984. "The Case for Band-Controlled Schools." *Canadian Journal of Native Education* 12(1):31–37.

Pemberton, Kim, 2014. "University of Victoria Puts First Nations Land Claim Mapping in the Spotlight." *Vancouver Sun,* August 11 (www.vancouversun.com/news/University+Victoria+puts+First+Nations+land+claim+mapping+spotlight/10109738/story.html#ixzz3CmKhuXAr).

Pentland, Clare. 1991. "The Transformation of Canada's Economic Structure." Pp. 296–310 in *Perspectives on Canadian Economic Development,* edited by G. Laxer. Toronto: Oxford University Press.

Perley, David G. 1993. "Aboriginal Education in Canada as Internal Colonialism." *Canada Journal of Native Education* 20(1):118–128.

Persson, Diane. 1986. "The Changing Experience of Indian Residential Schooling: Blue Quills, 1931–1970." Pp. 150–167 in *Indian Education in Canada,* vol. I: *The Legacy,* edited by J. Barman, Y. Hébert, and D. McCaskill. Vancouver: UBC Press.

Petitot, Father Emile. 1999. *Among the Chiglit Eskimos,* translated by E. Otto Höhn. Edmonton: Boreal Institute for Northern Studies.

Pevere, Geoff, and Greig Dymond. 1996. *Mondo Canuck: A Canadian Pop Cultural Odyssey.* Scarborough, ON: Prentice-Hall.

Pickett, Kate, and Richard Wilkinson. 2011. *The Spirit Level: Why Greater Equality Makes Societies Stronger.* London: Bloomsbury Press.

Piketty, Thomas. 2014. *Capital in the Twenty-First Century,* translated by A. Goldhammer. Cambridge, MA: Belknap.

Piven, Frances Fox. 2007. "The Neoliberal Challenge." *Contexts* 6(3):13–15.

Plain, Fred. 1988. "A Treatise on the Rights of the Aboriginal Peoples of the Continent of North America." Pp. 31–40 in *The Quest for Justice: Aboriginal Peoples and Aboriginal Rights,* edited by M. Boldt and J. A. Long. Toronto: University of Toronto Press.

Polanyi, Karl. 2001. *The Great Transformation: The Political and Economic Origins of Our Time.* Originally published in 1944. Boston: Beacon Press.

Ponting, J. Rick. 1986. "Relations between Bands and the Department of Indian Affairs: A Case of Internal Colonialism." Pp. 84–111 in *Arduous Journey: Canadian Indians and Decolonization,* edited by J. R. Ponting. Toronto: McClelland & Stewart.

Ponting, J. Rick. 1997a. "Getting a Handle on Recommendations of the Royal Commission on Aboriginal Peoples." Pp. 445–472 in *First Nations in Canada: Perspectives on Opportunity, Empowerment, and Self-Determination,* edited by J. R. Ponting. Toronto: McGraw-Hill Ryerson.

Ponting, J. Rick. 1997b. "The Socio-Demographic Picture." Pp. 68–114 in *First Nations in Canada: Perspectives on Opportunity, Empowerment, and Self-Determination,* edited by J. R. Ponting. Toronto: McGraw-Hill Ryerson.

Ponting, J. Rick, and Linda J. Henderson. 2005. "Contested Visions of First Nations Governance: Secondary Analysis of Federal Government Research on the Opinions of On-Reserve Residents." *Canadian Ethnic Studies* 37(1):63–86.

Porter, John. 1965. *The Vertical Mosaic*. Toronto: University of Toronto Press.

Porter, Joy. 2012. *Native American Environmentalism: Land, Spirit, and the Idea of Wilderness*. Lincoln, NE: University of Nebraska Press.

Potts, Karen, and Leslie Brown. 2012. "Becoming an Anti-Oppressive Researcher." Pp. 103–116 in *Rethinking Sociology in the 21st Century*, edited by M. Webber and K. Bezanson. 3rd ed. Toronto: Canadian Scholars' Press.

Poulantzas, Nicholas. 1973. *Political Power and Social Classes*, translated by T. O'Hagan. London: New Left Books.

Pratt, Larry, and Garth Stevenson, eds. 1981. *Western Separatism: The Myths, Realities, and Dangers*. Edmonton: Hurtig.

Purich, Donald. 1986. *Our Land*. Toronto: Lorimer.

Purich, Donald. 1992. *The Inuit and Their Land*. Toronto: James Lorimer and Company.

Putnam, Robert. 2000. *Bowling Alone: The Collapse and Revival of American Community*. New York: Simon & Schuster.

Ramonet, Ignacio. 2001. "The Changing Face of Separatism." *Le monde diplomatique* (February):1.

Ramos, Howard. 2006. "What Causes Canadian Aboriginal Protest? Examining Resources, Opportunities, and Identity, 1951–2000." *Canadian Journal of Sociology,* 31(2):211–234.

Ramp, William, and Trevor W. Harrison. 2012. "Libertarian Populism, Neoliberal Rationality, and the Mandatory Long-Form Census: Implications for Sociology." *Canadian Journal of Sociology* 37(3):273–294.

Ray, Arthur J. 1974. *Indians in the Fur Trade: Their Role as Trappers, Hunters, and Middlemen in the Lands Southwest of Hudson Bay, 1660–1870*. Toronto: University of Toronto Press.

Rea, K. J. 1968. *The Political Economy of the Canadian North*. Toronto: University of Toronto Press.

Reid, Scott. 1992. *Canada Remapped*. Vancouver: Pulp Press.

Resnick, Philip. 1991. *Toward a Canada–Quebec Union*. Montreal and Kingston: McGill-Queen's University Press.

Resnick, Philip. 2000. *The Politics of Resentment: B.C. Regionalism and Canadian Unity*. Vancouver: UBC Press.

Resnick, Philip. 2005. *The European Roots of Canadian Identity*. Peterborough, ON: Broadview Press.

Resnick, Philip, and Daniel Latouche. 1990. *Letters to a Quebecois Friend*. Montreal and Kingston: McGill-Queen's University Press.

Rice, James, and Michael Prince. 2013. *Changing Politics of Canadian Social Policy*. 2nd ed. Toronto: University of Toronto Press.

Richards, John, and Larry Pratt. 1979. *Prairie Capitalism: Power and Influence in the New West*. Toronto: McClelland & Stewart.

Richler, Noah. 2006. *This is My Country. What's Yours?* Toronto: McClelland & Stewart.

Richler, Noah. 2012. *What We Talk about When We Talk about War*. Fredericton, NB: Goose Lane Editions.

Rickman, H. P. 1961. "General Introduction." Pp. 11–63 in *Pattern and Meaning in History*, edited by W. Dilthey. London: Harper Row Publishers.

Riesman, David, with Reuel Denney and Nathan Glazer. 1950. *The Lonely Crowd: A Study of the Changing American Character*. New Haven, CT: Yale University Press.

Rioux, Marcel. 1978. *Quebec in Question*. Toronto: James Lorimer and Company.

Rioux, Marcel. 1993. "The Development of Ideologies in Quebec." Pp. 72–91 in *A Passion for Identity: An Introduction to Canadian Studies*, edited by D. Taras, B. Rasporich, and E. Mandel. Scarborough, ON: Nelson Canada.

Robbins, Richard H. 2014. *Global Problems and the Culture of Capitalism*. 6th ed. Toronto: Pearson.

Roberts, Joseph K. 1998. *In the Shadow of Empire: Canada for Americans*. New York: Monthly Review Press.

Robin, Martin. 1991. *Shades of Right: Nativist and Fascist Politics in Canada, 1920–1940*. Toronto: University of Toronto Press.

Robin, Martin. 1993. "British Columbia: The Company Province." Pp. 480–488 in *A Passion for Identity: An Introduction to Canadian Studies*, edited by D. Taras, B. Rasporich, and E. Mandel. Scarborough, ON: Nelson Canada.

Rodgers, Kathleen. 2014. *Welcome to Resisterville: American Dissidents in British Columbia*. Vancouver: UBC Press.

Romanow, Roy. 2006. "A House Half Built." *The Walrus* (June):48–54.

Romney, Paul. 1999. *Getting It Wrong: How Canadians Forgot Their Past and Imperiled Confederation*. Toronto: University of Toronto Press.

Ross, Rupert. 1992. *Dancing with a Ghost: Exploring Indian Reality*. Markham: Reed Books.

Rotstein, Abraham. 1978. "Is There an English-Canadian Nationalism?" *Journal of Canadian Studies* 13:109–118.

Rudmin, Floyd. 1993. *Bordering on Aggression*. Hull, QC: Voyageur Publications.

Rummel, R. J. 1994. *Death by Government*. New Brunswick, NJ: Transaction.

Russell, Dan. 2000. *A People's Dream: Aboriginal Self-Government in Canada*. Vancouver: UBC Press.

Ryan, Joan. 1995. *Doing Things the Right Way: Dene Traditional Justice in Lac La Martre, NWT*. Calgary: Arctic Institute of North America.

Said, Edward. 1993. *Culture and Imperialism*. New York: Vintage Books.

Sassan, Saskia. 2001. "Governance Hotspots: Challenges We Must Confront in the Post-September 11 World." Social Science Research Council (essays.ssrc.org/sept11/essays/sassen.htm).

Saul, John Ralston. 1997. *Reflections of a Siamese Twin: Canada at the End of the Twentieth Century*. Toronto: Penguin.

Saul, John Ralston. 2008. *A Fair Country: Telling Truths about Canada*. Toronto: Viking Press.

Saul, S. B. 1969. *The Myth of the Great Depression, 1873–1896*. London: The Macmillan Press.

Savoie, Donat, ed. 1970. *The Amerindians of the Canadian North-West in the 19th Century, as seen by Émile Petitot: The Loucheux Indian*, vol. II. Ottawa: Northern Science Group, Department of Indian Affairs and Northern Development.

Sawatsky, John. 1991. *Mulroney: The Politics of Ambition*. Toronto: Macfarland, Walter, and Ross.

Sayer, Derek. 1987. *The Violence of Abstraction: The Analytic Foundations of Historical Materialism*. Oxford: Basil Blackwell.

Schlesinger, Arthur, Jr. 1997. "Has Democracy a Future?" *Foreign Affairs* 76(5):2–12.

Schouls, Tim. 2003. *Shifting Boundaries: Aboriginal Identity, Pluralist Theory, and the Politics of Self-Government*. Vancouver: UBC Press.

Schultz, Marylou, and Miriam Kroeger, eds. 1996. *Teaching and Learning with Native Indians: A Handbook for Non-Native American Adult Educators*. Phoenix: Adult Literacy and Technology Resource Center.

Schwartz, Bryan. 1986. *First Principles, Second Thoughts: Aboriginal Peoples, Constitutional Reform, and Canadian Statecraft*. Montreal: Institute for Research on Public Policy.

Scott, John, and Gordon Marshall. 2005. "Post-Structuralism." Pp. 510–512 in *Oxford Dictionary of Sociology*, by J. Scott and G. Marshall. Oxford: Oxford University Press.

Scowen, Reed. 1999. *Time to Say Goodbye: The Case for Getting Quebec out of Canada*. Toronto: McClelland & Stewart.

Showalter, Dennis E., and Harold C. Deutsch, eds. 2010. *If the Allies Had Fallen: Sixty Alternate Scenarios of World War II*. New York: Skyhorse Publishing.

Siebert, John. 2014. "Canada and the Failure to End the 'Thousand Little Wars' in Afghanistan." *The Ploughshares Monitor* 35(2):4–9.

Sikotan (Flora Zaharia) and Mikai'sto (Leo Fox). 1995. *Kitomahkitapiiminnooniksi: Stories from Our Elders*, vol. 1. Kainaiwa Board of Education. Edmonton: Donahue House Publishing.

Sikotan (Flora Zaharia), Mikai'sto (Leo Fox), and Omahksipootaa (Marvin Fox). 2003. *Kitomahkitapiiminnooniksi: Stories from Our Elders*, vol. 4. Kainaiwa Board of Education. Edmonton: Donahue House Publishing.

Silver, A. I. 1997. *The French-Canadian Idea of Confederation 1864–1900*. 2nd ed. Toronto: University of Toronto Press.

Silver, Jim. 1996. *Thin Ice: Money, Politics, and the Demise of an NHL Franchise*. Halifax, NS: Fernwood.

Sinha, Vandna, and Anna Kozlowski. 2013. "The Structure of Aboriginal Child Welfare in Canada." *The International Indigenous Policy Journal* 4(2):1–21.

Skocpol, Theda. 1979. *States and Social Revolutions*. Cambridge: Cambridge University Press.

Sklair, Leslie. 2002. *Globalization: Capitalism and Its Alternatives*. Toronto: Oxford University Press.

Smith, Donald. 1998. *Beyond Two Solitudes*. Halifax, NS: Fernwood.

Smith, Goldwin. 1971. *Canada and the Canadian Question*. Originally published in 1891. Toronto: University of Toronto Press.

Smith, Graeme. 2013. *The Dogs Are Eating Them Now: Our War in Afghanistan*. Toronto: Alfred A. Knopf.

Smith, Melvin H. 1995. *Our Home OR Native Land? What Government Aboriginal Policy Is Doing to Canada*. Toronto: Stoddart.

Smylie, Janet, Deshayne Fell, Arne Ohlsson, and the Joint Working Group on First Nations, Indian, Inuit, and Métis Infant Mortality of the Canadian Perinatal Surveillance System

Surveillance System. 2010. "A Review of Aboriginal Infant Mortality Rates in Canada: Striking and Persistent Aboriginal/Non-Aboriginal Inequities." *Canadian Journal of Public Health* 101(2):143–148.

Sniderman, Andrew Stobo, and Adam Shedletzky. 2014. "Aboriginal Peoples and Legal Challenges to Canadian Climate Change Policy." *University of Western Ontario Journal of Legal Studies* 4(2) (ir.lib.uwo.ca/uwojls/vol4/iss2/1).

Snow, Chief John. 1988. "Identification and Definition of Our Treaty and Aboriginal Rights." Pp. 41–46 in *The Quest for Justice: Aboriginal Peoples and Aboriginal Rights*, edited by M. Boldt and A. Long. Toronto: University of Toronto Press.

Sprague, D. N. 1988. *Canada and the Métis, 1869–1885*. Waterloo, ON: Wilfred Laurier University Press.

Srebrnik, Henry F. 1998. "The Radical 'Second Life' of Vilhjalmur Stefansson." *Arctic* 51(1):58–60.

Stabler, Jack. 1989. "Dualism and Development in the Northwest Territories." *Economic Development and Cultural Change* 37(4):805–840.

Stacey, C. P., and Norman Hillmer. 1999. "World War II." Pp. 2551–2553 in *The Canadian Encyclopedia*. Toronto: McClelland & Stewart.

Standing, Guy. 2011. *The Precariat: The New Dangerous Class*. London: Bloomsbury Academic.

Standing, Guy. 2014. *A Precariat Charter: From Denizens to Citizens*. London: Bloomsbury Academic.

Stanford, Jim. 2006. "Modelling North American Integration: Pushing the Envelope of Reality." Pp. 151–182 in *Living with Uncle*, edited by B. Campbell and E. Finn. Toronto: James Lorimer and Company.

Stanford, Jim. 2014. "European Trade Deal Would Make a Bad Situation Worse for Auto Sector, with Spillover Effects throughout the Economy." *Canadian Centre for Policy Alternatives Monitor* 21(2):1, 10–12.

Stanley, George F. G. 1975. *The Birth of Western Canada: A History of the Riel Rebellion*. Originally published in 1936. Toronto: University of Toronto Press.

Staples, Steven, and William Robinson. 2008. *More Than the Cold War*. Ottawa: The Rideau Institute.

Statistics Canada. 1983. *Historical Statistics of Canada*. Cat. no. 11-516. Ottawa: Statistics Canada.

Statistics Canada. 2001. *Canada Year Book*. Cat. no. 11-402. Ottawa: Statistics Canada.

Statistics Canada. 2006a. "Population by Mother Tongue, by Province and Territory." *2006 Census*. Ottawa: Statistics Canada (www40.statcan.gc.ca/l01/cst01/demo11a-eng.htm).

Statistics Canada. 2006b. "Income Statistics (4) in Constant (2005) Dollars, Age Groups (5A), Aboriginal Identity, Registered Indian Status and Aboriginal Ancestry (21), Highest Certificate, Diploma or Degree (5) and Sex (3) for the Population 15 Years and Over with Income of Canada, Provinces, Territories, 2000 and 2005 - 20% Sample Data." Cat. no. 97-563-X2006008 Ottawa: Statistics Canada.

Statistics Canada. 2007a. *Canada Year Book 2007*. Ottawa: Statistics Canada.

Statistics Canada. 2007b. "Study: The New Underground Economy of Resources." *The Daily*, October 11.

Statistics Canada. 2008. "Imports, Exports, and Trade Balance of Goods on a Balance-of-Payments Basis, by Country or Country Grouping." Ottawa: Statistics Canada.

Statistics Canada. 2010a. "Population Projections for Canada, Provinces, and Territories 2009 to 2036." Ottawa: Statistics Canada (www.statcan.gc.ca/pub/91-520-x/91-520-x2010001-eng.pdf).

Statistics Canada. 2010b. "Life Expectancy." Ottawa: Statistics Canada (www.statcan.gc.ca/pub/89-645-x/2010001/life-expectancy-esperance-vie-eng.htm). Modified June 21, 2010.

Statistics Canada. 2011a. *Focus on Geography Series, 2011 Census.* Ottawa: Statistics Canada (www12.statcan.gc.ca/census-recensement/2011/as-sa/fogs-spg/Index-eng.cfm).

Statistics Canada. 2011b. "Detailed Mother Tongue (232), Knowledge of Official Languages (5), Age Groups (17A) and Sex (3) for the Population Excluding Institutional Residents of Canada, Provinces, Territories, Census Metropolitan Areas and Census Agglomerations, 2011 Census." *2011 Census of Population.* Cat. no. 98-314-XCB2011031. Modified November 26, 2013.

Statistics Canada. 2011c. "Religion (108), Immigrant Status and Period of Immigration (11), Age Groups (10) and Sex (3) for the Population in Private Households of Canada, Provinces, Territories, Census Metropolitan Areas and Census Agglomerations." *2011 National Household Survey.* Cat. no. 99-010-X2011032.

Statistics Canada. 2011d. "Population, Urban and Rural, by Province and Territory (Canada)." Ottawa: Statistics Canada (www.statcan.gc.ca/tables-tableaux/sum-som/l01/cst01/demo62a-eng.htm). Modified February 4, 2011.

Statistics Canada. 2011e. "Citizenship (5), Place of Birth (236), Immigrant Status and Period of Immigration (11), Age Groups (10) and Sex (3) for the Population in Private Households of Canada, Provinces, Territories, Census Metropolitan Areas and Census Agglomerations." *2011 National Household Survey.* Cat. no. 99-010-X2011026. Modified March 4, 2014.

Statistics Canada. 2011f. "Aboriginal Peoples in Canada: First Nations People, Métis and Inuit, Table 1: Aboriginal Identity Population, Canada, 2011." *2011 National Household Survey.* Cat. no 99-011-X2011001 (www12.statcan.gc.ca/nhs-enm/2011/as-sa/99-011-x/99-011-x2011001-eng.pdf).

Statistics Canada. 2011g. "Aboriginal Peoples in Canada: First Nations People, Métis and Inuit, Table 4: Age Distribution and Median Age for Selected Aboriginal Identity Categories, Canada, 2011." *2011 National Household Survey.* Cat. no. 99-011-X2011001 (www12.statcan.gc.ca/nhs-enm/2011/as-sa/99-011-x/2011001/tbl/tbl04-eng.cfm). Modified April 24, 2014.

Statistics Canada. 2011h. "Population Projections by Aboriginal Identity in Canada, 2006–2031." Demography Division of Statistics Canada. Cat. no. 91-552-X (www.statcan.gc.ca/pub/91-552-x/91-552-x2011001-eng.pdf).

Statistics Canada. 2011i. "Aboriginal Peoples in Canada: First Nations People, Métis and Inuit, Table 3: Distribution of First Nations People, First Nations People with and without Registered Indian Status, and First Nations People with Registered Indian Status Living on or off Reserve, Canada, Provinces and Territories, 2011." *2011 National Household Survey.* Cat. no. 99-011-X2011001 (www12.statcan.gc.ca/nhs-enm/2011/as-sa/99-011-x/99-011-x2011001-eng.pdf).

Statistics Canada. 2011j. "Table 1: Population with an Aboriginal Mother Tongue by Language Family, Main Languages within These Families and Their Main Provincial and Territorial

Concentrations, Canada, 2011." *2011 Census of Population*. Ottawa: Statistics Canada (www12.statcan.gc.ca/census-recensement/2011/as-sa/98-314-x/2011003/tbl/tbl3_3-1-eng.cfm).

Statistics Canada. 2012. "Final Report on 2016 Census Options: Proposed Content Determination Framework and Methodological Options." Ottawa: Statistics Canada (www12.statcan.gc.ca/census-recensement/fc-rf/reports-rapports/r2_index-eng.cfm). Modified December 18, 2012.

Statistics Canada. 2013a. "Table 1.1-1: Annual Population Estimates, July 1, National Perspective—Population." Ottawa: Statistics Canada (www.statcan.gc.ca/pub/91-215-x/2013002/t002-eng.pdf).

Statistics Canada. 2013b. "History of the Census of Canada." Ottawa: Statistics Canada (www12.statcan.gc.ca/census-recensement/2011/ref/about-apropos/history-histoire-eng.cfm).

Statistics Canada. 2013c. "Gross Domestic Product, Expenditure-Based, by Province and Territory." Ottawa: Statistics Canada (www.statcan.gc.ca/tables-tableaux/sum-som/l01/cst01/econ15-eng.htm). Modified December 20, 2013.

Statistics Canada. 2013d. "Energy Supply and Demand." *The Daily*, December 10 (www.statcan.gc.ca/daily-quotidien/131210/dq131210a-eng.htm).

Statistics Canada. 2013e. "Average Female and Male Earnings, and Female-to-Male Earnings Ratio, by Work Activity, 2011 Constant Dollars." Ottawa: Statistics Canada (www5.statcan.gc.ca/cansim/a05?lang=eng&id=2020102&pattern=2020102&searchTypeByValue=1&p2=35). Modified June 27, 2013.

Statistics Canada. 2013f. "2011 National Household Survey: Aboriginal Peoples in Canada: First Nations People, Métis and Inuit." *The Daily*, May 8 (www.statcan.gc.ca/daily-quotidien/130508/dq130508a-eng.htm?).

Statistics Canada. 2014a. "Labour Force, Employment and Unemployment, Levels and Rates, by Province, 2013." Ottawa: Statistics Canada (www.statcan.gc.ca/tables-tableaux/sum-som/l01/cst01/labor07a-eng.htm). Modified January 10, 2014.

Statistics Canada. 2014b. "Median Total Income, by Family Type, by Province and Territory (All Census Families)." *CANSIM* Table 111-0009. Ottawa: Statistics Canada (www.statcan.gc.ca/tables-tableaux/sum-som/l01/cst01/famil108a-eng.htm). Modified July 23, 2014.

Statistics Canada. 2014c. "Population of Census Metropolitan Areas." Ottawa: Statistics Canada (www.statcan.gc.ca/tables-tableaux/sum-som/l01/cst01/demo05a-eng.htm). Modified May 30, 2014.

Statistics Canada. 2014d. "Imports, Exports and Trade Balance of Goods on a Balance-of-Payments Basis, by Country or Country Grouping." Ottawa: Statistics Canada (www.statcan.gc.ca/tables-tableaux/sum-som/l01/cst01/gblec02a-eng.htm).

Statistics Canada. 2014e. "Survey of Financial Security, 2012." *The Daily* (www.statcan.gc.ca/daily-quotidien/140225/dq140225b-eng.htm). Modified February 25, 2014.

Statistics Canada. 2014f. "Aboriginal Peoples in Canada: First Nations People, Métis and Inuit." Ottawa: Statistics Canada (www12.statcan.gc.ca/nhs-enm/2011/as-sa/99-011-x/99-011-x2011001-eng.cfm). Modified March 28, 2014.

Statistics Canada. 2014g. "The Educational Attainment of Aboriginal Peoples in Canada." *2011 National Household Surveys*. Cat. no. 99-0012-X (http://www12.statcan.gc.ca/nhs-enm/2011/as-sa/99-012-x/99-012-x2011003_3-eng.cfm). Modified January 14, 2014

Statistics Canada. 2014h. "Education and Labour." *2011 National Household Surveys*. Statistics Canada Cat. no. 9-012-X2011037 9.

Stearns, P. N. 1975. *European Society in Upheaval*. 2nd ed. New York: Macmillan.

Steckley, John I., and Bryan D. Cummins. 2008. *Full Circle: Canada's First Nations*. 2nd ed. Toronto: Pearson Education Canada.

Steele, James, and Robin Mathews. 2006. "Canadianization Revisited: A Comment on Cormier's 'The Canadianization Movement in Context.'" *The Canadian Journal of Sociology* 31(4):491–508.

Stefansson, Vilhjalmur. 1921. *The Friendly Arctic*. New York: Macmillan.

Stefansson, Vilhjalmur. 1938. *Unsolved Mysteries of the Arctic*. New York: Collier.

Stein, Janice Gross, and Eugene Lang. 2007. *The Unexpected War: Canada in Kandahar*. Toronto: Viking Press.

Strange, Susan. 1996. *The Retreat of the State*. Cambridge: Cambridge University Press.

Stubbs, R., and G. R. D. Underhill, eds. 1994. *Political Economy and the Changing Global Order*. Toronto: McClelland & Stewart.

Stueck, Wendy. 2014. "Ruling over Land in B.C. Has Ripple Effects across Canada." *The Globe and Mail*, June 27 (www.theglobeandmail.com/news/british-columbia/ruling-over-land-in-bc-has-ripple-effects-across-canada/article19357334).

Surtees, R. J. 1969. "The Development of a Reserve Policy in Canada." *Ontario Historical Society* LXI:87–99.

Suzuki, David. 1992. "A Personal Foreword: The Value of Native Ecologies." Pp. xxi–xvi in *Wisdom of the Elders*, by P. Knudtson and D. Suzuki. Toronto: Stoddart.

Swedberg, Richard. 1990. *Economics and Society*. Princeton, NJ: Princeton University Press.

Tajfel, Henri, and John C. Turner. 1986. "The Social Identity Theory of Intergroup Behavior." Pp. 7–24 in *Psychology of Intergroup Relations*, edited by S. Worchel and W. A. Austin. Chicago: Nelson-Hall.

Taylor, Charles. 1993. *Reconciling the Solitudes*. Montreal and Kingston: McGill-Queen's University Press.

Taylor, J. Garth. 1974. *Netsilik Eskimo Material Culture: The Roald Amundsen Collection from King William Island*. Oslo: Universitetsforlaget.

Teeple, Gary. 2000. *Globalization and the Decline of Social Reform: Into the Twenty-First Century*. 2nd ed. Toronto: Garamond.

Tennant, Paul. 1988. "Aboriginal Rights and the Penner Report on Indian Self-Government." Pp. 321–332 in *The Quest for Justice: Aboriginal Peoples and Aboriginal Rights*, edited by M. Boldt and A. Long. Toronto: University of Toronto Press.

Thomas, Lewis H. 1977. "A Judicial Murder: The Trial of Louis Riel." Pp. 37–59 in *The Settlement of the West*, edited by H. Palmer. Calgary: Comprint.

Thompson, Dale. 1995. "Language, Identity, and the Nationalist Impulse: Quebec." Pp. 69–82 in *Being and Becoming Canada: The Annals of the American Academy of Political and Social Science* 538, edited by C. Doran and E. Babby.

Time. 2013. *Almanac 2013.* Chicago: Encyclopaedia Brittanica.

Titley, E. Brian. 1992. "Red Deer Industrial School: A Case Study in the History of Native Education." Pp. 55–72 in *Exploring Our Educational Past,* edited by N. Kach and K. Mazurek. Calgary: Detselig.

Tobias, John L. 1977. "Indian Reserves in Western Canada: Indian Homelands or Devices for Assimilation?" Pp. 89–103 in *Approaches to Native History in Canada,* edited by D. A. Muise. Ottawa: National Museum of Man Mercury Series.

Tobias, John L. 1983. "Protection, Civilization, Assimilation: An Outline History of Canada's Indian Policy." Pp. 39–55 in *As Long as the Sun Shines and Water Flows: A Reader in Canadian Native Studies,* edited by I. A. L. Getty and A. Lussier. Vancouver: UBC Press.

Tombs, George. 2013. "Translator's Preface." In *Canada's Forgotten Slaves: Two Hundred Years of Bondage,* by M. Trudel. Montreal: Véhicule Press.

Tönnies, Ferdinand. 1957. *Community and Society,* edited and translated by C. P. Loomis. Originally published in 1887. New York: Harper and Row.

Trent, John E. 1995. *The 1995 Quebec Referendum: A Practical Guide.* Ottawa: Dialogue Canada.

Trigger, Bruce G. 1969. *The Huron: Farmers of the North.* New York: Holt, Rinehart, and Winston.

Trofimenkoff, Susan. 1993. "For Whom the Bell Tolls." Pp. 380–392 in *Reappraisals in Canadian History: Pre-Confederation,* edited by A. D. Gilbert, G. M. Wallace, and R. M. Bray. Scarborough, ON: Prentice-Hall Canada.

Trudeau, Pierre. 1996. *Against the Current: Selected Writings 1939–1996,* edited by G. Pelletier. Toronto: McClelland & Stewart.

Trudel, Marcel. 2013. *Canada's Forgotten Slaves: Two Hundred Years of Bondage,* translated by G. Tombs. Montreal: Véhicule Press.

Turk, James L., and Allan Manson, eds. 2007. *Free Speech in Fearful Times: After 9/11 in Canada, the U.S., Australia, and Europe.* Ottawa: Canadian Association of University Teachers.

Turner, Chris. 2013. *The War on Science: Muzzled Scientists and Wilful Blindness in Stephen Harper's Canada.* Vancouver: Greystone.

Turner, Joanne. 1981. "The Historical Base." Pp. 49–57 in *Canadian Social Welfare,* edited by J. Turner and F. Turner. Don Mills, ON: Collier Macmillan Canada.

Turp, Daniel. 1993. "Solutions to the Future of Canada and Quebec after the October 26th Referendum: Genuine Sovereignties within a Novel Union." *Constitutional Forum* 4(2):47–49.

Ungar, Sheldon. 1991. "Civil Religion and the Arms Race." *Canadian Review of Sociology and Anthropology* 28(4):503–525.

United Nations. 2014a. *United Nations Intergovernmental Panel on Climate Change.* Fifth Assessment Report. New York: United Nations (www.ipcc.ch/index.htm).

United Nations. 2014b. *Human Development Reports.* New York: United Nations Development Programme (hdr.undp.org/en/content/table-2-human-development-index-trends-1980-2013).

United States Census Bureau. 2013. *Top Trading Partners—August 2013.* Washington, DC: United States Census Bureau (www.census.gov/foreign-trade/statistics/highlights/top/top1308yr.html).

United States Energy Administration. 2014. "Company Level Imports." *Petroleum and Other Liquids.* Washington, DC: United States Energy Administration. September 29 (www.eia.gov/petroleum/imports/companylevel).

Usalcas, Jeannine. 2011. "Aboriginal People and the Labour Market: Estimates from the Labour Force Survey, 2008–2010." Labour Statistics Division, Statistics Canada. Cat. no. 71-588-X, no. 3 (www.statcan.gc.ca/pub/71-588-x/71-588-x2011003-eng.pdf).

Valaskakis, Kimon, and Angeline Fournier. 1995. *The Delusion of Sovereignty: Would Independence Weaken Quebec?* Montreal: Robert Davies Publishing.

Vallee, Frank. 1971. "Eskimos of Canada: A Minority Group." Pp. 75–88 in *Native Peoples*, edited by J.E. Leonard. Don Mills, ON: Prentice-Hall of Canada.

Vallières, Pierre. 1971. *White Niggers of America*. Toronto: McClelland & Stewart.

van den Berghe, Pierre. 1992. "The Modern State: Nation-Builder or Nation-Killer?" *International Journal of Group Tensions* 22:191–208.

van Kirk, Sylvia. 1999. *Many Tender Ties: Women in the Fur Trade Society 1670–1870*. Winnipeg: Watson and Dwyer.

Vergano, Dan. 2013. "Half-Million Iraqis Died in the War, New Study Says." *National Geographic*, October 15 (news.nationalgeographic.com/news/2013/10/131015-iraq-war-deaths-survey-2013).

Villarreal, M. Angeles, and Ian F. Fergusson. 2014. *NAFTA at 20: Overview and Trade Effects*. A Report Prepared for Members and Committees of the U.S. Congress. Washington, DC: Congressional Research Service.

Wahl, Asbjørn. 2011. *The Rise and Fall of the Welfare State*. London: Pluto Press.

Waite, P. B. 1997. "In Loyalist Ontario: A Schoolboy's Recollections, 1930–1933." *The Beaver* 77(1):12–13.

Wall, Denis. 2000. "Aboriginal Self-Government in Canada: The Cases of Nunavut and the Alberta Métis Settlements." Pp. 143–166 in *Visions of the Heart: Canadian Aboriginal Issues*, edited by D. Long and O. P. Dickason. 2nd ed. Toronto: Harcourt Canada.

The Wall Street Journal. 2014. "The Short Answer: What is ISIS?" *The Wall Street Journal*, June 12 (blogs.wsj.com/briefly/2014/06/12/islamic-state-of-iraq-and-al-sham-the-short-answer).

Wallerstein, Immanuel. 1997. "World-Systems Analysis." Pp. 309–324 in *Social Theory Today*, edited by A. Giddens and J. Turner. Stanford, CA: Stanford University Press.

Wanner, Richard A. 1999. "Expansion and Conscription: Trends in Educational Opportunity in Canada, 1920–1994." *Canadian Review of Sociology and Anthropology* 36(3):409–442.

Warry, Wayne. 1998. *Unfinished Dreams: Community Healing and the Reality of Aboriginal Self-Government*. Toronto: University of Toronto Press.

Warry, Wayne. 2007. *Ending Denial: Understanding Aboriginal Issues*. Peterborough, ON: Broadview Press.

Waters, Malcolm. 1994. "Introduction: A World of Difference." *Australian-New Zealand Journal of Sociology* 30(3):229–234.

Watkins, Melville. 1963. "A Staple Theory of Economic Growth." *Canadian Journal of Economics and Political Science* 29(2):80–100.

Watkins, Melville. 1991. "The 'American System' and Canada's National Policy." Pp. 148–157 in *Perspectives on Canadian Economic Development*, edited by G. Laxer. Toronto: Oxford University Press.

Watkins, Melville. 1997. "Canadian Capitalism in Transition." Pp. 19–42 in *Understanding Canada: Building on the New Canadian Political Economy*, edited by W. Clement. Montreal and Kingston: McGill-Queen's University Press.

Wax, Murray, Rosalie Wax, and Robert V. Dumont, eds. 1964. "Formal Education in an American Indian Community." *Social Problems*, SSSP Monograph:1–126.

Weaver, Jace, ed. 1998. *Native American Religious Identity: Unforgotten Gods*. Maryknoll, NY: Orbis Books.

Webber, Jeremy. 1994. *Reimagining Canada*. Montreal and Kingston: McGill-Queen's University Press.

Weber, Max. 1958. *From Max Weber: Essays in Sociology*, edited by H. Gerth and C. W. Mills. New York: Oxford University Press.

Westfall, William. 1993. "On the Concept of Region in Canadian History and Literature." Pp. 335–344 in *A Passion for Identity: An Introduction to Canadian Studies*, edited by D. Taras, B. Rasporich, and E. Mandel. Scarborough, ON: Nelson Canada.

Whitaker, Reg. 1987. "Neo-Conservatism and the State." Pp. 1–31 in *Socialist Register*, edited by R. Miliband, L. Panitch and J. Saville. London: The Merlin Press.

Whitaker, Reg. 1991. *Canadian Immigration Policy Since Confederation*. Ottawa: Canadian Historical Association.

White, Deena. 1997. "Quebec State and Society." Pp. 17–44 in *Quebec Society: Critical Issues*, edited by M. Fournier, M. Rosenberg, and D. White. Scarborough, ON: Prentice-Hall Canada.

Whyte, Donald. 1992. "Sociology and the Constitution of Society: Canadian Experiences." Pp. 313–319 in *Fragile Truths: 25 Years of Sociology and Anthropology in Canada*, edited by W. Carroll, L. Christiansen-Ruffman, R. Currie, and D. Harrison. Ottawa: Carleton University Press.

Widdis, Randy. 1997. "American-Resident Migration to Western Canada at the Turn of the Twentieth Century." *Prairie Forum* 22(2):237–261.

Wilson, C. Roderick, and Carl Urion. 1995. "First Nations Prehistory and Canadian History." In *Native Peoples: The Canadian Experience*, edited by R. B. Wilson, and C. R. Morrison. 2nd ed. Toronto: McClelland & Stewart.

Wilson, Roger, ed. 1976. *The Land That Never Melts: Auyuittuq National Park*. Ottawa: Minister of Supply and Services.

Winegard, Timothy C. 2012. *For King and Kanata: Canadian Indians and the First World War*. Winnipeg: University of Manitoba Press.

Winks, Robin. 1998. *The Civil War Years: Canada and the United States*. 4th ed. Montreal and Kingston: McGill-Queen's University Press.

Wiseman, Nelson. 2007. *In Search of Canadian Political Culture*. Vancouver: UBC Press.

Wissler, Clark. 1923. *Man and Culture*. New York: Thomas Crowell.

Witt, Norbert. 1998. "Promoting Self-Esteem, Defining Culture." *Canadian Journal of Native Education* 22(2):260–273.

Wittington, Michael. 1985. "Political and Constitutional Development in the NWT and Yukon: The Issues and the Interests." Pp. 53–108 in *The North*, edited by M. Wittington. Toronto: University of Toronto Press.

Wolf, Naomi. 2007. *The End of America: Letter of Warning to a Young Patriot*. White River Junction, VT: Chelsea Green.

Wonders, William. 1993. "Canadian Regions and Regionalisms: National Enrichment or National Disintegration?" Pp. 345–366 in *A Passion for Identity: An Introduction to Canadian Studies*, edited by D. Taras, B. Rasporich, and E. Mandel. Scarborough, ON: Nelson Canada.

Woodsworth, J. S. 1972. *Strangers within Our Gates*. Originally published in 1909. Toronto: University of Toronto Press.

World Bank. 2014a. "Central Government Debt, Total (% of GDP): Canada." World Bank Group (data.worldbank.org/indicator/GC.DOD.TOTL.GD.ZS).

World Bank. 2014b. "Military Expenditure (% of GDP)." World Bank Group (data.worldbank.org/indicator/MS.MIL.XPND.GD.ZS).

World Bank. 2014c. "GNI per Capita in PPP Terms (Constant 2011 PPP$)." World Bank Group (hdr.undp.org/en/content/gni-capita-ppp-terms-constant-2011-ppp).

Wright, Eric Olin. 1985. *Classes*. London: Verso.

Wright, Ronald. 1993. *Stolen Continents: The New World through Indian Eyes*. Toronto: Penguin.

Wuttunee, William I. C. 1971. *Ruffled Feathers: Indians in Canadian Society*. Calgary: Bell Books.

Wynn, Graeme. 2012. "On the Margins of Empire 1760–1840." Pp. 181–276 in *The Illustrated History of Canada*, edited by C. Brown. Toronto: Key Porter Books.

Yazzie, Robert. 2000. "Indigenous Peoples and Post-Colonial Colonialism." Pp. 39–49 in *Reclaiming Indigenous Voice and Vision*, edited by M. Battiste. Vancouver: UBC Press.

York, Geoffrey. 1989. *The Dispossessed: Life and Death in Native Canada*. Toronto: Lester and Orpen Dennys.

Young, Robert A. 1995. *The Secession of Quebec and the Future of Canada*. Montreal and Kingston: McGill-Queen's University Press.

Young, Robert A. 1998. "Quebec Succession and the 1995 Referendum." Pp. 112–126 in *Challenges to Canadian Federalism*, edited by M. Westmacott and H. Mellon. Scarborough, ON: Prentice-Hall Canada.

Zinn, Howard. 1995. *A People's History of the United States 1492–Present*. New York: Harper Perennial.

COPYRIGHT ACKNOWLEDGEMENTS

INDEX